W9-AXN-981

VISUAL QUICKSTART GUIDE

FINAL CUT EXPRESS

FOR MAC OS X

Lisa Brenneis

 Peachpit Press

Visual QuickStart Guide
Final Cut Express for Mac OS X
Lisa Brenneis

Peachpit Press
1249 Eighth Street
Berkeley, CA 94710
510/524-2178
800/283-9444
510/524-2221 (fax)

Find us on the World Wide Web at: http://www.peachpit.com
To report errors, please send a note to errata@peachpit.com
Peachpit Press is a division of Pearson Education

Copyright © 2003 by Lisa Brenneis

Editor: Jeff Carlson
Production Editor: Connie Jeung-Mills
Illustrations: Jeff Tolbert
Copyeditor: Tonya Engst
Compositor: Owen Wolfson
Indexer: Caroline Parks
Cover Production: Nathalie Valette
Cover Design: The Visual Group

Notice of rights
All rights reserved. No part of this book may be reproduced or transmitted in any form
by any means, electronic, mechanical, photocopying, recording, or otherwise, without
the prior written permission of the publisher. For information on getting permission
for reprints and excerpts, contact permissions@peachpit.com.

Notice of liability
The information in this book is distributed on an "As Is" basis, without warranty. While
every precaution has been taken in the preparation of the book, neither the author nor
Peachpit Press shall have any liability to any person or entity with respect to any loss or
damage caused or alleged to be caused directly or indirectly by the instructions contained
in this book or by the computer software and hardware products described in it.

Trademarks
Visual Quickstart Guide is a registered trademark of Peachpit Press, a division of
Pearson Education.
Throughout this book, trademarks are used. Rather than put a trademark symbol in
every occurrence of a trademarked name, we state that we are using the names in an
editorial fashion only and to the benefit of the trademark owner with no intention of
infringement of the trademark.

ISBN 0-321-19912-X

9 8 7 6 5 4 3 2 1

Printed and bound in the United States of America

Dedication

For my folks, Jon and Aida Brenneis—from you I learned that if you treat your friends like family and your family like friends, you'll build a large friendly family.

You are the best.

Acknowledgments

Thanks to my Virtual Editorial Group:

Project Editor Jeff Carlson (Seattle), Copy Editor Tonya Engst (New York), Illustrator Jeff Tolbert (Seattle).

Is it just me, or are you the best team I've ever worked with?

Thanks to the Peachpit Press people:

Eternal thanks to Marjorie Baer, who cares deeply about making good books better. Thanks to production editor Connie Jeung-Mills (and I'm not just saying that); Jill Marts-Lodwig, Lisa Theobald, and Kelly Ryer, the editors of the previous editions of Final Cut Pro: VQP, who built a fine foundation for this edition.

Thanks to Jon Brenneis and to the Hsieh-Shaws for generously allowing the use of images that appear in this book.

Thanks to the whole Final Cut Pro/Express team at Apple Computer, particularly Brian Meaney and Erin Skitt—you are unfailingly helpful, gracious and professional.

Thanks to my collaborator and friend Brett Spivey, who consults on effects and compositing issues.

Thanks always to Lauren Ward (sharp eyes, sharp mind, sharp pencil) for all your help.

Thanks to all the men and women of the Final Cut Pro discussion forums: 2-pop.com, LAFCPUG.org, and Creative Cow. I started assembling a list by name, and it was too long to print. You lead the Final Cut community by example, and I am indebted to you. Keep posting.

Thanks to the deejays at internet radio beacon KVRX.org (University of Texas, Austin), where they play the best damn music by people you never heard of. Top fuel for weary fact-jockeys.

Finally, thanks to a group of very important people who defy classification: Ralph Fairweather, Michael Wohl, Charles McConathy, Cawan Starks, Ross Jones, Philip Hodgetts, Tom Wolsky, Kevin Monahan, Michael Horton, Ken Stone, Ned Soltz, Lowell Kay, Josh and Michelle Mellicker, Michael Rubin, Steve Martin and Ramy Katrib.

TABLE OF CONTENTS

TABLE OF CONTENTS

Chapter 9 **Editing in the Timeline
and the Canvas**   **237**

TABLE OF CONTENTS

INTRODUCTION

When the two Steves started Apple back in 1976, they dreamed of making a computer that people could use as a tool to change the world. In 1999, Apple released Final Cut Pro—a program worthy of the founders' vision. A community has formed around this tool, and people are making movies who weren't able to before. Final Cut Pro changed the way stories are told, because it changed who's telling them.

In 2003, Apple debuted Final Cut Express, a lower cost, entry-level, nonlinear editing and effects program built using the same code base as Final Cut Pro 3.

What a coincidence—I happen to have authored a compact reference guide to Final Cut Pro 3!

This book, *Final Cut Express for Mac OS X: Visual QuickStart Guide*, is adapted from my *Final Cut Pro 3 for Macintosh: Visual QuickPro Guide*. This edition has been re-organized in places to more accurately reflect the editing process, and includes basic orientation material here and there. More important, I've carefully revised the Final Cut Pro material to accurately reflect the way Final Cut Express works.

INTRODUCTION

Who should use this book

Final Cut Express for Mac OS X: Visual QuickStart Guide is designed to be used by intermediate to advanced Mac users with a little basic knowledge of video editing terms and procedures; explaining basic video production and editing is beyond the scope of this book. Final Cut Express (FCE) is designed to be easy to use and it's simpler than Final Cut Pro, but it's still a professional-level video editing and compositing program. If you are not new to the Macintosh, but you're completely new to video editing, consider some basic training in the fundamentals of video editing before you plunge into this program. If haven't done so already, try Apple's free iMovie program—it's a great way to get a taste of basic video editing in a stripped-down program that's a little easier for beginners to use.

What's in this book

The first part of the book starts with a quick feature overview for the entire program, followed by hardware setup, program installation, and preferences specification. Part I ends with a chapter devoted to managing an FCE project.

The next section introduces the Capture, Browser, and Viewer windows—the tools you use for capturing, importing and organizing media in preparation for an edit.

The third part of the book details the variety of ways you can use FCE's editing tools to assemble and refine an edited sequence. This section covers basic editing procedures and the operation of the Timeline, Canvas, and Trim Edit windows.

The fourth section is devoted to using the program's special effects and compositing tools. You'll find an overview chapter plus chapters devoted to creating motion effects, using filters, and creating titles and other generator effects.

The final section includes two chapters on finishing your FCE project: one discusses rendering techniques and strategies; the other lays out your options for outputting a final product.

How to use this book

This guide is designed to be a Final Cut Express user's companion, a reference guide with an emphasis on step-by- step descriptions of specific tasks. You'll encounter some of the following features:

◆ **"Anatomy" sections** introduce the major program windows with large annotated illustrations identifying interface features and operation. If you are not a step-by-step kind of person, you can pick up quite a bit of information just by browsing these illustrations.

◆ **"FCE Protocol" sidebars** lay out the protocols (the programming rules) that govern the way Final Cut Express works. These sections are highly recommended reading for anyone interested in a serious relationship with this program.

◆ **Sidebars** throughout the book highlight production techniques, project management ideas, and tips for streamlining your workflow.

◆ **Tips** are short bits that call your attention to a neat trick or a cool feature, or that warn you of a potential pitfall in the task at hand.

Learning Final Cut Express

Here are some tips to help you get up and running in Final Cut Express ASAP.

Basic theory

Two sidebars, one in Chapter 1 and another in Chapter 3, are referred to throughout this book. You don't absolutely have to read these to operate the program, but understanding some of the basic concepts underlying the design of the program will make Final Cut Express much easier to learn.

"What Is Nonlinear Nondestructive Editing?" in Chapter 1 explains how nondestructive editing works and how it affects the operation of Final Cut Express.

"FCE Protocol: Clips and Sequences" in Chapter 3 explains the protocols governing clip and sequence versions, which are key to understanding how Final Cut Express works.

FCE is context sensitive

The Final Cut Express interface is context sensitive, which means that the options available in the program's menus and dialog boxes can vary depending on any of the following factors:

◆ The external video hardware you have attached to the system

◆ The setup configuration you specify when you install the program

◆ The program window that is currently active

◆ The program selection that you just made

The logic behind the context-sensitive design is sound: to simplify your life by removing irrelevant options from your view. However, because the interface is context sensitive, the menus and dialog boxes in your installation of Final Cut Express may occasionally differ from those in the illustrations shown in this guide.

Keyboard commands

Final Cut Express was designed to support a wide variety of working styles ranging from heavy pointing, clicking, and dragging to entirely keyboard-based editing. More keyboard commands are available than those listed in the individual tasks in this book. You'll find a comprehensive list of keyboard commands in Appendix B.

Shortcut menus

Final Cut Express makes extensive use of shortcut menus. As you are exploring the program, Control-clicking items and interface elements is a quick way to see your options in many areas of the FCE interface, and it can speed up the learning process.

Refer to the manual

The official Final Cut Express User's Manual that ships with the program is available as 750-page PDF on the FCE Application CD. Apple's manual is a valuable reference tool, but be warned: you'll occasionally run across stray references to Final Cut Pro 3 features that don't exist in Final Cut Express. I'll occasionally refer you to specific sections of the official manuals that cover a topic in more detail that this book can accommodate. (Still, Apple did miss a few items covered here, and unlike the electronic-only manual, you can scribble notes in this *Visual QuickStart Guide*.)

Check out the Knowledge Base

Apple posts a steady stream of valuable Final Cut Express articles and updates in its Knowledge Base (formerly known as the Technical Information Library). The company also posts information about FCE "known issues" (that's corporate-speak for "bugs") as Knowledge Base articles. See Appendix A for information on locating the Knowledge Base online.

The Web is your friend

Using the World Wide Web is an essential part of using Final Cut Express. Apple, as well as the manufacturers of the video hardware you'll be using with Final Cut Express, relies on the Web to inform users of the latest developments and program updates, as well as to provide technical support. You'll find a starter list of online resources in Appendix A and specific web references sprinkled throughout this book. There are some great sources of information, technical help, and camaraderie out there. If you get stuck or encounter difficulties getting underway, go online and start asking questions. After you've learned the program, go online and answer questions. Helping other people is a great way to learn.

Where to find more information

Check out Appendix A, "Online Resources," for a list of helpful web sites.

Go forth and experiment

If you're new to video production—even if you're experienced but new to Final Cut Express—it would be wise to test your brand-new DV post-production system on a short, non-critical project before you plunge into that feature-length masterpiece that haunts your dreams. By knocking out a series of short projects, you build up your skills quickly as you learn from your mistakes. Have fun, keep moving, and don't be afraid to experiment.

LEARNING FINAL CUT EXPRESS

Part I:
Before You Begin

Part I:
Before
You Begin

The first part of this book covers all the "first day of school" business.

Chapter 1, "Welcome to Final Cut Express," contains an overview of the application's interface, points out major features, and outlines the production pathway of a typical FCE project from start to finish.

Chapter 2, "Installing and Setting Up," walks you through hardware setup as well as Final Cut Express installation and initial setup procedures. Even if you have already installed FCE, you should glance through this chapter—you'll find good information on managing hard disk space, external equipment, and more.

Chapter 3, "How to Manage an FCE Project," explains how FCE structures projects. You'll learn how to manage projects, sequences, and clips, how to delete files, and how to back up your project file. This chapter is a must-read for anyone contemplating a serious relationship with Final Cut Express.

WELCOME TO FINAL CUT EXPRESS

Welcome to Apple's Final Cut Express—a combination digital video editing, compositing, and special effects program. Final Cut Express is based on Final Cut Pro, Apple's wildly popular professional digital video editing program.

Final Cut Express is tightly integrated with Apple's G3 and G4 Macintosh processors, FireWire high-speed data transfer technology, and QuickTime multimedia format. FCE is designed to capture only DV-format video via FireWire, but allows you to export to most QuickTime formats. Final Cut Express provides professional editing functionality in a variety of styles, from strictly drag-and-drop edits to entirely keyboard-based editing.

Soon you'll be spending plenty of time working with clips, audio levels, and other editing minutiae, so let's start with the "Big Picture." This chapter contains a brief overview of Final Cut Express features, and tracks a basic FCE project from start to finish. You'll be introduced to the main interface windows used for editing and for creating effects, plus learn how to customize the arrangement of these windows.

Your First Final Cut Express Project: Start to Finish

Here's a roadmap you can use to chart a course through your first FCE project. This flowchart describes the production pathway of a typical project from hardware setup through output of the finished program. At each step, you'll find pointers to sections in this book that describe that part of the process in more detail.

1. **Set up hardware, install FCE, and choose an initial Easy Setup:** Use a FireWire cable to connect your DV camcorder to your computer. If you hook up your hardware before you install FCE, the program will select the correct initial settings automatically. (If you've already installed FCE, don't worry—those settings are easy to define at any time.)

   See Chapter 2, "Installing and Setting Up."

2. **Capture DV:** Use the controls in the Capture window to capture raw video and audio from your DV camcorder and save it to a hard disk.

   See Chapter 4, "Capturing Video."

3. **Import other media elements:** Add music or sound effects, or graphics elements such as digital stills or graphics created in Photoshop.

   See Chapter 5, "Importing Digital Media Files."

YOUR FIRST FINAL CUT EXPRESS PROJECT

4. Rough assembly: Review your raw video in the Viewer, and select the portions you want to use by marking In and Out points. Assemble the selected portions into a "rough cut" in an empty sequence in the Timeline. If your project includes narration, be sure to edit a "draft" narration into your rough cut. If you plan to base the rhythm of your cut on a piece of music, you should edit the music into the rough cut as well.

See Chapter 8, "Basic Editing."

ROUGH CUT

5. Fine cut: Revisit your rough cut, and make fine adjustments to edit points directly in the Timeline, the Trim Edit window, or by opening sequence clips and making adjustments in the Viewer.

See Chapter 10, "Fine Cut: Trimming Edits."

FINISHING

6. Finishing: When your fine cut is complete, use FCE's text generators to add titles, apply the Color Corrector filter to tweak the video's color balance, and fill out the audio tracks with effects and music.

See Chapter 13, "Compositing and Effects Overview."

OUTPUT

7. Output: Output your finished program to DV tape, to a DVD-mastering program like Apple's iDVD, or export in a compressed QuickTime format for distribution in another digital format like streaming Web video or CD-ROM.

See Chapter 18, "Creating Final Output."

YOUR FIRST FINAL CUT EXPRESS PROJECT

What Is Nonlinear, Nondestructive Editing?

Final Cut Express is a nonlinear, nondestructive editing program.

In a tape-based *linear* editing system, constructing an edit means selecting shots from one tape and then recording them in order on another tape. Once you've recorded the shots, you're limited to the shots as recorded and in the order recorded. If you want to go back and extend the length of a shot in the middle of your edited program, you'll also have to re-record every shot that came after it, because you can't slip the back end of your program down the tape to make room. A computer-based *nonlinear* editing system uses the computer's random access capabilities to allow editors to swap, drop, trim, or extend shots at any point in an edited sequence, without having to reconstruct any other portion of the program.

Some nonlinear computer editing programs, like iMovie, offer random access but modify the original media files on your hard disk when you change a clip (in iMovie's case, when you empty the Trash). This is called *destructive* editing.

Nondestructive editing is a basic concept that distinguishes Final Cut Express from other digital, nonlinear editing systems like iMovie. When you edit on a digital, nonlinear editing system like Final Cut Express, constructing a digital edit means constructing a playlist, much like a playlist you would construct in iTunes.

In iTunes, your archive of song files is stored in the iTunes Library; an iTunes playlist is a just a set of instructions that tells the iTunes jukebox how to sequence playback of songs you select. A single song file can appear in multiple playlists, and deleting a song from a playlist doesn't delete the actual song file from the Library. In Final Cut Express, sequences operate like iTunes playlists.

An FCE sequence is a collection of instructions to the program to play a certain bit of Media File A, then cut to a bit of Media File B, then play a later bit of Media File A, and so on. The full length of each file is available to the editor from within the edited sequence. That's because in Final Cut Express, the "clip"—the basic media element used to construct edited sequences—is only a set of instructions referring to an underlying media file. When you play back an edited sequence, it only looks as though it's been spliced together; in fact, Final Cut Express has assembled it on the fly. Extending a shot is simply a matter of rewriting the editing program's playlist to play a little more of Media File A before switching to Media File B. In Final Cut Express, you do this by modifying the clip's length in your edited sequence.

Nondestructive editing is key to editing in a program like Final Cut Express, which allows you to use media source files multiple times across multiple projects, or to access the same source file but process it in a number of different ways. Having many instances of a clip (which, in Final Cut Express, is just a set of instructions) all referring to the same media file saves disk space and offers flexibility throughout your editing process.

When you reach the limit of Final Cut Express's ability to assemble your edited sequence on the fly, it's time to render. The rendering process computes all the modifications, superimpositions, and transitions applied to the clip into a single new media file that resides on your hard disk and plays back as part of your edited sequence.

Touring Your Desktop Post-Production Facility

Four program windows form the heart of the Final Cut Express interface: the *Browser*, the *Viewer*, the *Canvas*, and the *Timeline* (**Figure 1.1**).

Because the program combines so many editing and effects creation capabilities in a single application, each of these windows performs multiple functions. Final Cut Express's elegant use of tabbed windows to stack multiple functions in a single window makes maximum use of your screen real estate.

A small, floating Tool palette contains tools you can use to make selections, navigate, and perform edits in the Timeline and the Canvas.

Figure 1.1 The four main program windows in Final Cut Express.

Useful features

Following are a few useful features that apply throughout the program:

Tabbed windows: Every major program window in Final Cut Express uses tabs. In the Viewer and Preferences windows, tabs give you access to multiple functions within the window (**Figure 1.2**). In the Canvas, Timeline, and Browser, tabs provide access to multiple sequences or projects (**Figure 1.3**). You can drag a tab out of the Browser, Viewer, Canvas, or Timeline and display the tab as a separate window. You can also return a tab to its original window by dragging the tab back to the tab header of the parent window. Review the sample screen layouts in "Customize Your Environment," later in this chapter.

Tooltips: You can use the tooltips feature to identify most of the control buttons in the Viewer and Canvas windows and on the Tool palette (**Figure 1.4**). Tooltips also display the keyboard shortcut for a tool or button. Rest the pointer over the button and wait a second, and a label will appear. Activate tooltips on the General tab of the Preferences window.

Figure 1.2 Tabs give you access to multiple functions in the Viewer window.

Figure 1.3 Tabs give you access to multiple sequences in the Timeline.

Figure 1.4 Rest the pointer over a button in the Tool palette, and a tooltip—a label with the tool's name—will appear. Tooltips also display keyboard shortcuts for tools and buttons.

Figure 1.5 Control-clicking a sequence clip in the Timeline calls up a shortcut menu with a list of functions related to that clip.

Menus, shortcuts, and controls

Final Cut Express offers several methods for performing video editing tasks. Some people work fastest using keyboard shortcuts; others prefer to use the menu bar or shortcut menus as much as possible. Apart from the menu bar and window buttons, you can use several other means to access Final Cut Express's functions; experiment to find out which control methods work best for you:

Shortcut menus: Shortcut menus can speed your work and help you learn Final Cut Express. Control-click an item in one of the four main interface windows and select from a list of common functions specific to that item (**Figure 1.5**). Control-click often as you learn your way around the program just to see your options in a particular area of the FCE interface.

Keyboard shortcuts: You'll find a complete list of keyboard shortcuts in Appendix B. You may find that these shortcut keys help you work more efficiently.

Timecode entry shortcuts: Final Cut Express provides a number of timesaving shortcuts for timecode entry. See "FCE Protocol: Entering Timecode Numbers" in Chapter 7.

YOUR DESKTOP POST-PRODUCTION FACILITY

Editing and Effects Windows

The following brief descriptions of the features and functions of each of the four main windows are simplified summaries of the full list of features. Final Cut Express's designers went all out to support a wide variety of editing styles, and they have produced a very flexible editing system.

The Browser

The Browser (**Figure 1.6**) is the window where you organize and access all the media elements used as source material for your projects. It also contains your projects' sequences: the data files that contain edited playlists.

The Browser's Effects tab is your source for effects, filters, and generators, including the text generator (**Figure 1.7**).

The Browser is not like a folder on your computer's Desktop—it's not a collection of actual files. Instead, a Browser item is a *pointer* to a file on your hard disk. It's important to keep in mind that file storage is independent of Browser organization. That means you can place the same clip in multiple Browser projects, and each instance of the clip will refer to the same media file on your hard drive. For detailed information about the Browser, see Chapter 6, "Organizing Clips in the Browser."

You can display over 30 sortable columns of information.

Different projects appear on separate tabs.

The Browser lists video and audio clips, sequences, and markers.

Figure 1.6 Use the Browser window to organize the media elements in your projects.

Figure 1.7 The Browser's Effects tab displays Final Cut Express's effects, filters, and generators as well as your own customized effects.

EDITING AND EFFECTS WINDOWS

The Viewer

The Viewer is bursting with functions. When you're editing, the Viewer acts as your source monitor; you can review individual video and audio clips and mark edit points. You can also load clips from the current sequence into the Viewer to refine your edits, apply effects, and create titles—and, as they say, much, much more.

The FCE interface offers a stack of tabs in the Viewer that organize and display audio and video plus provide controls for any effects you want to apply to a clip. Here are quick summaries of the functions available on each of the tabs.

The Viewer's Video tab

◆ **Video tab (Figure 1.8):** View video frames and mark and refine edit points. This is the default playback window for a video clip.

Different Viewer window functions appear on separate tabs

Enter a timecode in the Current Timecode field to navigate to a specific frame

Drag the playhead along the Scrubber bar to scrub through a clip

Use these controls to set In and Out points, markers, and keyframes

Use these onscreen transport controls, or use keyboard commands or timecode entry, to move around in your clips

Figure 1.8 The Viewer's Video tab.

The Viewer's Audio tab

◆ **Audio tab (Figure 1.9):** Audition and
mark edit points in audio-only clips.
Set level and pan or spread settings.
The Audio tab displays the audio portion
of an audio+video clip. Clips with two
channels display two audio tabs.

*Use the sliders to set your audio
levels and stereo spread*

*Drag this hand
icon; your handle
for performing
drag-and-drop
audio edits*

*The Audio tab
displays
waveforms of
your audio track*

Figure 1.9 The Viewer's Audio tab contains a few controls that don't
appear on the Video tab.

The Viewer's Effects tabs

- **Controls tab (Figure 1.10):** Adjust the settings for a generator effect, such as the text generator.

- **Filters tab:** Adjust the settings for any filter effects you have applied to a clip.

- **Motion tab:** Apply and modify motion effects.

- **Color Corrector tab:** Contains onscreen controls for adjusting the settings for the Color Corrector filter. This tab appears only on clips with the Color Corrector filter applied.

For more information on the Viewer, see Chapter 7, "Working with Clips in the Viewer."

To learn about creating effects, see Chapter 13, "Compositing and Effects Overview."

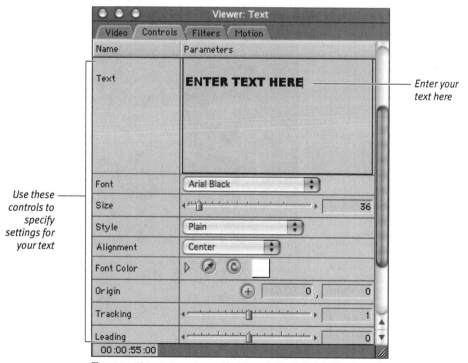

Figure 1.10 A text generator, on the Viewer's Controls tab. The Controls tab contains the tools you need to adjust the settings for a generator effect. The Filters and the Motion tab each perform the same function, but for different classes of effects.

The Canvas

The Canvas is a monitor where you view playback of your edited sequence. The Canvas and the Timeline work together; the Canvas always displays the frame at the current position of the Timeline's playhead.

The Canvas (**Figure 1.11**) looks similar to the Viewer and has many of the same controls. You can use the controls in the Canvas to play sequences, mark sequence In and Out points, add sequence markers, and set keyframes.

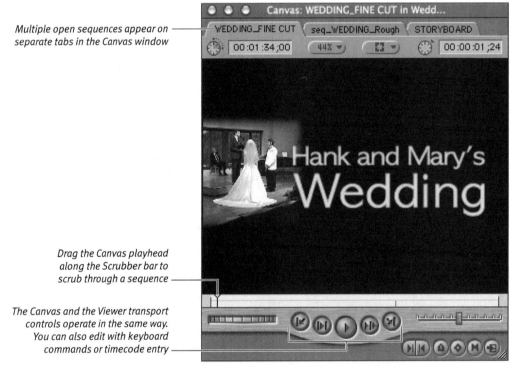

Multiple open sequences appear on separate tabs in the Canvas window

Drag the Canvas playhead along the Scrubber bar to scrub through a sequence

The Canvas and the Viewer transport controls operate in the same way. You can also edit with keyboard commands or timecode entry

Figure 1.11 The Canvas window.

In addition to using the Viewer-like marking controls, you can perform various types of drag-and-drop edits in the Canvas edit overlay (**Figure 1.12**), which appears automatically when you drag a clip into the Canvas. You can also use the Canvas's Image+Wireframe mode to plot motion effects.

For more information on the Canvas, see Chapter 9, "Editing in the Timeline and the Canvas."

Learn about applying motion effects in Chapter 14, "Motion."

Figure 1.12 The Canvas window, with the Canvas edit overlay displayed. Drag a clip from the Viewer or Browser and drop it on the type of edit you want to perform.

The Timeline

The Timeline displays your edited sequence as clips arrayed on multiple video and audio tracks along a time axis (**Figure 1.13**). The Canvas and Timeline are locked together; you view Timeline playback in the Canvas. If you have multiple sequences open, both the Timeline and the Canvas will display a tab for each sequence. You can edit by dragging clips directly from the Browser or the Viewer and dropping them in the Timeline; see Chapter 9.

Multiple open sequences appear on separate tabs in the Timeline window

Transitions appear in the same track as the clips they are applied to

Adjust a clip's opacity by dragging the clip overlay line up or down. Add keyframes to create dynamic changes in clip opacity

Drag the playhead along the ruler to scrub through a sequence

Shortcut menus provide information and task shortcuts for individual clips

Sequence clips appear on multiple tracks

Figure 1.13 The Timeline displays a chronological view of your edited sequence.

Figure 1.14 The Tool palette's pop-up selectors pack 24 tools into this tiny floating toolbar.

The Tool palette

The Tool palette (**Figure 1.14**) contains tools for selecting and manipulating items in the Timeline, Canvas, and Viewer. For a listing of each tool, see Chapter 9.

The Voice Over tool

Use the Voice Over tool (**Figure 1.15**) to record audio inside Final Cut Express. Specify a section of your sequence in the Timeline; then record voiceover as you play. See "Recording Audio with the Voice Over Tool" in Chapter 11.

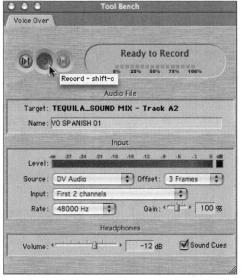

Figure 1.15 The Voice Over tool records synchronous audio directly into FCE.

Input and Output Windows

Although you perform most editing tasks in Final Cut Express's main editing and effects windows, you'll need to use a couple of other windows to shape your program's input and output.

Capture

Usethe Capture window (**Figure 1.16**) to capture video and audio media, from live video capture on the fly to project recapture with full device control. Capture functions are explained in detail in Chapter 4, "Capturing Video."

Figure 1.16 The Capture window supports three capturing techniques, including automated project recapture.

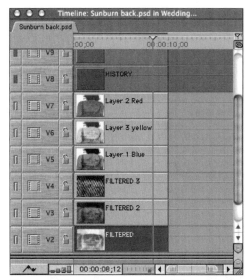

Figure 1.17 When you import a layered Photoshop file into Final Cut Express, you can maintain control over the individual layers.

Print to Video

Use Print to Video to output a Final Cut Express sequence or clip to videotape. The Print to Video function lets you configure pre- and post-program elements such as color bars and a 1-kHz tone, leader, slate, and countdown. Print to Video's loop feature allows you to print your sequence multiple times automatically.

For more information on the Print to Video window, see Chapter 18, "Creating Final Output."

Import and export options

Final Cut Express's media handling is based on Apple's QuickTime, and that means you have a lot of import and export format options. If QuickTime can handle it, so can Final Cut Express.

◆ You can import QuickTime-compatible media files into a Final Cut Express project.

◆ You can import an iMovie 3 project and convert it into an FCE project.

◆ You can import audio directly from a CD.

◆ You can import still images in a full range of formats.

◆ You can import a layered Adobe Photoshop file (**Figure 1.17**). Final Cut Express preserves the layers, importing the file as a sequence. Each layer in Photoshop corresponds to a video track in the sequence.

◆ You can export clips or sequences, or portions of either as QuickTime movies or in a variety of image and sound formats, including export to iDVD.

Customize Your Environment

The power of the Final Cut Express interface lies in its flexibility. You perform a wide range of tasks in FCE—database management, editing, effects design, titling, and many others. Here are a few sample screen layouts that can help you make the most of your screen real estate. Final Cut Express saves every detail of your workspace status each time you quit the program, so the next

time you relaunch, each program window contains the same project, sequence, clip, and frame—just as you left it.

Figure 1.18 is an example of a screen layout with a wide view of the Timeline.

Figure 1.19 is an example of a video editing layout, with large picture-viewing monitors.

Figure 1.18 Use a screen layout with a wide Timeline to see the big picture of your sequence layout.

Figure 1.19 This screen layout features large monitor views for video editing.

Figure 1.20 Choose Window > Arrange and then select from five preset and two custom screen layouts.

To select a preset screen layout:

◆ Choose Window > Arrange (**Figure 1.20**) and then select a screen layout from the five presets and two custom layouts available.

To customize a screen layout:

1. Arrange the four main windows in the layout and sizes you want.

2. Hold down the Option key and choose one of the two custom layouts from the Arrange submenu of the Window menu (**Figure 1.21**).

   The next time you open Final Cut Express, you can choose the layout you created from the Arrange submenu of the Window menu.

Figure 1.21 Holding down the Option key while selecting Custom Layout from the Arrange submenu of the Window menu saves the current screen layout as a custom preset.

Help Resources

The Final Cut Express application disk includes a 750-page manual in PDF format, but there's no printed manual and no onscreen help within FCE. There is, however, "Getting Started With Final Cut Express" (**Figure 1.22**), a DVD produced by Final Cut Pro training mavens DigitalFilm Tree. You should definitely view this basic orientation program.

Figure 1.22 "Getting Started With Final Cut Express" is a basic orientation program included with every copy of the Final Cut Express application.

Do You Need Final Cut Pro?

Final Cut Express is a very capable video editing program, but if you need any of the following features, you should learn more about Final Cut Pro, Apple's professional-grade digital editing program.

If you're knee-deep in a Final Cut Express project before you realize that the feature you need is only available in Final Cut Pro, fear not. Open a Final Cut Express project in Final Cut Pro and you'll find your FCE project intact—you can pick up where you left off and enjoy FCP features. (However, you cannot open a Final Cut Pro project within Final Cut Express.)

◆ **If you need to capture and edit video in a format other than DV:** Final Cut Pro allows you to capture and edit HD, SD, DV, and analog video and film-based projects.

◆ **If you need to log your video footage before capture:** Final Cut Pro supports logging your shots as you review your footage, then capturing all or selected clips in a batch process.

◆ **If you work with large amounts of source video and need to save storage space:** Final Cut Pro allows you to capture and edit in OfflineRT, a compressed format that requires much less storage space. FCP offers a number of options for trimming media files over the course of your project.

◆ **If you want to import and export project data for use in other editing systems:** In Final Cut Pro, you can export an Edit Decision List (EDL), used for recreating your edit on another editing system. You can export your audio tracks in Open Media Framework (OMF) format for finishing in an audio program like Digidesign's Pro Tools. FCP also supports After Effects plug-ins.

INSTALLING AND SETTING UP

This chapter walks you through the process of assembling the necessary hardware, hooking everything up, and installing Final Cut Express. Topics include Final Cut Express system requirements, and hardware selection and configuration for both a basic setup and a more full-featured system.

You'll also find a guide to the streamlined Easy Setup procedure and learn all about your options in the Preferences window.

The chapter ends with suggestions for optimizing performance, including recommendations for running Final Cut Express on a minimal "base-case" system and tips for troubleshooting Final Cut Express.

The perfect time to get the latest news on Final Cut Express and your hardware options is *before* you commit to a particular system. Web sites just for Final Cut Express users are in their early days, but there's a bustling community of resources for Final Cut Pro. FCP Web sites, FCP user group meetings, and reputable vendors are my favorite sources. See Appendix A for a list of some useful sites.

System Requirements

Final Cut Express has the same basic system requirements as its big brother Final Cut Pro, but because fast CPUs and built-in FireWire ports have spread throughout the Macintosh product line, FCE will run on just about any recent Mac.

Minimum software requirements:

◆ Mac OS X 10.2 or later

◆ QuickTime 6.0.2 or later

Minimum hardware requirements:

◆ Power Mac with a 300 megahertz (MHz) or faster G3 or G4 processor, with ATI built-in video support (required for DV)

◆ PowerBook G3, 400 MHz or faster, with built-in FireWire

◆ iMac DV, 350 MHz or faster

◆ iBook (dual USB), 500 MHz or faster, with built-in FireWire

◆ eMac

◆ Xserve

◆ 256 MB of RAM (though more is always welcome)

◆ CD-ROM or DVD-ROM drive

◆ 6 GB A/V (audio/video-rated) drive (20 GB or higher recommended)

◆ True color (24-bit) display

DV hardware requirements:

◆ A FireWire-equipped camcorder or DV deck for video capture

◆ FireWire cable plus any additional cables you may need for connecting your camcorder or deck to an external TV monitor and speakers

Real-Time System Requirements

FCE's G4 Real-Time Effects feature performs its effects-previewing magic without additional hardware, so you need a fast G4 to see the show. You'll need a 500-MHz or faster single (or 450-MHz dual) processor Power Mac G4 system with at least 384 MB of RAM to see any real-time previewing at all. FCE has been programmed to check the processor speed of your Mac, and to scale the quantity and quality of real-time effects available. Macs with faster processors (or dual processors) can process and preview multilayer scaling, motion effects, and selected transitions.

For more information on real-time system capabilities, see Chapter 17, "Rendering." Why are real-time effects discussed in the rendering chapter? Because you can preview all sorts of FCE effects while you're editing your show, but you still have to render them before you can output a full-resolution final program.

Storage Strategy for Final Cut Express

Digital video files are big—really, really big. In the Olde Days (five years ago), big hard drives were an expensive proposition; these days, $300 will get you a reliable 120 GB FireWire drive that will store eight hours of DV. If you're going to edit anything substantial at all, you should consider additional hard drive storage for your system.

Here are some overall considerations when selecting a storage option:

Any storage system you select must be fast enough to keep up with required data transfer rates (some experts recommend a minimum transfer rate of 7 or 8 MB per second). Many storage formats do meet the speed requirement, but as you weigh your speed/capacity/price trade-offs, don't short-change yourself in the speed department.

Hard disk storage is available in a variety of formats, and the number of formats is always growing. In place of a discussion about a variety of specific hard disk options, here's a set of strategic questions to help you steer to the storage option that's best for you.

How much space do I need?

DV requires 3.6 MB of storage space per second of program material.

That's 216 MB of storage space per one minute of DV, or 1 GB of storage space per five minutes of DV.

When calculating your storage needs, a good rule of thumb is to add the final program lengths of the total number of projects you want to keep online, and then multiply by four to accommodate any render files, undos, scratch copies, or test exports you may generate during your editing process. Be more generous if want to capture much more footage than you ultimately use.

Do I need a dedicated drive just for media storage?

A dedicated drive for storing your media will improve the performance of your system because it contains no operating system software, other applications, or other files that can fragment the disk. Fragmentation can interfere with the continuous data flow of video and audio to and from the disk.

Here's another reason to keep your media files and program files on separate drives: Your media drive, because it works harder, is more likely to crash than your program drive. In the event of a media drive crash, you may lose your media files, but you won't lose your edit data, which should make it easier to recover from the crash. A dedicated drive or drives for media storage is almost always a great investment.

Should I go with internal or external storage?

What kind of workflow do you anticipate? Whether to invest in internal drives (which could be less expensive) or external drives (which allow you to switch between projects quickly by swapping out drives on your workstation, or quickly move a project and its media from one workstation to another) depends on your individual needs.

Hardware Selection and Connection

You'll need a few additional items to transform your Macintosh into a video production studio. This section describes two possible setups—the basic system is the bare minimum required; the recommended setup is, well, highly recommended for anyone with more than a passing interest in making movies.

A basic hardware configuration (Figure 2.1) includes a DV camcorder or deck, a computer, and a high-resolution computer monitor. The beauty of the basic system is its simplicity—a DV camcorder connected to your Macintosh with a FireWire cable. That's all there is to it.

Here's a rundown on the function of each piece of the system.

DV camcorder or deck: The DV camera or deck feeds digital video and audio into the computer via FireWire and records DV output from Final Cut Express. During video capture, you must monitor audio through your camera or deck's audio outputs; computer speakers are muted.

Computer: Final Cut Express, installed on the Mac, captures and then stores digital video from the DV camera or deck on an A/V hard drive. Qualified Macs are equipped with FireWire; no additional video digitizing card is needed. You use your computer's speakers to monitor your audio. You edit your DV footage with Final Cut Express and then send it back out to tape through FireWire to your DV camcorder or deck.

DV Camcorder (or Deck)
- *DV tape playback is output to Final Cut Express*
- *Records Final Cut Express output to tape*
- *Monitors external video on viewfinder*

Computer Monitor
- *Monitors video in Viewer and Canvas windows*

Macintosh G3/G4 (FireWire equipped)
- *Final Cut Express captures DV*
- *Computer speakers monitor audio*
- *Internal hard drive stores DV and other media files, plus FCE application and project files*

FireWire Connection
One cable handles input and output of:
- *Digital video*   • *Device control*
- *Digital audio*   • *Timecode*

Figure 2.1 A basic FCE hardware setup.

HARDWARE SELECTION AND CONNECTION

High-resolution computer monitor: You view the results of your work on the computer's monitor.

A recommended setup (Figure 2.2) adds a dedicated hard drive to store your media, and enhances your monitoring capabilities with the addition of an NTSC or PAL video monitor and external speakers to the basic configuration.

◆ Adding a dedicated hard drive for your media files improves the performance as well as the media storage capacity of your system. For more information, see "Storage Strategy for Final Cut Express," earlier in this chapter.

◆ Most DV camcorders feature built-in LCD displays that you can use as an external video monitor, but if you're producing video projects to be viewed on television, you really should preview your video output on an NTSC monitor as you're editing. A real studio monitor is best, but even a consumer TV will give you a much more accurate idea of how your program looks and sounds. Connect the NTSC or PAL monitor to your video deck or camcorder using the component, S-video, or composite output jacks.

◆ External speakers, monitoring the audio output from your video camcorder or deck, will provide you with higher-quality audio output.

Figure 2.2 A recommended DV hardware configuration.

Connecting a DV camcorder

Connecting a DV camcorder or deck to your computer couldn't be simpler. All you need is a single FireWire cable, which transmits device control data, timecode, video, and audio between the DV device and your Mac.

To connect a DV device to your computer with FireWire:

1. Start with a 6-pin to 4-pin FireWire cable (**Figure 2.3**). Plug the 6-pin connector into the 6-pin FireWire port (**Figure 2.4**) and the 4-pin connector into your video device's DV port. (Ports on external devices are sometimes labeled IEEE 1394, DV IN/OUT, or iLink.) Both connectors snap into place when properly engaged.

2. Turn on the DV camcorder or deck.

3. Switch the DV device to VCR mode (sometimes labeled VTR).

Figure 2.3 A 6-pin to 4-pin FireWire cable. The 6-pin (big) end goes into your Mac's FireWire port; plug the 4-pin (small) end into your DV camcorder.

Figure 2.4 The FireWire logo labels the FireWire ports on the back of your computer.

FireWire Cables: Handle with Care

Before you hook up your FireWire connectors, take a careful look at the connector ends (the 4-pin connector is the smaller end). They are easy to connect, but the 4-pin connectors and ports can be especially fragile. Before connecting a 4-pin connector to its corresponding port, be sure to align it properly by matching an indent on the connector to the indent in the port. Do not force the two together.

The 6-pin connector (the larger end) plugs into one of the FireWire ports on the back of your Mac. Don't try to force the 4-pin connector into the computer's 6-pin FireWire port.

FCE Protocol: Disk Names

When naming hard drives, partitions, and folders that you intend to use with Final Cut Express, you should observe a special naming requirement—each hard disk must have a name that does not contain the entire name of another disk or partition. For example, disks named "Inferno" and "Inferno 1" could cause FCE to have trouble finding your files later.

What's the Difference Between DV and Digital Video?

When you refer to *digital video*, you could be talking about any video format that stores image and audio information in digital form—it's digital video whether you store it on a DV tape or on a DVD disc.

DV is a specific digital video format whose identifying characteristic is that conversion from analog to digital information takes place in the DV camera. So *DV* is a camera-based digital video format.

There are a few different flavors of DV; the differences between them come down to tape format and tape speed.

- DV usually refers to MiniDV, used by most consumer digital camcorders.

- DVCAM prints the same DV bitstream to a larger, more robust tape stock.

- DVC Pro uses a professional-grade tape as well, and it supports a high-quality mode—DVC Pro 50—which digitizes at twice the data rate as DV.

✔ Tips

- If your DV device is Apple FireWire compatible, connect it to the computer and turn it on before installing Final Cut Express to allow the installation program to automatically receive setup information from your DV camcorder or deck.

- Whenever you want to use a DV deck or camcorder, connect and turn on the device before opening FCE so the application can detect the device.

- If you want to use a camcorder as your playback/record deck, you must switch it to VCR mode. In VCR mode, the camcorder uses the video and audio connectors or FireWire for input and output. Because a camcorder in Camera mode has switched its inputs to receive information from the CCD sensor and microphone, Final Cut Express cannot record to the camcorder while it is in Camera mode.

HARDWARE SELECTION AND CONNECTION

Connecting an external NTSC or PAL video monitor

Final Cut Express is designed to use the audio and video outputs of your DV deck or camcorder to feed an external NTSC or PAL monitor. Because the monitor receives output from Final Cut Express through your device's outputs, you must have your device on and the FireWire connection established to your computer, or you won't be able to view output on your monitor while you work in Final Cut Express.

To connect an external NTSC or PAL monitor:

1. Position your video monitor at a comfortable viewing distance from your position in front of the computer.

2. *Do one of the following:*
   - Connect the audio and video outputs of your video deck or camcorder to the audio and video inputs of your NTSC or PAL monitor.
   - If you are using additional external speakers, or if your monitor has no speakers, connect only the video output from your video device to the video input of your video monitor. Use your video device's audio outputs to feed your external speakers.

3. After you install Final Cut Express, you can check or modify your viewing settings by choosing View > Video (**Figure 2.5**).

✔ Tip

- For more details on FCE's video output settings, see "FCE Protocol: Controlling External Video Output."

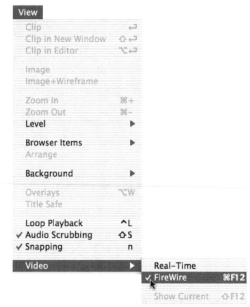

Figure 2.5 Choose View > Video to check or modify your external video output settings.

FCE Protocol: Controlling External Video Output

The external video display options in Final Cut Express require a little explanation. Using an external video monitor while editing is really the best way to work, so the program assumes you'll be working in this way and was designed to output video and audio via FireWire whenever a video device is connected to the system.

Here's the catch: you can preview real-time effects on your computer only when that video output is disabled.

The View > Video menu options control video output.

◆ View > Video > Real-Time disables the FireWire video output, thus enabling real-time effects preview on the computer monitor.

◆ View > Video > FireWire opens the video output feeding your DV camcorder, but disables real-time effects preview on the computer monitor.

◆ View > Video > Show Current renders the current frame only and displays it on your external video monitor. This option comes in handy when you're building effects and you want a quick "reality check" on your video monitor before you commit to a lengthy rendering process. The keyboard shortcut is Shift-F12.

If you monitor FCE's output through an external NTSC or PAL monitor, you may see a difference in the Canvas window playback quality. FCE gives CPU priority to the FireWire output to ensure that there are no dropped frames in that output signal, so the Canvas may play back at 15 frames per second (fps).

One day soon, you'll be able see your effects previewed in real time on your video monitor, but for now you'll have to choose. A keyboard shortcut (Command-F12) makes it easy to switch between video output and real-time effects preview.

FCE Protocol: Monitoring Audio Playback

◆ If you plan to use an external NTSC or PAL monitor as you edit, connect your external speakers to monitor the audio output of your camcorder or deck, so that the audio from the external speakers will be synchronized with the video displayed on the video monitor. You need to do this because audio from your computer's built-in audio outputs will be slightly out of sync with the NTSC or PAL monitor.

◆ FCE's default settings mute the audio feed to your computer's speakers whenever you're capturing video or whenever video signal is being output to your deck or camcorder via FireWire. So if you want to monitor audio and video through the computer, choose View > Video and select Real-Time, which turns off the external video feed.

Installing Final Cut Express

It's a good idea to set up and connect your additional hardware before you install the Final Cut Express software, because the type of DV deck or camcorder you use with Final Cut Express determines how the software is configured during installation. If you have not yet installed and configured the additional hardware you will be using with your computer, read "Hardware Selection and Connection," earlier in this chapter.

If you don't have your hardware yet, it's okay to proceed with the installation of the Final Cut Express software; you can always tweak the settings by hand later.

It's important to install your software in the recommended order.

To install Final Cut Express:

1. Be sure any external video hardware is connected and turned on before you start the installation procedure, so that Final Cut Express can automatically detect your video capture equipment.

2. If it's not already loaded, insert the Final Cut Express CD into your DVD or CD-ROM drive (**Figure 2.6**); then follow the onscreen installation instructions.

3. After reading the obligatory licensing agreement and ReadMe file, choose an install location from the Install Final Cut Express dialog box. Normally, you should choose the Applications folder on the startup disk; installing FCE in this folder gives all users of your computer access to the program (**Figure 2.7**).

Figure 2.6 The Final Cut Express application CD and installer. Don't forget to check out the Apple Final Cut Express User's Manual PDF in the Documentation folder.

Figure 2.7 If you install FCE into the Applications folder, any user of the computer can use the software.

Figure 2.8 You can install FCE into a private application folder within your Home directory.

Figure 2.9 For each user, FCE creates a Final Cut Express User Data folder. You can find it in each user's Preferences folder (in the user's Library folder).

However, if you want exclusive use of Final Cut Express, install the program in a private application folder you create inside your Home directory (**Figure 2.8**).

✔ Tips

- For each user, Final Cut Express creates a separate Final Cut Express User Data folder and generates a separate Custom Settings folder and Final Cut Preferences file (**Figure 2.9**).

- One big benefit of personal FCE Preference files is that your individual scratch disk preferences stay put, even when you're sharing your FCE system with the masses. As long as you remember to log in to your own identity before you start work, your preferences will load from your User Data folder when you launch FCE.

- Final Cut Express relies on QuickTime for its functionality, which is automatically installed under Mac OS X 10.2 and later. However, it's a good idea to check Apple's web site for the latest information on QuickTime updates and Final Cut Express version compatibility before you install FCE.

- You don't need to upgrade to QuickTime Pro to use Final Cut Express.

INSTALLING FINAL CUT EXPRESS

Where to Install FCE?

Here's a recommended installation configuration for a Final Cut Express system with two hard drives available:

You should leave your fastest drive completely free for media files only. Media files include captured audio and video, as well as rendered media files and any computer-generated graphics or motion graphics.

Keep your Final Cut Express project files on the same drive as the application.

You should also back up your project files to removable media with such frequency that your behavior seems obsessive to a casual observer. Go ahead, let 'em laugh.

Registering and choosing an initial setup

Be sure any external video hardware is connected and turned on before you launch Final Cut Express for the first time, so that FCE can detect your DV camcorder and streamline the Initial Setup process. With the standard hardware setup, your Initial Setup selections should correctly configure all your Final Cut Express audio and video settings automatically.

To register and choose your initial setup:

1. Open the Final Cut Express application and enter your registration information and serial number.

2. In the Choose Setup dialog box, choose an Easy Setup from the Setup For pop-up menu (**Figure 2.10**). Choose the setup that matches your system's video format and hardware. For more information, see "How to Choose an Easy Setup," later in this chapter.

   A brief description and summary of your selected Easy Setup appears below the pop-up menu (**Figure 2.11**).

Figure 2.10 In the Choose Setup dialog box, pick the Easy Setup that matches your system's video format and hardware.

Figure 2.11 After you choose an Easy Setup, a brief description and summary of its settings appears below its name.

Figure 2.12 Choose the disk you want to use to store your captured media from the Primary Scratch Disk pop-up menu.

3. From the Primary Scratch Disk pop-up menu, choose the disk you want to use to store your captured video, audio, render, and cache files (**Figure 2.12**). It is recommended that you save captured media files on a different disk than the disk where Final Cut Express is installed. For more information, see "Setting Scratch Disk Preferences," later in this chapter.

4. Click OK.

If you didn't connect a DV camcorder or deck during launch, Final Cut Express displays the External Video dialog box notifying you that it can't find an external device. Click Continue to dismiss it. If the dialog box appears and you did connect a device, see "Troubleshooting," later in this chapter.

Final Cut Express is now configured to use a standard set of preferences and preset controls based on information you supplied during initial setup. You may want to review the default preference settings before you dive into a project. For details on modifying preferences, read "Setting Preferences" later in this chapter.

Using Presets and Preferences

Capture, device control, and sequence settings are all organized into preset configurations, and these audio/video presets are grouped into master presets called *Easy Setups*.

FCE preference settings are accessed from two menu choices: Easy Setup and Preferences (**Figure 2.13**).

Figure 2.13 Preference settings are accessed from two Final Cut Express menu choices: Easy Setup and Preferences.

USING PRESETS AND PREFERENCES

How to "Trash Your Prefs"

FCE has made setting up preferences simple, but you may still find that you need to delete your FCE preferences files (or "trash your prefs") to force FCE to restore all your program settings to default values.

To find the three files you need to delete, go to: **User/Library/Preferences/** and remove the file called com.apple.FinalCutExpress.plist.

Then go to **User/Library/Preferences/Final Cut Express User Data/** and remove the other two preferences files, called Final Cut Express 1.0 Prefs and Final Cut Express MOA Cache, from the folder.

Relaunch Final Cut Express with all your external hardware on and connected. You'll see the Choose Setup dialog box. Here's your chance to reset your preferences from scratch.

Using Easy Setups

An Easy Setup is a single master preset configuration of multiple Final Cut Express settings: a Device Control preset, a Capture preset, a Sequence preset, and External Video settings. A preset is a group of saved settings that are automatically applied any time you create a new project or sequence. The beauty of a preset is that you can configure all your settings correctly with a single selection.

You selected an Easy Setup as part of the initial setup process. Your selected Easy Setup becomes your default setup, so all projects and sequences use these settings until you change them.

Once you have an Easy Setup that works for your Final Cut Express system, you shouldn't need to change it unless you change your video hardware or video format. If you do use your FCE system with a variety of different cameras or with footage shot in a different DV format, Easy Setups make it simple to switch configurations quickly and accurately.

In this section, you'll learn how to choose the correct Easy Setup and how to switch to a different Easy Setup.

Modifying the Settings of an Existing Item

If you switch to a different Easy Setup, or change your settings on the Timeline Options tab of the Preferences window, your change will be reflected in new projects, sequences, or items created after you changed the settings. Here's how and where you change the settings of a project, sequence, or clip you have already created:

- **Project Properties:** Open the project and then choose Edit > Project Properties.

- **Sequence Settings:** Control-click the sequence's icon in the Browser and then select Sequence Settings from the shortcut menu.

- **Item Properties:** Control-click the item's icon in the Browser or the Timeline and then select Item Properties from the shortcut menu.

For details on your settings options, see Chapter 3, "How to Manage an FCE Project."

How to choose an easy setup

The Easy Setups window displays the currently selected presets for each setting—Sequence, Capture, and Device Control, plus External Video—that make up your current Easy Setup, plus a brief description of when you should use the currently selected setup (**Figure 2.14**).

The DV-NTSC (or DV-PAL) setup will work for a majority of FCE users, but if you click the Easy Setups pop-up menu, you'll see a long list of other setups to choose from (**Figure 2.15**).

When should you switch to another Easy Setup? The basis for selecting a preset is always *matching*:

◆ You want your Capture preset to match the recorded format of the DV tape you're capturing. If the tape was recorded with 16-bit 48K audio, then the default DV-NTSC setup is fine. If you're capturing DV with 12-bit 32K audio, you'll need to switch to an Easy Setup with the same settings. If you're capturing DV that was shot in Anamorphic (wide-screen) format, switch to a setup set that includes Anamorphic.

◆ Your Sequence preset must match the format of your Capture preset. All Easy Setups in FCE take care of this for you.

◆ Your Device Control setting must match the requirements of the DV camcorder or deck you're controlling. Final Cut Express is pretty good at automatically selecting the correct device control setting, but if you're having trouble controlling your DV device from inside FCE, check the Final Cut Express Qualified Devices page at www.apple.com/finalcutexpress/qualification.html.

Figure 2.14 The Easy Setup window.

Figure 2.15 You'll find a long list of Easy Setups to choose from. Choose the one that matches the format of the video you want to capture.

USING EASY SETUPS

32 kHz refers to the alternate audio sample rate on most DV camcorders

Anamorphic refers to the alternate video aspect ratio: wide-screen (16:9)

FW Basic refers to the alternate FireWire device control setup

Figure 2.16 An Easy Setup's name indicates which alternates to the default preset are included. If a default preset is used, it's omitted from the name.

◆ Your External Video setting must match the video format (DV or PAL) of the device you're outputting video to.

◆ DV-NTSC, FCE's default setup, is designed to complement the recommended settings on most DV camcorders. (The default settings are the same in the two video standards that FCE supports: NTSC and PAL.)

✔ Tip

■ Unfortunately, many consumer DV camcorders come from the factory set to record audio at the lower quality 12-bit 32kHz setting. FCE assumes you'll be savvy enough to switch your camera settings to 16-bit 48kHz—the recommended higher quality audio setting. Check any source tapes you're capturing, and be aware that if your camera is set at 32kHz, choosing the default Easy Setup will result in a settings mismatch.

Here are the settings for DV-NTSC:

◆ **Sequence preset:** DV-NTSC 48 kHz

◆ **Capture preset:** DV-NTSC 48 kHz Capture

◆ **Device control preset:** FireWire NTSC

◆ **External video for playback and print to video:** Apple FireWire NTSC (720 x 480)

When an Easy Setup offers an alternate setting to any of these default presets, the alternate is listed in the Easy Setup's name. **Figure 2.16** dissects one example.

To switch to a different Easy Setup:

1. Choose Final Cut Express > Easy Setup.

2. From the Setup For pop-up menu, select an Easy Setup (**Figure 2.17**).

   A summary of your selected Easy Setup appears below the pop-up menu (**Figure 2.18**).

3. Click Setup.

   The new Easy Setup affects only new projects and sequences and doesn't change settings for existing projects and sequences.

✔ Tip

- Using FireWire Basic as your device control protocol will have no effect on the input or output quality of your digital video and audio.

Figure 2.17 From the Setup For pop-up menu, select an Easy Setup.

Figure 2.18 A summary of your selected Easy Setup appears below the pop-up menu.

USING EASY SETUPS

Apple FireWire vs. Basic FireWire

Apple FireWire is a high-speed serial bus that allows simultaneous transfer of digital video, digital audio, timecode information, and device control, all through a single cable. Nearly all Macintosh models of the past few years include built-in FireWire ports. FireWire's usefulness is not limited to digital video—a wide variety of hard drives, printers, scanners, audio mixers, and other peripheral devices take advantage of FireWire's high speeds and advanced features.

FireWire (IEEE 1394) serial bus technology is currently supported by many professional and consumer-level camcorders and decks. However, not all manufacturers have implemented the full FireWire specification in their products, so some devices don't fully support Final Cut Express's device control. That is why Final Cut Express provides two versions of the FireWire protocol in its Device Control presets: Apple FireWire and Apple FireWire Basic.

If your deck or camcorder uses FireWire, try selecting the Apple FireWire protocol first. With Apple FireWire selected, your device should support the most basic functions like returning timecode and accepting basic transport commands. If you discover that your device does not accurately go to specified timecodes or fails to execute special commands, switch to the FireWire Basic protocol.

Setting Preferences

Unlike the Easy Setup presets, which are largely dictated by your hardware and video format, a preference is a setting that specifies how *you* want to work with your media in Final Cut Express. The settings in the Preferences window affect all your Final Cut Express projects. The Preferences window contains four tabs: General (for general program behavior), Timeline Options, External Editors, and Scratch Disks.

To set general preferences:

1. Choose Final Cut Express > Preferences. The General tab appears as the front tab in the Preferences window (**Figure 2.19**).

2. Specify settings for the following:

◆ **Levels of Undo:** Specify the number of actions that can be undone. Specifying a large number of undos can make significant demands on your available RAM.

◆ **List Recent Clips:** Set the number of recently accessed clips available on the Viewer's Recent Clips pop-up menu (see Chapter 7).

◆ **Multi-Frame Trim Size:** Set the multiframe trim size by specifying the number of frames (up to nine) in this field. The specified number appears in the multiframe trim buttons in the Trim Edit window (see Chapter 10).

continues on next page

Figure 2.19 Specify a number of general program preferences on the General tab of the Preferences window.

♦ **Sync Adjust Movies Over:** Sync Adjust's only function is to compensate for audio sync problems in long, continuous clip captures from video shot on certain cameras, notably certain Canon models. *Unless you experience sync problems in long captures, turn off the Sync Adjust function by unchecking its box.* If you are capturing long clips from source tapes shot by cameras whose audio sampling rates are not exactly 48.000 KHz, enter a number of minutes in this field to specify a minimum capture length. Final Cut Express will sample-rate-convert the clip's audio on the fly to compensate for the sync problem. For details, see Chapter 4.

♦ **Real-Time Audio Mixing:** Specify the number of audio tracks that Final Cut Express mixes in real time. The default setting is 8 tracks. The maximum number of tracks you will be able to mix depends on multiple factors. Reduce the number of tracks if you experience audio playback problems, such as video stuttering or audio pops or dropouts (see Chapter 11).

♦ **Audio Playback Quality:** This pop-up menu allows you to choose the quality of the sample rate conversion when you import audio files with sample rates that differ from your sequence's rate. At the lowest playback quality, Final Cut Express can reserve more processing power for real-time mixing operations. If you choose the highest playback quality, your sample–rate-converted audio will sound better, but you won't be able to stack as many simultaneous audio tracks before FCE needs to mixdown (render) your audio. Higher quality settings will take more processing time, so the default is set to Low. In general, choose Low when editing. FCE automatically defaults to the highest audio quality during all rendering, audio mixdown, and printing to video operations,

so you won't need to switch the setting in the Audio Playback Quality pop-up menu when you're ready to output your sequence.

♦ **Still/Freeze Duration:** Enter a duration (in seconds) in this field to specify a default duration between In and Out points for imported still images, generators, and Adobe Photoshop files (see Chapter 5). Feel free to change this setting at will to increase your efficiency, for example, when you're producing a series of freeze frames of a uniform length.

♦ **Preview Pre-roll:** Enter a number of seconds in this field to specify how much media to play before the edit point when you click the Play Around Current button or the Play Around Edit-Loop button.

♦ **Preview Post-roll:** Enter a number of seconds in this field to specify how much media to play after the edit point when you click the Play Around Current button or the Play Around Edit-Loop button.

♦ **Thumbnail Cache (Disk):** Specify the amount of disk space to allocate for storing thumbnails.

♦ **Thumbnail Cache (RAM):** Specify the amount of memory to allocate for storing thumbnails. Increase this value to improve the program's performance.

♦ **RT Still Cache (RAM):** This preference appears only on Macs that support real-time effects. Specify the amount of memory to allocate for storing graphics. The recommended minimum is 25 MB, but you should increase this value if your projects include large numbers of graphics.

♦ **Show ToolTips:** Check this box to toggle the display of tooltip labels on buttons and tools.

◆ **Warn if Visibility Change Deletes Render File:** Check this box to display a warning dialog box whenever making tracks invisible would cause render files to be deleted (see Chapter 9).

◆ **Report Dropped Frames During Playback:** Check this box to display a warning dialog box whenever frames are dropped during playback.

◆ **Abort Capture on Dropped Frames:** Check this box to automatically stop the capture process if dropped frames are detected during the capture process (see Chapter 4).

◆ **Abort Capture on Timecode Break:** Check this box to automatically stop the capture process if a timecode break is detected during the capture process. If you leave this box unchecked, FCE will report the timecode break after your capture operation is complete, and it will retain that captured media file.

  ◆ **Prompt for Settings on New Sequence:** Check this box only if you want to see a list of sequence presets each time you create a new sequence. The default is unchecked.

◆ **Bring All Windows to the Front on Activation:** Under Mac OS X, the standard window behavior is to bring only the selected window to the front. Check this box to display all FCE windows when you make the program active.

◆ **Autosave Vault:** Check this box if you want FCE to save backup copies of all your open projects automatically at regular intervals. For more information, see "Using the Autosave Vault" in Chapter 3.

  ◆ **Save a Copy Every:** Enter a number of minutes in this field to specify a time interval between backup operations.

  ◆ **Keep at Most:** Enter a value to specify how many autosaved backup copies of each project file you want to store.

  ◆ **Maximum of:** Enter a value to specify the maximum number of projects you want to back up in the Autosave vault.
    If the number of open projects exceeds the number specified here, Final Cut Express overrides the maximum you set and autosaves all open projects.

✔ Tip

■ Increasing the Thumbnail Cache settings can improve performance in several areas. Displaying video on the computer monitor while printing to video taxes the computer's processing power and can cause performance problems. You also may want to increase the thumbnail cache sizes if you are working with a large number of clips and want to display thumbnails, or if you are using the Browser's Icon view. If you often scrub through thumbnails in the Browser's Icon view, you can optimize the performance of this feature by increasing the the thumbnail RAM cache. Set a location for the thumbnail disk cache on the Scratch Disks tab of the Preferences window.

Customizing the Timeline Display

The Timeline display options you specify on the Timeline Options tab in the Preferences window become the default display settings for subsequent new projects and sequences. If you want to modify these options for an existing sequence, you must make the change in the Sequence Settings window for that sequence. See "Changing the Settings of an Existing Sequence," in Chapter 3.

To customize your default Timeline display settings:

1. Choose Final Cut Express > Preferences.

2. Click the Timeline Options tab (**Figure 2.20**). You can modify the default settings for any of the following:

   ◆ **Track Size:** Choose a setting from this pop-up menu to specify a default track size.

◆ **Thumbnail Display:** Select one of three thumbnail display options from this pop-up menu:

   ◆ Name displays the name of the clip and no thumbnail images.

   ◆ Name Plus Thumbnail displays the first frame of every clip as a thumbnail image and then the name of the clip.

   ◆ Filmstrip displays as many thumbnail images as possible for the Timeline's current zoom level.

◆ **Show Keyframe Overlays:** Check this box to display opacity keyframe overlays on video clips and level keyframe graphs on audio clips in the Timeline.

◆ **Show Audio Waveforms:** Check this box to display the audio waveform along the audio clip in the Timeline.

◆ **Default Number of Tracks:** Specify the number of video and audio tracks to be included in a new sequence. Your custom Timeline display settings become the defaults for subsequent new sequences.

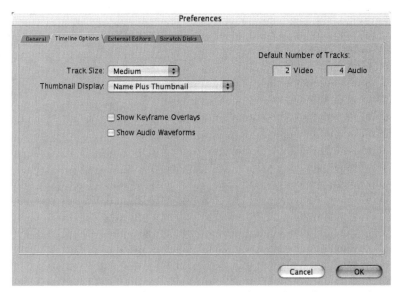

Figure 2.20 Customize your default Timeline display options on the Preferences window's Timeline Options tab.

Setting External Editors Preferences

When you're coaxing a stack of graphic elements you've created in a layered Photoshop file into a seamless match with your video elements, you may find yourself making many, many trips back and forth between FCE and Photoshop. The External Editors preferences are designed to speed the process of modifying a media file you've created in another application.

In this Preferences tab, you can specify which program will become the default editing application for each of three different media types: still image, video, and audio.

To specify external editors preferences:

1. Choose Final Cut Express > Preferences.

2. Click the External Editors tab.

3. Specify settings for the following (**Figure 2.21**):

   ◆ **Clear:** Click the Clear button to reset the External Editor for that file type to the default application used by Mac OS X.

   ◆ **Set:** Set a new external editor by clicking the Set button, navigating to the folder location of the editing application you want to specify, and clicking Open.

The path name and the application name appear next to the file type in the External Editors tab.

Figure 2.21 The path name and the application name appear next to the file type in the External Editors tab.

Setting Scratch Disk Preferences

A *scratch disk* is a folder on a hard disk where Final Cut Express stores your captured media source files and render files. The default scratch disk location is the hard disk where Final Cut Express is installed, but if possible you should specify another large-capacity disk as your primary scratch disk. You can specify multiple scratch disk locations to provide the necessary storage capacity for your project media.

You should use your fastest disk drives as your scratch disks. For best performance, avoid setting the startup disk as the scratch disk.

When you add a disk or folder to the scratch disk list, Final Cut Express automatically creates a folder on that disk called Final Cut Express Documents. That folder contains subfolders (one for each type of media file your project will generate) named Capture Scratch, Render Files, Audio Render Files, Thumbnail Cache Files, and Waveform Cache Files (**Figure 2.22**). Your captured media files are stored in a folder, bearing your project's name, inside the Capture Scratch folder.

✔ Tip

- Final Cut Express requires that each hard disk have a distinct name that does not contain the entire name of another media drive. For example, the program will not reliably distinguish between two drives named "Media" and "Media 1", but "Media 1" and "Media 2" are acceptable names. Bear this in mind when you assign names to hard drives.

Figure 2.22 The Final Cut Express Documents folder contains a subfolder for each type of media file that your project will generate.

To specify scratch disk preferences:

1. Choose Final Cut Express > Preferences.

2. Click the Scratch Disks tab.

3. Click the Set button to choose a hard disk to use as the scratch disk.

   To use more than one hard disk, click the next active Set button in the list. The Clear button removes a disk from the list.

4. Specify settings for the following (**Figure 2.23**):

   ◆ **Video Capture, Audio Capture, Video Render, and Audio Render:** Check these boxes to specify the types of files to be stored on each disk. (In FCE, DV video and audio are always captured to the same drive, which is why these checkboxes are linked.) Specify more than one disk for increased storage space. When the current disk runs out of space, Final Cut Express automatically switches to the next specified disk for storing capture files or to the disk with the most space available for storing render files.

   continues on next page

Figure 2.23 The Scratch Disks tab of the Preferences window.

SETTING SCRATCH DISK PREFERENCES

◆ **Waveform Cache:** Click the Set button
to specify a folder or disk to store waveform cache files (graphical representations
of audio signals).

◆ **Thumbnail Cache:** Click the Set button
to specify a folder or disk to store thumbnail cache files.

◆ **Autosave Vault:** Click the Set button to
specify a folder or disk to store FCE's automatic backup copies of your project files.

◆ **Minimum Allowable Free Space on
Scratch Disks:** Enter a limit value in
this field. When available disk space falls
below this minimum, a disk is no longer
used as a scratch disk, and files are stored
on the next disk in the list.

◆ **Limit Capture/Export File Segment
Size To:** Enter a limit value in this field.
The default value is 2,000 MB (2 GB).
Final Cut Express allows capture and
export of single files larger than 2 GB, but
if you plan to move your files to another
system that has a file size limitation,
or if you are sharing media files over a
network, you should enable this option.
Files that are larger than your specified
limit are spanned (written as separate,
but linked, files).

◆ **Limit Capture Now To:** Enter a value
in this field to control the maximum
time allowed by the Capture window's
Capture Now button. The default limit
is 30 minutes.

FCE Protocol: Scratch Disks

Unless you specify otherwise, Final Cut
Express uses the disk with the most available space as its storage area for rendered
files. If you specify multiple scratch disks,
Final Cut Express will use the next disk
in the list with the most available space
when the current disk runs out of space.
Specify separate disks for captured video
and audio files to obtain better capture
quality at higher data rates and improved
playback performance.

Zoom

Figure 2.24 If you see scroll bars on the edge of the Canvas's image area, you're zoomed in too far for optimum playback performance and your external video playback will be disabled. Choose Fit to Window from the Canvas Zoom pop-up menu to bring the entire frame back into view.

Optimizing Performance

Trying to eke out the best possible performance from Final Cut Express? Here's a rundown of settings and maintenance tips that can help FCE perform more efficiently:

Settings

◆ Turn off AppleTalk.

◆ Turn off file sharing.

◆ Avoid running processor-intensive operations in other open applications while you're working in Final Cut Express (especially when capturing video).

Display

◆ Make sure the entire image area is visible in windows playing video. If you see scroll bars on the edge of the Viewer or the Canvas (**Figure 2.24**), you're zoomed in too far for optimum performance.

◆ Don't place program windows so that they split across dual monitors.

Disk maintenance

◆ Store project files on your startup disk, and store media and rendered files on a separate hard disk.

◆ Defragment disk drives regularly, especially those used for capturing. You can use a defragmentation utility; or, make a complete backup of your data, erase the disk, and restore your data.

continues on next page

OPTIMIZING PERFORMANCE

- When a project is finished and archived, delete all files from the disk you used to create the project and defragment the drive. This helps prepare the disk for the next project.

- Final Cut Express performs poorly if you try to work with remote media files over a network connection. Copy files from the network to a local disk before importing them

- It's a good idea to run Disk First Aid, a component of Apple's Disk Utility application, once or twice a month to check your drive's data directory.

The Bottom Line: Running FCE on a G3-based Mac

To get the best performance possible from Final Cut Express running on a slower G3, you'll have to give up a little flexibility in your display options, but you may find that the improved responsiveness and playback quality are worth it.

1. Eliminate display scaling. Scaling the video to match the size of the playback window in the Viewer or the Canvas is handled by the computer's video card, but it takes a lot of processing power to pull off. To reduce the card's demands on your CPU, set your display option to match DV's native display format: 50 percent, non-square pixels. Go to the Zoom pop-up menu in the Canvas, set the View size to 50 percent, and then uncheck the View as Square Pixels box.

2. In the Monitors preference pane, set your monitor resolution to 1024 by 768 or lower and your color depth to Millions.

3. On the General tab of the Preferences window, reduce the number of undos as well as the number of recent items. These changes will free up more RAM.

4. Keep your projects lean by deleting old versions of sequences that you no longer need to reference. Smaller projects reduce the amount of RAM necessary to track an open project file.

5. Reinitialize your drives. Quite often, old drive software and/or drivers will impair performance.

Troubleshooting

You probably won't encounter any of these problems. But if you run into snags after installing Final Cut Express and configuring your hardware, the following tips may help.

Many of the tips presented here involve checking and adjusting preferences. But before you start changing individual preference settings, try this: Choose Final Cut Express > Easy Setup and make sure you're still using the correct Easy Setup for your video format and hardware.

Also, make sure you're running the latest version of Final Cut Express by checking Apple's web site.

You'll find a complete guide to setting preferences and presets earlier in this chapter.

You can't establish a device control connection with your camcorder or deck.

◆ Make sure the FireWire cable connecting your computer and DV camcorder is properly connected.

◆ Verify that the camcorder is set to VCR mode.

◆ If your device has a Local/Remote switch, be sure it's set to Remote.

◆ Turn the device off and back on and then restart Final Cut Express.

You can't control certain functions of your camcorder or deck.

◆ Make sure the FireWire cable connecting your computer and DV camcorder is properly connected.

◆ If you are using a device with FireWire, try switching the device control protocol from Apple FireWire to FireWire Basic.

◆ If your device has a Local/Remote switch, make sure it's switched to Remote.

◆ A few DV camcorders require special *DV tuner scripts*, little plug-ins that help FCE interpret the camera's device control protocols. The scripts should be available from Apple's Final Cut Express web site; check the site to see if your camcorder requires a script. If your camera requires a "tuner script" you should place it in FCE's Plug-ins folder.

You don't hear audio on your computer's speakers when playing video from your camcorder or deck.

◆ Make sure your audio cables are properly connected.

◆ When you enable your external video output to monitor video externally (by choosing FireWire from the View menu), your audio and video are routed to your external monitor or video device, and your computer's speakers are not receiving any audio. Make sure your external monitor and speakers are on and that the volume is turned up. To disable external video output, choose View > Video and select Real-Time.

Video is not visible on an external NTSC or PAL monitor.

◆ Make sure your cables are properly connected, and that your monitor is on.

◆ Verify that the camcorder is set to VCR mode.

◆ Confirm that external video output is enabled. Choose View > Video, and make sure that the FireWire option is checked.

◆ Make sure the Capture window is closed.

You notice dropped frames on your NTSC or PAL monitor during DV playback from the Timeline.

Like the common cold, dropped frames are frequently a symptom of an overworked system. Refer to the Appendix of the Final Cut Express User's Manual, *Solutions to Common Problems and Customer Support*, for a comprehensive list of possible causes for dropped frames. Here are a few easy things to try first:

◆ In the Canvas, choose Fit to Window from the Zoom pop-up menu to ensure that the image area displays the entire frame.

◆ Reduce the Canvas or Viewer view size to 50 percent.

◆ Disable Show as Square Pixels in the Zoom pop-up menu.

◆ Set the Audio Quality Playback to Low Quality and reduce the number of Real-Time Audio Mixing tracks specified on the General tab in the Preferences window.

◆ Turn off AppleTalk and file sharing.

◆ Make sure your media drives are fast enough to feed media files to FCE, and that the drives have not become so fragmented that their performance is impaired.

Video playback on the computer screen seems a little blurry.

◆ DV is set to play on older G3s at low quality, because these systems can't process software decompression any faster. You'll see the picture snap into focus when you stop DV playback in the Viewer or the Canvas. That's because FCE substitutes a high-quality still frame when you pause playback. So to play back DV at 29.97 fps in full quality, you need to connect an NTSC or PAL monitor to the video output of your external DV device.

You hear beeping that indicates unrendered audio playback of a single clip.

◆ Check which Audio Playback quality you have selected on the General tab of the Preferences window. If your audio clip's sample rate is not precisely 48000 kHz, Low quality playback is the only quality level that can sample-rate convert in real time.

Choose a higher quality setting and FCE will want to render your clip's audio before playback, so select Low quality (it won't affect the quality of your final audio, it's just for monitoring as you work. Besides, Low doesn't sound all that bad).

How to Manage an FCE Project

3

A Final Cut Express project is more than a collection of media files. The real power of Final Cut Express lies in the way the media is controlled by the intelligence of the program's data structuring. To take advantage of that power, you must take control of the data.

This chapter introduces Final Cut Express's system of organizing your video projects. You'll get an overview of Final Cut Express's organizing frameworks—projects, sequences, and clips.

Longer, more complex projects sometimes require a little extra care and feeding, so you'll find project management strategies, and techniques for building a project that contains multiple sequences. You'll also find tips on how to delete media files—and how to resurrect deleted files.

Final Cut Express is a nondestructive, nonlinear editing system, and that design has an impact on the way it handles file management. You'll be much more effective as a media manager if you understand how Final Cut Express tracks media files and project data before you use the project management techniques described in this chapter.

"FCE Protocol: Clips and Sequences," found in this chapter, explains the one rule in FCE you really need to know in order to understand how this program constructs edits.

Anatomy of an FCE Project

A Final Cut Express project breaks down into the following key components.

Project: The top level of the FCE organizing framework, a *project* file stores references (file location information) to all the media files you use to complete a particular program, along with the sequencing information (your "cut") and all settings for special effects you apply to any clip in the project. The project file contains no media—it's strictly the "brains" of your project—but this one file is your project's most valuable asset. All your editing genius is stored in this modest data file.

Sequence: The middle level of the Final Cut Express organizing framework, a *sequence* is an edited assembly of audio and video clips. A sequence is always part of a project, and you can have multiple sequences in a project, but you can't save a sequence separately from a project. However, you can copy a sequence from one project and paste it into another project.

Clip: The ground level of the FCE organizing framework, the *clip* represents an individual unit of media in Final Cut Express. A clip can stand for a movie, still image, nested sequence, generator, or audio file. Clip types appear in the Browser's Type column, and each type of clip displays an identifying icon.

Figure 3.1 diagrams the FCE organizing framework.

Figure 3.2 shows how FCE project structure plays out in the Browser and Timeline windows.

Project item types

On a project's Browser tab, you'll find quite a few different clip types, but you'll also find containers for holding clips— sequences and bins. The Browser's Effects tab contains other types of non-clip project items, audio and video filters and transitions, and generators. See "Browser Window Icons" in Chapter 6 for descriptions of each type of item you'll encounter in a project.

Figure 3.1 The project file is at the top level of FCE's organizing framework. You organize multiple clips and sequences inside a project file.

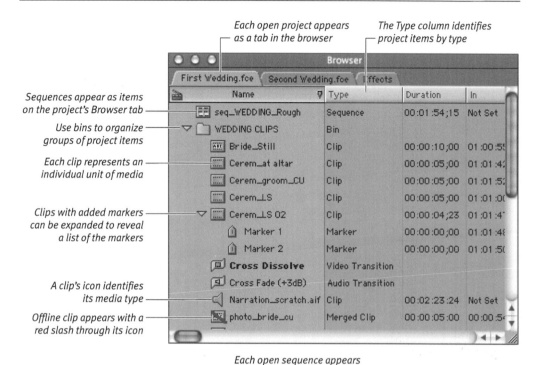

Each open project appears as a tab in the browser

The Type column identifies project items by type

Sequences appear as items on the project's Browser tab

Use bins to organize groups of project items

Each clip represents an individual unit of media

Clips with added markers can be expanded to reveal a list of the markers

A clip's icon identifies its media type

Offline clip appears with a red slash through its icon

Each open sequence appears as a tab in the Timeline

Figure 3.2 The Browser (top) and Timeline (bottom) interfaces provide a variety of information on items in your project.

ANATOMY OF AN FCE PROJECT

About Projects

Project files store disk location information for all the media files used in a program, along with the sequencing information for your edited program plus the settings for special effects applied to any clip in the project. The data stored in a project file is used to re-create the timing, sequencing, and transitions and effects you specify for a particular cut, *without altering or changing the storage location of your original source files.* (Note: If you haven't read the section "What Is Nonlinear Nondestructive Editing?" in Chapter 1, please do so now. It's key to understanding how Final Cut Express works.)

To get started in Final Cut Express, you create a new project and then start adding clips and sequences to the Browser window as you shape your project. Sequences can be exported independently as movies or clips, but they can't be saved separately from a project.

To create a new project:

◆ Choose File > New Project (**Figure 3.3**); or press Command-E.

A new project tab appears in the Browser window (**Figure 3.4**).

To open a project:

1. Choose File > Open; or press Command-O.

2. Locate and select the project file you want to open (**Figure 3.5**).

3. Click Choose.

Figure 3.3 Choose New Project from the File menu.

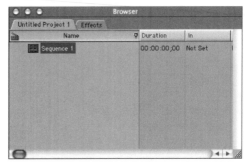

Figure 3.4 The Browser window with a new, untitled project. Sequence 1 appears automatically when you create a new project.

Figure 3.5 Locate the project file you want to open.

ABOUT PROJECTS

Figure 3.6 Choose Save Project As from the File menu.

Figure 3.7 After you've typed the new name for your project, click Save.

Figure 3.8 Choose Save All from the File menu.

To save a project:

◆ Choose File > Save Project; or press Command-S.

To save a project with a different name:

1. Choose File > Save Project As (**Figure 3.6**).

2. In the dialog box, type a name for the project in the Save Project As field.

3. Choose a destination folder.

4. Click Save (**Figure 3.7**).

To save all open projects:

1. Choose File > Save All (**Figure 3.8**).

2. If you created one or more new projects that haven't yet been saved, type a name for the first one in the dialog box.

3. Choose a destination folder.

4. Click Save.

   Repeat steps 2 through 4 for each new project that you want to save. Previously saved open projects are saved automatically.

ABOUT PROJECTS

Using Save As to Protect Your Work

Opening, modifying, and then saving the same project file day after day increases the chance that your precious project file will become corrupt and unusable.

Use the Save As command to back up your project file every day or so. Save As makes a fresh copy of the current version of your project file.

Give the original project file a version number, revert the name of your fresh duplicate to the base name of your project, and then continue working in the new duplicate version.

Because FCE automatically creates a new, separate capture folder every time you change the name of your project; to avoid the complications that arise from changing the name of your project file (multiple capture folders), you'll need to add an identifying version number to your older project file and then be sure that your active project file always has the same original name (**Figure 3.9**).

FCE's vault system, which automatically saves and then archives multiple versions of your project, provides you with a fail-safe backup, but some editors still prefer to retain control over the process. Good habits are hard to break.

Figure 3.9 Rename your older project file with an identifying version number and use the original project file name on your fresh copy.

Figure 3.10 Control-click a project's tab to bring up the shortcut menu; note the special cursor.

Figure 3.11 Control-clicking the project's tab will result in only one choice; choose Close Tab to close the project.

Figure 3.12 Click a project's tab to bring it to the front of the Browser.

To close a project:

1. In the Browser, Control-click the project's tab (**Figure 3.10**).

2. From the shortcut menu, choose Close Tab (**Figure 3.11**).

Or *do one of the following:*

- In the Browser, click the project's tab to bring it to the front (**Figure 3.12**). Then choose File > Close Project.

- In the Browser, press Command-W. For all projects you've modified, Final Cut Express will ask which projects you want to close.

✔ Tip

- To close all open projects, close the Browser window.

ABOUT PROJECTS

Viewing and Setting Project Properties

Each project has a set of properties that are saved with it. The project's properties apply to all sequences in a project and are independent of the project's sequence presets.

To view or change the Properties of a project:

1. In the Browser, click the Project tab.

2. Choose Edit > Project Properties (**Figure 3.13**).

3. In the Project Properties window (**Figure 3.14**), *do any of the following:*

- ◆ Display timecode or frames in the browser's Duration column. Choosing Frames displays the total number of frames for clips and sequences in the Duration column.

- ◆ Edit the heading labels for the Comment columns that appear in the Browser window.

4. After you make your changes, click OK.

To revert a project:

1. Choose File > Revert Project.

2. In the warning dialog box, click OK (**Figure 3.15**).

Final Cut Express reverts the current project file to its condition at the last time you saved the file.

Figure 3.13 Choose Project Properties from the Edit menu.

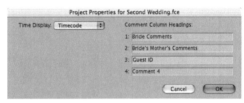

Figure 3.14 You can rename Comment column headings, and choose the timecode or frame display format from the Project Properties window.

Figure 3.15 After you choose File > Revert Project, you'll see a dialog box warning you that your unsaved changes will be lost.

ABOUT PROJECTS

Figure 3.16 Choose Restore Project from the File menu.

Figure 3.17 Select the archived project you want to restore; then click Restore.

To restore a project:

1. Choose File > Restore Project (**Figure 3.16**).

2. In the Restore Projects dialog box, select the archived project file you want to restore from the pull-down menu (**Figure 3.17**).

3. Click Restore.

   Final Cut Express opens the selected archived project from the Autosave vault.

✔ Tips

- If you want to replace the current version of your project with this dated archived version, you should save the archive copy with the same project name as your current version. This will maintain continuity in capture folders and Autosave archives.

- Final Cut Express 1.0.1 (the latest version as this book went to press) does not reliably locate the Autosave Vault. If you're in need of an archived project file, you'll need to open it from the Autosave Vault folder on your drive. Don't worry, your archived backups are in there.

Using the Autosave Vault

Final Cut Express's Autosave Vault feature automatically saves all open projects as you work, at a time interval that you select. The vault stores multiple, dated backup copies of your project. This archive can come in handy. For example, maybe you're at the point in a project where you are trying new approaches to refine your cut, and you want to discard your last experiment. Or maybe you and your collaborator just don't agree, and she's completely recut your program while you were away for the weekend.

Each autosaved version is a backup copy that includes all changes you've made (up to the last autosave time) in the project file that you're currently working on (that project file is modified only when you invoke the Save or Save All command). If you haven't made any changes in an open project file since the last backup copy was autosaved, FCE won't archive another backup in the Autosave vault until you do.

Setting Autosave vault location and preferences

You can set Autosave preferences on the General tab of the Preferences window. See "General Preferences Settings" in Chapter 2 for details on your settings options.

The backup copies of your project files are archived in a folder (**Figure 3.18**) located inside your Final Cut Express Documents folder. If you want to store your archive of backups elsewhere, specify another location on the Scratch Disks tab of the Preferences window (**Figure 3.19**).

Figure 3.18 In the Autosave vault, dated backup copies of your project files are archived in a folder.

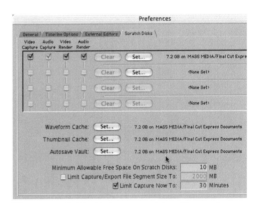

Figure 3.19 Set the Autosave vault location on the Scratch Disks tab of the Preferences window.

When the number of backup copies in the Autosave Vault reaches the limit you set in the preferences, FCE deletes the oldest Autosave file (or project folder) to make room for the newest Autosave file, unless the oldest project archived in the vault is currently open. FCE overrides the maximum projects limit you set if the number of open projects exceeds your specified limit when a scheduled Autosave occurs.

Using Autosave to recover from a crash

If your computer powers off or crashes while you're working, Final Cut Express will open the last saved version of your project file when you re-launch. The choice is yours—continue to work in your original file, or use the Restore Project command to open your most recent autosaved backup copy. Here's the drill:

To use Autosave to recover from a crash:

1. After you've restarted you should go to the folder where you archived your current original project file (that's the file you just crashed out of) and rename that file so it won't be overwritten and you can return to it, if need be.

2. Launch FCE, then use the Restore Project command to go to the Autosave Vault, and open the most recent Autosave backup version of your project file in FCE.

3. After you've checked out the integrity of the autosaved file in FCE, save the autosaved project file with your original project name.

✔ Tip

■ Due to a bug in FCE 1.0.1, you may need to navigate to the Autosave Vault outside the program and open the last autosaved project file manually.

You Need Backup

◆ The Autosave Vault should not be used as a substitute for your own systematic archiving of your project files. The Autosave Vault folder is not locked, and the oldest backups are purged regularly.

◆ Be consistent about where you store your project files. Make sure that all files relating to a project are stored in the same place.

◆ Back up project files on your FCE system and again on a removable disk or in another safe location to avoid losing files in case of a power outage or another technical problem. Project files contain all your time and hard work. Without the editing information in the project files, your media files have no sequencing information. Protect it. Okay—end of lecture.

USING THE AUTOSAVE VAULT

Undoing Changes

You can undo every type of action you perform in your projects, sequences, and clips, as well as redo actions that you have undone. FCE can store up to 32 actions across multiple projects—you set the number of Undos in the General Preferences window.

To undo the last action:

◆ Choose Edit > Undo (**Figure 3.20**), or press Command-Z.

To redo the last undone action:

◆ Choose Edit > Redo, or press Command-Y.

To specify the number of actions that can be undone:

1. Choose Final Cut Express > Preferences.

2. On the General tab of the Preferences window, set the levels of undo operations to a number between 1 and 32 (**Figure 3.21**).

Figure 3.20 Choose Edit > Undo to undo your last action.

Figure 3.21 You can set the levels of undo to any number between 1 and 32 on the General tab of the Preferences window.

FCE Protocol: Undoing Changes in Multiple Projects

FCE's Undo feature can track up to 32 changes across multiple projects, but it makes no distinction between projects.

If you are working with more than one sequence or project, check to be sure that you are in the correct one when you choose Undo. Even so, the change you undo may not occur in the current project, so take care when undoing multiple changes.

Reconnecting Offline Files

In Final Cut Express, the links between your clips and sequences in the Browser and the underlying media source files on disk are based on the media file's location. If you rename the source media files used in a project or sequence, the next time you open your project, you'll be greeted with the Offline Files window full of clips marked "missing." Don't panic. You can reconnect clips to media on your disk using the Reconnect Media command.

It's important to understand how Final Cut Express's protocols governing clip versions affect the reconnection process. Remember that the clips in your sequence are considered separate copies of the clips in the Browser. If a clip is used in a sequence, you must reconnect both the sequence version and the Browser version of the clip (**Figure 3.22**). This is a little tricky, because in FCE, the sequence icon in the Browser doesn't display the red diagonal offline indicator to warn you that it contains offline clips. When you are reconnecting offline files, be sure to select the sequence in the Browser as well as the clips. Selecting the sequence when you are reconnecting allows you to locate files for all offline clips in the sequence.

✔ Tip

- You can use Final Cut Express's Find function to search for all the offline clips and sequences in a project (set the search criteria to Offline (Y/N) Contains "Yes") and then select and reconnect the offline clips and sequences right in the Find Results window.

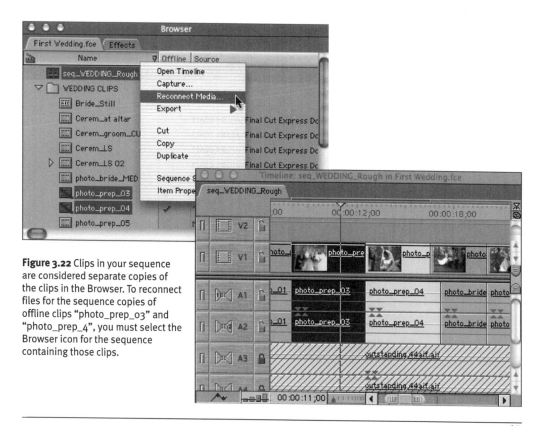

Figure 3.22 Clips in your sequence are considered separate copies of the clips in the Browser. To reconnect files for the sequence copies of offline clips "photo_prep_03" and "photo_prep_4", you must select the Browser icon for the sequence containing those clips.

To reconnect offline files:

1. Select the file or files to be reconnected (**Figure 3.23**). You can select a clip or sequence in the Browser, or clips in an open sequence in the Timeline.

2. *Do one of the following:*
   - ◆ Choose File > Reconnect Media.
   - ◆ Control-click the clip or sequence; then choose Reconnect Media from the shortcut menu (**Figure 3.24**).

3. In the Reconnect Options dialog box, three file options may be available, depending on your current selection: Offline, Online, or Render. Check the box for each type of file you want to reconnect; then click OK (**Figure 3.25**).

   In the Reconnect window, navigate to the folder location of the first file in your selection. Files not matching the name of the first offline clip are grayed out in the file window (**Figure 3.26**).

4. *Do any of the following:*
   - ◆ Select a file type from the Show pop-up menu to limit the file list display to the selected file type.
   - ◆ Check Matched Name Only to highlight only an exactly matching name in the file list display and gray out all non-matching names. Disable this feature to have access to a complete list of the folder's contents.
   - ◆ Select a drive or folder to search from the Search pop-up menu. Click the Next Volume button to move the next media drive.
   - ◆ Check Reconnect All Files in Relative Path to automatically reconnect any other clips in the sequence that are associated with files located in the same folder. You must reconnect the first file manually by clicking Select.

Figure 3.23 Select the clip you want to reconnect to its source media file.

Figure 3.24 Control-click the clip; then choose Reconnect Media from the shortcut menu.

Figure 3.25 In the Reconnect Options window, check the box for each type of file you want to reconnect; then click OK.

Figure 3.26 In the Reconnect window, navigate to the folder location of the first file in your selection. Files not matching the name of the first offline clip are grayed out in the file window.

◆ Click Skip File to bypass the clip currently displayed in the prompt at the top of the dialog box.

◆ Click Skip Remaining Files to bypass all remaining clips that can't be located automatically.

◆ Click Choose to reconnect the clip and its source media.

5. The prompt indicates the next file to locate. Continue until the dialog box closes.

✔ Tip

■ The prompt area at the top of the Reconnect dialog is often too small to display the full directory path for the clip you're searching for. When you're searching for many clips with similar names, the partial display is pretty useless. Where can you see the full directory path name for your stray clip? Your best bet is the Source column in the Browser (**Figure 3.27**).

Figure 3.27 The Browser's Source column displays the full directory path to the location of your files.

RECONNECTING OFFLINE FILES

Reconnecting online files

The Reconnect Media feature offers an option to reconnect online as well as offline files. Reconnecting missing or offline clips is the most common use of the Reconnect Media command, but you could have occasion to reconnect online files, too. For example, you may want to replace the media in a clip you've used in a sequence with a revised version of the same media element or with another element entirely.

Note that if you do want to relink a clip in your sequence with an entirely different source media file, the new file must be at least long enough to cover the current marked duration of the clip you're relinking it to. If your new source file is too short, you'll see an error message.

Using the Offline Files window to reconnect

Final Cut Express displays the Offline Files window to alert you that media files have gone missing since the last time you saved a project. Any time you open a project or switch back to FCE from the Finder, Final Cut Express rechecks the status of your media files. If FCE detects missing files, the Offline Files window appears automatically to alert you and offer you options for restoring order to your FCE project.

To reconnect using the Offline Files window:

1. Final Cut Express displays the Offline Files window (**Figure 3.28**), which contains a list of all media files missing from the current project and their most recent hard disk location. This listing could include:

   ◆ Missing source media files

   ◆ Render files lost because they reference a missing media file

   ◆ QuickTime Reference movies made invalid by a missing media file

   ◆ A segment of a spanned media file

Figure 3.28 The Offline Files window contains a list of all media files missing from the current project and their most recent hard disk location.

FCE Protocol: Broken Links

How did your clips get thrown offline? Here's a list things you might have done that severed the link between your FCE project and its source media files:

◆ You renamed your source media files.

◆ You renamed the folder containing your source media files.

◆ You moved your source media files to another disk.

◆ You deleted your source media on disk.

FCE is actually pretty good at tracking "unofficial" relocation of source media folders (try it some time), but forcing FCE to do so is not recommended procedure.

Figure 3.29 Use the Forget Files buttons to change the status of the files listed in the window from "missing" to "offline" and remove them from this list of missing files.

Figure 3.30 Click the Reconnect button to access the Reconnect Media feature and try to locate and reconnect the missing files.

FCE Protocol: Offline vs. Missing Clips

Missing clips and offline clips look the same in the Browser, Viewer, Timeline, and Canvas. What's the difference?

Offline clips are listed as offline in your project's item tracking data, so Final Cut Express doesn't look for them the next time you open that project.

Missing clips are listed as online in your project's item tracking data, but FCE can't find the clips' underlying media files. FCE will search for missing files each time you open a project until you reconnect the files or make them official offline files by clicking Forget in the Offline Files window.

---

2. *Do any of the following:*

♦ Use the Forget Files buttons (**Figure 3.29**) to change the status of the files listed in the window from "missing" to "offline" and remove them from this list of missing files. Final Cut Express will continue to post alerts about missing media each time you launch the project, until you reconnect the media and clips or make the clips offline.

- ♦ Click the Movie button to change the status of all the source media files in the list from "missing" to "offline." All clips referencing these files will be marked as offline clips in your project, but you can still relink the files later.

- ♦ Click the Render button to remove all of the render files from this list. If you choose to forget render files, you won't have the opportunity to reconnect them later.

3. To finish the process, *choose one of the following options:*

- ♦ Click the Reconnect button (**Figure 3.30**) to access the Reconnect Media feature and try to locate and reconnect the missing files. The Reconnect Media operation is described earlier in this chapter.

- ♦ Click OK to exit the Offline Files window, leaving all the files remaining in the list classified as missing or invalid. The next time you launch this project, FCE will display the Offline Files window again, and you can choose to reconnect or to take files offline at that time.

RECONNECTING OFFLINE FILES

Deleting Media

To delete media files, you have to go outside Final Cut Express, locate the files in the project's Capture Scratch folder, and move them to the Trash.

You delete unused render files from disk in the same way. You'll find render files in folders labeled Audio Render Files and Video Render Files. If you render frequently, you'd be surprised how much storage space your old render files can hog.

To delete a source media file from disk:

1. Save your project and quit Final Cut Express.

2. In the Finder, navigate to the project's Capture Scratch folder, and select the media file you want to delete.

3. Control-click the selected media file; then choose Move to Trash from the shortcut menu (**Figure 3.31**).

   The source media file is moved to the Trash.

4. Relaunch FCE and open the project.

   If you have not previously deleted the clips referencing the source media file, you'll see the Offline Files window listing the media file you moved to the Trash.

5. Click the Forget Movie button to update your FCE project's item tracking (**Figure 3.32**).

   To finally delete the files, you'll need to empty the Trash manually. If you change your mind later, before you empty the Trash, and want to retrieve the files, drag them out of the Trash and reconnect them to your project by using the Reconnect Media command. If you empty the Trash, your files are finally deleted.

Figure 3.31 In the project's Capture Scratch folder, control-click the media file you want to delete; then choose Move to Trash from the shortcut menu.

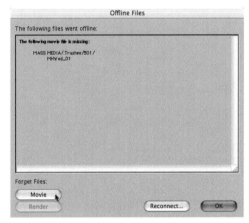

Figure 3.32 Clicking the Forget Movie button updates your FCE project's item tracking, removing the deleted file from the project's database.

✔ Tip

■ You can delete render files in the same way. With your Finder window in Column view, you can preview each media file in the QuickTime preview utility built right into the file window. Select the clip you want to preview and the QuickTime preview appears automatically. This trick works only in the Finder, though—not within the Reconnect dialog box in FCE.

FCE Protocol: Deleting Media

How do you delete media files from Final Cut Express the right way?

Before you toss that folder full of source media files in the Trash, take a moment to review the way Final Cut Express tracks files. Remember that the Browser clips you use to construct sequences in your project are not actually media files; they are pointers to the actual media files on disk, and Final Cut Express's links to those underlying source media files are location dependent. If you open the Item Properties window for any clip in Final Cut Express, you'll see the directory path to the underlying source media (the clip's directory path also appears in the Browser's Source column). If you have created subclips, repeated the same clip in a sequence, divided a clip with the razor tool, or created multiple versions of your sequence, you can have quite a few different clips all pointing to the same media file on disk.

If you delete a clip from the Browser bin or a Timeline sequence, you haven't thrown out the underlying media source file on disk. You can re-import the file to reconnect it to your project, or if you've already used that clip in a sequence, you can drag a copy of the sequence version of the clip back into the Browser. Dragging a clip from an open sequence in the Timeline back into the Browser places a copy of the sequence version of the clip in your project.

Your source media files stay on disk until you drag them to the Trash in the Finder. It's best not to delete media files linked to an open project while Final Cut Express is running.

You should save and close the project before you delete media files in the Finder. Determine your own comfort level here, but quitting Final Cut Express before you trash any media files would be the safest course.

Once you've deleted a source media file, all clips referring to that file are marked as offline. Final Cut Express warns you that the clips are offline each time you open the project until you delete the clip references, including any versions of the clips that appear in sequences, or tell FCE to "forget" the offline clips. See "Using the Offline Files window to reconnect," earlier in this chapter.

Project Maintenance Tips

Even if you are not forced to reorganize your project's media elements because you have run out of disk space, it's a good idea to streamline a project as you go, especially if you're working on a long, complex project. As your project accumulates clips, sequences, edits, render files, multiple tracks of audio, and effects, more and more of your available RAM is needed just to open the project. At some point, you could experience a drop in Final Cut Express's speed or video playback performance.

✔ Tip

■ Do you really need to preserve every scrap of media and every old duped sequence in your project? Redundant copies of project items may seem valuable now, but will you remember why you saved them when you return to this project in a year? Consider some project streamlining before you pack up and move. Check out the "Deleting media" section earlier in this chapter for ideas.

To streamline a project in progress:

1. With the project open in the Browser, choose File > Save All (**Figure 3.33**).
   The current version of the project is saved.

2. Choose File > Save Project As.
   The Save dialog box appears.

3. Navigate to the folder where you want to store your project file, enter a name for the new project version in the Save Project As field, and then click Save.
   The new version of your project replaces the older one on the front tab of the Browser window (**Figure 3.34**).

Figure 3.33 Choose File > Save All to save the current version of the project.

Figure 3.34 The new version of your project replaces the old one on the front tab of the Browser window.

Figure 3.35 Remove all but the most current versions of your sequences and delete any excess clips. If you need the old versions later, you still have them in the project version you saved in step 1.

Figure 13.36 Be careful which render files you delete. The Finder's built-in QuickTime player can help you ID the files you want to trash.

4. Remove all but the most current versions of your sequences and delete any excess clips (**Figure 3.35**). If you are short of disk space, you could choose to delete the clips' source media files as well, but you don't need to delete the source media files to get the benefits of a streamlined project.

5. In the Finder, navigate to the Render Files and Audio Render Files folders. They're located inside the Final Cut Express Documents folder where your media files are stored. Delete any obsolete render files.

6. With the new streamlined project open in the Browser, choose File > Save.

7. If you streamlined your project to improve Final Cut Express's performance, you'll need to close and then reopen the project to recapture the available RAM and start enjoying improved performance.

✔ Tip

■ Remember that the Render Files folder contains render files for all your projects, so be careful as you select the files you want to delete. Check each file's creation date and view any candidates for the trash bin on the Finder's built-in QuickTime preview player (**Figure 3.36**).

Editing in stages

If you are trying to assemble a long project in Final Cut Express on a modest system, you may find that you have much more media than hard drive space to store it on. Here are some project management strategies for editing a project in stages.

The simplest approach to a staged editing process is to edit one sequence at a time, print it to video, clear off the media, and then edit the next sequence.

Here's a checklist for taking a completed sequence offline and preparing your drives for the next sequence:

◆ After you have completed a sequence and printed it to tape, make sure you save the project file that contains the final version of your sequence.

◆ You should also save a backup copy of the project file on a Zip disk, CD, or some other form of removable media.

◆ Back up any media elements in your sequence, such as graphics files or digital audio from CDs, that won't be restored in a project recapturing process.

◆ In the Browser, select all the clips and sequences that reference media files you no longer need. Use the method for deleting media files described earlier in this chapter to delete all the unwanted media source files.

◆ The clips and sequences referring to the deleted media files will be marked offline, but the clip data remain in your completed project file. This clip and sequence data takes up very little room, so you don't need to delete it; you can store it in a single Browser bin.

◆ Capture the next batch of media files and start work on your next sequence.

The Last Mile: Tips for Final Assembly of BIG Projects

You can tell when the size of your project is taxing the limits of FCE's performance. Everything takes longer—opening and saving the project, screen refresh, even moving around the Timeline. If you have no choice but to press FCE's capacity to handle large amounts of media and multiple long sequences, try this:

◆ Split your show into a series of separate sequences and complete all rendering inside the individual sequences.

◆ Create a new project and drag just the finished individual sequences from your old projects into the new project; then close the old projects.

◆ Create the master sequence assembly of all your finished segment sequences in the brand-new project including just the master sequence and keep all other projects closed as much as possible.

◆ Back up your project file frequently.

Figure 3.37 Open the project you want to restore, then choose Capture Project from the File menu.

Figure 3.38 To restore non-DV media elements, follow the steps for reconnecting offline files.

Figure 3.39 To restore the render files, you must re-render any sequence material requiring rendering.

Restoring a sequence

If you find that you need to go back and modify a sequence after you have deleted its underlying media files, you can use the sequence data you saved in the project file to batch recapture your footage and re-create the sequence.

All filters, motion paths, keyframes, transitions, nested sequences, and audio mixing are reconstituted when you batch recapture the media files for a sequence. Your render files will be gone, however, and you'll need to re-render any sequence material requiring them.

To restore a project:

1. Open the project in the Browser and choose File > Capture Project (**Figure 3.37**).

2. Follow the steps in "Capture Project: Batch Recapturing" in Chapter 4 and batch recapture your footage from tape.

3. Restore to your hard disk any non-DV media elements in your sequence, such as graphics files or digital audio from CD, that won't be restored in the batch recapturing process.

4. Follow the steps described in "To reconnect offline files" earlier in this chapter (**Figure 3.38**) and reconnect any non-DV media elements you restored.

5. To restore the render files, re-render any sequence material requiring rendering (**Figure 3.39**).

PROJECT MAINTENANCE TIPS

Tracking used and unused clips

If you just want to do a little housecleaning in your project's media file folder, it's handy to have an inventory of every clip that's currently being used in a sequence in your project and another list of every element in your project that remains unused. How can you create complete lists of used and unused elements in your project? It's simple. You can use the Find feature to assemble these lists—you can even inventory multiple projects in a single Find operation. See "Searching for items in the Browser" in Chapter 6. Powerful stuff.

Figure 3.40 On each project's tab in the Browser, Command-click to select the sequences you want to include in your search.

To get a complete list of elements used in a group of sequences:

1. Open all the projects you want to search.

2. On each project's tab in the Browser, Command-click to select the sequences you want to include in your search (**Figure 3.40**).

3. Choose Edit > Find; or press Command-F.

4. In the Find window, configure the options as follows:

- ◆ Choose All Open Projects from the Search pull-down menu.

- ◆ Choose Used Media from the For pull-down menu and check the box next to In Selected Sequences.

- ◆ Choose Replace Find Results from the Results pull-down menu.

Figure 3.41 The Find window, configured to find unused clips in selected sequences. Click Find All to perform the search.

Waveform Cache: (Set...) 7.4 GB on MASS MEDIA/Final Cut Express Documents
Thumbnail Cache: (Set...) 7.4 GB on MASS MEDIA/Final Cut Express Documents

Figure 3.42 Looking for the Thumbnail and Waveform Cache folders? You'll find the directory path to their disk location listed on the Scratch Disk Preferences tab in the Preferences window.

5. Click Find All (**Figure 3.41**).

A list of all the clips used in the sequences you selected is displayed in the Find Results window. Final Cut Express does not support text export; the best you can do is to take a screen shot of the Find Results window and print it out.

✔ Tip

■ If your clip's name is different from the name of the underlying media file, you can find the underlying media file (and its location) for any clip in the clip's Item Properties window or the Browser's Source column.

Removing a project from your drives

Final Cut Express doesn't generate separate preview or temporary files when you use the Print to Video function (see Chapter 18). The only files you need to clean up after a project are the project file, media files, render files, and thumbnail and waveform cache files (**Figure 3.42**).

Setting Up for Multiple Projects and Users

Mac OS X was designed as a multi-user environment. The operating system's hierarchy of users and file access privileges is built on the assumption that multiple people are sharing the data and applications stored on your computer. For Final Cut Express users, this has a few specific effects.

File access

How you choose to set up your file access depends on your individual circumstances.

◆ If you are a solo user running Final Cut Express on a computer that you own, you should already be set up as the computer's Owner-User. This gives you access to any file in the system that you created.

◆ If you are collaborating on a project with a small group of trusted colleagues sharing Final Cut Express, you'll need to decide how you want to handle access to Final Cut Express's project and media files. You can choose to administer the project in OS X's multi-user domain and allow multiple users access to the project files, or you might find it simpler to create a single user ID for the entire group (**Figure 3.43**). In the latter case, everyone in the group logs in as that Project User and has the same read/write privileges to the project and media files.

◆ If you are sharing a Final Cut Express system with many users working on different projects, you'll want to configure your file access for maximum privacy.

Figure 3.43 Creating a single user ID for project collaborators to use can simplify file access on shared FCP projects.

Figure 3.44 Groups collaborating on a Final Cut Pro project should save common project files in the Shared folder so all group members have access to them.

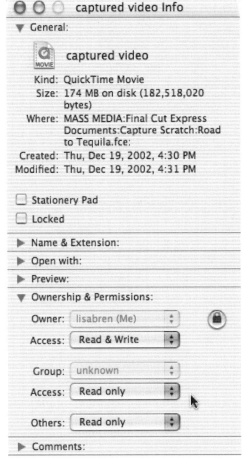

Figure 3.45 Mac OS X default file access for new files is Read & Write for the file's owner and Read Only for all other users.

Creating and saving files

Solo users can save their project files in a public or private Documents folder (save in your private Documents folder if you have any security concerns); groups collaborating on an FCE project should save common project files in the Shared folder, located inside the Users folder (**Figure 3.44**), so that all users can have access to the shared documents.

In FCE any time you create a new file—by saving a project file, capturing media, or creating graphics—that file's access privileges are set to the system default: Read & Write for the file's owner, and Read Only for all other users (**Figure 3.45**). You may occasionally need to modify file access privileges to allow other users access to your project and its media.

continues on next page

SETTING UP FOR MULTIPLE PROJECTS AND USERS

✔ Tips

■ A non-bootable hard disk may offer Read & Write privileges to all users by default, but that doesn't mean individual files and folders on that drive are accessible to all. To set open access for all files on a disk volume, check Ignore Ownership on This Volume in the drive's Info window (**Figure 3.46**).

■ Mac OS X considers FireWire drives to be removable media (because they're hot-swappable) and automatically offers Read & Write privileges to all users for the entire contents of the drive by default.

Figure 3.46 In the disk's Info window, check Ignore Ownership on This Volume to make all files on the volume accessible to all users.

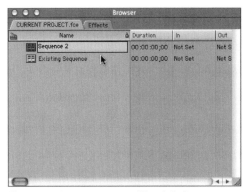

Figure 3.47 A new sequence with a default, highlighted name appears in the current bin.

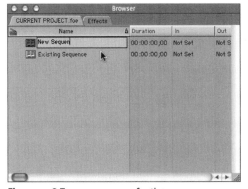

Figure 3.48 Type a new name for the sequence.

What's a Sequence?

A sequence is an edited assembly of audio and video clips. Sequences are the middle level of the Final Cut Express organizing framework. A sequence is always part of a project, and you can have multiple sequences in a project. Sequences can be exported independently as movies or clips, but they can't be saved separately from a project.

Once you've assembled a sequence, that sequence can be manipulated as if it were a single clip. You can open a sequence and play it in the Viewer, mark In and Out points, and insert all or part of that sequence into another sequence, just as if it were a clip. Inserting a sequence into another sequence creates what's known as a nested sequence. (See "Working With Multiple Sequences," later in this chapter.)

Creating a new sequence

A new project created in FCE automatically generates a new untitled sequence in your default sequence format.

Note that you probably won't need to change sequence presets unless you change your audio or video input device. Final Cut Express selects an Easy Setup with your default pre-set based on setup information you supplied when you installed the program. See "How to Choose an Easy Setup" in Chapter 2.

To add a new sequence to the current project:

1. Choose File > New > Sequence; or press Command-N.

    A new sequence with a default, high-lighted name appears at the top level of the current bin (**Figure 3.47**).

2. Type a new name for the sequence to rename it (**Figure 3.48**).

FCE Protocol: Clips and Sequences

A *clip* is the basic unit of media in Final Cut Express.

A clip can represent a movie, still image, nested sequence, generator, or audio file.

A clip is a reference to the actual media file stored on your hard disk. But a clip can also reference material that is not currently online. If you delete the original media file, the clip will still appear in the Browser and Timeline, but you won't see the frames and you won't be able to play it.

When you apply special effects and perform edits on clips, you are *not* affecting the media file on disk.

Using Clips in Sequences

When you insert a clip from a project into a *sequence*, the clip is *copied* into the sequence. The copy of the clip you placed in the sequence refers directly back to the actual media file on the disk and is not a reference to the clip in the project file.

This protocol is important to understand because it affects how and where you should make changes to your clips. So let's lay out the rules:

◆ You can open a clip from the Browser (outside a sequence) or from the Timeline (within a sequence).

◆ If you make changes to a clip in the Browser and then insert the clip into a sequence, the clip that is placed in the sequence *includes* the changes that have been made in the Browser.

◆ Any changes you make to a clip from within a sequence are *not* made to the clip in the Browser.

◆ After you've inserted a clip into a sequence, any further changes you make to that clip from the Browser will not be reflected in any sequence where the clip is used.

◆ Clips that appear in multiple sequences are independent of one another. Changes to one will not affect the others.

◆ If you want to make further revisions to a clip that's already in a sequence, open the clip from the Timeline and then make the changes.

◆ If you want to make changes to a clip and have the changes show up in all the sequences in which that clip is used, open the clip from the Browser and make the changes. Then reinsert the revised clip into each sequence in which you want the updated clip to appear.

◆ Final Cut Express identifies clips that have been opened from the Timeline by displaying two lines of dots in the Scrubber bar. No dots appear in the Scrubber bar of clips that have been opened from the Browser.

WHAT'S A SEQUENCE?

Figure 3.49 Double-click the sequence's icon in the Browser to open it for editing.

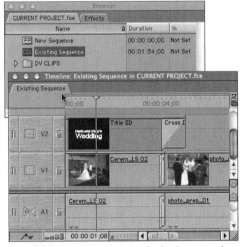

Figure 3.50 The sequence opens in the Canvas and the Timeline.

To open a sequence for editing:

Do one of the following:

◆ Double-click the sequence in the Browser (**Figure 3.49**).

◆ Control-click the sequence's icon; then choose Open Timeline from the shortcut menu.

◆ Select the sequence; then choose View > Sequence In Editor.

The sequence opens in both the Canvas and the Timeline (**Figure 3.50**).

Time Stamp for Sequences

The Last Modified column in the Browser makes it easy to find the most recently revised version of your sequence—a real life saver when you're returning to a project after a long absence.

To duplicate a sequence:

1. Select the sequence in the Browser (**Figure 3.51**).

2. Choose Edit > Duplicate (**Figure 3.52**); or press Option-D.

3. In the Browser, rename the sequence copy with a unique name (**Figure 3.53**).

✔ Tip

■ The copy procedure described here is a convenient way to "safety copy" a version of a sequence and associated media files after a long rendering process. With a safety copy of the rendered sequence, you can feel free to experiment with changes that could cause a re-render, because any changes you make to the duplicate sequence will not affect the original sequence or its render files.

To copy a sequence from one project to another:

1. Select the sequence in the Browser.

2. Choose File > Copy; or press Command-C.

3. Open the second project and select its tab in the Browser.

4. Choose File > Paste; or press Command-V.

   The sequence now appears in both projects. The two copies of the sequence reference the same source media files on disk, but you'll need to re-render any previously rendered sequence material in the new project location.

✔ Tip

■ You can also create a copy of a sequence by dragging it from one project window and dropping it on the destination project's Browser tab.

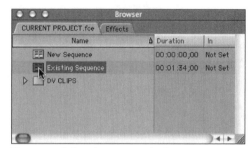

Figure 3.51 Select the sequence in the Browser.

Figure 3.52 Choose Edit > Duplicate.

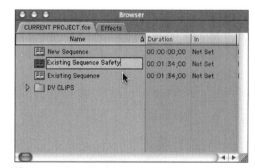

Figure 3.53 Rename the sequence copy.

WHAT'S A SEQUENCE?

Figure 3.54 Select the sequence; then choose Sequence > Settings.

Figure 3.55 The Sequence Settings window contains the same options as the Timeline Options tab in the Preferences window. Modifying settings in the Sequence Settings window changes the settings for that sequence only.

Changing the Settings of an Existing Sequence

You can open and review or modify Timeline display options for an existing individual sequence in the Sequence Settings window. The Sequence Settings window contains the same main display options as the Timeline Options tab in the Preferences window. You can also switch to a different sequence preset, but unless you're sure that's what you need to do, it's not advisable. When you modify settings for an individual sequence, you are changing the settings for that sequence only.

To change the settings for an individual sequence:

1. Make the sequence active by selecting it in the Browser or Timeline.

2. Choose Sequence > Settings (**Figure 3.54**); or press Command-0 (zero).

   The Sequence Settings window appears (**Figure 3.55**).

3. Review or modify any of the following sequence settings; then click OK.

   Track Size: Choose a setting from this pop-up menu to specify a default track size.

continues on next page

Thumbnail Display: Select one of three thumbnail display options from this pop-up menu:

◆ Name displays the name of the clip and no thumbnail images.

◆ Name Plus Thumbnail displays the first frame of every clip as a thumbnail image and then the name of the clip.

◆ Filmstrip displays as many thumbnail images as possible for the current zoom level of the Timeline.

Show Keyframe Overlays: Check this box to display opacity keyframe overlays on video clips and level keyframe graphs on audio clips in the Timeline.

Show Audio Waveforms: Check this box to display the audio waveform along the audio clip in the Timeline.

To switch a sequence's settings to a different sequence preset:

1. Make the sequence active by selecting it in the Browser or Timeline.

2. Choose Sequence > Settings.
The Sequence Settings window appears.

3. Click the Load Preset button.

4. Choose a different preset from the Select pop-up menu in the Select Sequence Preset dialog box (**Figure 3.56**); then click OK.

Figure 3.56 Choose a different sequence preset to replace the settings of your selected sequence.

Viewing and Setting Item Properties

The Item Properties window is the central location for information about an individual clip. Three tabs in the Item Properties window allow you to view or change the properties of a clip.

✔ Tip

■ What if you have changed the name of a clip and removed all traces of the original source media file it references? You can consult the Item Properties window for the renamed clip to trace the underlying source media file name and location.

To open a clip's Item Properties window:

1. Select the clip in the Browser or Timeline, or open it in the Viewer.
2. *Do one of the following:*
   - ◆ Choose Edit > Item Properties.
   - ◆ Control-click the item; then choose Properties from the shortcut menu.
   - ◆ Press Command-9.

To get information about the format of a clip:

1. In the clip's Item Properties window, click the Format tab (**Figure 3.57**) to open it. This tab displays data on the location of the clip's source media file, file size, and format characteristics.

continues on next page

Figure 3.57 The Format tab of the Item Properties window displays format information on an individual clip or sequence.

2. The following Format properties can be modified:

- **Field Dominance:** Specify the dominant field by making a selection from the pop-up menu.
- **Alpha Type:** Select an alpha channel type for the video clip.
- **Reverse Alpha:** Reverse the alpha channel of the video clip.
- **Composite Mode:** Select the mode to be used when compositing the video clip.
- **Pixel Aspect Ratio:** Select a pixel aspect ratio for this clip.
- **Anamorphic 16:9:** If your clip's source media is 16:9, checking this box ensures that FCE will interpret and display the clip's pixel aspect ratio properly.

To get information about the timing of a clip:

1. In the clip's Item Properties window, click the Timing tab to open it (**Figure 3.58**).

2. In the Clip section, you can modify the following Timing properties (on Browser clips only):

- **In:** Enter or modify the In point of a clip.
- **Out:** Enter or modify the Out point of a clip.
- **Duration:** Enter or modify the duration of a clip.

3. In the Media section of the Timing tab, you can view the total media length and the start and end timecode values of the clip's source media file.

4. In the Speed section of the Timing tab, you can view the clip's current speed and frame blending status.

Figure 3.58 The Timing tab of the Item Properties window.

To get logging information for a clip:

1. In the clip's Item Properties window, click the Logging Info tab (**Figure 3.59**). This tab provides logging information for a clip.

2. You can review or modify the following:

   ◆ **Reel:** Enter or modify the name of the clip's source tape.

   ◆ **Description:** Enter or modify descriptive details for a clip.

   ◆ **Scene:** Enter or modify tracking information for a clip.

   ◆ **Shot/Take:** Enter or modify tracking information.

   ◆ **Log Note:** Enter or modify a log note.

   ◆ **Capture:** Specify the status of a clip as Not Yet, OK, or Queued.

   ◆ **Mark Good:** Click the Mark Good check box to mark the clip as good.

   ◆ **Comments 1–4:** Enter or modify additional comments for the clip in these fields. Note: If you customized Comment column names in the Browser, they won't appear here.

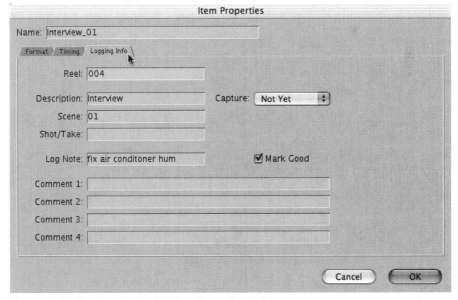

Figure 3.59 The Logging Info tab of the Item Properties window.

Working with Multiple Sequences

In Final Cut Express, you can edit a sequence into another sequence in the same way you would a clip: Drag the entire sequence from the Browser to another open sequence in the Timeline or Canvas. Alternatively, you can drag the sequence from the Browser and drop it on the Viewer's image area and then edit it into your open sequence as you would a clip.

Unlike clips, nested sequences are actually pointers or references to the original sequence, not copies. You can nest a sequence into multiple projects; then, if you change the original sequence, all the projects in which that sequence is nested will be updated.

Assembling multiple sequences into a master sequence is useful for a number of purposes, from reusing a previously edited and rendered segment such as a logo or a credit sequence to assembling a final master sequence from shorter segments produced by multiple editors.

Nesting and Sequences: A Glossary

What's the difference between a nested sequence and a sub-sequence? Here's a short glossary of terms related to nesting sequences as used in this book.

Main sequence: A sequence containing one or more nested sequences. Sometimes referred to as a *parent sequence*.

Nested sequence: Any sequence that has been nested within another sequence. Sometimes referred to as a *child sequence*. A nested sequence can range from a clip on a single track to an entire sequence. What designates a sequence as nested is its placement in a parent sequence. The word *nest* can also be used as a verb, as in "nest a sequence," which refers to editing all or a portion of an existing sequence into another sequence.

Sub-sequence: Can be used interchangeably with the term *nested sequence*. Nested sequences function as sub-sequences in their parent sequences.

Creating nested sequences

You can select a group of sequence clips or a portion of a Final Cut Express sequence and convert that selection to a self-contained sub-sequence. There's no simple "Nest Items" command—that's reserved for Final Cut Pro users—but you can achieve the same effect with a little more trouble by cutting and pasting your selected clips into an new empty sequence which you place in the clips' former location in the master sequence.

Converting a group of clips to a nested sequence has several advantages:

◆ Nesting a group of clips can simplify the process of moving them around within a sequence or placing them in another sequence.

◆ Converting a series of edited clips into a single nested sequence allows you to create a single motion path for the nested sequence rather than having to create separate motion paths for each clip.

◆ Nesting a group of clips allows you to apply and adjust a single copy of a filter to a series of clips, rather than having to apply and adjust filters for each individual clip.

◆ You can nest clips that are stacked on multiple tracks (such as layered title elements) and animate them as a single sub-sequence.

◆ You can nest a clip containing an element you want to blur. By increasing the frame size when you nest, you can create a roomier bounding box that will accommodate the larger size of your blurred element.

◆ Nested sequences can help preserve your render files—most render files associated with the nested sequence are preserved within the nested sequence, even if you move it around or change its duration. This feature is particularly useful in dealing with audio files, which lose their render files when they are moved unless they are contained in a nested sequence. For more information on nested sequences and rendering protocol, see "Using nested sequences to preserve render files" in Chapter 17.

◆ In a sequence with multiple effects applied, nesting a clip can force a change in the rendering order.

Copying and pasting from sequence to sequence

Moving selected clips into a new separate sequence is the first step in nesting a selection of clips inside your master sequence. Moving material from sequence to sequence is easy; simply copy (or cut) material from one sequence and paste it into another sequence. You can copy and paste the entire contents of a sequence, or you can select a single clip. Final Cut Express has a tricky protocol that governs copying between sequences: When you paste, the clips paste themselves into the new sequence in the same relationship to the target track that they held when they were copied. So you need to be aware of which track is targeted when you copy and also when you paste.

To copy and paste clips between sequences:

1. In the Timeline, set the target track controls to the track or tracks you are copying from (**Figure 3.60**).

2. Select the clips you want to copy into the destination sequence and then *do one of the following:*

   ◆ To copy the selected clips, press Command-C.

   ◆ To cut the selected clips, press Command-X.

3. In the destination sequence, set the target track control to the track or tracks you are pasting into; then press Command-V.

   The clips are pasted into your destination sequence (**Figure 3.61**).

✔ Tip

■ You can also select and then Option-drag items from one sequence to another.

Figure 3.60 In the Timeline, set the target track controls to the track or tracks you are copying from.

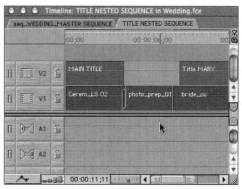

Figure 3.61 Press Command-V to paste the sequence tracks into your destination sequence.

Figure 3.62 To open a sequence in the Viewer, drag the sequence's icon from the Browser and drop it on the image area in the Viewer window.

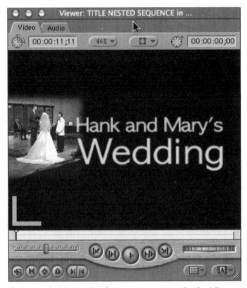

Figure 3.63 Your edited sequence opens in the Viewer window. You can edit the sequence into an open sequence in the Timeline, just as you would a clip.

Editing a sequence into another sequence

You can use sequences as source clips and edit them into another sequence. Your source clip sequence could be a preexisting sequence you drag into the Viewer or Timeline from the Browser, or it could be a nested sequence located inside a parent sequence in the Timeline. Opening a sequence in the Viewer is not quite as easy as opening a clip. Once you've loaded a sequence into the Viewer, however, you can edit it into a sequence just as you would a clip.

If you need more information on how to perform edits in Final Cut Express, see Chapter 6, "Editing in Final Cut Express."

To load a sequence into the Viewer:

◆ In the Browser, select the sequence you want to edit into your main sequence; then *do one of the following:*

◆ Choose View > Sequence.

◆ Drag the sequence's icon from the Browser and drop it on the image area in the Viewer window (**Figure 3.62**).

Your edited sequence opens in the Viewer, ready to be used as source media (**Figure 3.63**). If the sequence you select is open in the Timeline and the Canvas, it closes automatically when you load it into the Viewer.

WORKING WITH MULTIPLE SEQUENCES

To load a nested sub-sequence into the Viewer:

◆ In the Timeline, *do one of the following:*

  ◆ Control-click the nested sequence
    and then choose Open Viewer from
    the shortcut menu (**Figure 3.64**).

  ◆ Double-click the nested sequence
    while holding down the Option key.

  Your nested sequence opens in the
  Viewer window, ready to be used as a
  source clip.

✔ Tips

■ When you load a nested sequence from the
  Timeline and edit it back into your main
  sequence, you are creating a duplicate
  of the nested sequence—an independent
  copy of the original sequence that will
  not reflect changes you make to the original. If you want all copies of your nested
  sequence to update when you make
  changes, use the Browser version of your
  nested sequence as your source clip
  instead.

■ All nested audio appears as stereo pairs
  on two tracks, even if the sub-sequence
  contains only a single channel of audio.

■ Nesting audio tracks has its own set of
  advantages and its own protocols. For
  details on strategic use of nested audio
  tracks, see "Using nested sequences to
  preserve audio render files" in Chapter 17.

Figure 3.64 In the Timeline, control-click the nested
sequence, and then choose Open Viewer from the
shortcut menu.

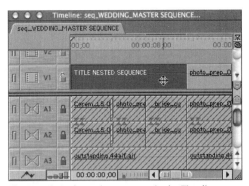

Figure 3.65 In the main sequence in the Timeline, double-click the nested sequence.

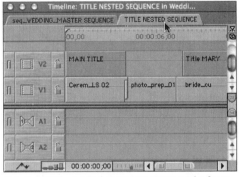

Figure 3.66 The nested sequence opens as the front tab of the Timeline.

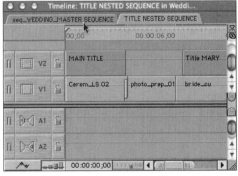

Figure 3.67 The main sequence is still open on the rear tab of the Timeline.

Making changes to a nested sequence

You can open a nested sequence and add, remove, or trim clips. When you return to your main sequence, you'll see that the nested sequence duration has been adjusted to reflect your changes. Clips to the right of the nested sequence will be rippled to accommodate the change to your nested sequence duration. You'll still need to open the nested sequence to make changes to the clips inside.

To make changes to a nested sequence:

Do one of the following:

◆ In the main sequence in the Timeline, double-click the nested sequence (**Figure 3.65**).

◆ In the Browser, double-click the icon for the nested sequence.

The nested sequence opens as the front tab of the Timeline (**Figure 3.66**). If you opened the nested sequence from inside the main sequence, the main sequence is still open on the rear tab (**Figure 3.67**).

To "un-nest" a sequence:

◆ There's no "Un-nest" command in Final Cut Express. If you want to replace a nested sequence that you have placed in your main sequence with the clips contained in that nest, you should first open the nest in the Timeline and then copy the clips from the open nest and paste them back over the nested sequence's original location in the main sequence. For more information, see "Copying and pasting from sequence to sequence," earlier in this chapter.

FCE Protocol: Updating Nested Sequences

When you insert a clip from the Browser into a sequence, the clip is copied into the sequence. The copy of the clip you placed in the sequence refers directly to the actual media file on the disk and is not a reference to the clip in the project file. Changes you make to the sequence version of the clip will not be reflected in the Browser version.

Nested sequences update globally

The protocol governing sequence versions is different, and it is also central to understanding the program. Unlike clips, sequences nested inside another sequence are actually pointers, or references, to the original sequence, not copies. *If you make changes to a sequence after you've edited it into a number of other master sequences, any changes you make to the original **will be reflected** every place you have used it. You'll need to make a duplicate of the sequence and make changes to the copy if you want to avoid a global update.*

For example, you could create a standard credit sequence and edit that sequence into every program in your series. If your credits require any last-minute changes, you can make the changes in the original sequence, and all the projects in which that sequence is nested will be updated.

But duplicate sequences are independent copies

Keep a close watch on nested sequences that you're using in multiple locations.

Multiple nested copies of the same sequence point to the original sequence IF (that's a big *if*) you always use the original Browser version of your sequence as your source when you nest the sequence in multiple locations.

*If you duplicate the original sequence in the Browser, the duplicate sequence you create is an independent copy of the original sequence that **will not reflect** changes you make to the original.* Duping a sequence is a good way to preserve render files, but bad news if you want to nest an identical sequence in multiple locations and take advantage of the global updating feature.

Copying and pasting a nested sequence to multiple locations within the master sequence in the Timeline produces the same result: independent duplicates of the original that don't update.If you need to place multiple copies of a nested sequence you created in the Timeline, always use the Browser version of your nested sequence to place the sequence in multiple locations.

Assembling Nested Sequences with Transitions

Building your program as a series of separate sequences and then assembling your sequence "scenes" into a final master sequence is a common post-production strategy. If you want to use transitions to join your scenes together, you'll need to allow extra media handles at the start and end of your nested sequences. When you're ready to assemble your master sequence, load each sub-sequence into the Viewer. Mark the frames you want to appear as the center point of your scene-to-scene transition as the sub-sequence's In and Out points before you edit them into the final master sequence (**Figure 3.68**).

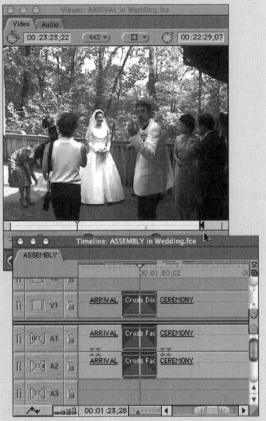

Figure 3.68 If you want to use a transition to join two sub-sequences, mark In and Out points that allow handles on your sub-sequences to establish the extra frames your transition will require.

Part II: Input

Part II:
Input

Before you can start editing, you need footage to work with. This section explains how to use the input features in Final Cut Express. The capture functions are limited to DV video and audio via a FireWire cable, but import of digital media files allows a much broader range of video and audio formats.

Take a moment to plan your route before you plunge into your project. There's a lot to think about when you start to assemble your project, and your media input strategy has a big impact on whether you get the most out of FCE.

CAPTURING VIDEO

Final Cut Express offers three video capture options, which use FireWire to transfer DV-format video and audio from a qualified DV camcorder or deck, or a qualified analog-to-digital converter box.

◆ **Capture Clip:** Capture clips one at a time. Set In and Out points to define the portion of the tape you want to capture, enter identifying information in the Logging tab, and capture the clip.

◆ **Capture Now:** Capture single clips without setting In and Out points. Use Capture Now to capture DV with or without device control, or to capture live video.

◆ **Capture Project:** A single, automated batch recapture process recaptures all the DV clips in a project. You need a device-controllable DV camcorder or deck to perform a Capture Project operation.

All three capture methods store the original DV timecode with the captured clip, but Final Cut Express assigns the same starting timecode (00:00:00:00) to all clips you are working with inside the program.

You will not be able to use FCE's automated capture and output features unless your external video hardware supports device control. You still can capture clips that are logged and manually captured while the tape is playing, but you won't be able to perform automated project recapture.

Capturing video is probably the first thing you'll want to do, but a little general knowledge of the FCE interface will make your first few captures go more smoothly.

If you are new to Final Cut Express, take a moment to read Chapters 6 and 7, which contain details on Browser and Viewer operation, before you start a capture process. You'll need to use both of these windows in the capture operation.

You may also want to review Chapter 2, "Installing and Setting Up," for details on preference and preset settings.

DV Timecode vs. FCE Timecode: What's the Difference?

On your original DV tape, each frame of the tape is assigned a unique number, called a *time-code number*. This system of timecode numbers has been the basis of video editing systems for over 30 years. In Final Cut Express, all captured clips are assigned the same starting time-code: 00:00:00:00. Each FCE clip, however, preserves the original timecode start and end numbers with the clip's media file. FCE accesses the original timecode numbers when you go back to the original DV tapes and recapture a project. If you open an FCE project in Final Cut Pro (FCE's big brother application), you'll have full access to the original DV timecode. In FCE, you can view the original start and end timecodes on the Timing tab of the clip's Item Properties dialog box (**Figure 4.1**). Want to see them? Select a clip, press Command-9, and click on the Timing tab.

You can look...but you can't touch.

Figure 4.1 A clip's original DV start and end timecodes appear on the Timing tab of the clip's Item Properties dialog box.

Figure 4.2 To open the Capture window, choose File > Capture.

Anatomy of the Capture Window

Use the Capture window to capture video and audio media in Final Cut Express. This window supports a range of capture options, from live video capture on-the-fly to automated project recapture with full device control.

To open the Capture window:

◆ Choose File > Capture (**Figure 4.2**); or press Command-8.

✔ Tips

■ The size of your Capture window is determined by the zoom level of the Canvas and Viewer windows in your workspace arrangement. If you're using a high zoom level for the Canvas and the Viewer, your Capture window will be large as well. Small Canvas and Viewer windows will result in a small Capture window. If you're using different sizes in the Viewer and Canvas windows, the Capture window appears at the size of the smaller one.

■ When you open the Capture window for the first time after launching FCE, the screen reads, "Preview Disabled." Don't freak out. That's standard operating procedure—the warning disappears when you click Play.

■ For best performance, the Capture window should be completely visible on your computer monitor, with nothing overlapping the window, not even the cursor.

■ If you have been capturing clips, FCE will not play back clips in your external monitor until you close the Capture window.

Preview section

Many of the controls in the Preview section of the Capture window also appear in the Viewer window. For more information, review "Anatomy of the Viewer" in Chapter 7.

Figure 4.3 shows an overview of the Capture window.

◆ **Current Timecode field:** This field displays the current timecode location of your source tape. Enter a timecode number in this field to shuttle the source tape to that timecode location.

◆ **Timecode Duration field:** This field displays the duration of the currently marked clip.

◆ **Free Space status display:** This display shows the amount of available hard disk space remaining.

◆ **Transport controls:** Use these buttons to control your deck or camcorder transport if you have device control enabled. Transport control operation is described in more detail in Chapter 7, "Working with Clips in the Viewer."

Figure 4.3 An overview of the Capture window.

◆ **Deck status display:** This display shows the status of communication between your deck or camcorder and Final Cut Express.

◆ **Go to In Point button:** Click to shuttle tape to the currently marked clip's In point.

◆ **Clip In Point field:** This field displays the timecode location of the currently marked clip's In point.

◆ **Mark In button:** Click to mark an In point for your capture.

◆ **Mark Out button:** Click to mark an Out point for your capture.

◆ **Clip Out Point field:** This field displays the timecode location of the currently marked clip's Out point.

◆ **Go to Out Point button:** Click to shuttle tape to the currently marked clip's Out point.

✔ Tip

■ Not only can you copy and paste timecodes from one field to another, you can Option-click and then drag and drop a timecode to copy it into another timecode field—a useful procedure while you're logging.

Capture controls

The Capture control buttons appear below the tabbed portion of the window. Each of the three buttons performs a different kind of capture operation.

◆ **Capture Clip button:** Click this button to capture a single clip immediately. Capture Clip requires that you enter identifying information in the Logging tab and set In and Out points before capturing the clip. For more information, see "Capture Clip: Capturing Video with Device Control," later in this chapter.

◆ **Now button:** Click this button to capture without setting In or Out points. Capture Now is useful if your camcorder or deck doesn't have device control, or if you want to capture long clips without setting the Out point in advance. For more information, see "Capture Now: Capturing Video without Device Control," later in this chapter.

◆ **Capture Project button:** Click this button to batch-recapture all the DV clips in your project. For more information see "Capture Project: Batch Recapturing," later in this chapter.

ANATOMY OF THE CAPTURE WINDOW

Logging tab

The Logging tab (**Figure 4.4**) contains fields and shortcut tools you use to enter the information you need to log a clip. Try to get into the habit of recording log information—you'll thank yourself when you need to sort through hundreds of clips to find a frame or short sequence.

◆ **Capture Bin button:** Click to open the current log bin (the Browser bin where captured clips are stored).

◆ **Up button:** Click to move the capture bin selection up a level from the currently selected capture bin.

◆ **New Bin button:** Click to create a new capture bin inside the currently selected capture bin.

◆ **Reel field:** Enter the name of your current source tape in this field. Control-click the text field to select from a list of recent reel names.

◆ **Reel Slate button:** Click to add a number at the end of the name for incremental labeling. Click again to increment the number by one. Option-click to clear the contents of the field. All the Slate buttons on the Logging tab perform the same functions for their respective fields.

◆ **Name display:** The name in this field is compiled from information entered in the Description, Scene, and Shot/Take fields. This is the name that appears in the Browser's Name column.

Figure 4.4 The Capture window's Logging tab.

◆ **Prompt check box:** Check this box for a prompt to name a clip when you click the Capture Clip button.

◆ **Description field:** Enter descriptive text in this field. Check the box at the right to include this description in the Name display.

◆ **Scene field:** Enter descriptive text in this field. Check the box at the right to include this description in the Name display.

◆ **Shot/Take field:** Enter descriptive text in this field. Check the box at the right to include this description in the Name display.

◆ **Log Note field:** Enter descriptive text in this field. Control-click the text field to select from a list of recent log notes.

◆ **Mark Good check box:** Check this box to place a marker in the Browser's Good column. When you're done capturing, you can use the Browser's sort function to group all the clips you've marked "Good."

◆ **Marker field:** Enter a marker name or remarks in this field. For more information, see "Using Markers" in Chapter 7.

◆ **Set Marker In field:** Click to set a Marker In point, or enter a timecode in the field.

◆ **Set Marker Out field:** Click to set a Marker Out point, or enter a timecode in the field.

◆ **Set Marker button:** Click to log the marker.

◆ **Update button:** Click to modify a previously entered marker.

◆ **Marker Comment window:** This window displays marker information for the current clip.

ANATOMY OF THE CAPTURE WINDOW

Setting Up for Capture

Apple's FireWire capture system has simplified video capture, but capturing still requires some preparation, because it puts your entire editing system through its paces.

Capturing is important, and you should set up for it correctly. Here's an overview of the setup procedure and your objectives in each step:

◆ **Review your selected Easy Setup.** You want to be sure that you've selected an Easy Setup that uses the proper combination of presets for this capture operation. Select an Easy Setup that uses the correct audio sample rate to match the media you want to capture. Your capture settings should match the video hardware and tape format you're using. Your device control settings should be compatible with your camcorder or deck.

◆ **Check scratch disk preferences.** You want to ensure that any media you capture will be written to the correct hard disk or folder, that your designated scratch disk is fast enough to handle the data transfer, and that you have enough space to accommodate the media files you want to capture.

◆ **Review capture-related options in the General tab of the Preferences window.** These options directly affect FCE's behavior during capture. If your system and source tapes are in perfect condition, you should leave these options checked. However, if you're unable to complete a capture because FCE is reporting trouble (and you're willing to risk some uncertainty about timecode or frame integrity), you should uncheck the safeguard preference that's aborting your capture attempts:

◆ Abort Capture on Dropped Frames automatically stops the capture process if dropped frames are detected.

◆ Abort Capture on Timecode Break automatically stops the capture process if FCE detects a timecode break during the capture process.

◆ Sync Adjust Movies compensates for audio sync problems in long clip captures from video shot on certain cameras, notably certain models of Canon cameras. See "FCE Protocol: Sync Adjust Movies Feature," later in this chapter, for more info.

◆ **Test device control settings.** You want to ensure that your video, audio, timecode, and device control connections between your deck or camcorder and Final Cut Express are operational.

✔ Tips

■ If you want to capture video by using a non-controllable device such as an analog-to-DV converter, switch to an Easy Setup that supports capture from converter boxes (available in FCE 1.0.1 and higher).

■ Before you start capturing footage, you should use color bars to check the image quality on your external video monitor as well. Your monitor is a critical tool for evaluating your footage, so set it up right—once you've calibrated it, leave the monitor's image settings alone. See Apple's online Knowledge Base article, "Final Cut Pro 3: How to Calibrate Your Broadcast Monitor," (article ID 36550) for instructions.

■ If your DV clips need image-quality adjustments, you can fix them post-capture by applying the appropriate image control filters. To learn how to use FCE's filters, see Chapter 15, "Filters and Compositing."

Is Your System Capture-Ready?

Capturing video puts your entire FCE system—including external hardware—to the test. Any conditions that impair its performance can show up as dropped frames, audio sync drift, or error messages—not a good start for your project.

Apple's Knowledge Base has a good article on the subject: "Final Cut Pro: Dropped Frames and Loss of Audio Sync" (article ID 58640).

Here's a checklist (summarized from the article) you can use to avoid the most common causes of capture troubles:

- ◆ AppleTalk should be off. Use the AppleTalk tab in the Network pane in your System Preferences to turn it off.

- ◆ The Canvas size should be set to Fit to Window or smaller. If you can see scroll bars in the Canvas, you have a problem. Analog capture cards may have other limitations on video scaling in the Canvas.

- ◆ Your computer monitor's refresh rate should be set to 75 Hz or higher in the Displays pane in your System Preferences.

- ◆ On PowerBook FCE systems, turn off processor cycling on the Options tab of the Energy Saver preference pane.

- ◆ You should be using FCE-qualified drives. If your drives are overly full, or if the data is too fragmented, drive performance can be impaired.

See "Optimizing Performance" in Chapter 2 and "Troubleshooting Capture Problems" later in this chapter for more tips on improving performance in Final Cut Express.

Entering Information on the Logging Tab

Logging is the process of reviewing your source video tapes, and labeling and marking the In and Out points of usable clips. Other logging data could include shot and take numbers, added markers at specific points in the action, and production notes. You can also mark clips as "Good," so that you can easily sort out the most promising takes.

In Final Cut Express you cannot store logging information for a clip without capturing it immediately. You must enter log information and then capture each clip in a single operation.

This section explains how to use all the logging features on the Capture window's Logging tab. You use these features the same way in all three types of video capture. You'll also learn how to select a *capture bin*—the bin your clips will be stored in after capture.

To use all the logging options in Final Cut Express, you need device control over your video deck or camcorder. If you don't have a controllable video device, you can log only the duration and In and Out points for individual clips, and you must enter the data manually.

Logging Tips

◆ Click the Capture Bin button to display the selected capture bin on the front tab of the Browser.

◆ Control-click the Reel field to access a pop-up menu displaying all the reel names you've used in the current project. Selecting your reel name from the pop-up list helps you ensure you're entering exactly the same name each time. That's critical to successful batch capture.

◆ Clear text from a field by Option-clicking the Slate button next to it.

◆ Use the Mark Good check box to mark your best stuff. You can use the Find feature to search the Browser's Good column and select only the clips you've marked "Good" for your first rough cut.

Figure 4.5 Click the New Bin button on the Logging tab to create a new bin inside the current capture bin and select it as the current capture bin.

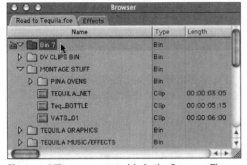

Figure 4.6 The new capture bin in the Browser. The clapstick icon indicates the current capture bin.

Figure 4.7 Control-click the bin; then select Set Capture Bin from the bin's shortcut menu.

Selecting a capture bin

A *capture bin* is the Browser bin where your clips are stored after capture. The default location for a new capture bin is the top level of a project tab in the Browser window. You can set the capture bin using the buttons in the Capture window or from a Browser window shortcut menu. Your choice of capture bin does not affect the location of the captured media files on your hard disk; instead, it specifies where in the Browser the clips referencing those media files appear.

To set a capture bin in the Capture window:

1. On the Logging tab of the Capture window, *do one of the following*:
   ◆ Click the New Bin button (**Figure 4.5**) to create a new bin inside the current capture bin and select it as the current capture bin (**Figure 4.6**).
   ◆ Click the Up button to set the bin hierarchically above the current capture bin as the new capture bin.

2. Click the Capture Bin button to switch to the Browser and open the new capture bin you created.

   A little clapstick icon appears in the Browser next to the current capture bin.

To set a capture bin in the Browser:

1. In the Browser, select the bin that you want to set as the capture bin.

2. Control-click the bin; then select Set Capture Bin from the bin's shortcut menu (**Figure 4.7**).

   A little clapstick icon appears next to the current capture bin.

Entering clip information on the Logging tab

To enter log information:

1. Load the source tape you want to capture into your camcorder or deck.

2. Choose File > Capture, or press Command-8.

3. In the Capture window, specify a logging bin using one of the methods described in the previous task.

4. In the Reel field, *do one of the following:*

   ◆ Enter a name for the reel (the tape or other video source you are currently logging).

   ◆ Click the Reel Slate button to add a numeric reel name.

   ◆ Control-click the Reel field; then choose from a pop-up list of recent reel names (**Figure 4.8**).

5. In the Description field, *do one of the following:*

   ◆ Enter a name for the clip.

   ◆ Select the Prompt check box if you want to name each clip as you log it (**Figure 4.9**).

6. In the Description, Scene, and Shot/Take fields, *do any of the following:*

   ◆ Click the check boxes next to the fields you want to incorporate into the clip's name.

   ◆ Enter any identifying text you want to use in the text field.

   ◆ Click the Slate button to automatically increment the corresponding text field's numeral (**Figure 4.10**).

Figure 4.8 Control-click the Reel field; then select from a list of recent reel names.

Figure 4.9 Check Prompt if you want to name each clip as you log it.

Figure 4.10 Click a Slate button to add an incremented numeral to its associated text field.

Figure 4.11 Click the Mark Out button to set an Out point for the capture.

Figure 4.12 Capture the clip using the Capture Clip or the Capture Now button.

The automatic naming function in Final Cut Express creates clip names by combining the fields you selected, such as Description_Scene01_01, into the Name field. This is the name that appears in the Browser's Name column, and it is the name of your source media file on disk.

7. Use the transport controls in the Capture window to control your source device and locate the footage to capture. If you have full device control enabled, you can also navigate to a specific timecode location on your source tape by entering a timecode value in the Current Timecode field.

8. Mark media In and Out points for a clip by *doing one of the following:*

   ◆ Click the Mark In and Mark Out buttons (**Figure 4.11**); or press I (the letter "i") to set the In point, and press O (the letter "o") to set the Out point.

   ◆ Enter specific timecodes in the timecode fields at the bottom of the Capture window. Enter the In point in the left timecode field and the Out point in the right timecode field.

9. Capture the clip using either the Capture Clip or the Capture Now button (**Figure 4.12**). Step-by-step instructions for each type of capture appear in the following sections of this chapter.

✔ Tip

■ Final Cut Express 1.0.1 doesn't automatically increment values as you capture successive clips. Until Apple repairs this feature, you'll need to click the Slate button of the last-checked field and increment the log information manually.

ENTERING INFORMATION ON THE LOGGING TAB

To add a marker to a clip while logging:

1. To access the marking controls, click the expansion triangle next to Markers at the bottom of the Logging tab.

2. Enter a marker name or comment in the Marker field.

3. To set the In and Out points of the marker, *do one of the following:*

   ◆ Enter timecode values in the In and Out timecode fields. You can Option-drag values from any timecode fields in the Capture window to copy them into these fields.

   ◆ Click the Mark In and Mark Out buttons.

4. Click Set Marker (**Figure 4.13**).

   The marker In and Out points and any information entered in the Marker field appear in the Marker Comment window.

   These markers appear as subclips in the Browser once a clip is captured (**Figure 4.14**).

✔ Tip

■ If you need to modify your marker data after you've set the marker, enter the revisions in the Marker fields and then click the Update button to save your changes.

Figure 4.13 Click Set Marker to enter the marker In and Out points as well as any information entered in the Marker field in the Marker Comment window.

Figure 4.14 The marker information appears within the captured clip.

FCE Protocol: Auto-Incrementing on the Logging Tab

The rules governing the behavior of the Description, Scene, and Shot/Take fields on the Logging tab are too many to list in this sidebar. Here, however, are a few handy rules that should help you get more efficiency out of the auto-entry features built into the Logging tab:

- The check box to the right of a field's name controls whether the field will be included in the clip's name.

- The last-checked field is the one that will increment automatically. Here are some examples:
  - If you check only the Description field, just the Description field will increment.
  - If Scene is the last-checked field, the scene number automatically increments, even if you entered a number in the Shot/Take field but left it unchecked.
  - If Shot/Take is the last-checked field, the Shot/Take field increments, and the scene number remains unchanged until you click its Slate button to increment it. Clicking the Scene field's Slate button resets the Shot/Take field to 01 (FCE assumes that your new scenes start with Take 01).

- You can include a Shot/Take number only if you include a scene number.

FCE Protocol: What Are Offline Clips?

An *offline clip* is a clip reference to a media file that has been deleted, moved, or renamed. If you log and capture a clip and then delete the clip's media file from disk, the clip "goes offline" and a red slash appears through the clip icon.

The offline clips appear in the Browser; you can even edit them, but you won't see or hear anything on the screen while you're editing. The only difference is that online clips are linked to captured media files on disk.

You can restore offline clips referencing deleted media by using the Capture Project feature, detailed later in this chapter, to recapture the media from tape.

You can use the Reconnect Media command to restore an offline clip's link to a moved or renamed media file.

Or you can delete a clip's media file deliberately to recapture some disk space, and recapture the clip's media only when you want to use it.

The Art of File Naming

When you capture or import media into Final Cut Express, you name each file as a part of the process. You'll be living with these file names for a long time. Since it's not a trivial matter to change file names once you've assigned them, you should develop a file naming system before you start your project. Write it down, distribute it to your production team, and stick to it.

Much of the logic behind file naming schemes involves constructing file names in a way that allows you to make use of the FCE's Sort and Find functions and to identify the file's content, file type, and version number. In Final Cut Express, an added level of flexibility is available to you because clips and their underlying media files do not need to have the same name.

A directory structure is the planned organization of folders you use to store your project's media elements. A complete file naming system should also be extended to the naming and organization of your files into folders. If you can, create your folder structure before you start acquiring your media elements. This will make it easier to file your elements correctly after the pace of production heats up.

Final Cut Express imposes an automated directory structure for captured media files, automatically generating folders named after your current project inside the Capture Scratch folder. This complicates the process of filing media elements according to your own system, but if you're organized, you can work around it. After you capture, you can move your captured clips into your own folder system and then import them into a project before you start assembling sequences.

Here are a few guidelines to help you develop file names that will remain useful throughout the life of your project:

♦ Incorporate file names into your shooting scripts, voice-over scripts, and storyboards early in production. Some projects actually enter the entire script into a database and use that script/database to track media elements.

♦ File names should contain the shot's scene and take numbers, if appropriate.

♦ Avoid duplicate file names.

♦ File suffixes are traditionally used as file type indicators. There are some standard file suffixes in use, but don't be shy about making up your own system of file type abbreviations. Be sure to document them.

♦ Audio file names should incorporate a code that indicates sample rate, file format, and whether the files are stereo or mono files.

♦ Your file naming system should include a code for version control. Don't rely on a file's creation or modification date as your only means of identifying the latest version of a file.

Figure 4.15 Choose
File > Capture.

Capture Clip: Capturing Video with Device Control

Capture clip combines logging tasks (marking In and Out points, naming the clip, entering comments) and capturing a single clip. Using a controllable DV camcorder or deck allows you to mark In and Out points at specific timecodes, and capture exactly the section you marked. Later on, you'll be able to recapture the exact same clip by using the Capture Project feature.

To capture a clip with device control:

1. Make sure your video device is properly connected and device control is operational. If you're using a camcorder, make sure it's switched to Play (VCR) mode; similarly, if you're using a deck with a Local/Remote switch, make sure the switch is set to Remote.

2. Choose File > Capture (**Figure 4.15**).

continues on next page

Capture Strategies to Manage Project Media

It's tempting to skip the time-consuming process of logging and capturing individual DV clips, and just hit the Capture Now button. Final Cut Express offers DV Start/Stop Detection and subclipping to handle extra-long clips (see the next section for details). So why not capture whole tapes and log them after you've captured?

The primary reason to go to the extra trouble of capturing shorter individual clips is because once you've captured a large clip, you can't easily delete the unused portions of its huge media file.

FCE's media management options are limited to manually deleting whole clips and their associated media files, and recapturing all DV project clips with the Capture Project feature. Neither of these options allows you to discard unused portions of the media file.

If you're desperate to reclaim some drive space, you can shed unused portions of a media file by exporting a clip that contains just the part of the media you want to keep, but you'll have to re-import the trimmed clip and then re-edit into your sequence. For more information on exporting a clip, see Chapter 18, "Creating Final Output."

CAPTURING VIDEO WITH DEVICE CONTROL

3. Use the transport controls in the Capture window to control the source device and locate the footage that you want to capture (**Figure 4.16**). If you have full device control enabled, you can also navigate to a specific timecode location on your source tape by entering a timecode value in the Current Timecode field.

4. In the Capture window, specify a capture bin using one of the methods described in the previous task.

5. Enter logging information for your clip (follow steps 4 through 6 in "To enter log information," earlier in this chapter).

Figure 4.16 Use the transport controls in the Capture window to control your video deck and locate the footage that you want to capture.

CAPTURING VIDEO WITH DEVICE CONTROL

Figure 4.17 Click the Mark Out button to set an Out point for the capture. You could also enter a timecode value in the Out point timecode field.

6. To mark a clip, *do one of the following:*

   ◆ Click the Mark In and Mark Out buttons (**Figure 4.17**); or press I to set the In point and press O to set the Out point.

   ◆ Enter specific timecodes in the timecode fields at the bottom of the Capture window. Enter the In point in the left timecode field and the Out point in the right timecode field.

7. Click the Capture Clip button located at the bottom of the window (**Figure 4.18**).

   Final Cut Express captures the clip, and the captured clip appears in a new Viewer window. Your captured clip is saved in the current project's designated capture bin.

Figure 4.18 Click the Capture Clip button located at the bottom of the Logging tab.

Capture Now: Capturing Video without Device Control

If you don't have a video device that your computer can control, you can still capture video in Final Cut Express by using the controls on your video deck or camcorder to search and play your source tape.

To log clips without the benefits of device control, you need to manually enter the clip's starting and ending timecodes and other information in the appropriate fields in the Capture window. That clip information is used to identify the clip when you save it.

If you enter log information before a Capture Now operation, the captured clip will be saved in your designated capture bin.

If you do not enter log information, the captured clip will be saved as an untitled clip in your designated capture bin.

✔ Tips

- Before you start capturing, check your Capture Now time-limit setting on the Scratch Disks tab of the Preferences window in FCE. The default limit is 30 minutes. Very long Capture Now time limits can increase the lag between the time you click the Capture Now button and the time that capture begins, so specify a time limit not much longer than the longest clip you're planning to capture.

- Analog-to-digital video converter boxes are handy for resurrecting treasured analog video footage, but if you're using a converter box with FCE to capture video you must use an Easy Setup configured specifically for that purpose—DV-NTSC (or PAL) 48kHz - DV Converter.

To capture a clip without device control:

1. Make sure your DV camcorder or deck is properly connected.

2. Choose File > Capture, or press Command-8.

3. In the Capture window, specify a capture bin by one of the methods described earlier.

4. To enter logging information for your clip, follow steps 4 through 6 in "To enter log information," earlier in this chapter.

5. Use your device's controls to locate the footage you want to capture, rewind 7 to 10 seconds, and then press the device's Play button.

6. Click the Capture Now button at the bottom of the Capture window 1 to 5 seconds before the device reaches the first frame in your clip (**Figure 4.19**).

   There's a slight delay after you click the button before capture begins—how long a delay depends on your Capture Now time limit and the number of scratch disks you have assigned to FCE.

continues on next page

Figure 4.19 Click the Capture Now button (at the bottom of the Capture window) 1 to 5 seconds before the first frame in your clip appears.

CAPTURING VIDEO WITHOUT DEVICE CONTROL

7. To stop capturing, press the Escape key (**Figure 4.20**); then stop playback on your device.

The captured clip appears in the designated capture bin on the project's tab in the Browser (**Figure 4.21**).

8. Play the clip to make sure it contains the video you want. You may need to close the Capture window—some video capture hardware won't play the captured clip while this window is open.

✔ Tip

■ If you're using a camcorder, you can use Capture Now to capture live footage. On most consumer DV models, your camcorder must be recording to tape as you capture the live footage in Final Cut Express.

Capturing analog audio

You can use FCE's Voice Over tool to digitize analog audio from a cassette player, TV, or other source and capture it in Final Cut Express. This can be a great convenience if you want to capture temporary rough voice-over or music. For more information, see "Recording Audio with the Voice Over Tool" in Chapter 11.

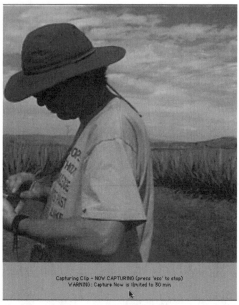

Figure 4.20 To stop capturing, press the Escape key.

Figure 4.21 The captured clip appears in the project's capture bin in the Browser.

Capture Project: Batch Recapturing

Use Capture Project to batch recapture DV clips and sequences you've previously captured with Final Cut Express. Capture Project captures all DV clips or just the offline clips in your project. Capture Project requires a camcorder or deck with device control.

This command is useful if you want to recapture several clips or an entire sequence in one automated batch recapture process—for example, when restoring a project you've removed from your hard disk. If you've accidentally deleted a few media files in the course of a project, you can use the Select Offline Items Only option to recapture just the footage you deleted.

Capture Project can only recapture DV clips from a source video tape. To restore an entire project, you must also restore all graphics, music, and any digital video that did not originate on a DV tape. For information on archiving and restoring FCE projects, see "Project Maintenance Tips" in Chapter 3.

Automated, unattended batch capture is limited to clips from one tape. You can set up an automated batch capture that involves clips from several reels, but you'll have to hang around and feed new tapes to your video deck during the process.

✔ Tip

- If you *really* want to recapture just a few selected clips, there's a way around Capture Project's "all or nothing" recapture limitation, but it's definitely a workaround: Create a new project, then copy and paste into that project only the few clips you want to recapture. Run the Capture Project process on the dummy project, then finally copy and paste the newly recaptured clips back to the original project. Hey, I said it was a workaround.

Preparing to recapture a project

Capture Project is an automated process. It's worthwhile to prepare carefully before you kick off an automated capture because, well, things can happen while your back is turned. Here are some suggestions:

◆ Check your currently selected Easy Setup and scratch disk preferences. Make any changes you want applied to this batch capture; you won't be able to change these settings after you open the Capture Project dialog box.

◆ Answer these questions: Are your capture settings correct for this batch capture, or are you capturing tapes in a different format? Is the estimated space available on your designated scratch disk sufficient to contain your incoming media files?

◆ Make a note of the available space estimate compared to the estimate of space needed in the Capture Project dialog box (**Figure 4.22**). This comparison can yield clues that can help you debug your batch capture list. For example, a 10-second subclip from a 20-minute master clip can throw your whole capture scheme out of whack; Final Cut Express would capture the entire 20-minute master clip.

◆ If you suspect that your tape contains timecode breaks, you should enable "Abort Capture on Timecode Break" in the General tab of the Preferences window before batch capturing clips. If you attempt to batch capture across a timecode break, Final Cut Express won't be able to accurately locate your offline clips, which can cause your batch capture to go seriously haywire. (Timecode breaks can be caused by shutting down the camera or ejecting your tape in midreel and not re-cueing on the last bit of previously recorded timecode.)

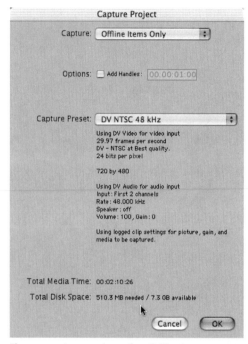

Figure 4.22 A comparison of available storage space and an estimate of the space needed for this batch capture appears in the Capture Project dialog box.

Figure 4.23 Click the Capture Project button in the Capture window to recapture all DV clips in the project.

Figure 4.24 The Selection Error dialog box appears if your project contains clips without reel numbers. Unless you need to re-examine reel settings for DV clips you want to recapture, click Continue to proceed.

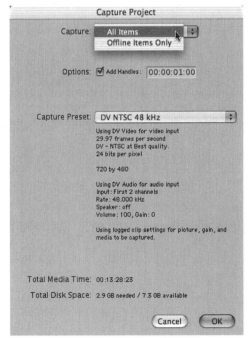

Figure 4.25 Select All Items to recapture the entire length of all offline and online DV clips in the project.

To batch recapture clips:

1. Choose File > Capture; or press Command-8.

2. In the Capture window, click the Capture Project button (**Figure 4.23**).

   If your project contains clips that lack reel numbers in their log information (this could be audio files or DV format clips you have imported from a digital source), the Selection Error dialog box appears.

3. Click Continue to proceed with the recapture (**Figure 4.24**). If you need to re-examine reel settings for DV clips you're planning to recapture, click Abort to interrupt the recapture operation.

4. In the Capture Project window's Capture pop-up menu, *do one of the following:*

   ◆ Select All Items to recapture all offline and online DV clips in the project (**Figure 4.25**).

   ◆ Select Offline Items Only to recapture just the offline DV clips in the project.

5. Enter a duration to set the handle size of offline clips (this is optional).

   Handles add extra frames beyond the In and Out points of a captured clip.

6. Select a capture preset option from the Capture Preset pop-up menu. This setting should match the video format and audio sample rate of the source tape you are recapturing.

7. Click OK.

   The Insert Reel dialog box appears, displaying a list of all the reels (tapes) required for this batch capture operation.

   continues on next page

8. Load the first tape you want to capture into your camcorder or deck, select it from the list, and click Continue (**Figure 4.26**).

9. To interrupt batch capture, press Escape or click the mouse button.

If you interrupt batch capture, Final Cut Express displays the Insert Reel dialog box again with a count of "aborted" clips—project clips that remain uncaptured (**Figure 4.27**).

10. Click Cancel to abort the Capture Project recapture, or click Continue to resume capture. If you cancel the process, you'll have to recapture all the clips in the current reel if you retry the Capture Project operation.

✔ Tip

- If you recapture online clips into the same scratch disk folder where the original clips' media files are stored, the original media files are overwritten. If you recapture into a different folder, the original media files are preserved.

Figure 4.26 Load the reel you want to capture into your deck, select it from the list, and click Continue. When it's finished capturing all the clips from that reel, FCE will prompt you to select the next reel.

Figure 4.27 The Insert Reel dialog box displays a count of "aborted" clips—project clips that remain uncaptured.

Figure 4.28 Choose Mark > DV Start/Stop Detection.

Figure 4.29 Final Cut Express places a marker at every point where it detects a Stop/Start signal in your clip's media file.

Using DV Start/Stop Detection

The DV Start/Stop Detection feature automatically sets markers in a previously captured DV clip each time it detects a Start/Stop (Record/Pause) signal in that clip. Because FCE can use markers to break a clip into individual subclips, you can use the technique outlined here to capture long sections of DV tape and break it into usable subclip chunks.

If you're accustomed to working in iMovie, DVD Start/Stop Detection is the closest thing to using iMovie's Import button with automatic scene detection enabled. Instead of getting a collection of separate clips, however, in Final Cut Express you end up with one large clip containing many markers, which can be converted to subclips. For more information, see "About Subclips" in Chapter 7.

To divide a captured DV clip into subclips based on starts and stops:

1. Open your previously captured DV clip in the Viewer.

2. With the Viewer active, choose Mark > DV Start/Stop Detection (**Figure 4.28**). Final Cut Express places a marker at every point where it detects a Stop/Start signal in the clip's media file (**Figure 4.29**).

3. If you want, add more markers at any point in the clip where you want to create a subclip.

continues on next page

4. Locate your clip's icon in the Browser; then click its expansion triangle to view the markers you just added to the clip (**Figure 4.30**).

5. If you want, rename markers with the names you want your subclips to have.

6. Select all of the markers; then choose Modify > Make Subclip.

New subclips, derived from your marked clip, appear in the Browser (**Figure 4.31**). If you renamed your markers, your new subclips use those names.

7. Review your new subclips and delete any with material you don't need.

✔ Tip

■ This DV Start/Stop technique is handy for converting a long clip into a group of smaller subclips, but when you're done, you still have a batch of subclips on your hands, and all of those subclips are still referencing the full length of your original media file.

Figure 4.30 Click the expansion triangle next to the clip to view the new markers. Select the markers you want to convert to subclips.

Figure 4.31 New subclips, derived from the markers in your marked clip, appear in the Browser.

USING DV START/STOP DETECTION

No Communication

Figure 4.32 The "No Communication" message appears in the Deck Status area of the Capture window if device control is disabled.

Troubleshooting Capture Problems

If you experience problems during video capture, you may see an error message. Final Cut Express monitors the state of controlled devices and reports an error if the problem is due to a camcorder or deck malfunction. Cancel the operation before proceeding and consult your camcorder or deck manual for troubleshooting information. Here are some basic troubleshooting tips that may help you get back on the road.

If the message "No Communication" appears in the Deck Status area of the Capture window (**Figure 4.32**), *do the following:*

◆ Check that your device is plugged in, switched on, and properly connected to your computer.

◆ Turn on the device and restart the computer. If your device's power was not switched on when you started your computer, the device may not have been recognized.

◆ Reconnect the FireWire cable and restart the computer. If the cable was not connected properly when you started your computer, the device may not have been recognized.

If you experience problems controlling your camcorder or deck:

◆ If your deck has a Local/Remote switch, be sure it's set to Remote.

◆ If you're using the Apple FireWire protocol, try Apple FireWire Basic instead. Switch to an Easy Setup that includes FireWire Basic (**Figure 4.33**).

◆ Check Apple's Final Cut Pro web site to see if your camcorder or deck requires a special DV Tuner script to work properly. Apple's Final Cut Pro Device Qualification page lists all qualified cameras (**Figure 4.34**); the DV camera information listed there applies to Final Cut Express as well. Tuner scripts should be available on the Final Cut Express web site.

Here's the URL for the Final Cut Pro 3 Device Qualification page: `www.apple.com/finalcutpro/qualification.html`.

Figure 4.33 If Apple FireWire doesn't provide reliable device control, switch to the Apple FireWire Basic protocol by switching to an Easy Setup that uses FireWire Basic.

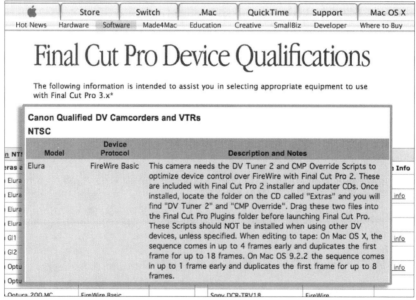

Figure 4.34 Check Apple's Final Cut Express web site to see if your video gear requires a DV Tuner script.

TROUBLESHOOTING CAPTURE PROBLEMS

If you encounter a "Bus error" message when you try to capture:

◆ Something went wrong when your captured data crossed the bus, the data delivery interface between your computer and the outside world. Bus errors can be caused by a number of things, but you can try making sure that your cables are hooked up completely and that any hardware cards in your computer are seated properly.

If you encounter a "Time Code Break" error message when you try to capture:

◆ Is there anything you can do to salvage a tape with timecode breaks? Certainly. You can dub the entire tape onto a tape with continuous timecode and start your logging and capturing process with the dubbed copy. If dubbing is not an option, you can assign separate reel numbers to each section and use those reel numbers as you log, but you won't be able to batch capture reliably on a tape with timecode breaks.

If your captured audio and video play back out of sync:

◆ The video displayed in the Viewer and the Canvas will not appear to play back in sync if you are monitoring your audio through external speakers connected to your camcorder or deck. The audio from the external speakers will be synchronized with video displayed on the video monitor.

◆ The audio sample rate of your original source tape must match the audio sample rate of your capture settings. Check the source tape's audio sample rate against your capture settings.

◆ Your FCE system may be dropping frames during capture or playback. See "Is Your System Capture-Ready?" earlier in this chapter for a list of possible causes for dropped frames.

FCE Protocol: Sync Adjust Movies Feature

The Sync Adjust Movies feature is designed to compensate for audio sample rate discrepancies in video tape that has been shot on certain cameras, notably certain models of Canon cameras.

When you enable the Sync Adjust Movies (SAM) feature in the General tab of the Preferences window, Final Cut Express checks the actual audio sample rate of any captured or imported media file whose duration is longer than the duration you specified in the preferences, and then it marks those files to be played back at a sample rate that will compensate for the sync problem.

Enabling the Sync Adjust Movies feature does not affect the sample rate during capture, but you will see the exact audio sample rate displayed in the Browser's Aud Rate column.

SAM restores synchronization by converting the audio sample rate of your captured clips on the fly and then playing back the result.

Note: Converting the sample rate of audio files in real time has a slight impact on performance and quality. If you have selected Medium or High Audio Playback quality in General Preferences, your audio will probably require rendering to play back. If you use the SAM feature and you don't want to render your audio for playback, choose the Low Audio Playback quality (Low quality doesn't sound all that bad).

If you're not using long sync takes and you don't perceive any sync problems, you might want to disable the Sync Adjust Movies feature.

However, if you are noticing audio/video sync drift in long takes, you might want to enable the SAM feature and see if that corrects your sync problem. The only serious downside to leaving SAM enabled is that you risk serious sync loss if you attempt to capture a tape with timecode breaks in it.

Because SAM doesn't flag files until after capture, you won't need to recapture clips to disable SAM.

However, because files are flagged at the time they are relinked or imported, even if you disable the Sync Adjust Movies feature in Preferences window after a clip has been imported or relinked, a SAM-flagged file will remain affected until you re-import or relink it.

IMPORTING DIGITAL MEDIA

One of most enchanting aspects of the DV revolution is the world of digital media elements that you can mix, match, and manipulate freely to spice up your video. Final Cut Express is exceptional in the wide latitude of digital file formats it accepts. You can import most types of QuickTime-compatible files into an FCE project, including video clips, still images, and sound files.

Apple's QuickTime web site contains a complete list of supported file formats at www.apple.com/quicktime/products/qt/specifications.html.

Here's a list of common FCE-supported QuickTime formats:

- ◆ **Graphics:** BMP, FlashPix, GIF, JPEG/JFIF, MacPaint (PNTG), Photoshop (PSD), PICS, PICT, PNG, QuickTime Image File (QTIF), SGI, TARGA (TGA), and TIFF

- ◆ **Video:** AVI, QuickTime Movie

- ◆ **Audio:** AIFF, Audio CD Data (Macintosh), Sound, and Wave

- ◆ **Other:** Macromedia Flash (video only)

You can import an entire folder or organization of multiple folders in a single operation. When you import a folder, Final Cut Express imports all files it recognizes in the folder, as well as all recognized files in any subfolders. Folders are imported with their internal hierarchies intact.

To import files or a folder:

1. Copy or move the file that you want to import into the desired media folder in your project (**Figure 5.1**).

2. In the Browser, select a destination for your incoming file by *doing one of the following*:

   ◆ To import files or folders into the top level of a project, click the project's Browser tab.

   ◆ To import files into a bin within a project, double-click the bin to open it.

3. *Do one of the following*:

   ◆ Choose File > Import; then choose Files (or Folder) from the submenu, select the items, and click Open.

   ◆ In the Browser or any Browser bin window, Control-click and then choose Import File (or Import Folder) from the shortcut menu.

   ◆ Drag the desired files or folders directly from your Desktop (**Figure 5.2**) to a project tab or to a bin within the Browser (**Figure 5.3**).

   ◆ Drag the desired files or folders from your Desktop to an open sequence in the Timeline. This places a clip reference to the media in the Timeline, but does not place a reference in the Browser.

Figure 5.1 Before you import a file, copy or move the file into the correct asset folder in your project.

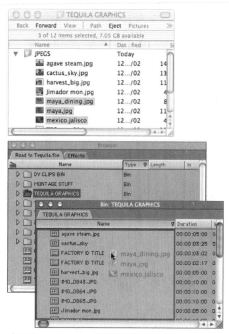

Figure 5.2 Drag the desired files or folders directly from your Desktop into Final Cut Express.

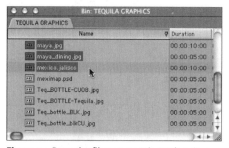

Figure 5.3 Drop the files on a project tab or in a bin within the Browser.

IMPORTING DIGITAL MEDIA

Figure 5.4 Imported still images have a default length of 2 minutes of identical video frames, with a duration of 10 seconds between In and Out points. The source media files for still image clips don't occupy 2 minutes' worth of drive space; you generate media only for the portions you render.

Importing Still Images

The default format for imported still images is a clip containing 2 minutes of identical video frames, with a default duration of 10 seconds between In and Out points (**Figure 5.4**). If you edit still images into a sequence, they won't be visible on your NTSC external monitor until they are rendered.

Final Cut Express supports all QuickTime-compatible graphics file formats. Check the QuickTime Read Me file or Apple's QuickTime web site for a complete list of compatible file formats.

✔ Tip

- Final Cut Express does not import EPS files.

FCE Protocol: File Location Is Critical

When you import a file into a Final Cut Express project, that file is not copied into the FCE project file. Importing a file places a clip in your Browser, but that clip is a reference to the current hard disk location of your imported media file at the time you import it.

In Final Cut Express, any clip's link to its underlying media file is entirely location based. If you move media files to another disk location after you've used them in a project, you break their links to the clip references in your FCE projects. You can use the Reconnect Media command to restore those clip-to-media file links, but a little forethought before you import files can save you a lot of hassle later. (The Reconnect Media function is discussed in Chapter 3, "How to Manage an FCE Project.")

Before you import a file into FCE, be sure to copy it to its permanent folder location in your project's media assets directory structure. Importing files directly from a removable media storage device (such as a Zip disk) will cause your file to be marked "Offline" in your project once you remove that disk from your system. The same principle applies to audio imported from a CD.

Setting the default duration for stills

Still images and generators are assigned a duration at the time they're imported into Final Cut Express. You specify the default duration for still images on the General tab of the Preferences window.

No matter what duration you set, your Final Cut Express clip references a single still image, so you won't create large, full-length video files until you render or export your stills at their edited lengths.

The default still duration is applied at the time you import the still into Final Cut Express. If you have imported a still image and want the duration to be longer, you must modify the preference setting and then re-import the still.

To change the default still duration:

1. Choose Final Cut Express > Preferences; or press Option-Q.

2. On the General tab of the Preferences window, enter a new default duration in the Still/Freeze Duration field (**Figure 5.5**).

3. Click OK.

✔ Tip

■ Modify the default still duration any time you're importing a large number of stills that you plan to cut to the same length. The stills will be imported at the final edited length and you can drop them directly into your sequence. *Molto bene.*

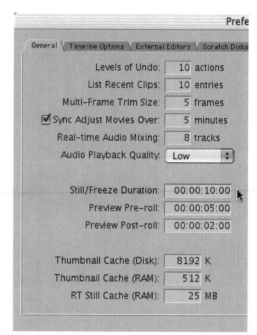

Figure 5.5 On the General tab of the Preferences window, type a new default duration in the Still/Freeze Duration field.

Working with Adobe Photoshop Files

Adobe Photoshop is the industry-standard tool for creating graphic elements for use in Final Cut Express. Its file format compatibility with Final Cut Express makes importing your artwork's layers and alpha channels easy.

When you're creating graphics for use in a video program, keep your final format's requirements in mind. Remember that video has title-safe requirements, a different pixel aspect ratio, and a different tolerance for color and contrast levels than still graphics.

Images that look beautiful in print or on a computer screen may not display well on a television monitor. The NTSC broadcast video standard cannot tolerate extreme contrast shifts on many of the colors that you can create and display in Photoshop.

Photoshop comes with an NTSC Colors filter that you can apply to your artwork to make it color safe for TV sets, and FCE has a Broadcast Safe filter that performs a similar function.

✔ Tip

- Photoshop's NTSC Colors filter is a fine tool, but it's easier to use the Broadcast Safe filter in Final Cut Express once the Photoshop files are incorporated into your sequence. For more information see Chapter 15, "Filters and Compositing."

Preparing a Photoshop file for use in FCE

The best way to preserve image quality in digital image formats is to maintain the same frame size and resolution from beginning to end. You will get best results by creating your art with the required pixel dimensions in mind, but if you create artwork on a computer for display on broadcast television, you'll find that you must jump through a few hoops.

The native frame size of DV is 720 by 480 pixels. However, if you create your artwork in Photoshop at that size, your image looks squeezed when it's displayed on a TV monitor after printing to video. This is because of a difference in the pixel aspect ratio between the computer world and the broadcast television world.

Computer monitors use square pixels, where the height is perfectly proportional to the width. NTSC television monitors use a system that has a non-square pixel aspect ratio of 1.33:1, where the height is just a little bit greater than the width.

To accommodate the difference between these two frame sizes, you must create your full-frame graphic elements at a slightly larger size than your target resolution and then size them down to the target resolution in Photoshop before you import your image into Final Cut Express. (Target resolution refers to the actual pixel count of an image's frame size in its final delivery, or target, format.)

To create a Photoshop file at DV NTSC target resolution:

1. In Photoshop, choose File > New; or press Command-N.

2. Enter a width of 720 pixels, a height of 534 pixels, and a resolution of 72 pixels per inch (**Figure 5.6**).

   This ratio of 720:534, or 1.33, is the proper proportion for creating text and graphics that will look the same on your NTSC monitor as on your computer monitor.

3. Create your image file (**Figure 5.7**).

4. Save the file as your original image file. Use this original graphic file to make any subsequent changes to the artwork.

5. Choose Image > Image Size (**Figure 5.8**).

6. In the Image Size dialog box, uncheck Constrain Proportions.

Figure 5.6 In the New dialog box, enter a width of 720 pixels, a height of 534 pixels, and a resolution of 72 pixels per inch.

Figure 5.7 The original Photoshop image at 720 by 534 pixels, before resizing.

Figure 5.8 Choose Image > Image Size.

WORKING WITH ADOBE PHOTOSHOP FILES

Figure 5.9 In the Image Size dialog box, specify a width of 720 pixels and a height of 480 pixels.

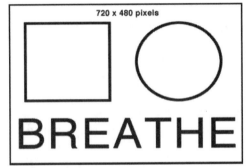

Figure 5.10 The "squashed" Photoshop image at 720 by 480 pixels, after resizing.

7. In the Pixel Dimensions section, enter a width of 720 pixels and a height of 480 pixels (**Figure 5.9**).

8. Click OK.

The vertical aspect of the image shrinks, which makes it look squashed (**Figure 5.10**).

9. Save the file as your production graphic file. Use this production graphic file in your project.

10. If you need to make changes to the artwork, use the original graphic file, which has the unaltered aspect ratio; then, when you're ready to save, repeat steps 4 through 9.

✔ Tips

■ You don't have to import an entire full-screen image if your image uses only a small portion of the frame. Arrange your elements in position in full-screen format, resize for the pixel aspect ratio difference, and then crop down the artwork.

■ If you're planning to zoom in on the image you're preparing, you should import a file with pixel dimensions that will allow the tightest framing to fill the entire video frame without scaling the image above 100%.

■ You can import a variety of file formats, but the most common are the native Photoshop format (for images with multiple layers) and the standard PICT format (for single-layer images with alpha channels).

■ You can also resize imported graphics clips and sequences in Final Cut Express, but you'll get better results using Photoshop's bicubic scaling for resizing because it uses a better resampling algorithm.

FCE Protocol: Updating Photoshop Files in FCE

It's easy to import Adobe Photoshop files into FCE, but if you need to change to a Photoshop file you've already used in a sequence, there are some hoops to jump through. Get ready to jump.

When you import a multilayer Photoshop file into your project for the first time, Final Cut Express constructs a description of this file that includes the number of layers and the frame size of each layer.

First hoop: It's not always easy to get Final Cut Express to update its description data of your Photoshop file. If you revise your existing image in Photoshop and save changes in the original file, you may not see the changes reflected when you return to Final Cut Express. FCE protocol dictates that the original proxy description of your Photoshop file is used.

How do you get FCE to refresh its memory and update your Photoshop file's description? Suggested workarounds include:

◆ After you've revised your Photoshop file, rename the file when you save your changes and then re-import it into FCE. Because you're re-importing the file with a new name, FCE creates a new description of it. The good news? Your Photoshop file revisions are showing up in FCE. The bad news? Now you have to manually replace the file with the revised file everywhere you've used it.

◆ If your file has the same number of layers, and those layers have the same frame size, you should be able to select the Photoshop clip wherever you've used it in your sequence and then use the Reconnect Media command to manually re-introduce the clip and the Photoshop source media file.

Second hoop: FCE uses the frame size data it recorded when you first imported your Photoshop file in all effect calculations that use X,Y coordinates—motion paths, scaling, warp filters, and so on. However (get ready to jump...), FCE does not include transparent pixels when it calculates a Photoshop layer's frame size. Say you have created text on a transparent background in Photoshop, imported your file into FCE, and then applied effects. Should you need to revise your text when you return to it, the frame size of your text layer has changed. Even if you successfully reconnect your revised Photoshop file to your FCE sequence, FCE will use the data description from the original import (with the old frame size) to calculate your effects. The result? Your text effects will look distorted, and you'll briefly consider quitting the business.

There's a workaround for this dilemma. It's not pretty, but you can save yourself some headaches down the road by anticipating changes to your text. Again, get ready to jump....

◆ When you build your original Photoshop file, place a single nontransparent pixel in each corner of the frame (**Figure 5.11**). You'll need to do this for each and every layer. FCE will use the rectangle created by those four placeholder pixels to calculate the frame size. You can change text to your heart's content inside the bounding box created by the four corner pixels, and your FCE frame size will not change. So if you can reconnect your Photoshop file, your effects will be calculated with the correct frame size data.

continues on next page

FCE Protocol: Updating Photoshop Files in FCE *continued*

Final Warning: Once you've imported a layered Photoshop file into FCE, you should avoid adding or subtracting layers from the file.

FCE identifies a Photoshop layer by its position relative to the file's bottom layer. Increase the total number of layers in the Photoshop file and FCE will ignore any layers numbered above the previous topmost layer. Deleting a layer from a Photoshop file that you've already imported could yield a variety of unpleasant results, so you should re-import any file with changes to the layer count.

The best workaround? Once you've imported your Photoshop graphics, don't change your mind. Or get ready to jump....

Figure 5.11 Place a single nontransparent pixel in each corner of each layer of your Photoshop composition. If you need to revise your Photoshop text later, those corner pixels will maintain a constant frame size, and when you re-import or reconnect your revised Photoshop file, FCE will recalculate your previously applied effects with the correct frame size. Hey—it's a workaround.

WORKING WITH ADOBE PHOTOSHOP FILES

Importing a layered Photoshop file into Final Cut Express

Final Cut Express preserves the layers in a layered Photoshop file, importing the file as a sequence. Each Photoshop layer is represented by a clip on a track in that sequence.

Double-click a Photoshop file sequence to open it in the Timeline, where you can choose individual layers to manipulate. Each layer is found on its own video track.

When you place a layered Photoshop file into your FCE sequence, you're actually *nesting* it: placing a sequence within another sequence. Nesting sequences is a powerful tool, and knowing the rules that govern the behavior of nested sequences will help you plan your work better. See "Working with Multiple Sequences" in Chapter 3.

To view individual layers in imported Photoshop files:

◆ In the Browser, double-click the Photoshop file, which appears as a sequence (**Figure 5.12**).

The Photoshop file opens as a sequence in the Timeline. Individual layers appear as clips aligned on separate video tracks (**Figure 5.13**).

Figure 5.12 A layered Photoshop file appears as a sequence when it's imported into Final Cut Express. Double-click the Photoshop file to open it.

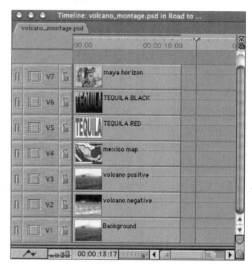

Figure 5.13 The Photoshop file opens as a sequence in the Timeline. Individual layers appear as clips.

Figure 5.14 To extend the total duration of a layered Photoshop file, open it as a sequence in the Timeline and adjust the length of the Individual layers.

✔ Tips

■ Once you've opened your multilayer Photoshop file as an FCE sequence, you can drag individual layer "clips" out of the sequence and drop them in the Browser. You can then use the individual layers as independent graphic clips.

■ To import a layered Photoshop file as a clip instead of a sequence, flatten the image in Photoshop before importing it.

■ Because imported layered Photoshop files appear in FCE as sequences, your Still/Freeze Image Duration preference will set the total length of the imported file, with no allowance for handles. If you want to increase its length after you import, you'll have to open the Photoshop file sequence and extend the length of the individual layers inside (**Figure 5.14**). Extending the length of multiple layer clips in one operation is a terrific use for the Extend edit. See "To perform an Extend edit in the Timeline" in Chapter 10.

WORKING WITH ADOBE PHOTOSHOP FILES

FCE Protocol: Layered Photoshop Files

◆ A layered Adobe Photoshop file imported into a Final Cut Express project retains its transparency information, visibility, and composite mode.

◆ Layer opacity settings and layer modes are preserved, but layer masks and layer effects are not.

◆ If a Photoshop layer mode has no corresponding compositing mode in Final Cut Express, the layer mode is ignored.

Importing Audio Files

Import digital audio files into Final Cut Express just as you do any other digital media. You can import files in any QuickTime-supported audio format.

You can capture audio at its originally recorded sample rate and use it in the same sequence with audio recorded at other sample rates. When you play back the sequence, Final Cut Express converts the sample rate in real time for any audio clips with sample rates that do not match the sequence settings.

Letting Final Cut Express convert the sample rates in real time is not always the best solution, however, as real-time sample-rate conversion is optimized for speed, not audio quality. You can convert the sample rate of your nonconforming audio by using the Export feature in Final Cut Express to make a copy of your audio file at the correct sample rate, or you can wait until you're ready to export your final product. FCE will sample-rate convert your nonconforming audio tracks using a higher quality, non-real-time conversion during the audio mixdown rendering process. See Chapter 18, "Creating Final Output."

To import an audio CD track into an FCE project:

1. In the Finder, double-click the audio CD to open it; then select and drag the .cdda audio files you want to import into your project's media folder (**Figure 5.15**).

Figure 5.15 Select and drag the .cdda audio files you want to import into your project's media folder.

Figure 5.16 Rename the file and then drag it directly into your FCE project.

2. Rename the files so you can remember where they came from.

3. Follow the steps outlined in "To import files or a folder" earlier in this chapter (**Figure 5.16**).

✔ Tips

- It is not recommended that you import audio tracks by dragging directly from an audio CD to the Browser window in Final Cut Express, because once you remove the CD from your computer, your project will no longer have access to the audio file.

- If you plan to sample-rate convert your CD audio to 48 kHz before you use it in your FCE project, check out the iTunes import method described in the next section.

Convert Audio to 48 kHz on Import with iTunes

Figure 5.17 Set your file conversion settings in the Importing pane of iTunes Preferences.

If you are using a lot of material from audio CDs in your FCE projects, consider using Apple's free iTunes, an audio jukebox application, to streamline sample-rate conversion. Here's how to set your preferences in iTunes to convert 44.1 kHz audio to 48 kHz as it imports the CD audio track directly to your project's media folder.

To set iTunes preferences:

1. Open iTunes, then choose iTunes > Preferences and click the Importing icon.

2. In the Importing pane, choose AIFF Encoder from the Import Using pop-up menu and Custom from the Configuration pop-up menu (**Figure 5.17**).

3. In the AIFF Encoder window, specify the following (**Figure 5.18**), then click OK.
   ◆ Sample Rate: 48.000 kHz
   ◆ Channels: Auto
   ◆ Sample Size: 16 bit

4. Back in the preferences window, click the Advanced icon.

Figure 5.18 In the AIFF Encoder window, make your settings match these.

Figure 5.19 Select your project's audio media folder as the destination folder for your sample-rate converted audio files.

5. In the Advanced pane, the iTunes Music Folder Location shows the currently selected destination folder for the CD audio you're about to import. Click the Change button (**Figure 5.19**), and navigate to your project's audio media folder. Click Choose, and then click OK.

6. In the iTunes playlist window, choose the tracks you want to import by ensuring their checkboxes are marked and click the Import button (**Figure 5.20**).

   The CD audio tracks are converted into 48 kHz AIFF files and appear in the destination folder you specified in Step 5, ready to import into your FCE project (**Figure 5.21**).

Figure 5.20 In the iTunes playlist window, check the tracks you want and click the Import button.

Figure 5.21 iTunes converts your CD audio tracks into 48 kHz AIFF files and places them in the specified folder.

Importing an iMovie 3 Project

Final Cut Express can import, open, and edit movies created in iMovie 3. When you import an iMovie project, the clips in the Browser are linked to the original source media files you captured in iMovie.

iMovie uses a different DV encoding method, which produces files in DV Stream format. DV Stream format differs from FCE's DV-NTSC (or DV-PAL) format, so you'll encounter a little extra work and a couple of limitations as you continue to work on a project that originated in iMovie 3:

◆ Once you've imported it, you must render all the media in your project to convert it to an FCE-compatible DV format.

◆ Your DV Stream iMovie files do not have timecode tracks, so you cannot recapture any media that originated in iMovie. Don't throw your iMovie media files away once you've rendered; you'll need them if you plan to continue editing.

◆ Final Cut Express may not play back your iMovie 3 DV files in real time unless you render them first.

◆ Your imported iMovie 3 project won't include any iMovie sound effects, titles, transitions, effects, or iDVD chapter markers.

To import an iMovie 3 project:

1. Choose File > Open.

2. Select the iMovie 3 project you want to open (**Figure 5.22**).

   The iMovie 3 project appears on a project tab in the Browser. The project contains the iMovie 3 sequence plus the individual clips from iMovie's clips shelf.

Figure 5.22 Choose File > Open, then select the iMovie 3 project file you want to import.

3. Double-click the sequence to open the iMovie 3 project sequence in the Timeline.

4. Choose File > Save Project As, and save your imported iMovie 3 project as a Final Cut Express project (**Figure 5.23**).

5. Render the sequence if necessary.

Figure 5.23 Once you've opened your iMovie 3 project in FCE and checked that your media and sequence information have imported successfully, choose File > Save Project As and save a new version of the project as a Final Cut Express project.

Part III: Getting Ready to Edit

Part III:
Getting Ready
to Edit

You've captured your video. You've imported your hunks of digital audio, your Photoshop titles, and your baby pictures. You're ready to edit. What's next?

Part III introduces the two program windows you'll use to review your source material in preparation for editing:

◆ The Browser, detailed in Chapter 6, offers powerful tools to track and organize your stuff.

◆ The Viewer, covered in Chapter 7, is your monitor to view, audition, mark, and apply effects to a clip.

You'll need a working knowledge of both windows to prepare your material for editing, so you might want to take a look at both chapters before you jump in.

Before the clips start flying, take a moment to organize your wonderland of little media bits. You'll be so glad you did.

ORGANIZE YOUR CLIPS IN THE BROWSER

6

The Browser is the window you use to organize and access clips, audio files, graphics, and offline clips—all the media elements you use in your project. It also includes the project's sequences—FCE objects that contain your edits.

The Browser performs these organizing tasks on your project's virtual clips and sequences— although they look like the files on your computer desktop, Browser items are *references* to media files, not the files themselves. It's very important to remember that copying, moving, or deleting a clip in the Browser does not affect that clip's source media file on disk. Moving a batch of clips from one bin to another in the Browser does not change the location of the clips' corresponding files on your hard drive. File storage is independent of Browser organization, so you can place the same clip in several Browser projects, and each instance of the clip will include a reference to the same media file on your hard drive.

See "What Is Nonlinear, Non-Destructive Editing?" in Chapter 1 for more background on nonlinear editing technology.

Anatomy of the Browser

When you open FCE for the first time, the Browser contains just two tabs:

◆ A new, Untitled Project tab with a single empty sequence.

◆ The Effects tab, which contains default copies of Final Cut Express's effects, filters, and generators, including the text generators. For information on using FCE's effects features, see Chapter 13, "Compositing and Effects Overview."

If you have multiple projects open, the Browser will display a tab for each open project. You can also open a Browser bin in a separate window, and then drag the bin's tab from the bin window into the main Browser window to display the bin as a tab.

Figure 6.1 shows the Browser window in List view. Note that FCE opens projects with the Browser in Icon view by default. Icon view is useful for organizing a storyboard, but doesn't provide the wealth of clip data available from the Browser columns in List view. To learn how to switch to List view, see "Customizing the Browser Display," later in this chapter.

Figure 6.1 The Browser window in List view.

Browser columns

The Browser window can display up to 32 columns of data, but you can customize the Browser to display only the columns you are using and hide the rest. Some columns accommodate remarks and other types of information that helps you track and sort information about your clips. **Table 6.1** contains a complete list of the columns available for use in the Browser.

Table 6.1

Browser Columns and Functions

COLUMN	FUNCTION	COLUMN	FUNCTION
Alpha	Alpha channel present	Log Note	Used for logging information
Anamorphic	Indicates whether clip is flagged to be displayed in anamorphic (16:9) aspect ratio	Name	Name of the media element; rename clips and sequences here
Aud Format	Bit rate (16-bit or 8-bit) and channel format (stereo or mono) of audio clip	Offline	Indicates clip's source media has not been captured yet, is missing, or has been deleted from disk.
Aud Rate	Sample rate of audio clip.	Out	Out point specified on a clip
Audio	Indicates number of audio channels for clips that include audio	Pixel Aspect	Pixel aspect ratio
Capture	Capture state of a clip in the Batch Capture list	Reel	Lists reel number entered at time of capture
Comment 1-4	Used for logging information	Reverse Alpha	Enable to reverse opaque and transparent area interpretation in clip's alpha channel
Composite	Composite mode used by this clip		
Compressor	Indicates compression codec	Scene	Displays information entered in Logging tab's Scene field
Data Rate	Rate of data flow per second	Shot/ Take	Displays information entered in Logging tab's Shot/Take field
Description	Displays information entered in Logging tab's Description field	Size	Source media file size, in megabytes
Duration	Duration between a clip's In and Out points	Source	Pathname of the media file on disk
Frame Size	Video frame size, in pixels	Thumbnail	Displays poster (or first) frame of the clip; click and drag a thumbnail to scrub through the clip
Good	Indicates a clip marked "Good" in Log and Capture window		
In	In point specified on a clip	Tracks	Number of video and audio tracks in the item
Last Modified	Displays the time and date of an item's last modification	Type	The type of each item; possible types: sequence, clip, subclip, bin, effect
Length	Length of the source media file on disk	Vid Rate	Video frame rate

ANATOMY OF THE BROWSER

Browser window icons

Along the left side of the window, you'll notice icons that accompany each item listed in the Browser. These icons represent file types in Final Cut Express:

 Sequence: An edited assembly of video and audio clips. Open sequences are displayed in the Timeline.

 Bin: Bins are folders used to organize clips and sequences. A bin can also contain multiple bins.

 Open Bin: A bin that is currently opened in a separate Browser window.

 Clip: A media file; can contain audio, video, graphics, or other media imported into Final Cut Express.

 Subclip: A portion of a clip defined by In and Out points; any number of subclips can be referenced to one master clip.

 Offline Clip: Placeholder clip referencing media not currently on the local hard drive.

 Audio Clip: Media clip composed of audio samples.

 Graphic: Clip is in a single-layer graphic file format (multilayer Photoshop files appear with a sequence icon).

 Marker: Reference point in a clip.

 Video Transition: Transition effect; can be applied to a video track.

 Audio Transition: Transition effect; can be applied to an audio track.

 Video Filter: Effects filter; can be applied to a video clip.

 Audio Filter: Effects filter; can be applied to an audio clip.

 Generator: Effects utility; generates screens, tones, and text for program transitions.

What Does "Not Set" Mean?

When you see "Not Set" displayed in the In (or Out) Browser column, it simply means that you haven't set an In (or Out) point in that clip. For instance, you could have inserted the full length of your clip into a sequence and then set In and Out points in the *sequence* version of the clip, or you could be using every captured frame of your clip in the sequence.

"Not Set" does not mean that you've somehow lost your source media file or that the clip has lost its timecode.

ANATOMY OF THE BROWSER

Using the Browser to Organize Your Project

The Browser is a powerful tool for organizing all your program elements in a way that makes sense to you. You could construct a multilevel folders-within-folders structure by organizing your material in multiple bins, or you could use one long list containing every element in the same display. You might want to keep separate bins for your live action footage, graphics, and music files; or, in a classroom situation, you might want to use a separate bin for each student's editing assignment.

You can search for your clips based on any clip property and sort from most Browser columns. Any markers you've placed in a clip will be noted in the Browser. You can use the Browser shortcut menu to modify some clip and sequence properties, or you can add or modify most clip information directly by double-clicking a Browser column entry.

To select an item in the Browser:

Do one of the following:

◆ Click the item you want to select.

◆ Use the arrow keys to step through the item list until you arrive at the item you want.

◆ Use the Tab key to move between items alphabetically from A to Z. Use Shift-Tab to move alphabetically from Z to A.

◆ Type the first few letters of an item's name, and the corresponding item will be highlighted.

✔ Tip

■ The Last Modified column shows a time/date stamp for clips and sequences, putting an end to guessing which version of a sequence you worked on last.

To select multiple items in the Browser:

Do one of the following:

- ◆ Command-click the individual items you want to select (**Figure 6.2**).

- ◆ Shift-click the first and last items in the list to select a range of items (**Figure 6.3**).

- ◆ Drag a bounding box around a group of list items or icons (**Figure 6.4**).

- ◆ To add or subtract single items from a multiple selection, Command-click the item.

✔ Tip

- ■ Item selection in FCE's Browser works in the same way as it does in the Mac OS X Finder: Command-click to select multiple items individually; Shift-click to select a range of items.

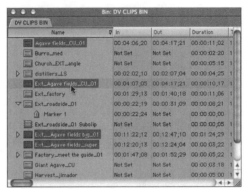

Figure 6.2 Command-click to select multiple Browser items individually.

Figure 6.3 Shift-click the first and last items to select a contiguous range of Browser items.

Figure 6.4 You can select a group of items by dragging a bounding box around them.

USING BROWSER TO ORGANIZE YOUR PROJECT

Figure 6.5 Click in the column header to sort by name; the direction of the tiny arrow to the right of the column name here indicates ascending order.

Figure 6.6 Click again to reverse the sort order; the arrow's direction now indicates a descending order.

Figure 6.7 Shift-click in a second column header to select a secondary sort column.

Sorting items

Final Cut Express allows you to sort by almost every column you see in the Browser. You can use a series of secondary sorts (up to eight) to further refine your list order.

To sort items in the Browser:

1. Click a column header to select the primary sort column (**Figure 6.5**).

   The primary sort column is indicated by a green arrow in the column header.

2. Click again to reverse the sort order (**Figure 6.6**).

3. Shift-click additional headers to select secondary sort columns (**Figure 6.7**).

4. A secondary sort column is indicated by a light blue arrow in the column header. Shift-click again to reverse the sort order.

✔ Tip

- If you've defined secondary sort columns by Shift-clicking, you'll need to click on a deselected column to clear the current sort before you can select a new primary sort column.

Customizing the Browser display

Different Browser display modes offer different functionality. List view, for example, offers a multitude of data, arranged in sortable columns, plus sexy scrubbable Thumbnail clips. Large Icon view allows you to drag your clips into any order you choose.

You can customize the Browser in the following ways:

◆ Make items appear as icons (**Figure 6.8**) or as a text list.

◆ In List view, rearrange, resize, hide, or show as many columns as you like. (Note: You can't hide the Name column.)

◆ Sort by most columns.

◆ Set a standard arrangement of columns and switch between that preset and another preset column arrangement for logging clips. Both presets are selectable from the column header's shortcut menu.

◆ Change the Comment column headers.

To display items as a list or as icons:

1. Control-click within the Browser window; if you're in the List view, Control-click within the Name column.

2. Choose a display option from the shortcut menu (**Figure 6.9**).

Or do this:

◆ Choose View > Browser Items and then select a display option from the submenu: As List, As Small Icons, As Medium Icons, or As Large Icons (**Figure 6.10**).

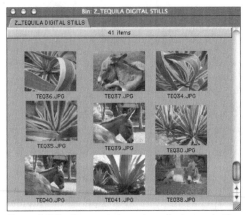

Figure 6.8 The Browser in Large Icon display mode. You can also select Medium Icon, Small Icon, or List view.

Figure 6.9 Control-click the Name column and then choose a display option from the shortcut menu.

Figure 6.10 Another way to choose a display option from the Browser Items submenu of the View menu.

Figure 6.11 Choose Show Thumbnail from the shortcut menu.

Figure 6.12 Click and drag your pointer across a thumbnail in the Browser; the thumbnail scrubs through the action in that clip.

Figure 6.13 Choose Hide Column from the shortcut menu.

To display thumbnails in List view:

1. In the Browser window, Control-click any Browser column except Name.

2. From the shortcut menu, choose Show Thumbnail (**Figure 6.11**).

✔ Tip

- You can scrub a clip's thumbnail in the Browser by clicking the thumbnail and then dragging in the direction you want to scrub (**Figure 6.12**). Initially, your thumbnail will display the clip's first frame, but you can select another poster frame by scrubbing through the clip until you locate the frame you want and then pressing the Control key before you release the mouse button. Very slick.

To hide a column:

1. In the Browser window, Control-click the column header.

2. From the shortcut menu, choose Hide Column (**Figure 6.13**).

USING BROWSER TO ORGANIZE YOUR PROJECT

To display a hidden column:

1. In the Browser window, Control-click the column header to the right of the place you want the hidden column to be displayed.

2. From the shortcut menu, choose the name of the column you want to display (**Figure 6.14**).

✔ Tips

- Final Cut Express initially hides some Browser columns by default. Check the shortcut menu in the Browser's column header for a complete list of available columns.

- You can keep your Browser columns narrow and still see a full-length entry in every column. Pause your pointer over a column entry to view a tooltip displaying the complete contents of the column.

To rearrange columns:

- Drag the column header to the new location (**Figure 6.15**).

To resize columns:

- Drag the right edge of the column header to the new width.

Figure 6.14 Choose the name of the column from the shortcut menu.

Figure 6.15 Drag a column to its new location.

USING BROWSER TO ORGANIZE YOUR PROJECT

Figure 6.16 Control-click the Comment column heading, and choose Edit Heading from the shortcut menu.

Figure 6.17 Type the new column header name and press Enter.

To edit the Comment column name:

1. In the Browser window, Control-click the Comment column header.

2. From the shortcut menu, choose Edit Heading (**Figure 6.16**).

3. Type the new column name (**Figure 6.17**).

4. Press Enter.

Or do this:

1. Choose Edit > Project Properties.

2. Type the new column name in the Comment text box and then click OK.

✔ Tip

■ Try double-clicking or Control-clicking clip information right in its Browser column. You will find that you can modify lots of clip settings without bothering to open the clip's Item Properties window. You can also modify clip settings for multiple clips in a single operation: Select the clips and then adjust the setting of just one of the selected clips.

Custom Browser Layouts on a Budget

Final Cut Express will save your custom Browser arrangement between sessions, but your custom arrangement does not propagate to new bins created within the project.

After you've been working in FCE for a while, you'll wish that your Browser bins retained the column layout of the parent project tab, thus saving you the labor of selecting columns and arranging their order each and every time you add a new bin to a project. With over 30 Browser columns to wrestle, custom Browser layouts would certainly be welcome. Custom Browser layouts are available in the Pro version of Final Cut, but here's a low-cost workaround that will save you time and hassle:

◆ When you start a project, make an empty template bin with your customized column selection, arrangement, and comment column names. Copy the template bin to create new bins, and your custom arrangement will be intact in the new bins.

◆ Create a template FCE project that contains your favorite Browser layouts, and copy and paste your customized bins from your template project file into your current project.

Searching for items in the Browser

Final Cut Express has a powerful search engine in its Find function. You can perform a simple name search, but you can also search for single or multiple items by timecode, by file type, or by comment, or you can search your project for unused clips—clips you have not yet used in any sequence. Take a moment to explore the search options available in the Browser and imagine how you might plan your project to make use of them.

To search for a single item:

1. Start in the Browser window. Choose Edit > Find (**Figure 6.18**); or press Command-F.

2. In the Find dialog box, type your search criteria or choose from the search criteria options available from the pull-down menus along the bottom of the window (**Figure 6.19**).

3. Click Find Next. Final Cut Express highlights the found item in the Browser (**Figure 6.20**).

Figure 6.18 Choose Find from the Edit menu.

Figure 6.19 This example searches the Road to Tequila project for any clip with the word "cute" appearing in any Browser column.

Figure 6.20 A clip with the word "cute" in the Comment column is highlighted in the Browser.

USING BROWSER TO ORGANIZE YOUR PROJECT

Figure 6.21 This example searches the Road to Tequila project for all clips that haven't been used in a sequence. The list of unused clips that match the search criteria will appear in the Find Results window.

Figure 6.22 You can set the Results option to Replace Find results.

Figure 6.23 The Find Results window with the list of clips that match your search criteria; note the two shortcut buttons at the bottom of the window.

To search for multiple items:

1. Start in the Browser window. Choose Edit > Find; or press Command-F.

2. In the Find window, type your search criteria, or select from the search criteria options available from the pull-down menus near the bottom of the window (**Figure 6.21**).

3. Select an option from the Results pull-down menu. You can choose to replace the results of your previous Find or add the new results to your previous list of found items (**Figure 6.22**).

4. Click Find All. The list of found items that match your search criteria appears in the Find Results window (**Figure 6.23**).

✔ Tip

■ Searching by the Name column in the Browser will return clips whose current name matches the search. But if you renamed your clips after capture, searching by both the Source and the Name columns will track down all the clips (including those pesky renamed clips) associated with a source media file.

Using the Find Results window

The Find Results window displays a list of found items that match your search criteria (**Figure 6.24**). This window displays the same clip information as the Browser, and it offers the same flexible sorting and display options. You can perform multiple searches in the Find window and assemble a collection of items in the Find Results window to *do any of the following:*

Figure 6.24 The Find Results window with the list of found clips; columns can be sorted just like in the Browser window.

- Copy or move found items to a single bin for assembly into an edited sequence.

- Delete found items from a project.

✔ Tips

- You can search within the Find Results window. If you've assembled a large group of items in the Find Results window and you want to refine your list or perform an additional search, you can choose Project: Find Results from the Search option pop-up menu (**Figure 6.25**).

Figure 6.25 Performing a search of the Find Results window.

- Can't remember the name of a clip, but you know what it looks like? The Find Results window can display in icon mode, just like the Browser. What a relief.

Search the Project or Search the Sequence?

You can perform two types of searches in Final Cut Express:

- Choose Edit > Find with the Browser window selected, and Final Cut Express will search all open projects for clips, sequences, graphics, and effects, but will not search for items located inside sequences.

- Choose Edit > Find with the Timeline selected, and your search will be limited to the currently open sequence. You'll want to search in the sequence if you are looking for the sequence version of a particular clip—a clip you applied effects to after you inserted it into a sequence, for example.

Searching for items in the Timeline is discussed in Chapter 9, "Editing in the Timeline and the Canvas."

Figure 6.26 Control-click to bring up the shortcut menu.

Figure 6.27 Select New Bin from the shortcut menu.

Figure 6.28 The current capture bin indicator is located at the left edge of the bin's Name column.

Working with Bins

Final Cut Express's Browser bins are similar to the folders you use to organize your Mac Desktop—with one crucial difference. When you make changes to the contents of a bin, such as moving, renaming, or deleting clips, the changes will not affect the disk files or the folders in which your source material is stored. If you delete a clip from the bin, it is not deleted from the disk. Creating a new bin does not create a corresponding folder on your hard drive. The bin exists only within your project file. (See "What Is Nonlinear, Nondestructive Editing?" in Chapter 2 for more information.)

To add a new bin to a project:

◆ In the Browser window, Control-click an empty portion of the Name column (**Figure 6.26**).

Or do this:

1. From the shortcut menu, choose New Bin (**Figure 6.27**).

2. Choose File > New > Bin.

What's That Little Doodad?

The tiny clapboard icon (**Figure 6.28**) indicates that the current bin is set as the *capture bin*, the Browser bin where your captured clips will be stored. For details, see "Selecting a capture bin" in Chapter 4.

To open a bin and create a Browser tab for it:

1. In the Browser window, double-click a bin name.

2. In the newly opened Bin window, drag the tab from the bin header into the area above the Name column in the Browser window (**Figure 6.29**).

   The bin appears as a tab in the Browser window (**Figure 6.30**).

To move items between bins in List view:

1. Drag the items you want to move onto your destination bin (**Figure 6.31**).

2. Release the mouse button and drop the items into the bin.

✔ Tip

■ To move any item to the top level of a project, drag the item to the Name column header in the Browser window.

Figure 6.29 The bin opens as a new window; drag the tab to the Browser window.

Figure 6.30 The bin is now accessible from its own tab in the Browser window.

Figure 6.31 Drag selected items to a different bin.

Figure 6.32 Hold down the Option key as you drag an item to copy it to a new location.

Figure 6.33 The item is copied and appears in both locations.

Figure 6.34 Control-click the item you want to delete, then choose Cut from the shortcut menu.

To make a copy of a Browser item:

1. Hold down the Option key as you drag the item you want to copy (**Figure 6.32**).

2. In the new location, release the mouse button.

   The item is copied and appears in both locations (**Figure 6.33**).

To remove a Browser item from a project:

1. Select the item.

2. Press Delete.

Or do this:

1. Control-click the item you want to delete.

2. From the shortcut menu, choose Cut (**Figure 6.34**).

✔ Tip

■ Remember—when you cut a clip from the Browser, you're not deleting the media file on disk, just the virtual reference that points to the file on disk. See Chapter 3, "How to Manage an FCE Project" for details on how to delete media files on disk.

To modify clip properties in the Browser:

1. Control-click the clip you want to modify.

2. From the shortcut menu, choose Item Properties (**Figure 6.35**).

To make changes to multiple Browser items or entries:

1. Command-click to select the items or entries you want to modify (**Figure 6.36**).

2. Control-click one of the selected items.

3. From the shortcut menu, specify the change you want to make (**Figure 6.37**).

✔ Tip

■ Heads up—Final Cut Express allows you to select multiple items in the Browser and then make a shortcut selection, but FCE will not allow batch processing of most of the functions on the Browser shortcut menu. For example, you can cut, copy, or drag multiple clips to the Viewer, but you can't capture or export multiple clips in a single operation.

Figure 6.35 Control-clicking an item is the quickest way to access the Item Properties window.

Figure 6.36 Command-click to select multiple items to modify.

Figure 6.37 Specify a change in the shortcut menu.

WORKING WITH BINS

Figure 6.38 First, select the item you want to rename.

Figure 6.39 Click again on the item's name to open the field, then type a new name.

To rename clips, sequences, and bins:

1. Click to select the item you want to rename (**Figure 6.38**).

2. Click again on the item's name.

3. Type a new name (**Figure 6.39**).

WORKING WITH CLIPS IN THE VIEWER

You'll be spending a lot of time in the Viewer window. Not only do you use the Viewer to play clips and mark edit points and keyframes, you also work in the Viewer to sculpt audio and video with effects and filters.

The Final Cut Express interface uses tabs in the Viewer window to organize and display the clip controls. You'll see only the tabs that are relevant to the clip that's currently open; not all tabs are open by default. Following are summaries of the functions available on each tab:

+ **Video tab:** View video frames and set In and Out points and keyframes. This is the default playback window for a video clip.

+ **Audio tab:** Audition and mark edit points in audio-only clips. This is where you can set level and pan or spread settings. The Audio tab will display the audio portion of an audio+video clip. Clips with two channels of audio will display two Audio tabs: one for each audio channel. To learn more about working in the Audio tab, see Chapter 11, "Audio Tools and Techniques."

+ **Filters tab:** Adjust the settings for any video or audio filter effects you have applied to a clip.

+ **Controls tab:** Adjust the settings for a generator you have opened. A text entry field for a text generator appears on this tab.

+ **Color Corrector tab:** Use the onscreen controls for FCE's color correction filters. The Color Corrector tab appears only on clips with a color correction filter applied. To learn about applying filters and effects, see Chapter 15, "Filters and Compositing."

+ **Motion tab:** Apply and modify motion effects to a clip. You can create animated effects by using a combination of keyframes and changes to motion settings. To learn about creating motion effects, see Chapter 14, "Motion."

Anatomy of the Viewer

The Final Cut Express Viewer has a wide variety of tools for navigating and marking your clips: transport controls, clip-marking controls, pop-up selectors, view selectors, and timecode navigation displays (**Figure 7.1**).

All the Viewer controls listed here, except the pop-up selectors, appear in the Canvas window as well. The controls operate in the same way in the Canvas window as they do in the Viewer.

The next few sections discuss the onscreen controls you'll encounter in the Viewer.

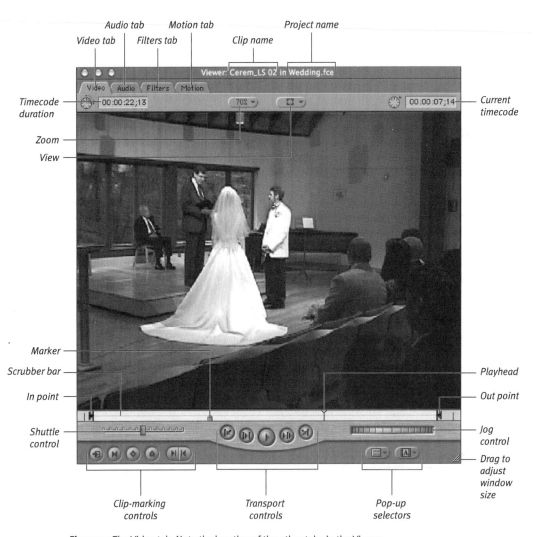

Figure 7.1 The Video tab. Note the location of the other tabs in the Viewer.

ANATOMY OF THE VIEWER

Transport controls

Figure 7.2 shows the transport controls that lie horizontally across the bottom of the Viewer window. The transport controls are located in the middle of the bottom section of the Viewer:

◆ **Previous Edit button:** Click to jump the playhead back to the previous edit (In or Out point).

◆ **Play In to Out button:** Click to play the clip from the In point to the Out point.

◆ **Play button:** Click to play the clip from the current position of the playhead. Click again to stop playback.

◆ **Play Around Current button:** Click to play the part of the clip immediately before and after the current position of the playhead. The pre-roll and post-roll settings (in the Preferences window) determine the duration of the playback.

◆ **Next Edit button:** Click to move the playhead to the next edit.

◆ **Shuttle control:** Drag the control tab away from the center to fast forward or rewind (**Figure 7.3**). Speeds vary depending on the control tab's distance from the center. A green control tab indicates normal playback speed.

◆ **Jog control:** Drag to the left or right (**Figure 7.4**) to step through your clip one frame at a time.

◆ **Scrubber and playhead:** The Scrubber is the strip that stretches horizontally below the image window. Move through a clip by dragging the playhead, or click on the Scrubber to jump the playhead to a new location (**Figure 7.5**).

Previous Edit *Play In to Out* *Play Around Current*
Play *Next Edit*

Figure 7.2 The Viewer's transport control buttons.

Figure 7.3 The Shuttle control.

Figure 7.4 The Jog control.

Figure 7.5 The Scrubber and playhead.

✔ Tip

■ The Viewer's transport and clip-marking controls all have keyboard shortcut equivalents. Use the tooltip feature to learn keyboard shortcuts for onscreen controls you use regularly.

Clip-marking controls

All the onscreen controls you use to mark clips are grouped in the lower-left corner of the Viewer (**Figure 7.6**):

- **Match Frame:** Click to match the frame currently showing in the Viewer with the same frame as it appears in your sequence. The sequence frame appears in the Canvas window. Match Frame is useful for synchronizing action.

- **Mark Clip:** Click to set In and Out points in the sequence. Edit points will be set at the outer boundaries of the clip at the position of the playhead in the target track.

- **Add Keyframe:** Click to add a keyframe to the clip at the current playhead position.

- **Add Marker:** Click to add a marker to the clip at the current playhead position.

- **Mark In (left) and Mark Out (right):** Click to set the In point or the Out point for the clip at the current playhead position.

Pop-up selectors

Two buttons at the lower right of the Viewer window provide convenient access to source materials (**Figure 7.7**):

- **Recent Clips:** Select recently used clips directly from this pop-up menu.

- **Generators:** Select a generator effect from this pop-up menu. (To read about generators, see Chapter 16, "Titles and Generators.")

Figure 7.6 The Viewer's clip-marking controls.

Figure 7.7 Pop-up selectors.

Figure 7.8
The Zoom selector.

Figure 7.9
The View selector.

Figure 7.10
The Timecode Duration display.

Figure 7.11 The Current Timecode display.

View selectors

The selectors directly above the Viewer's image area allow you to adjust the window's view.

◆ **Zoom:** Adjust the Viewer's image display size (**Figure 7.8**). (This pop-up selector does not affect the actual frame size of the image.)

◆ **View:** Select a viewing format (**Figure 7.9**). Title Safe and Wireframe modes are accessible from this pop-up menu. (For more information, see "Viewing Overlays" later in this chapter.)

Timecode navigation and display

Two timecode displays appear in the upper corners of the Viewer window. They are useful for precisely navigating to specific timecode locations.

◆ **Timecode Duration:** This displays the elapsed time between the In and Out points of a clip. If no edit points are set, the beginning and end of the clip serve as the In and Out points (**Figure 7.10**). Control-click the Timecode Duration display to switch the elapsed time view among Drop, Non-drop, and Frames view.

◆ **Current Timecode:** This displays the timecode at the current position of the playhead. You can enter a time in the display to jump the playhead to that point in the clip (**Figure 7.11**).

Working with Clips in the Viewer

You can open clips from the Browser or from the Timeline. You can open single and multiple clips, or open clips you have viewed recently. You can also open clips from outside an open project.

When you open an audio+video clip, it appears in a Viewer window with the Video tab selected.

To open a clip in the Viewer:

Do one of the following:

◆ Double-click the clip's icon in the Browser or Timeline.

◆ Control-click the clip's icon and choose Open Viewer from the shortcut menu (**Figure 7.12**).

◆ Select the clip's icon and press Enter.

◆ Drag a clip's icon from the Browser and drop it in the image area of the Viewer.

To open a clip in a new window:

1. Select the clip in the Browser or Timeline.

2. Choose View > Clip in New Window.

✔ Tips

■ It's common practice in Final Cut Express to load an entire sequence into the Viewer and edit it into another sequence, just as if it were a clip. To do this, select the sequence in the Browser; then choose View > Sequence, or drag the sequence's icon from the Browser and drop it in the image area of the Viewer.

■ You can learn more about constructing a project with multiple sequences in Chapter 3, "How to Manage an FCE Project."

Figure 7.12 Control-click the clip's icon and choose Open Viewer from the shortcut menu.

■ If loading a sequence into the Viewer causes the Canvas and Timeline to disappear, that means you loaded a sequence that was currently open in the Timeline. The Timeline closes because FCE protocol dictates that you cannot edit a sequence into itself.

Figure 7.13 Command-click to select multiple clips.

Figure 7.14 Drag the clips to the Viewer and then drop them on the image area.

Figure 7.15 The first clip is opened in the Viewer; the rest are listed in the Recent Clips pop-up selector.

To open multiple clips:

1. Command-click to select multiple clips in the Browser (**Figure 7.13**).

2. Drag the clips to the Viewer (**Figure 7.14**).

   The first clip opens in the Viewer, and the other selected clips are listed in the Recent Clips control (**Figure 7.15**).

To open a recently viewed clip:

◆ Select the clip name from the Recent Clips control's pop-up list (**Figure 7.16**).

✔ Tip

■ You can load an entire Browser bin of clips into the Viewer in one move by dragging the bin from the Browser and dropping it in the image area of the Viewer. The clips in the bin will show up in the Recent Clips control (as long as your List Recent Clips preference is set high enough to cover the folder's item count).

Figure 7.16 Select a clip from the Recent Clips control's pop-up list.

To open a clip from the Timeline or Canvas:

1. Select the clip in the Timeline.

2. *Do one of the following:*

   ◆ Choose View > Clip to replace the current contents of the Viewer with the selected clip (**Figure 7.17**).

   ◆ Choose View > Clip in New Window to open a new Viewer containing the selected clip (**Figure 7.18**).

   ◆ Control-click the clip in the Timeline; then choose Open (clip name) from the shortcut menu.

   The clip opens in the Viewer. If you positioned the Timeline's playhead over a frame in the clip, the clip opens with the Viewer's playhead located at the same frame.

To open an imported clip in its original application:

1. Open the clip in the Viewer or Canvas window.

2. Choose View > Clip in Editor (**Figure 7.19**).

   Clips created in an application other than Final Cut Express will open in that application (**Figure 7.20**). If the application used to create the clip is not installed on your computer, a dialog opens that allows you to choose an application in which to edit the clip.

✔ Tip

■ You can specify default applications for editing imported graphic, video, and audio files on the External Editors tab of the Preferences window. For more information, see "Setting External Editors Preferences" in Chapter 2.

Figure 7.17 Choose View > Clip to open a clip selected in the Timeline or Canvas window in the Viewer.

Figure 7.18 Choose View > Clip in New Window to open a clip selected in the Timeline or Canvas window in a new Viewer window.

Figure 7.19 Choose View > Clip in Editor to open a clip in the application you used to create it.

Figure 7.20 This clip, captured in Final Cut Express, has opened in QuickTime Player, because Final Cut Express clips are QuickTime-format files.

Figure 7.21 Click a project's tab to bring that project to the front of the Browser window.

Figure 7.22 Drag a clip into a project in the Browser window. Clip changes will be saved with the project.

To open a clip outside the current project:

1. Choose File > Open.

2. Locate the clip's media file on disk.

3. Select the file and click Open.

To save changes in a clip outside the current project:

1. In the Browser window, select a project in which to save your modified clip by clicking the tab of that project.

   This brings your selected project to the front of the Browser window (**Figure 7.21**).

2. Click and drag from the image area in the Viewer to the project's tab in the Browser.

   Your clip is now inserted in that project, and your changes will be saved with that project (**Figure 7.22**).

FCE Protocol: Saving Clip Changes

Say you have marked edit points and placed some other markers in a clip you opened outside of your project. To save the changes you made to that clip, you'll need to do the following:

◆ Insert the modified clip into a project that's currently open.

   or

◆ Export the clip.

Remember that FCE will save the changes you make only if the clip has been placed in a project or exported as a new file. If you mark changes and close the Viewer window without taking the steps listed here... bye-bye changes. There's no warning dialog, so take care. One exception to this rule: any modification of a clip's reel number will be written to the clip's media file immediately.

To open a generator effect in the Viewer:

1. Start in the Browser window with the Effects tab selected.

2. *Do one of the following:*
   - ◆ Double-click the generator icon in the Browser or Timeline (**Figure 7.23**).
   - ◆ Select a generator icon and press Enter.

✔ Tip

- ■ You can select generator effects directly from the Generators pop-up menu in the Viewer window (**Figure 7.24**).

To play a clip in the Viewer:

1. Start with an open clip and the Viewer window active.

2. Click the Play button (**Figure 7.25**); or press the Spacebar; or press L.

3. To stop playback, click the Play button; or press the spacebar; or press K.

To play a clip in reverse:

1. Start with an open clip and the Viewer window active.

2. Shift-click the Play button; or press Shift-spacebar; or press J.

3. To stop playback, click the Play button; or press the spacebar; or press K.

Figure 7.23 Double-click a generator icon to open the generator effect in the Viewer.

Figure 7.24 Choose a generator effect from the Generators pop-up menu.

Figure 7.25 Click the Play button to start clip play. Click Play again to stop play.

Figure 7.26 Click the Play In to Out button to play the section of the clip between the In and Out points.

Figure 7.27 Click the Play Around Current button to play a section of the clip before and after the current playhead position.

Figure 7.28 Choose Mark > Play > Every Frame to play every frame of a clip.

To play a clip between In and Out points:

1. Start with an open clip and the Viewer window active.

2. Click the Play In to Out button (**Figure 7.26**); or press Shift-\ (backslash).

3. To stop playback, click the Play button; or press the spacebar; or press K.

To play a clip from the current playhead position to the Out point:

◆ Command-click the Play button.

To play a clip before and after the current playhead position:

◆ Click the Play Around Current button (**Figure 7.27**); or press the backslash key (\).

The clip plays back the specified pre-roll duration before the playhead location, and it plays back the post-roll duration after the playhead location.

✔ Tip

■ You can set the duration of video playback using the pre-roll and post-roll settings in the General tab of FCE's Preferences window.

To play every frame:

◆ Choose Mark > Play > Every Frame (**Figure 7.28**); or press Option-P.

✔ Tip

■ If you've applied complex effects to a clip, use the Play Every Frame command to preview the clip without rendering it first. Playback is slower than normal, but you'll get a rough idea.

To loop playback in all playback modes:

1. Choose View > Loop Playback (**Figure 7.29**).

2. Choose View > Loop Playback again to turn off looping.

✔ Tip

■ You can toggle looped playback on and off from your keyboard by pressing Control-L.

Figure 7.29 Choose View > Loop Playback to loop clip playback. Choose View > Loop Playback again to toggle looping off.

JKL Keys: The Way to Move

"JKL Keys," a swift and efficient system for controlling variable-speed playback from your keyboard, is an import from expensive, pro digital editing systems. Learn it, and you'll be whipping through your footage like the pros do. Here's how it works.

The J, K, and L keys are in a row on your keyboard, and you use them to control playback speed and direction. The I and O keys, which you use for setting In and Out points, are located just above JKL. The comma (,) and period (.) keys, which you can use to trim edits, are located below JKL. The semicolon (;) and apostrophe (') keys control Previous and Next Edit. This arrangement makes it easy to edit because it places the most commonly used keyboard shortcuts under one hand. It's easy to see how editors get attached to this system.

Here's the rundown on J, K, and L keyboard command functions:

◆ **Press J to play in reverse.** Tap J twice to double the reverse shuttle speed. Tap J three times for 4x reverse shuttle speed. Tap J four times for 8x reverse shuttle speed.

◆ **Press K to stop or pause.**

◆ **Press L to play forward.** Tap L twice to double the forward shuttle speed. Tap L three times for 4x forward shuttle speed. Tap L four times for 8x forward shuttle speed.

◆ **Hold down K and tap J or L to get slow-motion shuttling in either direction.** A single J or L tap, with the K key held down, steps you forward or backward one frame at a time.

Figure 7.30 Drag the playhead across the Scrubber to scrub through a clip.

Figure 7.31 Drag the Jog control to step through a clip one frame at a time.

Figure 7.32 Drag the Shuttle control to scan a clip at a range of speeds from slow to fast.

Other ways to move: jogging, scrubbing, and shuttling

While editing, you may find yourself spending more time playing your material at fast and slow speeds than at normal speed. Use the following tools for high- and low-speed navigation:

◆ To scrub through a clip, drag the playhead along the Scrubber bar above the transport controls (**Figure 7.30**).

◆ To jump the playhead to a location within the clip, click in the Scrubber bar.

◆ To move the playhead frame by frame, use the arrow keys.

◆ To jump the playhead in one-second increments, press Shift as you use the arrow keys.

◆ To jog one frame at a time, drag the Jog control (**Figure 7.31**). You can drag off the control area if you continue to hold down the mouse button.

◆ To play a clip at various speeds, drag the Shuttle control (**Figure 7.32**). Drag further from the center to increase the playback speed. Drag right to play forward; drag left to play in reverse.

FCE Protocol: Entering Timecode Numbers

Final Cut Express uses the standard time-code format of Hours:Minutes:Seconds:Frames, and employs a number of convenient shortcuts for timecode navigation. For example, typing 01241315 sets the timecode to 01:24:13:15. You don't need to include the colons when you type. You need to type only the numbers that change. Numbers that don't change, such as the hour or minute, don't need to be entered. Let's look at some examples.

Example 1

1. Start at timecode location 01:24:13:15.

2. To jump to timecode 01:24:18:25, type 1825(for 18 seconds, 25 frames) and press Enter.

The playhead jumps to timecode location 01:24:18:25. The hour and minute don't change for the new timecode location, so you don't need to reenter the hour or minute.

Example 2

The same idea applies to a new timecode minutes away from your current location.

1. Again start at timecode location 01:24:13:15.

2. To jump to timecode 01:27:18:25, type 271825 (for 27 minutes, 18 seconds, 25 frames) and press Enter.

The playhead jumps to timecode location 01:27:18:25.

Entering Durations

Say you want to move 12 seconds, 27 frames back in your clip. You don't need to calculate the new timecode number yourself.

Type –1227, and your clip jumps back 12 seconds and 27 frames. You can enter the timecode value preceded by a + (plus) or – (minus) sign, and FCE will change the current time by that amount.

You can jump to a new location using the + (plus) and – (minus) keys in two ways: using time (Hours:Minutes:Seconds:Frames) or using the total number of frames, which Final Cut Express converts into time plus frames. Here are some examples using time:

- Typing –3723 jumps back 37 seconds and 23 frames.

- Typing +161408 moves ahead 16 minutes, 14 seconds, and 8 frames.

In the Frames position in the timecode, any two-digit value between 30 and 99 is converted to the correct number of seconds (30 frames = 1 second). Here are some examples using the frame count:

- Entering –69 frames jumps back 69 frames, which is 2 seconds and 9 frames.

- Entering +36 frames jumps ahead 1 second, 6 frames, which is 36 frames.

One More Shortcut

There's one other keyboard shortcut: You can substitute a period (.) for zeros in a timecode value. Each period replaces a set of two zeros in a timecode number. Here's an example:

- To jump to timecode location 00:07:00:00, type 7.. (7 and two periods). The periods insert 00 in the Frames and Seconds fields.

- Type 11... to move to 11:00:00:00.

Sure beats typing all those colons, huh?

Figure 7.33 Current Timecode display in the Viewer window.

Figure 7.34 Adding 1 second, 15 frames (45 frames), to the current timecode position using a timecode entry shortcut.

Figure 7.35 The playhead is repositioned 1 second, 15 frames later, and the Current Timecode display is updated.

Figure 7.36 Timecode Duration display in the Viewer window. The current clip duration is 10 seconds.

Figure 7.37 Adding 1 second (30 frames) to the current clip duration using a timecode entry shortcut.

Figure 7.38 The Out point is extended by 1 second, and the Timecode Duration display is updated.

Navigating with Timecode

Moving around using timecode values can be the most efficient way to work, especially if your sense of timing is tuned to "frames per second." Final Cut Express's timecode input functionality is quite flexible. If you know exactly where you want to go, this is the way to get there. Timecode navigation works the same way in both the Viewer and Canvas.

To navigate using timecode values:

1. Start with your clip open and the Viewer window selected. **Figure 7.33** shows the timecode location before repositioning.

2. Enter a new timecode number (or use the shorthand methods detailed in the nearby Tips and sidebar). You don't need to click in the field to begin entering a new timecode—just type the numbers (**Figure 7.34**) and then press Enter.
   The playhead moves to the location that matches the new timecode value, and the new timecode position displays in the Current Timecode field in the upper-right corner of the Viewer (**Figure 7.35**).

To change the Out point using timecode:

◆ To change the Out point for a clip or sequence, enter a new timecode value in the Duration field, in the upper-left corner of the Viewer; then press Enter. (See **Figures 7.36–7.38**.)

✔ Tips

■ In the Viewer or Canvas, press Tab once to select the Duration field or twice to select the Current Timecode field.

■ You can copy the timecode from one field and paste it into another if the timecode is valid in the location where it is being pasted. You can also drag a timecode from one field to another by pressing Option while dragging.

Working with In and Out Points

The In and Out points determine the start and end frames of the clip portion that is used when the clip is edited into a sequence. Determining the usable part of a clip and setting In and Out points is the first step in assembling your edit. Many editing functions are performed by adjusting these points, either within the clip itself or from within a sequence.

To set In and Out points for a clip in the Viewer:

1. In the Browser, double-click the clip to open it in the Viewer.

2. Press the Home key to position the playhead at the beginning of the clip.

3. Use the Play button or the spacebar to start playing the clip from the beginning.

4. Click the Mark In button (**Figure 7.39**), or press I, when you see (or hear) the beginning of the part you want to use.

5. Click the Mark Out button (**Figure 7.40**), or press O, when you see (or hear) the end of the part you want to use.

6. Click the Play In to Out button, or press the vertical bar key (|, or Shift-\), to check your In and Out points (**Figure 7.41**).

✔ Tips

- You don't need to have the clip playing to set its In and Out points. You can drag the playhead to locate a particular frame and then set the edit point.

- To some iMovie users, the concept of using In and Out points may seem strange—in iMovie, you trim the clip to define where it begins and ends. One time-saving advantage of using In and Out points is that you can easily add frames to your clip in the Viewer without restoring the clip and trimming it again.

Figure 7.39 Set an In point by clicking the Mark In button.

Figure 7.40 Set an Out point by clicking the Mark Out button.

Figure 7.41 Click the Play In to Out button to review the edit points you have marked.

Figure 7.42 Use the Scrubber bar's shortcut menu to set and clear edit points.

Figure 7.43 Pressing Shift while dragging an edit point slides both the In and Out points.

To change In and Out points in the Viewer:

Do one of the following:

◆ Play the clip again and click Mark In or Mark Out at the new spot.

◆ Drag the In or Out point icon along the Scrubber bar to change the point's location.

◆ Drag the In or Out point icon off the Scrubber to remove the point.

✔ Tip

■ You can use the shortcut menu to set and clear edit points. Control-click in the Scrubber and choose an option from the shortcut menu (**Figure 7.42**).

To move the In and Out points simultaneously:

1. Start in the Viewer.

2. Click either edit point indicator in the Scrubber.

3. Press and hold Shift while dragging the edit point indicator (**Figure 7.43**).

   The marked duration of the clip is not changed, but the frames included in the marked clip shift forward or backward. Modifying an edit in this way is called *slipping*.

Other Ways to Set In and Out Points

If you open FCE's Mark menu, you'll see a number of additional ways to set and clear In and Out points. Most of the marking shortcuts work only in the Timeline, but they'll come in handy after your sequence is assembled.

Mark Clip: Sets In and Out points at the boundaries of a selected Timeline clip. You can also use Mark Clip to mark a Timeline gap. Place the Timeline playhead over the gap, then press X.

Mark to Markers: Place your Timeline playhead between two markers, and FCE will use the markers' locations to set In and Out points.

Mark Selection: Sets In and Out points at the boundaries of a selected area of the Timeline.

About Subclips

Subclips are shorter clips you create from a longer master clip. You can create multiple subclips from a single master clip. For example, you can open a 15-minute clip in the Viewer and subdivide it into as many subclips as you need.

As you create subclips, the master clip remains open in the Viewer. Once you've created a subclip, you can open it in the Viewer and work with it in the same way as any other clip. Changes you make to a subclip won't affect the master clip.

Final Cut Express places new subclips in the same project bin as the master clip, automatically naming each clip as you create it. For example, if the master clip is named "Whole Thing," the first subclip is named "Whole Thing Subclip," the second is "Whole Thing Subclip 2," and so on.

Once you create a subclip, you can rename it and trim the edit points, but you cannot extend the subclip's In and Out points beyond the In and Out points of its master clip.

If you need to extend a subclip's edit points beyond its current duration, you must remove the subclip's limits, restoring your subclip to the full length of the master clip, and then set new In and Out points.

Figure 7.44 Mark an Out point for your subclip.

Figure 7.45 Choose Modify > Make Subclip.

Figure 7.46 A new subclip appears in the Browser, below the master clip.

To create a subclip:

1. Double-click a clip in the Browser or Timeline to open it in the Viewer window.

2. Mark the clip's In and Out points (**Figure 7.44**).

3. Choose Modify > Make Subclip (**Figure 7.45**); or press Command-U.

   A new, automatically named subclip appears in the Browser, below the master clip (**Figure 7.46**).

To adjust a subclip's length:

1. Select a subclip in the Browser or a sequence subclip in the Timeline.

2. Choose Modify > Remove Subclip Limits.

3. Open the subclip in the Viewer.

   The full length of the master clip appears. If you have selected a Timeline subclip, the current In and Out points will still be displayed.

4. Set new In and Out points for the subclip.

To find a subclip's master clip:

1. Double-click a subclip in the Browser or Timeline to open it in the Viewer window.

2. Choose Mark > Go To > Master Clip; or press Shift-F.

✔ Tip

■ A word of caution: If you choose to recapture a project containing a subclip, Final Cut Express will recapture the entire length of the master media file containing the subclip. For tips on project recapture, see Chapter 3, "How to Manage an FCE Project."

Using Markers

Markers are reference pointers in a clip or sequence that have a variety of uses. You can:

◆ Quickly jump the playhead to markers in clips or sequences.

◆ Align the clip marker to a marker in the sequence.

◆ Align a filter or motion keyframe to the marker.

◆ Mark a range of the clip to use as you might a subclip.

◆ Align other clip markers, clip boundaries, or transition boundaries to a marker in the Timeline.

To learn more about using markers in sequences see Chapter 9, "Editing in the Timeline and the Canvas."

To add markers to a clip or sequence in the Viewer:

1. Open the clip in the Viewer.

2. Play the clip or sequence.

3. When playback reaches the place where you want to set a marker, click the Add Marker button (**Figure 7.47**); or press M.

4. To add a custom label or comments to the marker, click Add Marker (or press M) a second time to display the Edit Marker dialog (**Figure 7.48**).

✔ Tip

■ Save keystrokes! Shift-click the Add Marker button to set a marker and open the Edit Marker dialog in one move. However, a bug in version 1.0 prevents you from using this shortcut to create new markers in the same clip after you've set one.

Figure 7.47 Click the Add Marker button to set a marker in your clip.

Figure 7.48 Click Add Marker again to call up the Edit Marker dialog.

Figure 7.49 Choose Mark > Markers > Delete to remove a marker from your clip.

Figure 7.50 Choosing a marker from the shortcut menu. Control-click the Current Timecode display to see the shortcut menu listing of all markers in a clip.

Figure 7.51 Rename a marker or add comments in the Edit Marker dialog; then click OK.

To delete a marker:

1. Move the playhead to the marker.

2. *Do one of the following:*
   - Choose Mark > Markers > Delete (**Figure 7.49**).
   - Press Command-` (accent grave, which shares a key with the tilde [~]).
   - Option-click the Marker button.

To move the playhead to a marker:

Do one of the following:

- Drag the playhead in the Scrubber bar to the marker location.

- Control-click the Current Timecode field in the Viewer and choose a marker from the shortcut menu (**Figure 7.50**).

- Choose Mark > Previous > Marker (or Mark > Next > Marker).

To rename a marker:

1. Move the playhead to the marker.

2. Press M to open the Edit Marker dialog.

3. Type a new name or comment in the corresponding text box (**Figure 7.51**).

4. Click OK.

To extend the duration of a marker:

1. Move the playhead to the marker.

2. Press M to open the Edit Marker dialog.

3. Now, extend the marker's duration by entering a duration value (**Figure 7.52**).

   An extended duration marker appears as a marker icon with a bar extending along the Scrubber bar (**Figure 7.53**).

To create a subclip from a marker:

1. In the Browser, click the marked clip's expansion triangle to reveal a list of its markers; then select the desired marker (**Figure 7.54**).

2. Choose Modify > Make Subclip; or press Command-U.

   The new subclip appears in the Browser. The subclip will have a duration equal to the extended marker's duration (**Figure 7.55**). If the marker has no extended duration, the subclip will extend to the next marker in the clip.

✔ Tips

- You can place extended duration markers on audio tracks to visually mark the location and duration of key dialogue or a specific passage in a music track.

- DV Start Stop Detection is akin to the popular "scene detection" feature in iMovie. FCE will automatically set markers in your captured clip each time it detects a Start/Stop (Record/Pause). Because FCE can use markers to break a clip into individual subclips, you can use the technique outlined here to capture long sections of DV tape and break them into usable subclip chunks. To learn how, see "Using DV Start/Stop Detection" in Chapter 4.

Figure 7.52 Extend a marker's duration by entering a value in the Duration field of the Edit Marker dialog.

Figure 7.53 The marker icon displays its duration on the Scrubber bar.

Figure 7.54 Click the clip's expansion triangle; then select the desired marker from the list.

Figure 7.55 The new subclip appears in the Browser. Note that the subclip's duration is equal to the extended marker's duration.

USING MARKERS

Working with Clips in the Viewer

Figure 7.56 Choose Mark > Markers > Extend.

Figure 7.57 The marker's duration now extends to the playhead position.

Figure 7.58 Move the playhead to the new desired location for your marker.

To extend the marker duration to the playhead location:

1. Position the playhead where you want the endpoint of your extended marker to go.

2. Choose Mark > Markers > Extend (**Figure 7.56**); or press Option-` (accent grave, which shares a key with the tilde [~]).

   The marker's duration will extend from the original location of the marker to the location of the playhead (**Figure 7.57**).

To move a marker forward in time:

1. Move the playhead to where you want to reposition the marker (**Figure 7.58**).

   You can move a marker only forward.

2. Choose Mark > Markers > Reposition (**Figure 7.59**); or press Shift-` (accent grave).

✔ Tip

■ To extend or reposition a marker on the fly during playback, use the keyboard shortcuts listed in the previous sections. Tap the keys when you see the frame you want to make your new marker location.

Figure 7.59 Choose Mark > Markers > Reposition.

195

Marking Shortcuts

FCE offers lots of ways to mark In and Out points. This is something editors do all day long, so it may be worthwhile to try these shortcuts and see which work best for you.

To mark the In point:

Do one of the following:

- Press I on the keyboard.

- Click the Mark In button in the Viewer.

- Press / (slash) on the keypad.

- From the Mark menu, choose Mark In.

To mark the Out point:

Do one of the following:

- Press O on the keyboard.

- Click the Mark Out button in the Viewer.

- Press * (asterisk) on the keypad.

- From the Mark menu, choose Mark Out.

To delete edit points:

Do one of the following:

- To clear both In and Out points, press Option-X; or Option-click the Mark Clip button.

- To clear In points, press Option-I; or Option-click the Mark In button.

- To clear Out points, press Option-O; or Option-click the Mark Out button.

To jump the playhead to edit points:

Do one of the following:

- To go to the In point, press Shift-I; or Shift-click the Mark In button.

- To go to the Out point, press Shift-O; or Shift-click the Mark Out button.

USING MARKERS

Figure 7.60 Choose a magnification level from the Zoom pop-up menu.

Figure 7.61 Select the Zoom In tool from the Tool palette.

Figure 7.62 Drag a marquee around the area you want to zoom in on.

Adjusting the Viewer Display

You can set up the Viewer to show your clips in a variety of display formats and magnifications. Final Cut Express is also designed to overlay an array of useful information on your clip image, but you can turn off the overlay. View settings are clip specific and are stored with each clip.

Changing magnification and window size in the Viewer or Canvas

Final Cut Express has an ambitious interface. Unless you work with a dual monitor setup, you'll occasionally want to juggle window sizes in order to get a closer look at your work.

To zoom in:

Do one of the following:

◆ Choose a higher magnification level from the Zoom pop-up menu at the top of the Viewer or Canvas (**Figure 7.60**).

◆ Select the Zoom In tool from the Tool palette and click inside the Viewer or Canvas.

◆ From the View menu, choose a zoom-in amount from the Level submenu.

◆ Select the Zoom In tool from the Tool palette (**Figure 7.61**). Click the image area and drag a marquee to zoom in on the desired area of the image (**Figure 7.62**).

Note that clips will not play smoothly when you have zoomed in on a clip in the Viewer.

To view different parts of a magnified image:

Do one of the following:

◆ Select the Hand tool from the Tool palette and drag it over the image to move the view (**Figure 7.63**).

◆ Use the scroll bars to move around the image.

To zoom out:

Do one of the following:

◆ Choose a lower magnification level from the Zoom pop-up menu at the top of the Viewer.

◆ Select the Zoom Out tool from the Tool palette and click inside the Viewer or Canvas.

◆ From the View menu, select a zoom-out amount from the Level submenu (**Figure 7.64**).

To fit a clip into the window size:

◆ From the Zoom pop-up menu at the top of the Viewer, choose Fit to Window.

Figure 7.63 Drag the Hand tool over a magnified image to move it in the Viewer window.

Figure 7.64 Choose View > Level and select a zoom-out level.

Figure 7.65 Choosing Fit All from the Zoom pop-up menu.

To fit all items into the view plus a 10 percent margin:

Do one of the following:

◆ From the Zoom pop-up menu at the top of the Viewer, choose Fit All (**Figure 7.65**).

◆ Choose View > Level > Fit All.

✔ Tip

■ Choosing Fit All causes FCE to zoom out enough to show all objects in a multilayered composited sequence, including those outside the screen area (**Figure 7.66**).

To view at actual size:

◆ From the Zoom pop-up menu at the top of the Viewer, choose 100%.

Figure 7.66 The Viewer showing all of the objects in a multilayered composited sequence. Selecting Fit All is the only way to get the Viewer zoom level to go below 12.5 percent.

To shrink the window to the current clip size:

1. Make the Viewer active (**Figure 7.67**).

2. Double-click the Zoom In tool in the Tool palette (**Figure 7.68**).

   The viewer window will shrink to fit the current clip size (**Figure 7.69**).

Figure 7.67 Click the Viewer to make it active.

Figure 7.68 Double-click the Zoom In tool in the Tool palette.

Figure 7.69 The Viewer shrinks to fit the current clip image size.

ADJUSTING THE VIEWER DISPLAY

Viewing Overlays

Overlays are icons or text displayed on top of the video when the playhead is parked on a significant frame. Overlays indicate significant points, such as In and Out points, in a clip or sequence. Overlays appear only when the Viewer and Canvas are in Pause mode and are not rendered to output. Final Cut Express displays the following overlays by default (**Figure 7.70**):

◆ **In and Out Points:** These icons appear when the playhead is positioned on the In or Out point frame.

◆ **Start and End of Media:** The filmstrip symbol along the left or right side of the video frame indicates the start or end of the video media.

◆ **Start and End of Edits (not shown):** An L shape at the lower left indicates the start of an edit, and a backward L shape at the lower right indicates the end of an edit. These icons appear only in the Canvas.

◆ **Marker:** A marker overlay appears as a translucent box displaying the marker's name and comment text.

The Title Safe and Action Safe overlays are not displayed by default, and they have their own display controls in the View menu:

◆ **Title Safe and Action Safe:** Title Safe and Action Safe boundaries are rectangular boxes around the edges of the video.

In Point overlay

Out Point overlay

Title Safe overlay

Start of Media overlay

Action Safe overlay

Marker overlay

Figure 7.70 Viewer overlays.

VIEWING OVERLAYS

To view or hide overlays:

◆ Choose Overlays from the View pop-up menu at the top of the Viewer or Canvas to toggle the display of all overlays (**Figure 7.71**).

Viewing Title Safe and Action Safe boundaries

Most NTSC (National Television Standards Committee) television sets don't display the full video image on their screens. Use the Title Safe and Action Safe overlays to be sure that crucial parts of your composition or titles are not cut off at the edges when displayed on a television screen.

✔ Tip

■ Consumer TV sets may trim the edges of your video, but web video displays the whole frame, so if you are aiming your show at both web and TV, you'll need to watch the edges of your frame .

To view or hide Title Safe and Action Safe boundaries:

Do one of the following:

◆ Choose View > Title Safe.

◆ From the View pop-up menu at the top of the Viewer, choose Title Safe (**Figure 7.72**).

◆ Choose Title Safe again to toggle the overlay.

Figure 7.71 Turn off all overlay displays in the Viewer by unchecking Overlays in the View pop-up menu.

Figure 7.72 Choose Title Safe from the View pop-up menu to display the Title Safe overlay.

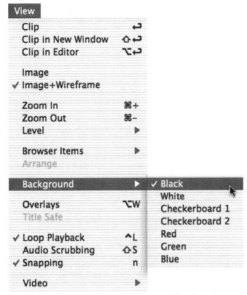

Figure 7.73 Select a black background by choosing View > Background > Black.

Viewing with different backgrounds

If you are working with a clip that has an alpha channel—say some black generated text that you want to superimpose over video—you can change the default black background of your black text to white, to make the text more visible while you are working with it. Translucent clips will be more visible if you choose a background that emphasizes them. When a clip is rendered, the background is always set to black.

To choose a background for viewing a clip:

◆ From the View menu, select the desired background from the Background sub-menu (**Figure 7.73**).

Wireframes in the Viewer

Image+Wireframe mode lets you view schematic diagrams of the motion effects you apply to a clip or sequence. Wireframe mode is available in both the Canvas and Viewer. You can use the Viewer's View pop-up menu to switch on Image+Wireframe mode, but you're more likely to be using Wireframe mode in the Canvas. For details on Wireframe mode operation, see Chapter 13, "Compositing and Effects Overview."

Part IV: Editing

Part IV: Editing

Final Cut Pro was designed to appeal to working editors. The program's designers went to great lengths to design an editing process that is both efficient and flexible, and the experience of editing in Final Cut Pro has been preserved intact in Final Cut Express.

Because FCE offers so many ways to assemble and fine-tune an edit, this section requires a few chapters to lay out your choices. Chapter 8 covers basic editing technique, Chapter 9 details the features in the Timeline and the Canvas windows where you assemble edited sequences. Chapter 10 is devoted to FCE's professional array of trim edit types and techniques (if you're coming to Final Cut Express from iMovie, prepare to be amazed).

Part IV rounds out with a pair of special topic chapters: one devoted to audio editing and finishing, and the other describing the art of the FCE transition.

Somewhere in all this wide world of choice, you'll find a combination of editing techniques that feels right for you, and for your project.

BASIC EDITING

Everything up to this point has been preamble—by now you're familiar enough with Final Cut Express that you can jump in and start the actual work of editing. But there's more to it than just slicing and rearranging clips. In this chapter, you'll learn not only basic procedures for performing edits in FCE, including how to use the seven edit types available, but also the underlying concepts and protocols that govern editing: sequences, three-point editing, multiple media tracks, and various edit types.

You assemble an edited sequence in the Timeline window, which displays a chrono-logical view of a sequence. All the media elements you've assembled to create a sequence appear in the Timeline as elements that diagram the sequencing and layering of audio and video tracks. As you drag the playhead along the Timeline ruler, the current frame of the sequence updates in the Canvas window. The Canvas window is the viewer you use to play back the edited sequence you've assembled in the Timeline. (A more detailed discussion of Timeline and Canvas window operations appears in Chapter 9, "Editing in the Timeline and the Canvas.")

Once you've assembled a first draft of an edited sequence, known as a *rough cut* (isn't that a great expression?), you'll probably want to go back and *trim* (fine-tune) your edits. Final Cut Express's edit trimming tools and techniques are outlined in Chapter 10, "Fine Cut: Trimming Edits."

If you need a review of FCE's project structure and media elements basics before the clips start flying, see Chapter 3, "How to Manage an FCE Project."

Basic Editing Overview

Figure 8.1 summarizes the steps involved in performing a drag-and-drop-style edit that uses the Canvas overlay. The next section offers a step-by-step breakdown of the same edit.

4. Drag clip from viewer to Canvas
- Canvas edit overlay will appear
- Drop clip on the Overwrite edit type area

3. Set In and Out points
- Press I to set In point
- Press O to set Out point

2. Open first clip in viewer
- Double-click to open in Viewer

1. Start in the Browser
- Press Command-N to create a new sequence
- Double-click sequence to open in Timeline

Figure 8.1

5. Clip is added to sequence
- Timeline's playhead location determines In point for clip's sequence

Figure 8.2 Double-click the new sequence's icon in the Browser to open it for editing. Examine the open sequence in the Timeline to check that target tracks are assigned and that the playhead is positioned at the beginning of the sequence.

Figure 8.3 Double-click the clip to open it in the Viewer, then mark In and Out points to specify which portion of the source clip you want to use.

Basic Editing Step-by-Step

Here's a step-by-step breakdown of a simple rough-assembly-style edit in Final Cut Express. After you've reviewed this basic editing procedure, find out how to perform more specific types of edits in the sections that follow.

To add the first clip to your sequence:

1. In the Browser, press Command-N to create a new sequence.

2. Double-click the new sequence to open it in the Canvas and the Timeline (**Figure 8.2**).

   The new empty sequence opens in the Timeline window. The Timeline's playhead is positioned at the beginning of the sequence.

   Before you insert a clip in a sequence, you need to check the target tracks (the destination tracks for your clip in the sequence).

3. In the Timeline, check the target track assignment for your first clip. In a new sequence, default target tracks will already be assigned to V1, A1, and A2. If necessary, you can specify different target tracks by clicking the target track controls.

4. In the Browser, double-click the first clip you want to insert in your new sequence; that clip opens in the Viewer.

5. In the Viewer, select the portion of the clip you want to use in the sequence by setting In and Out points on your source clip (**Figure 8.3**). (See "Working with In and Out Points" in Chapter 7.)

continues on next page

6. Click the Viewer's image area and drag the clip to the Canvas window.

The Canvas edit overlay menu appears.

7. Drop the clip on the Overwrite edit area (**Figure 8.4**). (Overwrite is the default edit type in FCE unless you specify another type.)

The clip will be inserted at the beginning of your new sequence (**Figure 8.5**).

Figure 8.4 Drag the source clip from the Viewer to the Canvas edit overlay; then drop the clip on the Overwrite edit area.

Figure 8.5 The source clip has been added to the sequence. The Timeline playhead position was used as the sequence In point, so the clip's In point is located at the Timeline playhead position.

Many Ways to Make an Edit

Dragging your source clip to the Canvas edit overlay is just one way to execute an edit. Once you have defined your edit points, you can also do the following:

◆ Drag the clip directly from the Viewer to the Timeline (**Figure 8.6**).

◆ Drag one or more clips directly from the Browser to the Timeline (now *that's* a rough edit).

◆ Use a keyboard shortcut to perform the edit The keyboard shortcut for each edit type is listed in "Performing Edits in the Canvas," later in this chapter.

Figure 8.6 You can edit by dragging a clip directly from the Browser or Viewer and dropping it into a sequence in the Timeline.

BASIC EDITING STEP-BY-STEP

Figure 8.7 Position the Timeline playhead where you want your second clip to start, then press I to set a sequence In point.

Figure 8.8 The second source clip, displayed in the Viewer with In and Out points set.

Figure 8.9 Drag the second source clip to the Canvas edit overlay; then drop the clip on the Overwrite edit area.

To insert additional clips:

1. In the Timeline, park the playhead on the frame where you want your new clip to start (**Figure 8.7**). You can press I to set a sequence In point on that frame, but it's not required.

2. In the Viewer, set In and Out points on your second clip (**Figure 8.8**).

3. Click and drag the clip from the image area of the Viewer to the Canvas window.

   The Canvas edit overlay menu will appear.

4. Drop the clip on the Overwrite edit area (**Figure 8.9**).

   The second clip will be inserted starting at the sequence In point (**Figure 8.10**).

Figure 8.10 The sequence displayed in the Timeline, with the second clip inserted at the sequence In point.

FCE Protocol: Three-Point Editing

In a three-point edit, you can define any three points of an edit, and Final Cut Express will calculate the fourth point for you. Here's an example:

1. Specify In and Out points for your source clip.

2. Park the playhead in the Canvas at the sequence In point (the point where you want your new clip to start).

When you insert the new clip into your sequence, Final Cut Express uses the duration of the new clip insert to calculate the sequence Out point.

At least three edit points must be set in the Viewer and Canvas to perform an edit. But if you specify fewer than three points and perform an edit, FCE will calculate your edit based on the following protocols:

◆ If no In or Out point is set in the Canvas, the Canvas playhead location is used as the sequence In point.

◆ If no In or Out point is set in the source, FCE assumes that you want to use the entire source clip. The playhead's location in the sequence (Timeline and Canvas) is used as the sequence In point. FCE calculates the Out point for the sequence.

◆ If one edit point (In or Out) is set in a source clip, the second point is the beginning or the end of the media (depending on whether the user-defined point is an In or an Out point). The Canvas playhead is used as the sequence In point, and FCE calculates the Out point.

There are three exceptions to the three-point editing rules:

◆ Fit to Fill editing requires four user-specified points, because FCE adjusts the speed of the specified source clip to fill a specified sequence duration.

◆ Replace editing ignores the In and Out points set in the source clip and uses the boundaries of the clip under the Canvas playhead as sequence In and Out points. Replace edits affect the target-track media. To replace an audio track, turn off targeting for all video tracks.

◆ If In and Out points are set for both the source clip and the sequence, FCE ignores the source clip's Out point and uses the clip's In point and the sequence's In and Out points.

Figure 8.11 The target track controls in the Timeline.

Figure 8.12 Set a target track by clicking an Audio Target Track control. The control is highlighted in yellow when targeting is on.

Specifying target tracks

Each time you add clips to a sequence, you can specify which tracks the media will occupy. You specify target tracks using the Timeline's target track controls (**Figure 8.11**): the speaker and film icons located at the left of the Timeline. You can specify a maximum of three target tracks at a time: one for video and two for audio.

Audio-Target Track controls are shaped like speakers (or are they little bow ties?); click the left side to assign the track to channel 1, select the right side for channel 2.

To select target tracks in the Timeline:

◆ In the Timeline, click the target track control at the left side of the track you want to use.

The control is highlighted in yellow when targeting is on (**Figure 8.12**).

FCE Protocol: Target Tracks

◆ Once you specify target tracks, your edits will use the same target tracks until you change your target selection.

◆ When you insert a clip into a sequence by dragging it to a specific track in the Timeline, the clip will be placed on that track even if you did not target it previously.

◆ If the target track is locked, it will not accept any additional audio or video.

To use audio only from an audio+video clip:

◆ Click to turn off the video target track before you perform your edit (**Figure 8.13**).

To use one channel of two-channel audio from the source clip:

◆ Click to turn off the target indicator of the track you want to exclude (**Figure 8.14**).

✔ Tips

■ Once you've used the target track controls to route your source clips to their proper tracks, you might want to lock the tracks to prevent further changes to edited clips on that track. See "Lock versus Target" in Chapter 9 to learn the hows and whys of track locking.

■ When you are ready for big-time multi-track editing, be aware that FCE offers a raft of keyboard shortcuts for target track selection. Check them out in Appendix B, "Keyboard Shortcuts."

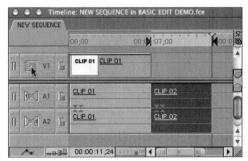

Figure 8.13 Click to turn off the Video Target Track control. Audio tracks remain targeted.

Figure 8.14 With A2 targeting turned off, channel 2 audio is excluded from the sequence.

FCE Protocol: Editing Multiple Tracks in Final Cut Express

Final Cut Express sequences can have multiple video and audio tracks. The first video clip you add to a sequence will be the base layer (V1). Video frames you place on track 2 (V2) are superimposed over any video frames at the same point in time on track 1. In a sequence with multiple layers, the base track becomes the background, and media on each higher-numbered track obscures the media on tracks below it. The result appears in the Canvas (after a little rendering).

Audio tracks A1 and A2 are the designated base tracks for stereo audio. Final Cut Express can mix and play back several audio tracks in a sequence in real time.

How Many Audio Tracks?

The number of audio tracks you may mix in real time depends on your Macintosh's configuration (available RAM, processor speed, hard drive data transfer rate, and so on), the number of audio files requiring real-time sample rate conversion, and how many simultaneous audio transitions you have included in your sequence. You can specify how many tracks you want FCE to attempt to handle in real time by setting the Real-Time Audio Mixing preference (see "Using Presets and Preferences" in Chapter 2). However, increasing your real-time audio track budget is no guarantee that you'll be able to play back the number of tracks you specify, and if you set this preference too high, you could trigger dropped frames during playback or dropouts in audio.

Eight tracks of real-time audio is the FCE default setup, but you can have up to 99 tracks in a sequence.

In calculating the number of audio tracks you need for a sequence, note that each simultaneous audio crossfade or transition increases the track count by one. So if your sequence requires seven audio tracks, adding a pair of crossfades increases the count to nine tracks. It also requires rendering to preview.

You can reduce your audio track overhead by choosing Mixdown Audio from the Sequence menu. Mixdown Audio renders all the audio tracks in a sequence along with their transitions, and it filters and consolidates them into one render file. For more information on working with audio in FCE, see Chapter 11, "Audio Tools and Techniques."

Moving the playhead

You can jump the playhead to the edit point of your choice with a single keystroke or mouse click. Most of these shortcuts work in the Viewer as well.

To move the playhead to the In point:

◆ Press Shift-I; or Shift-click the In point icon in the Canvas Scrubber bar.

To move the playhead to the Out point:

◆ Press Shift-O; or Shift-click the Out point icon in the Canvas Scrubber bar.

To jump the playhead to an adjacent edit point:

Do one of the following:

◆ Click the Previous Edit or the Next Edit button in the transport controls.

◆ Press the Up or the Down Arrow key.

◆ Open the Mark menu and choose from the Next or Previous submenu.

◆ Press Option-E (to go to the previous edit point) or Shift-E (to go to the next edit point).

Using FCE's Many Edit Types

When you drag a clip directly into the Canvas image area, the Canvas edit overlay appears with fields for each type of edit (**Figure 8.15**). Select the type of edit you want to perform by dropping your clip on the corresponding overlay area. The default type is an Overwrite edit.

Keep reading to find a rundown of the types of edits you can perform in FCE, along with variations they impose on the basic editing procedure.

Selected target track indicators

Insert edit area

Insert with Transition edit area

Overwrite edit area

Overwrite with Transition edit area

Replace edit area

Drag the incoming source clip from the Viewer

Fit to Fill edit area

Superimpose edit area

Figure 8.15 The Canvas edit overlay allows drag-and-drop editing for seven types of edits.

Figure 8.16 Position the Timeline playhead to set your sequence In point.

Figure 8.17 Drag the source clip from the Viewer to the Canvas edit overlay; then drop the clip on the Insert edit area.

Figure 8.18 The completed Insert edit in the Timeline. Clip 02, inserted between Clip 01 and Clip 03, pushes Clip 03 to the right.

Insert edit

When you perform an Insert edit, the sequence clips at the In point move to the right to make room for the new source clip. Any clips that span the In point are automatically split to accommodate the new clip.

✔ Tip

- Insert edits can also be performed by dragging the source clip directly to the Timeline. See "Performing Edits in the Timeline," later in this chapter.

To perform an Insert edit:

1. Set the sequence In point by positioning the Canvas (or Timeline) playhead where you want the edit to occur (**Figure 8.16**).

2. Drag the clip from the Viewer to the Insert edit area in the Canvas overlay (**Figure 8.17**); or press F9.

   The source clip is inserted into the sequence (**Figure 8.18**).

USING FCE'S MANY EDIT TYPES

Overwrite edit

In an Overwrite edit, the source clip over-writes sequence clips past the sequence In point. Overwrite edits use the source In and Out points to calculate the edit duration, replacing sequence material with the incoming source clip, with no time shift in the existing sequence.

✔ Tip

■ You can also perform Overwrite edits by dragging the source clip directly to the Timeline. See "Performing Edits in the Timeline," later in this chapter.

To perform an Overwrite edit:

1. Set the sequence In point by positioning the Canvas (or Timeline) playhead where you want the edit to occur (**Figure 8.19**).

2. Drag the source clip from the Viewer to the Overwrite edit area in the Canvas overlay (**Figure 8.20**); or press F10.

   The source clip is added to the sequence, overwriting any existing sequence material on the targeted tracks that falls between the sequence In and Out points (**Figure 8.21**).

Figure 8.19 Position the Timeline playhead to set your sequence In point.

Figure 8.20 Drag the source clip from the Viewer to the Canvas edit overlay; then drop the clip on the Overwrite edit area.

Figure 8.21 The completed Overwrite edit in the Timeline. Clip 02 overwrites the portion of Clip 01 that extends beyond the sequence In point, without moving Clip 03.

Replace edit

A Replace edit replaces the contents of a sequence clip with source clip material.

The Replace edit uses the playhead position in the Viewer, not the source In and Out points, to calculate the Replace edit; your source In and Out points will be ignored. If you don't set sequence In and Out points, FCE uses the boundaries of the clip under the Timeline playhead.

You can use a Replace edit to simply replace a shot in a sequence with footage from another shot with the same duration. Replace editing can also be a powerful tool for matching action; for example, when you're cutting between multiple-camera coverage of different angles on the same action (in your big-budget dreams). Park the Canvas playhead at the point in the action that you want to match in your source clip. Find the source clip frame that matches the action in the sequence frame. Mark In and Out points in the Canvas to select the section of the sequence you want to replace with the new material. The material between the sequence In and Out points is replaced by corresponding material from the source clip on either side of the frame that was matched.

continues on next page

Hate Your Edit? Do Undo

Undo is one of the great technological contributions to civilization. Especially when you're editing.

As you build your edited sequence, keep in mind that the fastest way to repair your sequence after you've done something brilliant but basically bad is to use the Undo feature. You can set your FCE preferences to allow up to 32 Undos—10 is the default.

Undo is particularly useful when you've just performed an unsuccessful (or accidental) Overwrite edit and replaced some clips in your sequence. Deleting the clips that wiped out part of your sequence won't restore your original footage, but if you Undo (Command-Z) your Overwrite edit, your sequence footage will be restored.

So, go forth and be bold. Experiment with your edit. You can always Undo.

To perform a Replace edit:

1. Position the Viewer playhead on the frame you want to match with a frame in the Canvas (**Figure 8.22**).

2. Position the Canvas playhead on the frame you want to match with the one selected in the Viewer. If you want to specify the duration of the replacement clip, set sequence In and Out points (**Figure 8.23**).

Figure 8.22 Position the Viewer playhead on the frame you want to match with a frame in the Canvas.

Figure 8.23 Position the Canvas playhead on the frame you want to match with a frame in the Viewer.

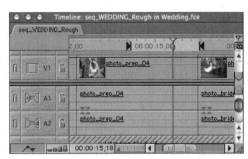

Figure 8.24 The sequence before the Replace edit in the Timeline.

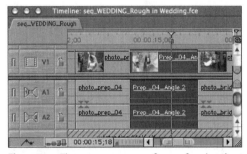

Figure 8.25 The same sequence after performing the Replace edit. The new clip replaces the old, using the match frame you selected as the sync point.

3. Drag the source clip from the Viewer to the Replace edit area in the Canvas overlay; or press F11.

Figure 8.24 shows the Timeline before the Replace edit; **Figure 8.25** shows the Timeline after the Replace edit.

✔ Tip

- Use the Replace edit technique to replace a clip with an offset copy of itself. This is a shortcut to adjust the timing of action in a clip or to sync action to music.

What's a Backtime Edit?

Say you're filling a gap in your edited music video sequence. The In point of the clip you want to use is not critical, but you know exactly where you want this clip to end—and you want the clip to fit your gap exactly. In this case, set up a *backtime* edit by marking the gap as your sequence In and Out points, along with the source Out point you identified in your source clip. FCE will calculate the other In point and back your clip in so it fits the gap perfectly.

Fit to Fill edit

In a Fit to Fill edit, the speed of the source clip is modified to fill the duration specified by the sequence In and Out points; the clip must be rendered before the edit can be played back.

To perform a Fit to Fill edit:

1. In the Timeline, set sequence In and Out points to define the sequence section you want to fill (**Figure 8.26**).

2. In the Viewer, set source In and Out points to define the part of the source clip you want to speed-modify so it fits between your edit points in the sequence (**Figure 8.27**).

3. Drag the source clip in the Viewer to the Fit to Fill edit area in the Canvas overlay; or press Shift-F11.

   The source clip is speed-modified to fit between the sequence In and Out points (**Figure 8.28**).

✔ Tip

■ You've just added a clip to your sequence—but it's too short to fill the gap you're trying to fill. Here's a slick trick: perform Fit to Fill on a clip that's already edited into your sequence by double-clicking the clip to open it in the Viewer, then dragging it to the Fit to Fill edit area. Voilà! Perfect fit.

Figure 8.26 Marking a sequence Out point in the Timeline. Setting the sequence In and Out points defines the section you want to fill.

Figure 8.27 Marking a source Out point in the Viewer. Setting source In and Out points defines the section you want to fit into the sequence.

Figure 8.28 The source clip is speed-modified to fit between the sequence In and Out points. Note that the speed change appears on the clip.

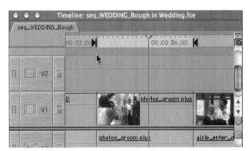

Figure 8.29 Use the Mark Clip keyboard shortcut (X) to mark In and Out points at the clip boundaries of the clip you want to superimpose over.

Figure 8.30 In the Viewer, set source In and Out points to specify the part of the source clip that you want to superimpose on the sequence.

Figure 8.31 Drag the source clip from the Viewer to the Canvas edit overlay; then drop the clip on the Superimpose edit area.

Superimpose edit

In a Superimpose edit, the source clip is placed on a new track above the target track, starting at the sequence In point. The target track is not changed. If the clip has audio, the source audio is added to new tracks below the target audio track.

To perform a Superimpose edit:

1. Position the Canvas playhead or set a sequence In point where you want the source clip to start (**Figure 8.29**).

2. In the Viewer, set source In and Out points to define the part of the source clip you want to add to the sequence (**Figure 8.30**).

3. Drag the source clip from the Viewer to the Superimpose edit area in the Canvas overlay (**Figure 8.31**); or press F12.

   The source clip is placed on a new track above the target track, starting at the sequence In point (**Figure 8.32**).

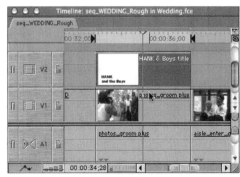

Figure 8.32 The source clip is placed on a new track above the target track, starting at the sequence In point.

USING FCE'S MANY EDIT TYPES

223

Transition edits

You may not always want to cut abruptly
between clips in a sequence, which is why
FCE offers two types of edits that incorporate transitions: Insert with Transition and
Overwrite with Transition. A transition edit
automatically places a cross dissolve (FCE's
default transition) at the head of the edit.
When using either of the transition edit types,
you'll need at least 15 extra frames in each
clip at the edit point where the transition is
applied in order to create the transition. (The
additional frames necessary are equal to half
of the default transition's 30-frame duration;
see Chapter 12, "Creating Transitions," for
more on using transitions.)

To perform a Transition edit:

1. Set the sequence In point by positioning
   the Canvas (or Timeline) playhead where
   you want the edit to occur (**Figure 8.33**).

2. In the Viewer, set source In and Out
   points to define the part of the source
   clip you want to add to the sequence
   (**Figure 8.34**).

Figure 8.33 Positioning the Timeline playhead to set a
sequence In point.

Figure 8.34 In the Viewer, set source In and Out
points to specify the part of the source clip that you
want to use.

Figure 8.35 Drag the source clip from the Viewer to the Canvas edit overlay; drop it on either of the Transition edit areas.

Figure 8.36 The Timeline, showing the source clip inserted into the sequence with the default transition at the head.

3. Drag the source clip from the Viewer to either the Insert with Transition or the Overwrite with Transition edit area in the Canvas overlay (**Figure 8.35**).

The source clip is inserted in the sequence with a one-second cross dissolve at the sequence In point. (**Figure 8.36**).

✔ Tips

■ If you're working on a slower Mac that doesn't support real-time effects preview, you must render transition edits before you can play them back.

■ If you've customized a transition in your sequence that you want to reuse, select it in the Timeline and drag it to your Favorites folder on the Effects tab in the Browser. You can copy a Favorite transition from the folder and paste it into a sequence wherever you want it. Setting up a customized Favorite transition is easy, so it's worth doing even if you're building a fairly short sequence.

Deleting clips from a sequence

Two types of edits can be used to remove material from a sequence:

◆ **Lift** removes the selected material, leaving a gap.

◆ **Ripple Delete** removes the selected material and closes the gap.

To perform a Lift edit:

Do one of the following:

◆ Select the clip in the Timeline and press Delete.

◆ Select the clip in the Timeline and then choose Sequence > Lift.

◆ Select the clip in the Timeline and press Command-X (Cut).

◆ Control-click the selected clip in the Timeline; then choose Cut from the shortcut menu. (Cut also lets you paste the deleted clip in another location in the sequence.)

Figure 8.37 shows a sequence in the Timeline before a Lift edit; **Figure 8.38** shows the same sequence after a Lift edit.

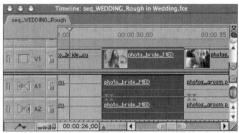

Figure 8.37 A clip selected in the Timeline. Press Delete to perform a Lift edit by deleting the clip from the sequence; or press Command-X to cut the clip for pasting elsewhere.

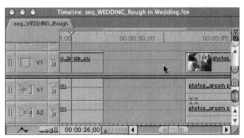

Figure 8.38 The sequence after a Lift edit. The rest of the sequence clips hold their positions.

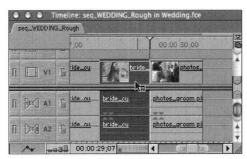

Figure 8.39 Control-click the selected sequence clip to access the shortcut menu.

Figure 8.40 From the shortcut menu, choose Ripple Delete.

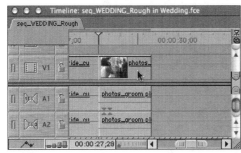

Figure 8.41 The sequence after a Ripple Delete edit. Material to the right of the deleted clip has been pulled up to close the gap.

To perform a Ripple Delete edit:

Do one of the following:

◆ Select the clip in the Timeline and press Shift-Delete.

◆ Select the clip in the Timeline; then choose Sequence > Ripple Delete.

◆ Control-click the selected clip in the Timeline (**Figure 8.39**); then choose Ripple Delete from the shortcut menu (**Figure 8.40**).

The clip is deleted from the sequence, and the material on all unlocked tracks to the right of the sequence pulls up to close the gap (**Figure 8.41**).

✔ Tip

■ You can delete a precisely defined section of a sequence by setting sequence In and Out points to mark the section you want to remove and then pressing Delete to lift the section, or pressing Shift-Delete to ripple delete it.

Performing Edits in the Timeline

Editing in the Timeline can be a faster way to go, particularly when you're in the early stages of assembly.

You have a number of ways to control the size and time scale of the Timeline window. You need the Timeline's "big picture" view when you deploy multiple tracks of visual or sound effects, but you can also zoom way in when performing precise work. See Chapter 9, "Editing in the Timeline and the Canvas," for details.

Figure 8.42 Using Large Icon view in the Browser, arrange clip icons in storyboard order.

◆ You can assemble a sequence by dragging clips directly to the Timeline from the Browser or Viewer.

◆ You can use the Browser Sort function to sort your takes by timecode or by shot number, and then drag a whole group of clips from the Browser directly to the Timeline. FCE will place the clips in the Timeline based on your Browser sort order.

◆ You can construct a storyboard in the Browser's Large Icon view (**Figure 8.42**), and then drag all the clips into the Timeline (**Figure 8.43**). If the Browser tab from which you drag the clips is in Icon mode, the clips are placed in left-to-right order, from top to bottom (**Figure 8.44**).

Figure 8.43 Select all clips in the Browser and drag them to the Timeline.

◆ You can designate target tracks in an edit just by dragging a source clip directly to the destination track.

◆ Drag a source clip to the space above your existing tracks, and FCE will automatically create a new track.

Figure 8.44 The sequence assembles clips in storyboard order.

Figure 8.45 Dragging a clip to the upper third of the Timeline track performs an Insert edit.

Figure 8.46 Dragging a clip to the lower two-thirds of the Timeline track performs an Overwrite edit.

Figure 8.47 When you drop a clip directly into the Timeline, the Canvas displays details about the two clips adjacent to your edit point.

To perform an Insert edit:

◆ Drag the source clip from the Viewer or Browser to the upper third of the Timeline track (**Figure 8.45**).

The pointer changes to indicate the type of edit.

To perform an Overwrite edit:

◆ Drag the source clip from the Viewer or Browser to the lower two-thirds of the Timeline track (**Figure 8.46**).

✔ Tips

■ If you drag a clip to the Timeline when it is set to the smallest timeline track size, you'll perform an Overwrite edit. Hold down the Option key to perform an Insert edit.

■ When you drag a clip from the Browser onto a clip or transition in the Timeline, a two-up display appears in the Canvas. This two-up display shows the frame just before your insert on the left, and it shows the frame just after your insert on the right. The names of the sequence clips adjacent to your edit point appear at the top of each display, and the time-code of the displayed frames appears at the bottom (**Figure 8.47**).

Performing Split Edits

A split edit sets different In and Out points for video and audio in a single clip (**Figure 8.48**).

To mark a split edit:

1. With the clip open in the Viewer, position the playhead where you want the video to begin.

2. Control-click the Scrubber bar; then choose Mark Split > Video In from the shortcut menu (**Figure 8.49**).

3. Reposition the playhead at your desired Out point and choose Mark Split > Video Out from the shortcut menu.

4. Repeat the process to set your Audio In and Out points (**Figure 8.50**). You could also switch to your clip's Audio tab and mark the audio there.

Figure 8.48 Split edit points as they appear in the Viewer's scrubber bar.

Figure 8.49 Control-click anywhere on the Scrubber bar to call up the shortcut menu; then choose Mark Split > Video In.

Figure 8.50 Using the Scrubber shortcut menu to mark the Audio Out point. (Alternatively, you can switch to the clip's Audio tab to do this.)

Figure 8.51 Moving split In points by dragging them in the Scrubber. The Audio and Video In points will shift in tandem. Video edit points appear in the top half of the Scrubber; audio points appear in the bottom half.

Figure 8.52 Shift-dragging moves all four points at once. The timecode readout in the Viewer displays the current In point location of the point that you drag.

To move split edit points:

◆ Open the clip in the Viewer. In the Scrubber bar, click and drag either the In points or the Out points to a new position.

 The video and audio edit points move in tandem in a split edit (**Figure 8.51**).

To slip all split edit points at once:

◆ In the Scrubber bar, press Shift while dragging any of the edit points.

 All of the edit points *slip*, or move in unison (**Figure 8.52**).

 The respective video and audio durations specified in the split edit don't change, but the frames that are included in the marked clip shift.

✔ Tip

■ As you slip a split edit, the updated In point frame with the timecode for the edit point you selected displays on the Viewer image, and the edit's Out point frame with timecode displays on the Canvas. Awesome.

Tips for Quicker Split Edits

Split edits are commonly used in cutting synchronized dialogue scenes. You can mark a split edit before you insert a clip into a sequence for the first time (as shown here), but a common split edit approach to a dialogue sequence starts by making straight cuts of both video and audio tracks based on the rhythm of the dialogue and then going back and using the Roll tool to adjust the edit points on the video track only. Hold down the Option key as you click the edit point to select only the video track of your clip. Check out "Tips on Tools" in Chapter 10 for more info.

Another approach is to include only video or only audio in your edit by targeting only the video or audio track in the Timeline.

As you play back your footage, you can use one of these keyboard shortcuts to mark a split edit on the fly:

◆ Mark Video In: Control-I

◆ Mark Video Out: Control-O

◆ Mark Audio In: Command-Option-I

◆ Mark Audio Out: Command-Option-O

To move only one edit point in a split edit:

◆ In the Scrubber bar, press Option while dragging the edit point you want to modify (**Figure 8.53**).

A display pops up as you drag to indicate the duration of the offset between Video In and Audio In, or Video Out and Audio Out. The Scrubber bar in the Viewer updates to reflect the new edit points.

To remove a split edit point:

◆ In the Scrubber bar, Control-click; then choose Clear Split and, from the shortcut submenu, select the point you want to clear (**Figure 8.54**).

Figure 8.53 Option-click and drag to shift only one edit point in a split edit. The pop-up display shows the offset duration between Video and Audio In points.

Figure 8.54 Clearing a Video Out point using the Scrubber shortcut menu. Control-click the Scrubber bar to access this menu.

Figure 8.55 In the Timeline, place the playhead over the clip that you want to use to mark the sequence.

Figure 8.56 Check that the selected clip is on the target track. The target track icon is highlighted in yellow.

Figure 8.57
Choose Mark > Mark Clip.

Figure 8.58 The sequence In and Out points are set to match the boundaries of the clip.

Shortcuts for Marking Sequence Edit Points

Use the same commands and keyboard shortcuts that you use to mark In and Out points in the Viewer to mark your sequence In and Out points in the Timeline and the Canvas.

FCE also offers a couple of handy commands specifically for marking edit points in a sequence:

◆ Use the Mark Clip command to set the sequence In and Out points to match the edit points of a particular clip in the sequence.

◆ Use Mark Selection to set the sequence In and Out points to match a multiple-clip selection or a selection that includes only part of a clip.

To use the Mark Clip command:

1. Place the playhead over a clip in the Timeline (**Figure 8.55**).

2. Check that your selected clip's track is the target track (**Figure 8.56**).

3. Choose Mark > Mark Clip (**Figure 8.57**); or press X.

   The sequence In and Out points are set to match the boundaries of the clip (**Figure 8.58**).

✔ Tip

■ Mark Clip is a quick way to mark sequence In and Out points if you want to super-impose something over a particular clip.

SHORTCUTS FOR MARKING SEQUENCE EDIT POINTS

To use the Mark Selection command:

1. Make a selection in the Timeline. The selection can range from an entire sequence to a part of a single clip (see Chapter 9 for information on using the Tool palette's selection tools) (**Figure 8.59**).

2. Check that your selection's track is the target track (**Figure 8.60**).

3. Choose Mark > Mark Selection (**Figure 8.61**).

   The sequence In and Out points are set to the boundaries of the selection (**Figure 8.62**).

Figure 8.59 Selecting a region of the sequence. Use Range Select from the toolbar if you want to include just part of a clip.

Figure 8.60 Check that the selected region is on the target track. The target track icon is highlighted in yellow.

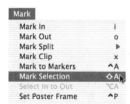

Figure 8.61 Choose Mark > Mark Selection.

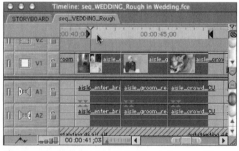

Figure 8.62 Sequence In and Out points are set to match the boundaries of the selected region.

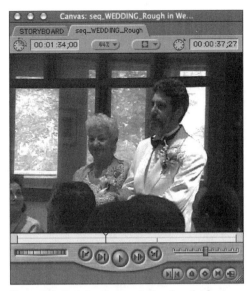

Figure 8.63 Park the Canvas playhead on the frame that you want to match in the source clip.

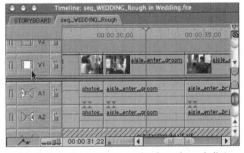

Figure 8.64 In the Timeline, make the selected clip's track the target track. The target track icon is highlighted in yellow.

Figure 8.65 Click the Match Frame button in the Canvas.

Locating a Match Frame

The Match Frame command opens a copy of the source clip for the frame at the play-head position on the target track. This is a convenient way to locate the source video for a clip.

To find a particular frame of video in a clip in the sequence:

1. In the Canvas or the Timeline, park the playhead on the frame for which you want to locate the source clip (**Figure 8.63**).

2. Set the target track to the track that contains the desired frame (**Figure 8.64**).

3. Click the Match Frame button in the Canvas (**Figure 8.65**); or press F.

   The source clip opens in the Viewer with the In and Out points set. The current frame in the Viewer matches the current frame on the target track in the Canvas (**Figure 8.66**).

Figure 8.66 The source clip that matches the sequence clip opens in the Viewer. The frame displayed in the Viewer matches the current frame displayed in the target track in the Canvas.

Editing in the Timeline and the Canvas

The previous chapter introduced basic editing procedures in Final Cut Express; this chapter outlines your display, navigation, and editing options in the Timeline and the Canvas windows. You'll also learn about the Tool palette, a deceptively tiny floating toolbar that's packed with editing, selection, and display tools. The Tool palette is key to efficient workflow in the Timeline.

The Timeline and the Canvas work together, but they present two different views of your edited sequence. The Timeline displays a chronological diagram of all the clips in your sequence; the Canvas is a monitor where you view playback of an edited sequence. That's why the Canvas and Timeline playheads are locked together. The Canvas always displays the frame at the current position of the Timeline's playhead.

When you open a sequence, it appears simultaneously in the Timeline and the Canvas. Any changes you make to the sequence in the Timeline reflect in the Canvas playback, and any changes you make in the Canvas reflect in the Timeline display.

Double-clicking a sequence clip in the Timeline opens it in the Viewer; sequence clips are identified in the Viewer by two lines of dots in the Scrubber bar. Why the identification? Remember that when you insert a clip into a sequence, you are inserting a copy of the clip from the Browser. If you change the sequence version of the clip, your changes will be reflected in the sequence only. Opening the same clip directly from the Browser in a Viewer window opens a different copy of the clip. If you change the Browser copy (for example, by making audio-level adjustments or adding motion effects), these changes will not affect the copy of the clip in the sequence. It's important to understand the difference between working with clips that have been opened from the Browser and clips that have been opened from the Timeline. (For more information, see "FCE Protocol: Clips and Sequences" in Chapter 3.)

Anatomy of the Canvas

The Canvas window (**Figure 9.1**) looks like the Viewer and has many of the same controls. You can use the controls in the Canvas window to play edited sequences, mark sequence In and Out points, add sequence markers, and set keyframes. In addition to the Viewer-like marking controls, the Canvas features a pop-up overlay where you can perform various types of drag-and-drop edits. The Canvas edit overlay appears only when you drag a clip from the Browser or the Viewer to the Canvas.

You can also use the Canvas window to plot out effects. Learn about applying filters and effects in Chapter 13, "Compositing and Effects Overview."

✔ Tips

- You can use the tooltips feature to identify most of the control buttons in the window. Place your pointer over a button and then wait a second, and a name label will appear. (Enable tooltips in the Preferences window if they're not showing up.)

- Two playback options don't have interface controls: Play Every Frame (Option-P) and Loop Playback (Control-L).

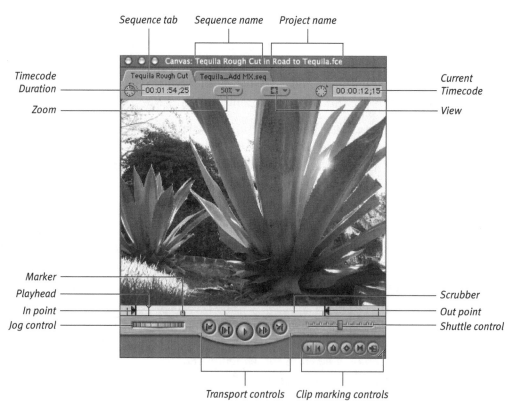

Figure 9.1 An overview of the Canvas window. Use the Canvas to play sequences, perform edits, and set keyframes.

Previous Edit *Play In to Out* *Play Around Current*
Play *Next Edit*

Figure 9.2 The Canvas's transport controls.

Figure 9.3 The Shuttle control.

Figure 9.4 The Jog control.

Figure 9.5 The Scrubber and playhead.

Onscreen controls and displays

The Canvas controls include transport controls, Canvas display options, and editing controls.

Note that all the Canvas controls listed here (except the editing buttons and the overlay) appear in the Viewer window as well and operate in the same way.

Transport controls

The Canvas's transport controls are shown in **Figure 9.2**.

◆ **Previous Edit:** Click to jump the playhead back to the previous edit, the In point, or the Out point.

◆ **Play In to Out:** Click to play the clip from the In point to the Out point.

◆ **Play:** Click to play the clip from the current position of the playhead. Click again to stop playback.

◆ **Play Around Current:** Click to play the part of the clip immediately before and after the current position of the playhead. The pre-roll and post-roll settings (in the Preferences window) determine the duration of the playback.

◆ **Next Edit:** Click to move the playhead to the next edit, the In point, or the Out point.

◆ **Shuttle control:** Drag the control tab away from the center to fast forward or rewind. Speeds vary depending on the tab's distance from the center. A green control tab indicates normal playback speed (**Figure 9.3**).

◆ **Jog control:** Click and drag your mouse to the left or right to step through a sequence one frame at a time (**Figure 9.4**).

◆ **Scrubber and playhead:** The Scrubber is the strip immediately below the image window. Move through the sequence by dragging the playhead, or click the Scrubber to jump the playhead to a new location (**Figure 9.5**).

Clip-marking controls

All of the onscreen controls you use to mark clips are grouped in the lower-right corner of the Canvas (**Figure 9.6**):

◆ **Mark In (left) and Mark Out (right):** Click to set the In point or the Out point for a sequence at the current playhead position.

◆ **Add Marker:** Click to add a marker to the sequence at the current playhead position.

◆ **Add Keyframe:** Click to add a keyframe to the sequence clip at the current playhead position.

◆ **Mark Clip:** Click to set the sequence In and Out points at the outer boundaries of the clip at the position of the playhead in the target track.

◆ **Match Frame:** Click to display in the Viewer the frame currently showing in the Canvas. This control is useful for synchronizing action.

View selectors

◆ **Zoom:** Adjust the Canvas's image display size (**Figure 9.7**). (This pop-up selector does not affect the actual frame size of the image.)

◆ **View:** Select a viewing format. You can access Title Safe and Wireframe modes from this pop-up menu (**Figure 9.8**).

Figure 9.6 The Canvas's clip marking controls.

Figure 9.7 The Zoom pop-up selector.

Figure 9.8 The View pop-up selector.

ANATOMY OF THE CANVAS

Figure 9.9 The Timecode Duration display.

Figure 9.10 The Current Timecode display.

Figure 9.11 The Current Timecode pop-up menu. Select a sequence marker from the list to jump to that marker's location.

Figure 9.12 You can access the same list of sequence markers by Control-clicking on the Timeline ruler.

Timecode navigation and display

Two timecode displays, located in the upper corners of the Canvas window, are useful for precisely navigating to specific timecode locations.

- ◆ **Timecode Duration:** This display shows the elapsed time between the In and Out points of a clip. If no edit points are set, the beginning and the end of the sequence serve as the In and the Out points (**Figure 9.9**).

- ◆ **Current Timecode:** This display shows the timecode at the current position of the playhead. You can enter a timecode in this display to jump the playhead to that point in the sequence (**Figure 9.10**).

✔ Tips

- ■ Control-click the Current Timecode field to see a pop-up selector of sequence markers in the current sequence. Select one to jump the playhead to that marker's location (**Figure 9.11**). The same list of sequence markers is available from the Timeline ruler's shortcut menu (**Figure 9.12**).

- ■ You can use keyboard shortcuts to step through both sequence and clip markers in the Timeline, but you must open a clip in the Viewer to make changes to that clip's markers. For details, see "Using Markers in the Timeline and the Canvas," later in this chapter.

Anatomy of the Canvas Edit Overlay

When you drag clips from the Viewer and drop them on the Canvas, the edit overlay appears (**Figure 9.13**). The edit overlay and its related edit procedures are detailed in Chapter 8, "Basic Editing." You can perform the following types of edits:

◆ **Insert edit:** This type of edit inserts a source clip into a sequence by pushing back the part of the sequence that's past the sequence In point, making room for the new source clip.

◆ **Overwrite edit:** The source clip over-writes sequence clips past the sequence In point. Overwrite uses the source In and Out points to calculate the edit duration. The incoming source material replaces the sequence material; there is no time shift in the existing sequence.

◆ **Transition edits:** The source clip is inserted into the sequence with the default transition at the source clip's head.

◆ **Replace edit:** This edit type replaces the contents of a sequence clip with the source clip material. It allows you to specifically align single frames in the source clip and sequence. The material between the sequence In and Out points is replaced by corresponding material from the source clip on either side of the frame that was matched.

◆ **Superimpose edit:** The source clip is placed on a new track above the target track, starting at the sequence In point. The target track is not changed. If the clip has audio, the source audio is added to new tracks below the target audio track.

◆ **Fit to Fill edit:** The speed of the source clip will be modified to fill the duration specified by the sequence In and Out points; the clip must be rendered before the edit can be played back.

◆ **Target track indicators:** These show which tracks have been targeted for this edit.

Selected target track indicators

Insert edit area — Insert

Insert with Transition edit area

Overwrite edit area — Overwrite

Overwrite with Transition edit area

Replace edit area

Fit to Fill edit area

Superimpose edit area

Figure 9.13 The Canvas edit overlay allows drag-and-drop editing for seven types of edits.

ANATOMY OF THE CANVAS

Figure 9.14 Selecting Image+Wireframe from the View pop-up selector.

Figure 9.15 Motion paths, filters, and scaling can be directly applied in the Canvas window.

Using the Canvas Window

The Canvas and the Viewer windows operate in much the same way. If you review the sections in Chapter 7, "Working with Clips in the Viewer," that detail operating the Viewer window, you'll know how to use the Canvas window as well.

Editing in the Canvas is detailed in Chapter 8, "Basic Editing."

So what does that leave for this section? Just a few odds and ends.

To open a sequence in the Canvas:

◆ Start in the Browser. Double-click the sequence icon. The sequence opens in the Canvas and the Timeline.

To composite or add effects to a sequence in the Canvas:

1. Start in the Canvas with your sequence cued to the location to which you want to add effects.

2. Choose Image+Wireframe from the View selector in the Canvas (**Figure 9.14**).

   The Canvas acts as your monitor as you compose and review effects or create motion paths (**Figure 9.15**). Learn more about creating effects in Chapter 13, "Compositing and Effects Overview."

Creating and exporting still frames

It's easy to turn any single video frame into a freeze-frame image and use it in a sequence. If you want to convert this image into a graphic file and work with it outside of FCE, you'll need to export it using the Export command on the File menu.

To create a still image from a Canvas frame:

1. In the Canvas, position the playhead on the desired frame.

2. Choose Modify > Make Freeze Frame.

   The new freeze-frame image opens in the Viewer window as a clip. It has the default duration for stills, as specified on the General tab of the Preferences window. You can modify the freeze-frame clip's duration by setting In and Out points before you edit it into your sequence.

To export a still image from a Canvas frame:

1. In the Canvas, position the playhead on the desired frame.

2. Choose File > Export > QuickTime.

3. In the dialog box, type a new name for your exported still image in the Name field.

4. Select a destination folder.

5. Select Still Image from the Format pop-up menu (**Figure 9.16**).

6. To set export format options, click the Options button.

7. In the Export Image Sequence Settings dialog box, select an export format from the pop-up menu at the top (**Figure 9.17**); click OK. You can ignore the frame rate settings because you are exporting a single frame.

8. Back in the Save dialog box, click Save.

Figure 9.16 Select Still Image from the Format pop-up menu.

Figure 9.17 Select an export format for your still image from the pop-up menu.

Figure 9.18 Select a time display option from the shortcut menu in the Canvas's Current Timecode display.

To set the time display view:

◆ In the Canvas, Control-click either time-code display field; then select a time display option from the shortcut menu (**Figure 9.18**).

✔ Tip

■ Changing the timecode display in the Canvas won't alter your sequence's time-code settings. That's why the timecode display shortcut menu says, "View as."

Adjusting the Canvas Display

You can set up the Canvas to show clips in a variety of display formats and magnifications. Final Cut Express also lets you overlay an array of useful information on your clip image, or you can turn off everything.

Display options operate the same way in the Canvas and the Viewer. Learn more about Canvas display options by reading "Adjusting the Viewer Display" in Chapter 7.

Anatomy of the Tool Palette

The Tool palette contains tools for selecting and manipulating items in the Timeline, Canvas, and Viewer. As you work in the Timeline with an assembly of clips in a rough sequence, you use the tools in the palette to do the following:

◆ Select anything, from a sliver of a single clip to all the tracks in your sequence.

◆ Select and adjust edit points in your sequence.

◆ Adjust the scale of the Timeline so you can see what you are doing.

◆ Crop or distort an image.

◆ Add and edit keyframes in the Timeline.

Figure 9.19 shows the Tool palette as it appears in the program.

Figure 9.20 shows the Tool palette with all of its pop-up selectors fully extended. When you actually use the Tool palette to select a tool, you will see only one of these selectors at a time, but they are assembled in this illustration to show the location of every available tool.

Figure 9.19 The Tool palette as a compact floating toolbar.

Figure 9.20 The Tool palette with every pop-up selector displayed. You'll see only one of these bars at a time, when you select a tool.

Here's a complete rundown of the tools you"ll find in the Tool palette.

Selection tools

 Selection: Selects individual items.

 Edit Selection: Selects just the edit points inside your selection.

 Group Selection: Selects whole clips or groups of whole clips.

 Range Selection: Selects the area inside the selection marquee you draw. Select partial clips with this tool.

 Select Track Forward: Selects all of the contents of the track after the selection point.

 Select Track Backward: Selects all of the contents of the track before the selection point.

 Track Selection: Selects the entire contents of a single track.

 Select All Tracks Forward: Selects the contents of all tracks after the selection point.

 Select All Tracks Backward: Selects the contents of all tracks before the selection point.

Edit tools

 Roll: Rolls edit points.

 Ripple: Ripples edit points.

 Slip: Slips a clip's In and Out points.

 Slide: Slides a clip in a sequence.

 Razor Blade: Cuts a single clip into two sections.

 Razor Blade All: Cuts clips on all tracks at the selection point into two sections.

Learn more about performing these edits in Chapter 10, "Fine Cut: Trimming Edits."

View tools

 Zoom In: Zooms in on an image or within the Timeline.

 Zoom Out: Zooms out from an image or within the Timeline.

 Hand: Moves the Timeline or image view from side to side.

 Video Scrub Hand: Scrubs the thumbnail image displayed on Timeline clips.

Image modifiers

 Crop: Crops the edges of an image in the Viewer or the Canvas (in Wireframe mode).

 Distort: Distorts a selection by click-dragging corner points.

Keyframe tools

 Pen: Adds a keyframe.

 Pen Delete: Deletes a keyframe.

 Pen Smooth: Smoothes a curve by adding Bézier handles to the selected keyframe.

You can use the Pen tools in keyframe graphs on the Viewer effects tabs, in keyframe overlays in the Timeline, and on a motion path in the Canvas or the Viewer.

ANATOMY OF THE TOOL PALETTE

Using the Tool palette

When you click and hold the mouse on a tool in the palette, the Tool palette extends to display multiple tools on pop-up selectors. Each pop-up displays all of the tools available from its palette button. After you've made a selection from the pop-up, your selected tool will display on the palette.

✔ Tip

■ See Appendix B for a complete list of keyboard shortcuts for tool selection. Shortcuts are also listed in tooltips and on FCE menus.

Figure 9.21 Click a tool to select it from the Tool palette.

To select a tool from the palette:

Do one of the following:

◆ Click the tool to select it (**Figure 9.21**).

◆ Click and hold on the tool icon; then make a selection from the pop-up display of related tools (**Figure 9.22**).

◆ Use a keyboard shortcut. To quickly see the proper key, rest the pointer over the tool icon in the palette. A tooltip displaying the name of the tool and its shortcut will appear (**Figure 9.23**).

Figure 9.22 Select a tool from the pop-up display of related tools.

Figure 9.23 Rest the pointer over a tool to display its tooltip.

Anatomy of the Timeline

The Timeline displays multiple video and audio tracks along a time axis (**Figure 9.24**). The base layers of video (V1) and audio (A1 and A2) appear toward the center of the Timeline window. Additional audio tracks extend below the base layer; additional video tracks stack above the base layer.

If you have multiple sequences open, the Timeline and the Canvas display a tab for each sequence.

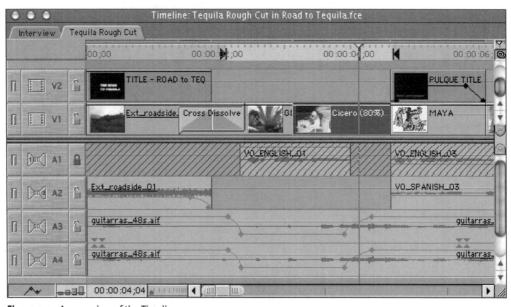

Figure 9.24 An overview of the Timeline.

Cool Timeline Features

Final Cut Express's Timeline is a marvel of visual interface. Bits of useful information appear out in the open . Here are some interface highlights you won't want to miss:

◆ **Linked Selection control:** The Linked Selection indicator controls whether linked selection is active or disabled.

◆ **Snapping control:** Use this control to toggle snapping and check snapping status.

◆ **Speed change:** If you modify a clip's playback speed, the new speed setting appears next to the clip's name in the Timeline.

◆ **Multiple-clip level control for audio:** This feature is nice. You don't need to nest your audio to set levels on multiple audio clips. Select the clips in the Timeline (you can select all of the audio tracks in your sequence if you like) and use the Modify > Levels menu command.

◆ **Opacity level control for multiple clips:** This works like the multiple-clip audio level command. You can adjust opacity by a relative or absolute percentage.

◆ **Video Scrub Hand tool:** Select the Video Scrub Hand tool and drag across the Timeline clip's thumbnail image. The tiny thumbnail image plays as moving video.

Onscreen controls and displays

Use the controls in the Timeline window to move the playhead, view the tracks in your edited sequence, and perform edits and keyframe adjustments. Timeline controls and displays include track icons, sequence edit points, and clip and sequence markers (**Figures 9.25**, **9.26**, and **9.27**).

◆ **Sequence tabs:** Each open sequence in the Timeline has its own sequence tab. To make a sequence active, click its tab.

◆ **Track Visibility control:** Click to make a track invisible. When the track is invisible, the contents remain in the Timeline but are not played or rendered with the sequence. Invisible tracks appear dimmed in the Timeline. Caution: Render cache files are deleted if the track is made invisible.

◆ **Target Track controls:** Click to select the target tracks (one video track and up to two audio tracks) before performing an edit.

◆ **Lock Track control:** Lock a track to prevent any changes to its contents. Locked tracks are crosshatched in the Timeline.

◆ **Clip Overlays control:** Click to toggle the display of Audio Level line graphs over audio clips and Opacity Level line graphs in video clips.

continues on next page

Sequence tabs

Track Visibility control

Target Track controls

Lock Track control

Clip Overlays control

Track Size control

Current Timecode field

Figure 9.25 Detail of the left side of the Timeline.

ANATOMY OF THE TIMELINE

- **Track Size control:** Click to switch among the four track display sizes in the Timeline.

- **Current Timecode field:** This field displays the timecode at the current position of the playhead. You can enter a time in the display to jump the playhead to that point in the clip. This display/control operates like the Current Timecode boxes in the Viewer and the Canvas.

- **Timeline ruler:** This displays the timecode for the current sequence and sequence In and Out points. Edit-point overlays are displayed along the ruler. Adjust the ruler's time scale with the Zoom slider or the Zoom control.

- **Render status bars:** Two render status bars indicate which parts of the sequence have been rendered. The upper bar is for video tracks, and the lower bar is for audio tracks. Red bars indicate material that requires rendering to be played back. Gray bars indicate material that does not require rendering. A blue-gray bar indicates material that has already been rendered. On real-time capable systems, a green status bar indicates that the material can be played back in real time, and yellow indicates real-time play back with a proxy (lower-quality) version of the material.

Figure 9.26 Detail of the center section of the Timeline.

◆ **Clips:** You can display clips as solid bars or as video frames. Clips that have clip visibility turned off appear dimmed in the Timeline. Clips on locked tracks are crosshatched in the Timeline. Clips with a speed change applied display the current speed setting.

◆ **Zoom control:** Click to jump between different time scale views.

◆ **Zoom slider:** Use this slider to scroll through your sequence and to adjust the time scale of your view.

◆ **Playhead:** The playhead reflects the chronological position in the sequence of the frame displayed in the Canvas. The playhead in the Timeline always moves in tandem with the Canvas playhead.

◆ **Vertical scroll bars:** This two-part scroll bar allows the video and audio tracks to scroll independently. Adjust the thumb tabs between the scroll controls to create a static area in the center of the Timeline.

◆ **Out-of-Sync indicators:** This display indicates the number of frames by which a clip's video and audio tracks are out of sync.

◆ **Link indicators:** Linked clips display in the Timeline with underlined names. When a linked clip is selected, moved, or trimmed, items linked to it are affected in the same way. Linked selections can be switched on and off as a sequence preference.

continues on next page

Figure 9.27 Detail of the right side of the Timeline.

ANATOMY OF THE TIMELINE

◆ **Stereo Pair indicators:** These indicators appear as two triangles. These two audio clips are linked as a stereo pair.

◆ **Linked selection control:** The Linked selection indicator controls whether linked selection is active or disabled. Note: This control toggles the Linked selection feature, not Link/Unlink. One click on this tiny icon does not permanently unlink the linked clips in your sequence. You typically disable linked selection to select just the audio or video track of a linked AV clip—to adjust a split edit in a sync sequence, for example.

◆ **Snapping control:** Click to toggle snapping on and off.

Color coding in the Timeline

Final Cut Express uses a color coding system to identify the various clip and sequence types found in the Timeline. **Table 9.1** lists the file types and their colors.

Table 9.1

Color Coding in the Timeline	
COLOR	ITEM
Purple	Video sequences
Cyan	Video clips
Aquamarine	Video graphics
Green	Audio clips
Light green	Audio sequences
White	Offline video or audio clips

Figure 9.28 Choose Sequence > Settings to open the Sequence Settings window.

Figure 9.29 Select a name display option from the Thumbnail Display pop-up menu.

Customizing Timeline Display Options

Every sequence is different, which is why you can customize Timeline display options for each one—perhaps you don't need to see thumbnails in a complicated sequence, or maybe it's easier to edit a short montage using larger tracks. These display settings are modified in the Sequence Settings window. Your custom display settings will apply only to the currently open sequence; if you want the same appearance every time you create a new sequence, you can specify your preferred Timeline display setup on the Timeline Options tab of the Preferences window. For preferences setting details, see Chapter 2, "Installing and Setting Up."

To set clip display mode on video tracks for the current sequence:

1. Make the Timeline active; then choose Sequence > Settings (**Figure 9.28**).

2. From the Thumbnail Display pop-up menu, select from three thumbnail display options (**Figure 9.29**):

   ◆ Name displays the name of the clip with no thumbnail images.

   ◆ Name Plus Thumbnail displays the first frame of every clip as a thumbnail image and then the name of the clip.

   ◆ Filmstrip displays as many successive thumbnail images as possible for the current zoom level of the Timeline.

3. Click OK.

To show or hide audio waveforms for the current sequence:

1. In the Sequence Settings window, click the Show Audio Waveforms box to toggle the display of waveforms in the Timeline (**Figure 9.30**).

2. Click OK.

To set the track display size:

1. In the Sequence Settings window, choose a size (Reduced, Small, Medium, or Large) from the Track Size pop-up menu.

2. Click OK.

✔ Tips

■ The Timeline's audio waveform display is really useful for tweaking your audio edits, but Timeline display performance suffers when waveforms are displayed. If you want to quickly look at the waveforms without taking a trip to the Sequence Settings window, press Command-Option-W.

■ It's easier to change the track size by clicking one of the four size option icons on the Track Size control, located in the lower-left corner of the Timeline (**Figure 9.31**).

To customize your default Timeline display settings:

1. Choose Final Cut Express > Preferences.

2. In the Preferences window, click the Timeline Options tab.

3. On the Timeline Options tab, set your preferred display options (**Figure 9.32**). Your custom Timeline display settings will be the defaults for subsequent new sequences.

Figure 9.30 In the Sequence settings window, check the Show Audio Waveforms to toggle display of waveforms in the Timeline.

Figure 9.31 Select from the four track display sizes by clicking one of the icons in the Track Size control.

Figure 9.32 Set your preferred default Timeline display options on the Timeline Options tab of the Preferences window.

CUSTOMIZING TIMELINE DISPLAY OPTIONS

Figure 9.33 Click and drag a thumb control of the Zoom slider to adjust the scale of your Timeline view.

Figure 9.34 Click the Zoom control to jump to a new time scale.

Timeline scaling and scrolling

Final Cut Express has state-of-the-art Zoom features and scroll bars. The time scale in the Timeline is continuously variable; you can transition smoothly from viewing several minutes of your sequence down to a single frame. The horizontal scroll bar—the Zoom slider—is a combination Zoom and scroll control. The Zoom control is handy—you can jump to any time scale with a single mouse click.

The vertical scroll bar separating the video and audio tracks allows you to set a static area in the center of the Timeline window, so your base tracks are always in view.

To adjust the time scale of the Timeline display:

Do one of the following:

◆ The thumb controls are the ribbed-looking ends of the Zoom slider. Click a thumb control and drag it to shrink the time scale and expose more of your sequence (**Figure 9.33**). Shift-click and drag to adjust both ends of your view simultaneously.

◆ Click the Zoom control to the left of the Zoom slider to jump to a different time scale (**Figure 9.34**).

To zoom the view of the Timeline:

1. From the Tool palette, select the Zoom In or the Zoom Out tool (**Figure 9.35**); or press Z.

2. Click in the Timeline or drag a marquee around the section you want to display (**Figure 9.36**).

Or do one of the following:

◆ Use a keyboard shortcut. (See Appendix B for a complete list of shortcuts.)

◆ Choose View > Zoom In (or Zoom Out).

✔ Tips

■ When the Timeline is zoomed in or out to the maximum, the plus sign (+) or minus sign (–) disappears from the Zoom tool's pointer.

■ Pressing Option while using the Zoom In tool toggles it to Zoom Out.

Figure 9.35 Click the Zoom In tool to select it from the Tool palette.

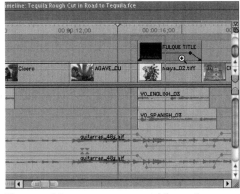

Figure 9.36 Drag a marquee around the section you want to zoom in on.

Best Zoom Shortcuts

Final Cut Express has a jillion ways to zoom and scroll program windows. Which shortcuts are most useful in the Timeline?

◆ **Option-+ (plus) / Option- – (minus):** This keyboard combo zooms the Timeline even if the Canvas is currently selected, and it keeps the selected clip (or the playhead, if no clip is selected) centered in the Timeline as it scales. This shortcut is the best way to zoom in and out of the Timeline.

◆ **Command-+ (plus) / Command- – (minus):** This shortcut works like Option plus and minus, but it zooms the selected program window.

◆ **Shift-Z:** This key combination adjusts the time scale to fit the entire sequence in the Timeline window.

◆ **Shift-Page Up / Shift-Page Down:** This shortcut scrolls the Timeline one full length of the Timeline window at the current scale.

CUSTOMIZING TIMELINE DISPLAY OPTIONS

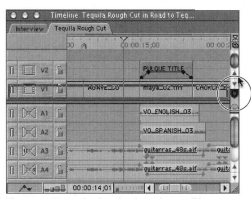

Figure 9.37 Drag the thumb tab up the scroll bar to create a static display area for a video track in the Timeline.

Figure 9.38 Drag the thumb tab down the scroll bar to create a static display area for an audio track in the Timeline.

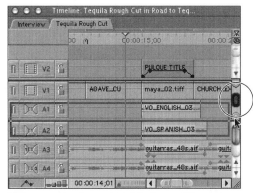

Figure 9.39 Use the center tab in the scroll bar to move the static display area up or down the Timeline display.

To scroll through your sequence:

◆ Drag the Zoom slider across the scroll bar.

To set up the vertical scroll bars:

1. In the Timeline, click and hold the uppermost thumb tab near the center of the vertical scroll bar. Drag the thumb tab up the scroll bar to create a static area for as many video tracks as you want to keep in constant view (**Figure 9.37**).

   You can use the upper scroll bar to scroll through higher video tracks in the upper portion of the Timeline window.

2. Click and hold the lowest thumb tab in the vertical scroll bar. Drag the thumb tab down the scroll bar, creating a static area for as many audio tracks as you want to keep in constant view (**Figure 9.38**).

   You can use the lower scroll bar to scroll through additional audio tracks in the lower portion of the Timeline window.

3. Once you have set up your static view area, use the center tab on the scroll bar to move the static area up or down in the window (**Figure 9.39**).

CUSTOMIZING TIMELINE DISPLAY OPTIONS

Navigating in the Timeline

Many of the tasks described here can be accomplished with the help of keyboard shortcuts. Final Cut Express has an army of key commands; many professional editors prefer a keyboard-intensive working style. This section demonstrates some other ways to approach the Timeline interface because, frankly, keystrokes don't make good illustrations. Check out the keyboard shortcuts in Appendix B. Before you flip to the back of the book, though, consider the alternatives in this section. You keyboard diehards might find something here you actually like.

✔ Tips

■ Use the "gear-down dragging" option to make precision adjustments to clips, levels, or edits in the Timeline—hold down the Command key while dragging an item.

■ You can use the playhead's locator line to help identify the exact timecode location of an item way down at the bottom of the Timeline window. Set the playhead's locator line on the point you want to identify, and the Current Timecode display will give you its exact timecode location.

Figure 9.40 Drag the playhead along the Timeline ruler to scrub through your sequence.

Figure 9.41 Click a point in the Timeline ruler to jump the playhead to that location.

Positioning the playhead in a sequence

The playhead in the Timeline can be positioned by the same methods as the Canvas and the Viewer playheads.

The playhead sits on the Timeline ruler and has a vertical locator line that extends down through the Timeline track display.

To scrub through a sequence in the Timeline:

◆ Drag the playhead along the Timeline ruler (**Figure 9.40**).

To jump the playhead to a new location:

◆ Click the location on the Timeline ruler to move the playhead to that location (**Figure 9.41**).

Navigating with timecode in the Timeline

Just as in the Viewer, using timecode values to position the playhead in the Timeline and the Canvas will result in frame-accurate positioning. Final Cut Express's timecode input function is very flexible (see "FCE Protocol: Entering Timecode Numbers" in Chapter 7 for protocol and entry shortcuts).

NAVIGATING IN THE TIMELINE

To navigate using timecode values:

1. Start in the Timeline. Make sure all clips are deselected, or you'll move the selected clip and not the playhead.

2. Enter a new timecode number or use the shorthand methods detailed in Chapter 7. You don't need to click in the field to begin entering a new timecode; just type the numbers (**Figure 9.42**).

3. Press Enter.

   The playhead moves to the new timecode value, and the new timecode position displays in the Current Timecode field in the lower-left corner of the Timeline (**Figure 9.43**).

To jump the playhead from edit to edit:

Do one of the following:

◆ Press the Up Arrow key (for the previous edit) or the Down Arrow key (for the next edit).

◆ In the Canvas, click the Previous Edit button or the Next Edit button.

◆ Choose Mark > Previous (or Next) > Edit.

◆ Press Option-E (for the previous edit) or Shift-E (for the next edit).

The playhead jumps to the first frame of the clip. If you've enabled Show Overlays on the View menu, an L-shaped icon appears in the lower left or right of the Canvas window, indicating that you are on the first or last frame of the sequence clip (**Figure 9.44**).

Figure 9.42 Typing +4.00 to move the playhead 4 seconds later in the sequence.

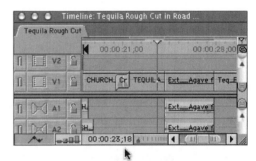

Figure 9.43 The playhead is repositioned 4 seconds later in the sequence.

Figure 9.44 An L-shaped icon in the lower left of the Canvas indicates the first frame of a clip after an edit point.

NAVIGATING IN THE TIMELINE

Figure 9.45 The Timeline with snapping turned on. The current position indicator displays arrows to show that it has snapped to an edit.

Figure 9.46 You can activate Timeline snapping by clicking the Snapping control on the right side of the Timeline. The control turns green when snapping is enabled.

Figure 9.47 Snapping a clip to an edit point. You can toggle Timeline snapping even in mid-edit by pressing N at any time.

About snapping in the Timeline

Snapping is an interface state that makes certain points in the Timeline "sticky." With snapping turned on, the edges of clips will snap together, or a clip will snap to an edit point on an adjacent track when dragged close to it. The playhead snaps to edits, clip and sequence markers, and keyframes (if displayed) on all visible tracks. If you drag the playhead across the Timeline ruler, it snaps to items in the Timeline when it encounters them. A small arrow appears above or below the edit, marker, or keyframe, showing you what the playhead has snapped to (**Figure 9.45**).

To turn snapping on or off:

Do one of the following:

◆ Choose View > Snapping.

◆ Click the Snapping control located in the upper right corner of the Timeline window (**Figure 9.46**).

To toggle snapping on or off on the fly:

◆ Press N; then drag the playhead, or your selected clip, to the new location (**Figure 9.47**).

Snapping remains in the toggled state until you press the N key again. Snapping can be toggled at any time, even in mid-edit.

Using markers in the Timeline and the Canvas

Final Cut Express has two types of markers:

♦ Clip markers appear on individual clips in the Timeline.

♦ Sequence markers appear on the Timeline ruler.

If you open a Timeline clip in the Viewer, the clip markers appear in the Viewer Scrubber bar.

You can learn more about working with markers in Chapter 7, "Working with Clips in the Viewer."

To set a sequence marker:

1. In the Timeline, position the playhead at the point where you want to set the marker. Make sure no clips are selected at the playhead's location.

2. Press M.

   A sequence marker appears in the Canvas scrubber and on the Timeline ruler.

✔ Tips

■ You can set a sequence marker only if no clips are selected at the playhead position in the Timeline. With a selected Timeline clip under the playhead, your marker will be set as a clip marker on that clip.

■ You can delete sequence markers only if no clips are selected in the Timeline.

■ Any two adjacent sequence markers can be used to locate sequence In and Out points. Just position your Timeline playhead anywhere between the two markers you want to use and choose Mark > Mark to Markers; or press Control-A.

Figure 9.48 Choosing a marker from the Timeline ruler's shortcut menu.

Figure 9.49 Selecting the marker jumps the playhead to that marker's location.

To position the playhead on a specific sequence marker:

◆ Control-click the Timeline ruler; then choose a marker from the list of sequence markers in the shortcut menu (**Figure 9.48**).

The playhead jumps to the selected marker's position (**Figure 9.49**).

To jump the playhead to the next or the previous sequence marker:

Do one of the following:

◆ Choose Mark > Previous (or Next) > Marker.

◆ Press Option-M for the previous marker.

◆ Press Shift-M for the next marker.

These are the same commands you use to locate clip markers in the Viewer; when you use them in the Canvas or the Timeline, FCE looks for sequence markers only, unless you have selected a Timeline clip. With a Timeline clip selected, these commands will locate both clip and sequence markers in the selected clip.

To position the playhead on a specific Timeline clip marker:

◆ In the Timeline, Control-click the clip; then choose a marker from the list of clip markers in the shortcut menu (**Figure 9.50**).

The playhead jumps to the selected marker's position.

✔ Tip

■ Say you have a specific phrase in the middle of a narration track that you'd like to align with an action in your video track. You can place a clip marker in the audio track and a sequence marker in the video clip at a key point; then, grab the audio clip by its marker and drag it to align it to your video clip marker (**Figure 9.51**). This procedure works best with snapping enabled.

Figure 9.50 Selecting a clip marker from a Timeline clip's shortcut menu jumps the playhead to that marker's location.

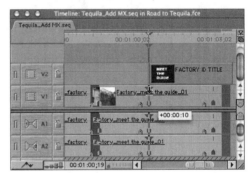

Figure 9.51 You can grab a Timeline clip by its marker and drag it to align it to another marker or to an edit point.

Figure 9.52 A sequence in the Timeline. Note the open space above the last video track.

Figure 9.53 Adding a new video track to the sequence. The location specified is after the last track.

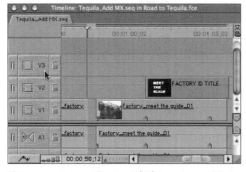

Figure 9.54 A new video track (V3) have been added at the specified location above V2.

Working with Timeline Tracks

Editing operations in Final Cut Express frequently involve configuring tracks. Timeline tracks can be locked, unlocked, targeted, added, deleted, and made visible or invisible. There is a difference between tracks and the contents of tracks. The procedures described in this section affect whole tracks. To learn about editing procedures that affect individual sequence clips, edit points, and keyframes, see "Working with Items in the Timeline," later in this chapter.

To add tracks to a sequence:

1. Open the sequence in the Timeline (**Figure 9.52**).

2. Choose Sequence > Insert Tracks.

3. In the Insert Tracks dialog box, enter the number of new video or audio tracks. Final Cut Express supports up to 99 tracks for video and 99 tracks for audio. (Select the appropriate checkbox if the Insert field is inactive.)

4. Select from options for inserting tracks:
   - Choose Before Base Track to insert your tracks before the first track in the Timeline.
   - Choose After Target Track or After Last Target Track to insert your tracks after the current target track for video or after the last target track for audio in the Timeline.
   - Choose After Last Track to insert your tracks after the last track in the Timeline (**Figure 9.53**).

5. Click OK to insert the tracks.
   The new tracks are added at the specified location (**Figure 9.54**).

To add a track to a sequence quickly:

Do one of the following:

◆ Drag a clip to the area above the top video track or below the bottom audio track (**Figure 9.55**).

A new track will be added to the sequence automatically (**Figure 9.56**).

◆ Control-click anywhere on the track header; then choose Add Track from the shortcut menu.

To delete a single track from a sequence:

◆ Control-click anywhere on the track header; then choose Delete Track from the shortcut menu (**Figure 9.57**).

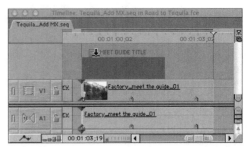

Figure 9.55 Drag and drop a clip in the area above the top video track.

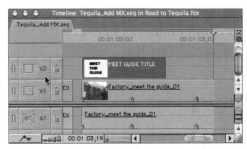

Figure 9.56 A new track is created automatically, and the clip is added to the sequence.

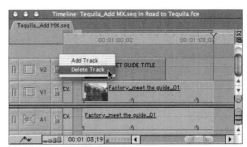

Figure 9.57 In the Timeline, delete a track by Control-clicking the track's header and then choosing Delete Track from the shortcut menu.

WORKING WITH TIMELINE TRACKS

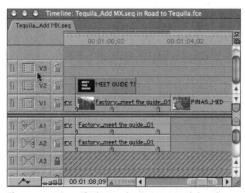

Figure 9.58 Specify the track you want to delete by making it the target track; then choose Sequence > Delete Tracks.

Figure 9.59 Select Current Target Track from the options in the Delete Tracks dialog box.

Figure 9.60 The target track is deleted from the sequence.

To delete multiple tracks from a sequence:

1. Open the sequence in the Timeline. To delete a specific track, make that track the target track (**Figure 9.58**).

2. Choose Sequence > Delete Tracks.

3. In the Delete Tracks dialog box, select from options for deleting tracks:
   - ◆ As needed, click the Video Tracks and Audio Tracks check boxes to select track types.
   - ◆ Choose Current Target Track to delete the current target track in the Timeline (**Figure 9.59**).
   - ◆ Choose All Empty Tracks to delete every empty track in the Timeline.
   - ◆ Choose All Empty Tracks at End of Sequence to delete all empty tracks after the last track used in the Timeline.

4. Click OK to delete the tracks.

   The selected track is deleted from the sequence; remaining tracks are renumbered consecutively (**Figure 9.60**).

WORKING WITH TIMELINE TRACKS

To lock a Timeline track:

Do one of the following:

◆ In the Timeline, click the Track Lock control on the left side of the track. Click again to unlock the track (**Figure 9.61**).

◆ To lock an audio track, press F4 plus the track number of the track you are locking.

◆ To lock a video track, press F5 plus the track number of the track you are locking.

To lock all Timeline video tracks:

◆ To lock all video tracks in the sequence, press Shift-F5.

To lock all Timeline audio tracks:

◆ To lock all audio tracks in the sequence, press Shift-F4.

✔ Tip

■ Option-click a Track Lock control to toggle locking on all other audio or video tracks except the selected track.

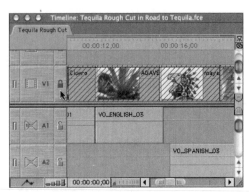

Figure 9.61 Lock a Timeline track by clicking the Track Lock control. Click again to unlock the track.

FCE Protocol: Lock vs. Target

One of the tasks when learning a new program is getting in sync with the logic behind the program design. If you are coming to Final Cut Express from another editing system, there are probably a few things that FCE does differently. Understanding the difference between locking and targeting is important to your editing happiness, so let's get this straight.

Locking a track keeps it out of trouble. So unless you're working on a particular track, you might as well keep it locked so that your editing operations don't have unforeseen consequences, like trimming or moving tracks that are stacked above or below the base tracks, out of your Timeline view (spooky music here). You have to take the responsibility for locking tracks because FCE defaults to unlocked tracks (unlike other editing systems, which may disable tracks by default until you enable them).

Lock 'em. Just do it. You're welcome.

Even if you've selected a specific edit on one track with the selection tool, any unlocked track is capable of responding to changes you make to that edit. If you have locked all the tracks that you don't want cut or moved, this capability is a great thing. For example, you can make multi-track cuts, moves, and lifts to dialogue tracks or multicamera sync setups and leave your locked music track right where it is.

Target track controls are a scheme for mapping each source clip to its proper Timeline track. Even though you don't always need to specify a target track to perform an edit, it's a good habit to check your target assignments whenever you perform an edit.

FCE also uses targeting as a way to specify the track when you perform a specific operation. For example, you target a track when you are getting ready to delete it.

Making a Timeline track invisible

You can temporarily hide a track by making it invisible so that the contents of that track do not appear in the sequence when you play it back. This is useful when you tweak multilayered composited sequences.

You can also single out a track by making all of the other tracks in the sequence invisible. This allows you to focus on the contents of a single track temporarily. You can single out video and audio tracks independently.

Note that changing the visibility of a track will cause a loss of any render files associated with the track. A warning dialog box appears when you attempt to change visibility on a track.

If you've invested a lot of rendering in a sequence, you can use a couple of workarounds to avoid re-rendering just because you turned a track off for a moment:

◆ You don't need to turn off the entire track. You can make an individual clip invisible by Control-clicking the clip in the Timeline and unchecking Clip Visibility in the shortcut menu. If you are interested in a short section of your sequence, you can turn off just the clips you want to hide, and you'll sacrifice only the render file for that clip, preserving your render files for the rest of the sequence.

◆ Undo and Redo might work. FCE has many layers of undo, and if you haven't been messing around too much in the interim, you can revert to the state before the render file loss.

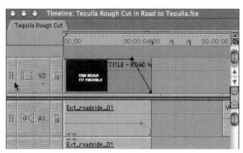

Figure 9.62 Click the Track Visibility control to make a track invisible.

Figure 9.63 If making a track invisible will cause a loss of render files, you'll see this warning.

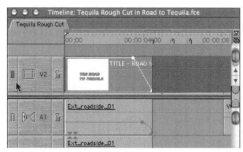

Figure 9.64 The invisible track will be excluded from playback.

Figure 9.65 Audio track A1 will play back alone. All other audio tracks are muted.

To make a track invisible:

1. In the Timeline, click the Track Visibility control at the far left of the track you want to affect (**Figure 9.62**).

2. If the sequence has been rendered, a dialog box will appear warning you about impending loss of render files (**Figure 9.63**). If you don't need your render files click Continue.

3. The track is made invisible (**Figure 9.64**). The Render status bar updates to show which sections of your sequence have been altered and may require re-rendering.

✔ Tips

■ You can still edit invisible tracks. Lock invisible tracks if you don't want them to respond to edits.

■ Next time you build a sequence involving multiple takes or a multicamera shoot, try loading your synchronized clips into tracks above and below the base layer (V1 and A1 to A2), keeping the base layer clear to assemble your cut. You can turn on single tracks for viewing and then copy and paste your selections into the base layers.

To single out a track for visibility:

Do one of the following:

◆ Option-click the Track Visibility icon.

◆ Select items in the track, then choose Sequence > Solo Item(s); or press Control-S.

The contents of all of the video or the audio tracks except the selected one are dimmed in the Timeline, and are hidden from view in the Canvas (**Figure 9.65**).

WORKING WITH TIMELINE TRACKS

Working with Items in the Timeline

This section covers Timeline editing procedures that affect individual sequence clips, edit points, and keyframes. Manipulation of Timeline items makes extensive use of the tools available in the Tool palette. Final Cut Express boasts some great selection tools, but very few keyboard equivalents. If you haven't used the Tool palette yet, review "Anatomy of the Tool Palette" earlier in this chapter.

Selecting items in the Timeline

All of the selection tasks described here use tools from the Tool palette.

Items you can select in the Timeline:

◆ **Clips,** including multiple clips or ranges of clips

◆ **Transitions,** which can then be trimmed or deleted

◆ **Edits,** which can then be modified in several ways

◆ **Gaps,** which can be closed or filled with media

Items you cannot select in the Timeline:

◆ **Overlay keyframes:** You can move these in the Timeline by dragging them.

◆ **Tracks:** You can't select a track, but the contents of a track can be selected.

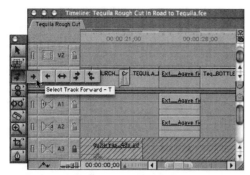

Figure 9.66 Choose the Select Track Forward tool from the Tool Palette.

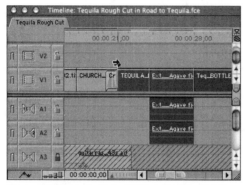

Figure 9.67 Using the Select Forward tool to click the first clip on any track to be included in the selection.

Selecting items with the track selection tools

The track selection tools offer a variety of ways to select the contents of one or more tracks. Don't forget: If you select an item that you've included in a linked selection, all the items involved in that linked selection will be affected by whatever operation you're about to perform.

✔ Tip

- Deselect an individual Timeline item from a group selection by Command-clicking the item.

To select all items on a single track:

◆ From the Tool palette, choose the Select Track tool and click anywhere in the track.

To select all items on a single track forward or backward from the selected point:

1. From the Tool palette, choose the Select Track Forward or the Select Track Backward tool (**Figure 9.66**).

2. In the Timeline track, click the first clip to include in the selection.

   That entire selected clip plus all the items in front of it or behind it are selected (**Figure 9.67**).

To select all items on all tracks forward or backward from the selected point:

1. From the Tool palette, choose the All Tracks Forward or the All Tracks Backward tool (**Figure 9.68**).

2. In the Timeline, click the first clip on any track that should be included in the selection.

   The contents of all tracks from that point forward or backward are selected.

Figure 9.68 Choose the All Tracks Forward tool from the Tool Palette to select clips on all tracks forward from the selection point.

✔ Tips

- The Track Forward and Track Backward tools select entire clips only; they do not make range selections.

- When you have one of the Select All Tracks tools active, you can quickly switch to the corresponding Select Track tool by holding down the Shift key.

To select an entire clip:

1. From the Tool palette, choose the Selection tool; or press A.

2. In the Timeline, use the Selection tool to click the clip you want to select.

   The Canvas indicates the selection by displaying a cyan border around the video of the selected clip.

To select part of a clip or a larger selection including partial clips:

1. From the Tool palette, choose the Range Selection tool (**Figure 9.69**).

2. In the Timeline, drag a marquee around the range to select it (**Figure 9.70**).

   A two-up display in the Canvas shows the first and last frames of your selection.

Figure 9.69 Choose the Range Selection tool from the Tool palette.

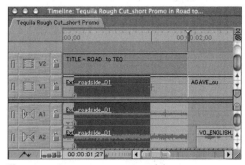

Figure 9.70 Drag a marquee around the range you want to select. You can select partial clips with this tool.

Figure 9.71 Choose the Group Selection tool from the Tool palette.

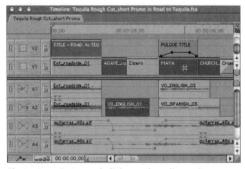

Figure 9.72 Command-click to select discontinuous clips in the Timeline or to deselect an individual clip from a group selection.

Figure 9.73 Set a sequence Out point in the Canvas.

To select multiple whole clips:

1. From the Tool palette, choose the Group Selection tool (**Figure 9.71**).

2. In the Timeline, drag a marquee around all the clips you want to select. You don't need to include the entire clip; any clip you touch will be included in its entirety.

To select multiple noncontiguous clips:

1. From the Tool palette, choose the appropriate selection tool.

2. In the Timeline, Command-click the items you want to select (**Figure 9.72**). Command-click again on a selected item to deselect it.

To select all items between the In and Out points:

1. Set the sequence In and Out points in the Timeline or in the Canvas (**Figure 9.73**).

2. In the Timeline, specify the target tracks (**Figure 9.74**).

3. Choose Mark > Select In to Out; or press Option-A.

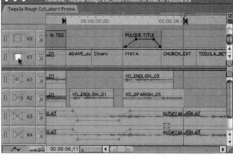

Figure 9.74 Click to turn on the Target Track control for the track where you want to make the selection.

To set In and Out points around a selected part of a sequence:

1. From the Tool palette, choose the Range Selection tool. If your desired selection is composed of whole clips, use the Group Selection tool.

2. In the Timeline, drag a marquee around the range you want to select.

3. Choose Mark > Mark Selection; or press Shift-A.

   The bounds of the selection become the sequence In and Out points (**Figure 9.75**).

To set In and Out points at two markers:

1. Position the Timeline playhead anywhere between the two markers you want to use.

2. Choose Mark > Mark to Markers; or press Control-A.

   Sequence In and Out points are now set at the markers' Timeline locations.

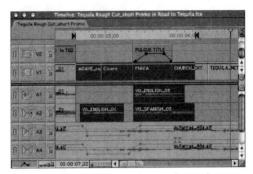

Figure 9.75 The boundaries of your selection become the sequence In and Out points.

WORKING WITH ITEMS IN THE TIMELINE

Figure 9.76 Select the sequence clips you want to link in the Timeline.

Linking clips

Linking clips is Final Cut Express's scheme for grouping clips. When clips are linked, any action performed on one clip affects the other clips as well. Check out the sidebar, "FCE Protocol: Linked Clips," later in this chapter for the rules governing linked clips and the operation of linked selections.

To link a group of unrelated clips:

1. In the Timeline, select the clips you want to link (**Figure 9.76**).

   You can select one video and up to two audio clips from different tracks.

2. Choose Modify > Link; or press Command-L.

   In the Timeline, an underline appears under the linked clips' names indicating their linked status.

To permanently unlink a group of linked clips:

1. Select an item.

2. Choose Modify > Link; or press Command-L.

   In the Timeline, the underline under the linked clips' names disappears, indicating their unlinked status.

Using linked selection

You can temporarily override the rules that govern a linked clip's selection. Editors frequently disable linked selection to select just the video (or just the audio) track of a linked clip, in order to create a *split edit* (that's an edit where a clip's audio and video tracks have different lengths).

You can disable linked selection for the entire sequence or for a single selection operation.

To turn linked selection on or off:

Do one of the following:

◆ Click the Linked Selection control on the right side of the Timeline window. (**Figure 9.77**).

◆ Choose Sequence > Linked Selection.

◆ Press Shift-L to toggle linked selection on and off.

To select an item without selecting any items that are linked to it:

◆ Hold down the Option key when you select the item.

Figure 9.77 Activate linked selection by clicking the Linked Selection control. The control turns green when linked selection is enabled.

FCE Protocol: Linked Clips

Here is how Final Cut Express handles linked clips:

◆ Video and audio clips that originated from the same media file are linked automatically.

◆ You can set up multiple linked clip groups.

◆ You can switch linked selection on or off.

◆ When linked selection is turned on, FCE treats your linked items as a single entity for most operations.

◆ If you switch linked selection off, all your linked items will be treated as if they were unlinked, with the following exception: Audio and video clips that were captured in sync continue to reference each other even when linked selection is disabled and will display out-of-sync indicators if moved out of sync with each other.

◆ Locking a track overrides a linked selection. If a linked item is on a locked track, it won't be modified, even if you modify an item it's linked to.

◆ Moving a linked clip's video to a higher track (for example, from track V1 to track V2) will automatically move the clip's audio to higher-numbered audio tracks (for example, from tracks A1 and A2 to tracks A3 and A4).

Figure 9.78 Dragging a clip to a new location. The pop-up indicator shows the offset from the clip's original location.

Figure 9.79 Dropping the clip performs an Overwrite edit in the new location.

Figure 9.80 Hold down the Shift key while dragging the clip from V1 to V2. The selection pointer has changed to a down-pointing arrow, indicating that an Overwrite edit will be performed when you drop the clip.

Moving Timeline clips

As with most things in Final Cut Express, you have a choice of methods for moving clips within and between sequences. There are a variety of drag-and-drop methods, plus the timecode entry method, which offers greater precision and a little less flexibility.

To drag a clip to a new position:

1. In the Timeline, select the clip and drag it to a new position (**Figure 9.78**).

2. In the new position, *do one of the following*:
   - ◆ Drop the clip to perform an Overwrite edit (**Figure 9.79**).
   - ◆ Drop the clip while holding the Option key to perform an Insert edit.

To shift a clip to another track at the same timecode location:

1. In the Timeline, select the clip you want to move.

2. Hold down the Shift key while dragging the clip vertically to another track (**Figure 9.80**).

   The clip maintains its timecode position at the new track location.

To copy a clip to a new location:

1. In the Timeline, select the clip you want to move.

2. Hold down the Option key while dragging the clip to another location (**Figure 9.81**).

   A copy of the selected clip is edited into the new location.

✔ Tips

- You can make copies of sequence clips by dragging them from the Timeline into the Browser. Drag multiple clips to make a copy of each clip. Remember that this clip copy will include any changes you have made to the clip in the sequence.

- A quick way to make a Browser copy of every clip you've used in a sequence is to select the entire sequence in the Timeline (Command-A) and then drag the clips over to a Browser bin. Don't worry about wiping out your sequence—remember, you're making copies.

To copy and paste a clip into the Timeline:

1. In the Timeline, select the clip (**Figure 9.82**); or use the Group Selection tool from the Tool palette to select clips from multiple tracks.

2. Cut or copy the selected material to the clipboard.

3. Target the destination track, and position the playhead where you want to paste the clip (**Figure 9.83**).

Figure 9.81 Press the Option key as you start to drag to copy the clip from V1 to V2. Continue pressing Option as you drop the clip copy to perform an Insert edit; or release the key before you drop to perform an Overwrite edit.

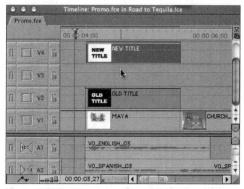

Figure 9.82 Select the clip you want to copy and paste.

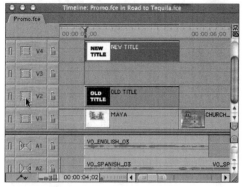

Figure 9.83 Position the playhead where you want the pasted clip to start; then target the track you want to paste into.

WORKING WITH ITEMS IN THE TIMELINE

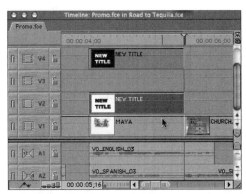

Figure 9.84 The pasted clip overwrites the contents of the target track.

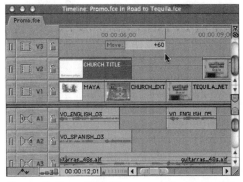

Figure 9.85 Type +60 and then press Enter to reposition the clip 60 frames (2 seconds) later in the sequence.

4. Choose Edit > Paste; or press Command-V.

The pasted material overwrites the sequence clips, starting at the playhead location in the target track and extending for the duration of the pasted material (**Figure 9.84**).

✔ Tip

■ Press Shift-V to insert-edit the pasted material in the new sequence location.

To reposition an item in the Timeline by entering a timecode:

1. In the Timeline, select the clip you want to move.

2. Enter a new timecode number; or use the shorthand methods detailed in Chapter 7, "Working with Clips in the Viewer."

As you type, a text entry window appears below the Timeline ruler (**Figure 9.85**).

3. Press Enter.

The clip is repositioned, if there is space at the new timecode location.

If an edit tool had been selected from the Tool palette before timecode entry, the edit is performed in the direction indicated by the timecode.

WORKING WITH ITEMS IN THE TIMELINE

Finding and closing gaps

As you assemble a sequence, all that cutting and pasting and slipping and sliding may create gaps in your sequence tracks. Sometimes the gaps are too small to see in the Timeline, but a gap of even a single frame is easily detectable in Canvas playback.

This section contains a repertoire of techniques for detecting and closing gaps and explains FCE protocol for defining gaps.

To find gaps in a sequence:

1. Make the sequence active; then press the Home key to position the playhead at the beginning of the sequence (**Figure 9.86**).

2. Choose Mark > Next > Gap; or press Shift-G.

   The playhead moves to the beginning of the first gap found (**Figure 9.87**).

3. If you want to close the gap, use one of the procedures described in the next section, "To close a gap."

4. Repeat steps 2 and 3 until you reach the end of the sequence.

✔ Tip

■ Press Option-G to jump the playhead back to the previous gap.

Figure 9.86 Pressing the Home key positions the playhead at the beginning of the sequence.

Figure 9.87 The playhead jumps to the start of the first gap found.

FCE Protocol: Gaps and Track Gaps

Final Cut Express defines two classes of gaps: gaps and track gaps.

◆ A gap is any empty spot across all unlocked video or audio tracks.

◆ A track gap is any empty spot on an individual track in a sequence; if you have a gap on one track, but a clip bridges the gap on a higher or lower track, FCE defines that as a track gap.

Some gap-closing techniques, such as Ripple Delete, work only with gaps, not track gaps. To close track gaps, lock all other tracks, leaving the gapped tracks as the only unlocked tracks in your sequence.

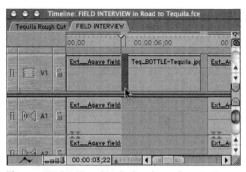

Figure 9.88 Position the playhead anywhere in the gap you want to close.

Figure 9.89 Control-click the gap; then choose Close Gap from the shortcut menu.

Figure 9.90 Clips to the right of the gap shift left to close the gap.

To close a gap:

1. Make the sequence active; then position the playhead anywhere in the gap (**Figure 9.88**).

2. *Do one of the following:*
   - Select the gap and press Delete.
   - Control-click the gap; then select Close Gap from the shortcut menu (**Figure 9.89**).
   - Choose Sequence > Close Gap.

   Clips to the right of the gap will shift left to close the gap. These clips adjust their timecode location to occur earlier, and the sequence duration may change (**Figure 9.90**).

✔ Tips

- When you fine-tune gaps in sequences, take advantage of the Zoom tools to scale your view so you can see what you're doing. You may also find that turning on snapping will simplify selection and manipulation of gaps and track gaps.

- You can get a quick reading of the duration of a gap by Control-clicking the gap and then choosing Fill with Slug from the shortcut menu. Now you can Control-click the slug, and the duration will appear in the shortcut menu. When you're done, just select the slug and press Delete—your gap's back, and you can decide what to do next.

To find track gaps in a Timeline track:

1. In the Timeline, click the Target Track control of the track you want to search to make it the target track (**Figure 9.91**).

2. Press the Home key to position the playhead at the beginning of the sequence.

3. Choose Mark > Next > Track Gap.

   The playhead moves to the beginning of the first track gap found (**Figure 9.92**).

To close a track gap:

Do one of the following:

◆ Open the shortcut menu over the gap and choose Close Gap (**Figure 9.93**).

◆ Select the gap and press the Delete key.

◆ Position the playhead anywhere within the gap; then choose Sequence > Close Gap.

✔ Tip

■ Sometimes a gap can't be closed because clips don't have space to shift back. If the command can't be completed, the Close Gap command is dimmed. Try the track locking technique discussed next.

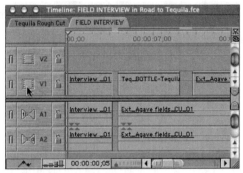

Figure 9.91 To select a track to search for track gaps, click to turn on the Target Track control.

Figure 9.92 The playhead jumps to the start of the first track gap found.

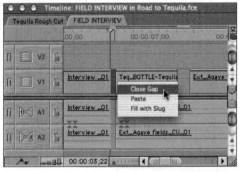

Figure 9.93 Control-click the track gap; then choose Close Gap from the shortcut menu.

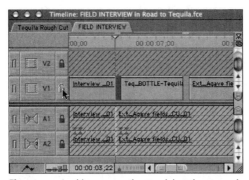

Figure 9.94 Locking every other track but the gapped track allows you to close the gap by shifting material on the unlocked track only.

Figure 9.95 Control-click the gap; then choose Close Gap from the shortcut menu.

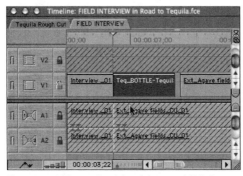

Figure 9.96 Clips to the right of the gap shift left to close the track gap. Clips on the locked tracks have not moved.

To close a track gap without affecting other tracks in a sequence:

1. Press Shift-F4 to lock all video tracks in your sequence.

2. Press Shift-F5 to lock all audio tracks in your sequence.

3. Click the Track Lock control of the gapped track.

   Your selected track is now the only unlocked track in the sequence (**Figure 9.94**).

4. *Do one of the following:*
   - ◆ Select the gap and press Delete.
   - ◆ Control-click the gap; then select Close Gap from the shortcut menu (**Figure 9.95**).
   - ◆ Choose Sequence > Close Gap.

   Clips to the right of the gap will shift left to close the gap. These clips adjust their timecode locations to occur earlier, and the sequence duration may change (**Figure 9.96**).

5. If you want to unlock your sequence tracks after closing the gap, press Shift- F4 and Shift-F5 again to toggle track locking off.

WORKING WITH ITEMS IN THE TIMELINE

To close a track gap with the Select Forward tool:

1. Snapping must be on; if necessary, choose View > Snapping to turn it on.

2. From the Tool palette, choose the Select Track Forward tool; then click the first clip to the right of the track gap (**Figure 9.97**).

   The clips to the right of the sequence are selected, and the cursor changes to a four-headed arrow pointer.

3. Drag the selected clips to the left until they snap to close the gap; then drop them as an Overwrite edit (**Figure 9.98**).

To close a gap by extending an adjacent clip (an Extend edit):

◆ In some cases, you may prefer to close a gap in a sequence by extending the duration of a clip that's adjacent to the gap. One advantage of an Extend edit is that all the clips in your sequence can stay put, and you won't develop sync problems. To learn how to perform an Extend edit, see Chapter 10, "Fine Cut: Trimming Edits."

Figure 9.97 Use the Select Track Forward tool to click the first clip to the right of the track gap.

Figure 9.98 Drag the selected clips to the left until they snap to close the gap; then drop them as an Overwrite edit.

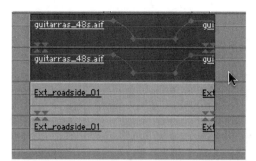

Figure 9.99 Select the clip whose attributes you want to copy; then press Command-C.

Figure 9.100 Selecting audio levels in the Paste Attributes dialog box.

Copying and pasting clip attributes

A clip's *attributes* comprise the settings applied to a particular media file in Final Cut Express. You can paste all the attributes of one clip onto another clip, or you can select and paste some of the settings of a clip onto another clip without affecting other attributes. For example, you can apply just the filter settings from clip A to clip B without changing the video frames of clip B. Conversely, you can replace the video frames of clip B without disturbing the filters that have been applied to it by pasting only the video frames from another clip. If you just paste into a sequence without selecting a clip in the Timeline or the Canvas, the clip's media contents and selected attributes are included.

The Remove Attributes command is an easy way to strip selected settings from a clip or to remove selected settings from multiple clips in a single operation.

To paste the attributes of a copied clip into another clip:

1. In the Timeline or the Browser, select a clip whose attributes you want to copy (**Figure 9.99**); then press Command-C to copy it to the clipboard.

2. Select the clip that will inherit the attributes; then choose Edit > Paste Attributes.

3. In the Paste Attributes dialog box, select the attributes that you want to transfer to the selected clip (**Figure 9.100**).

    Scale Attribute Times: Check this box to adjust the timing of the incoming keyframes to fit the duration of the clip inheriting the attributes. If this option is not selected, leftover keyframes will be cropped off the end.

continues on next page

Video Attributes: Check this box if you want to paste any video attributes from the following list:

- ◆ **Content:** Paste the video frames only. If the receiving clip is a different length, incoming video frames are cropped or lengthened to match the duration of the receiving clip. The clip speed is not affected.

- ◆ **Basic Motion, Crop, Distort, Opacity, Drop Shadow, Motion Blur,** and **Filters:** You can pick and choose among these options to apply the parameter values and keyframes you have set for each attribute.

- ◆ **Speed:** Apply the same speed settings.

- ◆ **Clip Settings:** Paste all capture settings that are logged with a clip. (You can review these settings on the Clip Settings tab of the Log and Capture window.)

Audio Attributes: Check this box if you want to paste any of the audio attributes from the following list:

- ◆ **Content:** Paste the audio waveform only. If the receiving clip is a different length, the incoming audio file is cropped or lengthened to match the duration of the receiving clip. The clip speed is not affected.

- ◆ **Levels, Pan,** and **Filters:** Apply the parameter values and keyframes you have set for each attribute.

4. Click OK.

The selected attributes are pasted into the receiving clip (**Figure 9.101**).

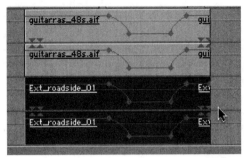

Figure 9.101 The audio levels from Voiceover Subclip 1 have been copied and pasted into Voiceover Subclip 2.

✔ Tip

- ■ Pasting audio levels can be a quick way to add an audio element—say, another sound effects track—to a scene you have already mixed. You can "borrow" the mix levels from a track that has already been adjusted to match action and paste those levels onto your new effects track. You can apply the same idea to video compositing: Paste the motion path from one video layer to another that you want to track the same path; or, paste and then offset the timing of the motion path.

Figure 9.102 Check the attributes you want to remove; then click OK.

Figure 9.103 Selecting multiple audio clips with the Select Track Forward tool.

Figure 9.104 Adjusting the audio levels relative to their current levels.

To remove attributes from a clip:

1. In the Timeline, select the clip or clips whose attributes you want to remove.

2. Choose Edit > Remove Attributes.

3. In the Remove Attributes dialog box, check the attributes you want to remove (**Figure 9.102**); then click OK.

Making multiclip adjustments

Two commands in the Modify menu allow adjustments on multiclip selections:

◆ Use Modify > Levels to adjust levels for a group of audio clips.

◆ Use Modify > Opacity to adjust opacity levels for a group of video clips.

To adjust audio levels for a group of clips:

1. In the Timeline, select a group of audio clips whose levels you want to adjust (**Figure 9.103**).

2. Choose Modify > Levels.

3. In the Gain Adjust dialog box, *do one of the following:*

   ◆ Choose Relative from the pop-up menu; then use the slider to adjust each clip's volume relative to its current level by the dB value indicated next to the slider (**Figure 9.104**).

   ◆ Choose Absolute from the pop-up menu; then use the slider to set each clip's volume to the dB value indicated next to the slider.

4. Click OK.

✔ Tip

■ Use FCE's audio level meters to check your audio level adjustments. Choose Window > Audio Meters to display the meters.

To adjust opacity levels on a group of clips:

1. In the Timeline, select a group of clips whose levels you want to adjust.

2. Choose Modify > Levels.

3. In the Opacity Adjust dialog box, *do one of the following:*

   ◆ Choose Relative from the pop-up menu; then use the slider to adjust each clip's opacity relative to its current level by the percentage value indicated next to the slider.

   ◆ Choose Absolute from the pop-up menu; then use the slider to set each clip's volume to the percentage value indicated next to the slider (**Figure 9.105**).

4. Click OK.

Figure 9.105 Setting opacity levels to 80 percent for all selected clips.

Changing the playback speed of a clip

Changing the playback speed of a clip adjusts its duration by duplicating or skipping clip frames and creates either a slow-motion or a fast-motion effect. For example, if you start with a 1-minute clip and set the playback speed to 50 percent, Final Cut Express will duplicate each frame, doubling the clip length to 2 minutes. Your adjusted 2-minute clip will appear to play back at half speed. If you start with the same 1-minute clip and increase the playback speed to 200 percent, the adjusted clip will skip every other frame and appear to play back at double speed in 30 seconds. You can specify frame blending when modifying a clip's speed to smooth out the slow-motion or fast-motion effect. (Yes, adjusting the speed requires rendering before you can play back the clip.)

Figure 9.106 Select the clip in the Timeline.

Figure 9.107 Modify your clip's speed by a percentage or specify a duration; then click OK.

Figure 9.108 The size of the clip's icon increases to reflect the duration change caused by modifying the playback speed, and the adjusted speed appears next to the clip's name. You must render the clip to review the speed change.

To change the playback speed of a clip:

1. Select the clip in the Timeline (**Figure 9.106**).

2. Choose Modify > Speed; or press Command-J.

3. Choose from the options in the Speed dialog box:
   - ◆ You can modify the clip speed by a percentage or specify a duration for the adjusted clip. Changing the clip speed or duration automatically adjusts the other value.
   - ◆ The Frame Blending option smoothes motion at slow or fast speeds.
   - ◆ The Reverse check box renders the clip's frames in reverse order; the adjusted clip plays in reverse.

4. Click OK (**Figure 9.107**).
   The adjusted duration of the modified clip will be calculated based on the clip's original In and Out points (**Figure 9.108**).

✔ Tip

- ■ If you want to apply speed effects to only a portion of a clip, first use the Razor Blade tool to break out the portion of the clip that you want to process. Speed effects can be applied only to whole clips.

WORKING WITH ITEMS IN THE TIMELINE

Working with Keyframes in the Timeline

Keyframes indicate that effects parameters are changing over time. Think of a keyframe as a kind of edit point: You stamp a keyframe at the point where you want to change the value of an effect's parameter. This section covers Timeline functions relating to keyframes.

Final Cut Express has two types of keyframes:

♦ **Keyframe overlays** indicate clip opacity for video clips and volume level for audio clips. Keyframe overlays are displayed as line graphs right on top of the track display in the Timeline (**Figure 9.109**).

♦ **Motion Effect Keyframes** appear in the Canvas (or Viewer). You can view, add or modify motion keyframes only when the window is in Image+Wireframe mode. (**Figure 9.110**). Working with keyframes to create motion effects in the Canvas is covered in Chapter 14, "Motion."

✔ Tip

■ The Pen tool selects only keyframes, so it's the best tool to use if you need to adjust a keyframe overlay near an edit point—for example, when you fine-tune a fade.

Figure 9.109 Keyframe overlays allow you to sculpt audio levels right in the Timeline.

Figure 9.110 Apply keyframes to sculpt motion effects in the Canvas's Image+Wireframe mode. See Chapter 14, "Motion," for details.

WORKING WITH KEYFRAMES IN THE TIMELINE

Figure 9.111 Click the Clip Overlays control in the Timeline window to toggle the display of keyframe overlays.

Figure 9.112 Use the Pen tool to add a keyframe to a clip's keyframe overlay graph.

Figure 9.113 A tooltip displaying the current audio level updates as you adjust the keyframe.

To display keyframe overlays in the Timeline:

◆ In the Timeline, click the Clip Overlays control in the lower-left corner (**Figure 9.111**).

To add an overlay keyframe to a track:

1. From the Tool palette, select the Pen tool.

2. On the selected clip's overlay keyframe graph, click where you want to place the keyframe (**Figure 9.112**).

   A new keyframe is added to the overlay.

✔ Tip

■ Did you just add one keyframe too many? Press Option, and your Pen tool toggles to Pen Delete mode. Click on that extra keyframe to delete it; then release the Option key.

To adjust the values of individual overlay keyframes:

Do one of the following:

◆ Click and drag overlay keyframes vertically to adjust their values. As you drag, a tooltip appears, displaying the parameter's value (**Figure 9.113**).

◆ Shift-drag the graph line between two overlay keyframes to adjust its position.

To delete overlay keyframes:

◆ Drag keyframes off the track completely to delete them.

◆ With the Pen Tool selected, press the Option key to toggle to the Pen's Delete mode. Click the keyframe you want to delete.

   The keyframes (except for the last one) are removed, and the keyframe path adjusts to reflect the change.

Searching for Items in the Timeline

The Final Cut Express search engine is built to search for other items beyond clips and sequences. Use FCE's Find command to search the Timeline for clip names, marker text, and clip timecodes. You can search for items forward or backward. You can also search for and close gaps in all tracks in a sequence or in individual tracks.

Figure 9.114 Position the playhead at the beginning of the section you want to search.

✔ Tip

- This might be a good time to mention that when you place a clip in a sequence, the new sequence clip is a separate version from the one that stays in the Browser, even though the two clips may have the same name. So if you are searching for the sequence version of a clip, you need to search in that sequence.

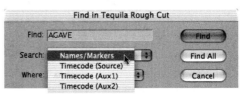

Figure 9.115 Specifying a search for clips or markers with "agave" in their names.

To search for items in the sequence:

1. Open the sequence in the Timeline.

2. *Do one of the following:*
   - ◆ To search the entire sequence, position the playhead at the start of the sequence.
   - ◆ To search a selected portion of the sequence, set the sequence In and Out points to specify the search area; or position the playhead at the beginning of the section you want to search (**Figure 9.114**).

3. Choose Edit > Find; or press Command-F.

4. From the Search pop-up menu, choose the type of item to search for (**Figure 9.115**):
   - ◆ **Names/Markers:** Search for the text in clip names, marker names, and marker comments.
   - ◆ **Timecode Options:** Search for any source or auxiliary timecode in a clip.

Figure 9.116 Specifying a search of the sequence from the sequence In to the sequence Out point.

Figure 9.117 Specifying Find All causes FCE to highlight all clips in the sequence that match the search criteria.

Figure 9.118 Three clips whose names contain the phrase "agave" are highlighted in the Timeline. Only the section between the sequence In and Out points has been searched.

5. Choose which tracks to search from the Where pop-up menu:
   - **All Tracks:** Search all tracks in the sequence.
   - **Target Tracks:** Search only the current target tracks.
   - **From In to Out:** Search between the sequence In and Out points on all tracks (**Figure 9.116**).

6. To perform the search, *do one of the following:*
   - Click Find to find the item.
   - Click Find All to find all occurrences of clips that match the search criteria (**Figure 9.117**).

   All clips that match the search criteria are selected in the Timeline (**Figure 9.118**). If the search returns a marker, the playhead is positioned on the marker.

To cycle through items in the Timeline that match the criteria:

- Follow the search procedure outlined in the preceding steps; then press F3.

To search for an item backward from the position of the playhead:

- Follow the search procedure outlined in the preceding steps; then press Shift-F3.

FINE CUT: TRIMMING EDITS

What's the difference between performing an edit and trimming an edit? An edit adds new material to a sequence; a trim adjusts previously assembled sequence material. The development of nonlinear editing has expanded the repertoire of trim edit types. Some trim edit types (like Ripple and Roll) date back to the tape-to-tape days of video editing; others (like the Slide edit) could not have existed before the advent of non-linear systems.

In this chapter, you'll learn about the types of trim edits available in Final Cut Express. Each can be performed in a variety of ways (with tools, with timecode entry, or with keystrokes) and in a few different locations (the Timeline, the Trim Edit window, and the Viewer), so you'll learn how and where you can perform each type. This chapter also introduces the Trim Edit window, a specialized work environment for making fine adjustments to your edits.

Note that when editors talk about performing certain types of edits, the edit type is used as a verb, as in, "Roll that cut forward 30 frames." That's easier to say than, "Perform a Roll edit on that edit point which will move the edit point forward 30 frames." In the editing suite, time is money.

Types of Trimming Operations

Each trim edit type can solve a particular editing problem, so it's a good idea to become familiar with the whole palette—maybe even try them all in advance. (If you would like to review FCE's basic editing types, return to Chapter 8, "Basic Editing.")

Figure 10.1 A Ripple Left edit, as performed in the Timeline.

◆ **Ripple:** A Ripple edit adjusts the length of one clip in a sequence by changing either the In or the Out point of that clip. A Ripple edit accommodates the change by rippling (or shifting) the timecode location of the clips that come after the adjusted edit without affecting their duration. Use a Ripple edit if you want to adjust the length of a clip in a sequence without losing sync or creating a gap. Locked tracks will not be rippled. As an example, the Close Gap command in the Timeline performs a Ripple Delete edit.

Figure 10.1 shows a Ripple Left edit, in contrast to **Figure 10.2**, which shows a Ripple Right edit. Note the differences in the cursor and in the selected edit points.

Figure 10.2 A Ripple Right edit, as performed in the Timeline.

◆ **Roll:** A Roll edit (**Figure 10.3**) adjusts the location of an edit point shared by two clips. A rolling edit makes the change by subtracting frames from clip A on one side of the edit to compensate for the frames added to clip B on the other side of the edit. The overall duration of the sequence remains unchanged, but the location of the edit in the sequence is changed.

Figure 10.3 A Roll edit, as performed in the Timeline.

◆ **Slip:** A Slip edit (**Figure 10.4**) is an adjustment made within a single clip. When you slip a clip, you select a different part of that clip to include in the sequence, while maintaining the same clip duration and timecode location in the sequence. Surrounding clips are not affected, and the sequence duration does not change.

Figure 10.4 A Slip edit, as performed in the Timeline. The selected portion of the clip has shifted –14 frames.

Figure 10.5 A Slide edit, as performed in the Timeline. The selected clip has slid 1 second, 1 frame earlier in the sequence.

Figure 10.6 A Swap edit, as performed in the Timeline. The two clips will swap positions.

Figure 10.7 An Extend edit. Select the edit point of the clip you want to extend to the playhead position.

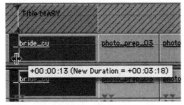

Figure 10.8 Resizing a clip in the Timeline. Drag an edit point with the Selection tool to adjust clip duration.

◆ **Slide:** A Slide edit (**Figure 10.5**) moves a single clip in relation to those before and after it, so that the durations of the clips on either side change, but the In and Out points of the clip you're sliding remain the same. The clips immediately adjacent to the sliding clip accommodate the change; the overall sequence duration does not change.

◆ **Swap:** A Swap edit (**Figure 10.6**) doesn't alter any sequence clips, but it does change the order in which they appear in the sequence. Perform a Swap edit in the Timeline by selecting a clip, dragging it to a new location, and placing it into the sequence using an Insert edit.

◆ **Extend:** An Extend edit (**Figure 10.7**) moves a selected edit point to the playhead position by extending the clip's duration, rolling over any gaps or clips that are encountered. You can extend an edit only to the maximum length of that clip's media. An Extend edit is a useful way to fill sequence gaps without affecting the sequence duration.

◆ **Resize:** The Selection (or Arrow) tool can be used to resize a clip in the Timeline by dragging an edit point. You can drag the edit point to create a gap (by making the duration of the clip smaller; **Figure 10.8**) or to cover an existing gap.

✔ Tip

■ Press the Command key to "gear down" the onscreen tools while performing fine adjustments to a trim. With the Command key engaged, your manipulation of the onscreen trim tools will result in much smaller adjustments to your edit points.

Selecting an Edit for Trimming

The first step in trimming an edit in the Trim Edit window or the Timeline is selecting the edit. If you use a trimming tool from the Tool palette to select the edit, you can select and define the type of trim to perform at the same time. You can select only one edit per track.

If an edit point you select for trimming has been linked to others, the edit points of the linked items are also selected. Any adjustments you make will be applied to all clips in the linked selection, so if you find that you can't trim an edit point, the conflict may be with one of the linked items. You can toggle linked selection off by holding down the Option key as you select the edit.

With snapping turned on, edit points will stick to markers, keyframes, the playhead, and edit points on other tracks. Snapping can simplify alignment of edits in the Timeline. To toggle snapping on the fly, press the N key while dragging edit points.

✔ Tips

- Many trim operations will ripple all of your unlocked tracks as part of the trim process. If you don't want your tracks taking unplanned trips when you are trimming, lock all tracks except the ones you want to adjust.

- If FCE refuses to execute a trim edit that would ripple your unlocked tracks backward, check to see if clips on other tracks in your sequence can't move back in time without bumping into other clips.

Tips on Tools

FCE's edit tools get a heavy workout when you transform your rough assembly into a fine cut. You can review the contents of the Tool palette's selection and edit tools in "Anatomy of the Tool Palette" in Chapter 9, but here are some other ideas for making efficient use of these tools:

- Use the keyboard shortcuts to call up an edit tool. See **Table 10.1** for a list of basic selection shortcuts. Check out Appendix B for more shortcuts.

- Once you've selected an edit tool, press U to cycle through the three principal trim types: Roll, Ripple Left, and Ripple Right.

- You can use the Ripple and Roll tools to directly select the edit you're adjusting. With one click, you've selected the edit and specified the edit type.

- Pressing the Option key to override linked selection works on all edit tools, not just the Selection arrow.

- Pressing the Command key while dragging an edit tool on a selected edit in the Timeline will "gear down" the tool and allow you to make fine adjustments.

- Turn off Snapping to make fine adjustments that don't align with an existing edit point, marker, or clip boundary.

- Turn on Snapping to align an edit to another existing edit point or marker.

Figure 10.9 Choose the Edits Selection tool from the Tool palette. This tool is designed to detect and select edits only.

Table 10.1

Tool Selection Shortcuts	
TOOL	SHORTCUT
Roll Edit	R
Ripple Edit	R+R
Slip Item	S
Slide Item	S+S
Razor Blade	B
Razor Blade All	B+B
Selection	A
Edit Selection	G

To select an edit in the Timeline:

Do one of the following:

◆ From the Tool palette, choose the Edits Selection tool (**Figure 10.9**); or press G. Then click an edit point in the Timeline. The Trim Edit window opens.

◆ From the Tool palette, choose the Selection tool; then click the edge of the clip in the Timeline. Double-click the edit if you want the Trim Edit window to open as well.

◆ From the Tool palette, choose the Ripple tool or the Roll tool; then click the edge of the clip in the Timeline.

◆ Press V to select the edit point nearest the playhead's location.

✔ Tips

■ If you are having trouble selecting Timeline edit points, use the Zoom slider to magnify your view, or try again with the Ripple tool or the Roll tool; they're designed to select edit points only, so you can't accidentally select a clip.

■ Using the Option key to override linked selection works with any edit tool, just as it does with the Selection tool.

Quick Navigation Keys

Option and Shift modifier keys are used throughout FCE's keyboard shortcuts for navigation. Here's a set of keyboard shortcuts to help you motor through your sequence while you fine-tune your edit.

KEY	SHIFT + KEY	OPTION + KEY	NO MODIFIER
I	Go to In	Clear In	Set In
O	Go to Out	Clear Out	Set Out
M	Next Marker	Previous Marker	Set Marker
E	Next Edit	Previous Edit	Extend Edit
G	Next Gap	Previous Gap	
K	Next Keyframe	Previous Keyframe	

To select multiple edits in the Timeline:

Do one of the following:

- From the Tool palette, choose the Edits Selection tool; then draw a marquee around the edit points of one or more Timeline tracks (**Figure 10.10**). You can select one edit per track; the selected edits don't have to be aligned in time.

  The Trim Edit window opens as you release the mouse button.

- From the Tool palette, choose the Selection tool; then Command-click the edge of the clips in the Timeline. Double-click any selected edit if you want the Trim Edit window to open as well.

- From the Tool palette, choose the Ripple tool or the Roll tool; then Command-click the edge of the clips in the Timeline.

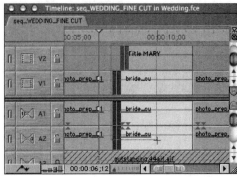

Figure 10.10 Draw a marquee around edit points you want to select.

All Keys: Mouseless Trimming in FCE

You can work your way through your edit without touching the mouse. Here's one possible scenario:

1. Press Shift-E to jump the playhead to the next edit in the Timeline.

2. Press V to select the nearest edit.

3. Press \ (backslash) to play the sequence before and after the selected edit point.

4. Press R to select the Roll tool.

5. Press + (plus) or – (minus) and then enter a number of frames to roll the edit.

So many keyboard shortcuts in FCE—and so many ways to speed your work while you give your mouse hand a rest. To learn more, check out the Keyboard shortcuts in Appendix B.

Anatomy of the Trim Edit Window

The Trim Edit window is a work environment optimized for making fine adjustments to a single edit point. You can trim the selected edit by one frame or several frames, quickly switch between Ripple and Roll edits, and play back the edit to review your trim adjustments. The Play Around Edit button is designed to loop playback of your edit while you fine-tune it. The looping is not seamless, though; there is a slight interruption in the playback when you nudge the edit point.

Figure 10.11 shows an overview of the Trim Edit window.

- ◆ **Outgoing clip name:** Displays the name of the outgoing clip.

- ◆ **Outgoing clip duration:** Displays the elapsed time between the In and Out points of the outgoing clip. This value updates to reflect trim adjustments.

- ◆ **Outgoing clip current timecode:** Displays the clip's source timecode at the current position of the playhead.

continues on next page

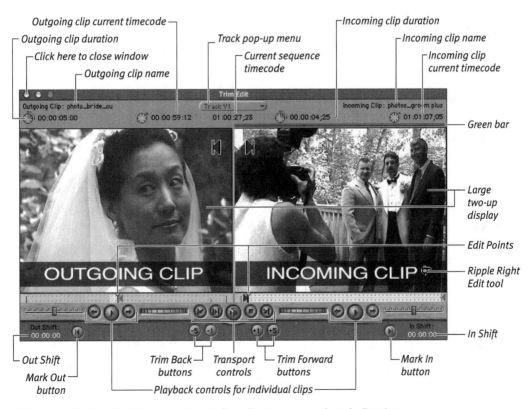

Figure 10.11 Use the Trim Edit window to make fine adjustments to a selected edit point.

◆ **Track pop-up menu:** Displays a list if multiple edits have been selected. Select the track you want to edit in the Trim Edit window.

◆ **Current sequence timecode:** Displays the sequence timecode location of the edit point. Enter + or – and a duration to roll the edit point. You don't need to click the field; just start typing.

◆ **Incoming clip current timecode:** Displays the clip's source timecode at the current position of the playhead.

◆ **Incoming clip duration:** Displays the elapsed time between the In and Out points of the incoming clip. This value updates to reflect trim adjustments.

◆ **Incoming clip name:** Displays the name of the incoming clip.

◆ **Large two-up display:** The left screen displays the last frame before the edit. The right screen displays the first frame after the edit.

◆ **Green bar:** Indicates which side of the edit you are trimming.

◆ **Edit points:** Indicate the current Out and In points for the two clips in the Trim edit window. You can trim by dragging the outgoing clip's Out point or the incoming clip's In point with an edit tool.

◆ **Playback controls for individual clips:** The outgoing and incoming clips have separate playback controls. Use these controls to play only that clip without changing the current edit point location.

◆ **Out Shift:** Indicates the number of frames that the Out point has been adjusted.

◆ **Mark Out button:** Click to set a new Out point for the outgoing clip at the current playhead position.

Play In to
Out button

Stop
button

Previous
Edit button

Play Around
Edit Loop button

Next Edit
button

Figure 10.12 Trim Edit window transport controls detail.

◆ **Trim Back buttons:** Nudge the selected edit point to the left. Trim by single-frame increments or by another frame increment you specify on the General tab of FCE's Preferences window.

◆ **Trim Forward buttons:** Nudge the selected edit point to the right.

◆ **Mark In button:** Click to set a new In point for the incoming clip at the current playhead position.

◆ **In Shift:** Indicates the number of frames that the In point has been adjusted.

Figure 10.12 shows the Trim Edit window's transport controls.

◆ **Previous Edit button:** Click to move the previous edit into the active area of the Trim Edit window.

◆ **Play In to Out button:** Click to play from the start of the first clip to the end of the second clip.

◆ **Play Around Edit Loop button:** Click to loop playback of the edit point plus the specified pre-roll and post-roll. Playback loops until you click Stop. You can continue trimming the edit while playback is looping.

◆ **Stop button:** Click to stop playback and position the playhead on the edit point.

◆ **Next Edit button:** Click to move the next edit into the active area of the Trim Edit window.

ANATOMY OF THE TRIM EDIT WINDOW

Using the Trim Edit Window

The Trim Edit window offers plenty of flexibility to accommodate your editing style; you can mix and match trimming methods in a single trim operation. This window features two good-sized screens displaying the clips on either side of the edit you are adjusting, as well as Duration and Current Timecode displays for each side.

✔ Tip

■ If you're using Timecode entry in the Trim Edit window, you can cancel an edit by pressing the Esc key while the Timecode field is still active. You can also undo an edit at any time by pressing Command-Z.

FCE Protocol: Trimming Error Messages

When you attempt a trim operation that can't be executed, Final Cut Express will warn you by displaying one of the following error messages:

◆ **You cannot set the In point later than a disabled Out point:** When you're adjusting an In or Out point in the Trim Edit window, you can't position your clip's In point later than its Out point. Likewise, Out points cannot be placed before In points. The word *disabled* in the message refers to Trim Edit window protocol. Only the outgoing clip's Out point and the incoming clip's In point are active while you're in the Trim Edit window.

◆ **Clip collision:** A trimming operation would cause clips to collide or one clip to overwrite another. Specifies the track number where the error occurred.

◆ **Transition conflict:** A transition duration adjustment would be required to accommodate the trimming change. Specifies the track number where the error occurred.

◆ **Media limit:** The source clip does not include sufficient media to complete the edit as specified. Specifies the track number where the error occurred.

◆ **Insufficient content:** The same as the "Media limit" error; the source clip does not contain sufficient media to complete the edit.

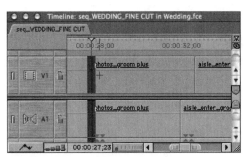

Figure 10.13 Click an edit point in the Timeline with the Edits Selection tool.

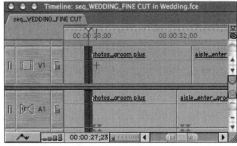

Figure 10.14 The Trim Edit window opens automatically.

Figure 10.15 Close the Trim Edit window by clicking the Close button in the upper-left corner.

To open the Trim Edit window:

Do one of the following:

◆ Press Command-7.

The playhead jumps to the closest edit on the target track, and the Trim Edit window opens with a Roll edit selected.

◆ In the Timeline, click an edit with the Edits Selection tool (**Figure 10.13**).

The edit is selected, and the Trim Edit window opens automatically (**Figure 10.14**).

◆ Choose Sequence > Trim Edit.

◆ In the Timeline, double-click an edit.

To close the Trim Edit window:

Do one of the following:

◆ Move the Timeline or the Canvas playhead away from the edit.

◆ Click anywhere in the Timeline away from an edit to deselect all edits in the Timeline.

◆ Click the close button in the upper-left corner of the Trim Edit window (**Figure 10.15**).

✔ Tip

■ All the plus and minus adjustments you make in the Trim Edit window refer to the location of the edit point, not the duration of either clip. That's especially important to remember when you're making adjustments on the right side of the edit point.

To trim an edit in the Trim Edit window:

1. Select one or more edit points to trim, using any of the methods described earlier in this section. Then, if the Trim Edit window has not opened automatically, press Command-7 to open the Trim Edit window.

2. In the Trim Edit window, select the type of trim operation by clicking in the appropriate image area (the pointer changes to indicate whether you've selected Ripple Left, Roll, or Ripple Right):

   ◆ Click the left image to trim the outgoing clip with a Ripple Left edit.

   ◆ Click the right image to trim the incoming clip with a Ripple Right edit (**Figure 10.16**).

   ◆ Click the area between the images to select a Roll edit.

   A green bar appears above the clip image, indicating that that side of the edit is selected for trimming.

3. Trim the edit using any of the following methods:

   ◆ Use the trim buttons to move the edit point to the left or right by frame increments (**Figure 10.17**).

   ◆ Trim the edit point by typing + or − and a duration to add or subtract. You don't need to click the field—just start typing and then press Enter. The type of trim performed depends on the edit selection you made in step 2.

   ◆ Click and drag an edit point in the Scrubber bar.

   ◆ Use the individual playback controls under either clip to play the clip; then mark a new Out point for the outgoing clip or a new In point for the incoming clip.

Figure 10.16 Click the image on the right in the Trim Edit window to select a Ripple Right edit.

Figure 10.17 Clicking this Trim Forward button moves the edit point to the right by single-frame increments.

Figure 10.18 Click the Play Around Edit Loop button to loop playback of your edit point plus the specified pre-roll and post-roll.

The In Shift and Out Shift fields update to show the total cumulative shift in the edit point. These fields will track the shift, even if you perform the trim as several small adjustments. The Timeline display updates to reflect your trim.

4. Use the transport controls to review your edit.

◆ Click the Play In to Out button to play from the start of the first clip to the end of the second clip.

◆ Click the Play Around Edit Loop button to loop playback of the edit point plus the specified pre-roll and post-roll (**Figure 10.18**).

◆ Click the Stop button to stop playback and position the playhead on the edit point.

5. When you finish trimming, close the Trim Edit window.

✔ Tips

■ You can use the Previous Edit and Next Edit buttons in the Trim Edit window to move to the next edit on the current track without leaving the Trim Edit window.

■ If you have selected multiple edits to trim, use the Track pop-up menu to select the track to view in the Trim Edit window.

USING THE TRIM EDIT WINDOW

To slip an edit in the Trim Edit window:

1. To open the Trim Edit window, select an edit in the Timeline with the Edits Selection tool (**Figure 10.19**); or press Command-7.

2. In the Trim Edit window, Shift-drag the active edit point on either Scrubber bar to slip that clip (**Figure 10.20**); or drag the edit point with the Slip tool.

   The Current Time display switches to show the adjusted timecode location for the edit point you are slipping.

3. Release the mouse button to complete the Slip edit.

   The Current Time display reverts to displaying the timecode location at the clip's current playhead position.

4. When you finish trimming, close the Trim Edit window.

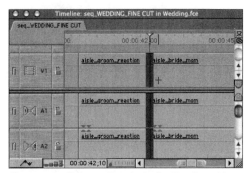

Figure 10.19 Click an edit point in the Timeline with the Edits Selection tool, and the Trim Edit window will open.

Figure 10.20 Shift-dragging an active edit point in the Trim Edit window slips the selected clip. During the slip, the display changes to show the new In and Out points.

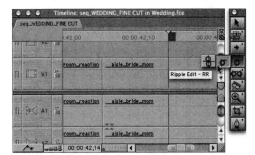

Figure 10.21 Choose the Ripple Edit tool from the Tool palette.

Figure 10.22 After selecting the edit you want to ripple, type + or – followed by the number of frames to add or subtract from the edit point.

Trimming Edits in the Timeline

The Timeline can be a good place to trim your sequence if you need to keep tabs on multiple tracks in relation to one another. You can perform all types of trim edits in the Timeline: Ripple, Roll, Slip, Slide, Extend, Swap, and Resize.

✔ Tip

- Set up your Timeline display to optimize the efficiency of your trim operation. Things to check include the time scale, track size, snapping, and vertical scroll bar setup. You'll find details on Timeline display options in Chapter 9, "Editing in the Timeline and the Canvas."

To perform a Ripple edit in the Timeline:

1. From the Tool palette, choose the Ripple Edit tool (**Figure 10.21**).

2. In the Timeline, select the edit by clicking near the edge of the clip.

   The selected side of the edit will be highlighted.

3. Ripple the edit using *one of the following methods:*

   ◆ Click and drag the edit to adjust the duration of the clip in the sequence.

   ◆ Type + or – followed by the number of frames to add or subtract from the current edit point (**Figure 10.22**); then press Enter.

TRIMMING EDITS IN THE TIMELINE

To perform a Ripple edit on multiple tracks simultaneously:

◆ Command-click to select multiple edit points; then use the Ripple Edit tool to perform the Ripple edit across all the tracks (**Figure 10.23**).

✔ Tip

■ Holding down the Shift key while you perform a trim toggles the cursor between the Ripple Edit and Roll Edit tools.

To perform a Roll edit in the Timeline:

1. From the Tool palette, choose the Roll Edit tool (**Figure 10.24**).

2. In the Timeline, select the edit point.

3. Roll the edit using *one of the following methods:*

   ◆ Click and drag in either direction. As you drag, the Canvas display changes to two smaller screens showing the Out point of the outgoing clip on the left and the In point of the incoming clip on the right (**Figure 10.25**).

   ◆ Type + or − followed by the number of frames to add or subtract from the current edit point; then press Enter.

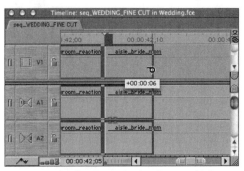

Figure 10.23 Performing a Ripple edit on multiple tracks in the Timeline.

Figure 10.24 Choose the Roll tool from the Tool palette.

Figure 10.25 During a Roll edit, the Canvas window converts to dual-screen mode, displaying the outgoing Out point on the left and the incoming In point on the right.

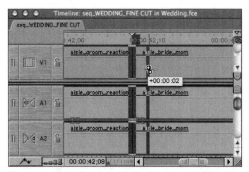

Figure 10.26 Performing a Roll edit across multiple tracks in the Timeline.

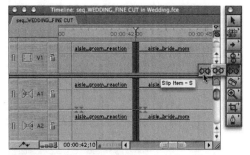

Figure 10.27 Choose the Slip Item tool from the Tool palette.

Figure 10.28 During the Slip edit, the Canvas window converts to dual-screen mode, displaying the In point frame on the left and the Out point frame on the right.

To roll multiple tracks simultaneously:

◆ Command-click to select multiple edit points; then use the Roll Edit tool to perform the Roll edit across all of the tracks (**Figure 10.26**).

✔ Tip

■ If you're still dragging but your Roll edit stops rolling, your clip has reached the end of the media.

To slip a clip in the Timeline:

1. In the Tool palette, choose the Slip Item tool (**Figure 10.27**).

2. In the Timeline, select the clip and drag it left or right. As you drag:

   ◆ An outline of the complete clip appears, indicating the amount of media available.

   ◆ The Canvas display changes to two smaller screens showing the In point frame on the left and the Out point frame on the right (**Figure 10.28**).

3. Release the mouse button when you have positioned the clip at its new location.

✔ Tip

■ Try turning off snapping in the Timeline before you slip your clip. Your clip will slip more smoothly.

TRIMMING EDITS IN THE TIMELINE

To slip a clip in the Timeline using numerical timecode entry:

1. Select the clip in the Timeline.

2. In the Tool palette, choose the Slip Item tool.

3. Type + or – and the number of frames to slip; then press Enter.

To slide a clip in the Timeline:

1. In the Tool palette, choose the Slide Item tool.

2. In the Timeline, select the entire clip (**Figure 10.29**) and drag it left or right. As you drag:

   ◆ An outline of the complete clip appears, indicating the amount of media available (**Figure 10.30**).

   ◆ The Canvas display changes to two smaller screens showing the Out point frame of the clip to the left of the sliding clip and the In point frame of the clip to the right of the sliding clip.

3. Release the mouse button when you have positioned the clip at its new location (**Figure 10.31**).

To slide a clip in the Timeline using numerical timecode entry:

1. In the Tool palette, choose the Slide Item tool.

2. Select the clip in the Timeline.

3. Type + or – and the number of frames to slide; then press Enter.

Figure 10.29 Select the clip with the Slide tool.

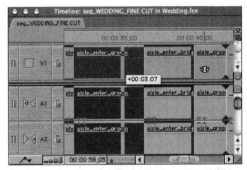

Figure 10.30 During the Slide edit, an outline of the complete clip appears in the Timeline, indicating the amount of media available outside the clip's edit points.

Figure 10.31 The clip in its new sequence location.

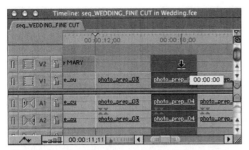

Figure 10.32 Drag the clip out of its sequence location.

Figure 10.33 Use snapping to help you line up the head of the clip you are moving with the edit point where you want to insert the clip.

Figure 10.34 As you drop the clip into the Timeline, the pointer changes to a curved arrow. Drop the clip at the insertion point.

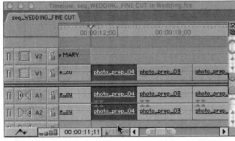

Figure 10.35 The inserted clip pushes the rest of the sequence clips down without altering any sequence durations.

To perform a Swap edit in the Timeline:

1. In the Timeline, select the clip you want to move.

2. Drag the clip out of the Timeline track (**Figure 10.32**).

3. Align the head of the selected clip with the head of the clip in the Timeline at the insert location (**Figure 10.33**); then press Option without releasing the mouse button.

   The pointer becomes a curved arrow.

4. Drop the selected clip at the insertion point you selected (**Figure 10.34**).

   The inserted clip swaps out with the sequence clip's position; no sequence clip durations are altered (**Figure 10.35**), but the order in which they appear has changed.

✔ Tips

- The Swap edit is one way to go if you want to preserve render files you've already created. The swapped clips don't change duration, and they maintain the linkage to their previously rendered files.

- You can perform Swap edits only with single clips.

To perform an Extend edit in the Timeline:

1. Check the Snapping control to make sure snapping is on. (An Extend edit is a little easier with snapping turned on.)

2. From the Tool palette, choose the Edits Selection tool (**Figure 10.36**).

3. In the Timeline, click the edit of the clip you want to extend (**Figure 10.37**).

4. Move the playhead to the position that the edit will extend to (**Figure 10.38**); then press E on your keyboard.

The clip with the selected edit extends to the playhead position. An Extend edit will overwrite any gaps or clips it encounters, up to the position of the playhead (**Figure 10.39**).

If there is not enough media to reach your selected playhead position, an "insufficient content for edit" error message appears, and the edit is canceled.

✔ Tip

■ Use an Extend edit to create a split edit on the fly. In the Timeline, select the edit you want to adjust by Option-clicking it; then, play back your sequence and press the E key when you see your new edit location. The edit point will move to the playhead's position at the moment you press E—if you have enough media in your clip to extend it to that point.

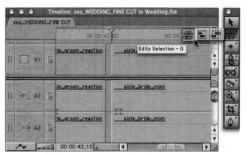

Figure 10.36 Choose the Edits Selection tool from the Tool palette.

Figure 10.37 Click the edit of the clip you want to extend.

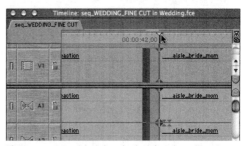

Figure 10.38 Position the playhead at the edit point on the other edge of the gap; then press E.

Figure 10.39 The clip on the left lengthens, extending to the playhead position and filling the gap.

TRIMMING EDITS IN THE TIMELINE

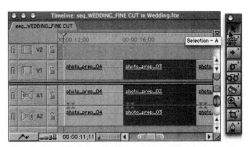

Figure 10.40 Choose the Selection tool from the Tool palette. The Selection arrow changes to a Resize pointer when you position it near an edit point.

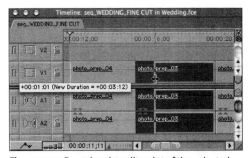

Figure 10.41 Dragging the edit point of the selected clip in the Timeline resizes the clip.

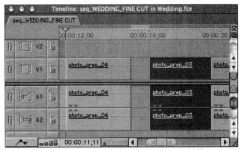

Figure 10.42 The clip, resized to a shorter duration, leaves a gap in its Timeline track.

To resize the duration of a clip in the Timeline:

1. In the Tool palette, choose the Selection tool (**Figure 10.40**).

2. In the Timeline, select an edit point and drag it (**Figure 10.41**).

    You can drag the edit point to create a gap (by making the duration of the clip shorter; **Figure 10.42**) or cover an existing gap (by making the duration of the clip longer).

To divide (razor-blade) a clip in the Timeline:

1. Set your target track to the one that contains the clip you want to divide (**Figure 10.43**).

2. In the Timeline, position the playhead at the point where you want to divide the clip (**Figure 10.44**); then press Control-V to add an edit point.

   The added edit point will create an additional clip that starts at the playhead position (**Figure 10.45**).

   Or, do this:

   Press B to select the Razor Blade tool; then click at the point where you want to divide the clip.

✔ Tips

- Both halves of a divided clip will have the same name as the original, so if you plan on keeping both of them around, you may want to give them new names that reflect their history as two halves of a bladed clip—for instance, bride_cu_1.1 and bride_cu_1.2.

- Use the Razor Blade All tool to divide clips on all Timeline tracks at the same point.

Figure 10.43 Target the track that contains the clip before you select its division point.

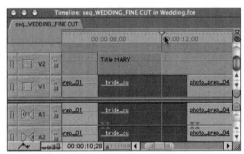

Figure 10.44 Position the playhead at the point where you want to divide the clip.

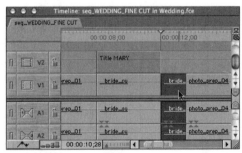

Figure 10.45 The clip divides at the playhead position. The added edit point creates an additional clip that starts at the playhead position.

Figure 10.46 Dragging the Out point with the Ripple Edit tool. The edit point will be rippled to the left.

Trimming Edits in the Viewer

You can perform four types of trim operations in the Viewer: Ripple, Roll, Slip, and Resize. Remember that you can perform trim operations only on sequence clips, so all of these trim operations require you to open the sequence clip in the Viewer by double-clicking it in the Timeline.

To perform a Ripple edit in the Viewer:

1. From the Tool palette, choose the Ripple Edit tool.

2. In the Timeline, double-click the clip to open it in the Viewer.

3. In the Viewer's Scrubber bar, drag either the In or the Out point to ripple the clip (**Figure 10.46**).

To perform a Roll edit in the Viewer:

1. From the Tool palette, choose the Roll Edit tool.

2. In the Timeline, double-click the clip to open it in the Viewer.

3. In the Viewer's Scrubber bar, drag either the In or the Out point to roll the edit.

   If you run out of media to accommodate the shift in your edit point, an overlay appears on the image in the Viewer warning you of a "media limit" error on the track that's run out of frames.

To slip a clip in the Viewer:

1. From the Tool palette, choose the Slip Item tool.

2. In the Timeline, double-click the clip to open it in the Viewer.

3. In the Viewer's Scrubber bar, drag either the In or the Out point to slip the clip.

   As you slip, the Viewer displays the first frame of the clip; the Canvas displays the last frame of the clip (**Figure 10.47**).

Figure 10.47 As you slip the edit, the Viewer displays the first frame of the clip, and the Canvas displays the last frame.

✔ Tip

■ You can also slip a clip in the Viewer by Shift-dragging either the In or the Out point with the Selection tool.

To resize a clip in the Viewer:

1. In the Tool palette, choose the Selection tool.

2. In the Timeline, double-click the clip to open it in the Viewer.

3. In the Viewer's Scrubber bar, drag either the In or the Out point to resize the clip (**Figure 10.48**).

   You can drag the edit point to create a gap (by decreasing the duration of the clip) or cover an existing gap (by increasing the duration of the clip).

Figure 10.48 Dragging the edit point in the Viewer's Scrubber bar resizes the selected clip.

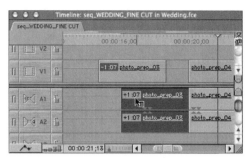

Figure 10.49 Control-click the out-of-sync indicator on the part of the clip you wish to reposition.

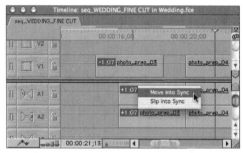

Figure 10.50 Choose Move into Sync from the shortcut menu.

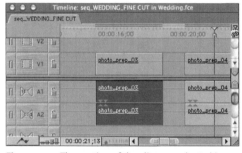

Figure 10.51 The portion of the clip you selected is repositioned in the Timeline so sync is corrected. Note that you can move a clip into sync only if there is a gap in the track to accommodate the move.

Correcting Out-of-Sync Clips

When you insert a sync clip into a sequence, the audio and video are automatically linked. That means you'll have to go out of your way to knock them out of sync, because linked items are selected and moved together. However, if you have turned linked selection off, it's possible to knock a sync clip out of sync.

Boxes appear on the clips that are out of sync. These indicators display the number of frames that the audio and video portions of the clip are out of sync in relation to each other.

Final Cut Express offers two options for correcting a sync problem:

◆ You can move a clip into sync, which repositions the selected portion of the clip so that the sync is corrected.

◆ You can slip a clip into sync, which corrects the sync problem by performing a Slip edit on the selected portion of the clip (keeping the clip in the same position and shifting the contents of the clip).

Occasionally, you'll want to move a clip out of sync intentionally—for example, when you combine the video from one take with substitute audio from another take.

You might want to mark the video and the substitute audio as being in sync. In that case, you can mark a clip as in sync if the sync does not need to be corrected and you don't want to be warned of a sync problem.

To move a clip into sync:

◆ In the Timeline, Control-click the out-of-sync indicator (the red box on the clip; **Figure 10.49**); then choose Move into Sync from the shortcut menu (**Figure 10.50**). The portion of the clip you selected is repositioned to correct the sync (**Figure 10.51**).

To slip a clip into sync:

◆ In the Timeline, Control-click the out-of-sync indicator (the red box) on the clip portion you want to slip into sync; then choose Slip into Sync from the shortcut menu (**Figure 10.52**).

To mark a clip as in sync:

◆ In the Timeline, select the audio and video clips you want to mark as in sync (**Figure 10.53**); then choose Modify > Mark in Sync.

The two selected clips are marked as in sync, without shifting their positions in the Timeline (**Figure 10.54**).

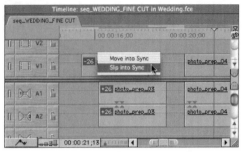

Figure 10.52 Control-click the out-of-sync indicator; then choose Slip into Sync from the shortcut menu.

Figure 10.53 Select the audio and video clips you want to mark as in sync.

Figure 10.54 The clips do not shift position, but are marked as in sync.

AUDIO TOOLS AND TECHNIQUES

11

The basic editing and finishing features in Final Cut Express operate in the same way for video or audio clips. This chapter covers the few tools and techniques unique to audio editing, audio effects, and mixing.

You can learn about other aspects of audio elsewhere in this book. Capturing audio is covered in Chapter 4, "Capturing Video." Steps for importing digital audio from CDs or other digital sources appear in Chapter 5, "Importing Digital Media Files," and exporting audio back to tape or to another digital format is covered in Chapter 18, "Creating Final Output." Also, rendering audio is explained in Chapter 17, "Rendering."

The FCE interface has four areas where you edit and finish audio.

◆ **The Audio tab in the Viewer:** The Audio tab displays audio-only clips, as well as the audio portion of audio+video clips. This is where you can audition and mark edit points in audio clips, and use keyframes to set audio level and pan or spread settings. The audio tab is the only place in FCE where you can get a large view of your audio clip's waveforms and make sub-frame adjustments to edit points.

◆ **The Audio tracks in the Timeline:** The Timeline is the only place where you can view all of your audio tracks at once. Turn on the Timeline's audio waveform display (it's off by default) and you can edit audio quite nicely; you can do everything from basic assembly to fine trimming. You can use keyframes to set and sculpt audio levels using the Timeline's clip overlays. Playback in the Audio tab and the Trim Edit window is independent of Timeline/Canvas playback, so the Timeline is the only place you can trim audio on the fly as you watch your sequence play back.

◆ **The Trim Edit window:** If the Trim Edit window displayed large-size waveforms as you fine-tuned your audio edits, it would be a great place to do fine dialogue or music cutting. Unfortunately, you can't see waveforms in this window, so it's not a top choice for tight audio editing.

◆ **The Voice Over tool:** FCE's audio recording tool can record multiple tracks of sync audio as FCE plays back a selected portion of your sequence. Sounds complicated, but it's easy to use and very useful.

Audio Tracks vs. Timeline Tracks

One small clarification: "audio track" is an old expression describing an audio recording, such as a soundtrack or an album track.

In Final Cut Express, "track" refers to an empty layer in the Timeline where you assemble video and audio clips, but not the clips themselves.

In an attempt to avoid confusion, this book uses the term *CD track* to refer to an audio recording on CD, *audio tracks* to refer to Timeline tracks that hold audio clips, *audio clips* to refer to the individual items you manipulate in FCE, and *audio files* to refer to the source media files those audio clips reference.

So—are we avoiding confusion yet?

Figure 11.1 Ch 1 + Ch 2 audio format appears in the Viewer with two Audio tabs. Each channel is distinct and can be independently adjusted.

Figure 11.2 The two audio channels that make up a stereo pair appear in a single Audio tab. Any adjustments made to one channel are automatically applied to both channels.

FCE's Audio Formats

In the audio world, "format" has entirely too many meanings.

There are media formats, such as DV, VHS, or DAT, which describe the media used to record the original audio. There are also digital audio file formats, such as AIF, MP3, or WAV.

And then there are the audio formats discussed here, which describe the structure of multiple channel audio recordings, such as stereo or mono. These audio formats apply to the audio captured with video, as well as to imported clips or audio-only clips captured with the Voice Over tool:

◆ **Ch 1 + Ch 2:** Both channels have been captured but are distinct and can be adjusted independently of one another. Two audio tabs appear in the Viewer (**Figure 11.1**). All clips captured in FCE are formatted as Ch 1 + Ch 2.

◆ **Mono Mix:** The audio consists of both channels from the tape mixed into a single track. A single Audio tab appears in the Viewer.

◆ **Stereo:** Both channels have been captured as a stereo pair. Stereo pairs are always linked, so anything applied to one track applies to both. Waveforms for the two channels that make up the stereo pair appear in a single Audio tab (**Figure 11.2**).

◆ **Ch 1:** The audio consists of only the left channel from the tape (Ch 1), with pan centered. A single Audio tab appears in the Viewer.

◆ **Ch 2:** The audio consists of only the right channel from the tape (Ch 2), with pan centered. A single Audio tab appears in the Viewer.

Modifying Audio Channel Formats

Two linked audio clips behave differently than two linked audio clips defined as a stereo pair.

◆ Two linked audio clips will be selected together, but their levels and filters must be controlled separately. Two linked audio clips can appear on two separate Audio tabs in the Viewer.

◆ Two audio clips defined as a stereo pair share everything except their audio content and their Timeline tracks. The two stereo channels appear on a single Audio tab in the viewer, and they are always selected together. Any filter, panning, or level modification applied to one stereo channel is automatically applied to the other.

You can modify the audio format of captured audio using the Modify > Stereo Pair and Modify > Link commands. For example, toggling Stereo Pair off will convert a pair of clips captured as a stereo pair to two linked clips in Ch 1 + Ch 2 format.

✔ Tip

■ Converting two single audio clips to form a stereo pair is a quick way to apply identical level changes to a couple of clips. You can always toggle stereo off after you have made your level adjustments.

Figure 11.3 Select the stereo audio clip in the Timeline then choose Modify > Stereo Pair (or press Option-L) to toggle stereo off.

Figure 11.4 The stereo audio clip converted to Ch 1 + Ch 2 format. Note that the small triangles that indicate a stereo pair are gone, but the clip names remain underlined because the two audio channels remained linked.

To convert a stereo pair to Ch 1 + Ch 2 format:

◆ Select the stereo audio clip in the Timeline (**Figure 11.3**), then choose Modify > Stereo Pair to toggle stereo off.

The stereo audio clip is converted to Ch 1 + Ch 2 format, but the two audio channels remained linked (**Figure 11.4**). If you want to convert these to two completely independent audio clips, select the linked audio clips in the Timeline, then choose Modify > Link to toggle linking off.

To convert two audio clips to stereo pair format:

◆ Select the two audio clips in the Timeline, then choose Modify > Stereo Pair to toggle stereo on.

FCE Protocol: Want Stereo? You'll Have to Make It Yourself

FCE's Capture window only captures video+audio clips, and it formats stereo audio channels as Ch 1 + Ch 2. If you want your clip's audio to be formatted as a stereo pair, you'll need to select the two channels of your audio clip in the Timeline, then choose Modify > Stereo Pair to toggle stereo on.

The Browser's Audio format columns

You'll find four Browser columns devoted to info about the formatting of your audio clips (**Figure 11.5**); this summary will help you decode what each column is telling you about your audio files.

◆ **Tracks:** The number of audio and video tracks used in a clip or sequence. Note the higher total number of tracks in the sequences.

◆ **Audio:** The audio clip's format as defined inside FCE. "A1+A2" indicates the Ch 1 + Ch 2 format, FCE's default audio capture format.

◆ **Aud Format:** The audio format of the audio's source media file. The number (8, 12, 16) indicates the audio's bit depth.

◆ **Aud Rate:** The sample rate of the audio's source media file.

Figure 11.5 Audio format information columns displayed in the Browser.

FCE's Audio Formats

What's Bit Depth and Sampling Rate Got to Do with My Audio Quality?

Digital audio is recorded at a bit depth and a sampling rate.

Bit depth indicates the fidelity of the recording's dynamics (volume levels), and sample rate determines the fidelity of the recording's frequency response.

The bit depth defines the resolution of the dynamic range—the number of possible steps between the softest and loudest sound—of the recording.

An 8-bit digital audio recording uses 256 levels. A 16-bit digital recording has a range of 65,536 levels to represent the possible dynamic range.

The recording's sampling rate tells you how many times per second audio samples are saved to memory or disk. A 22kHz sample rate means 22,000 audio samples were recorded each second; in contrast, a 48kHz sample rate recording would take 48,000 audio samples each second.

Remember: your audio recording's fidelity is set at the time you record the original; you can't improve a recording by choosing a higher sample rate later, but you can convert an audio file to a lower bit depth and sample rate.

If you're looking for audio fidelity, more is better, so go for the highest bit depth and sampling rate when you record original audio.

✔ Tips

- Don't use compressed audio as source media when you edit in FCE. Compressed audio will be distorted during playback and in your final output. It's all right to compress your final output audio when exporting (see Chapter 18, "Creating Final Output" for more on exporting).

- Final Cut Express allows you to mix audio tracks with different sample rates within the same sequence. The program can convert the sample rate of nonconforming audio on the fly as you play back a sequence. Real-time sample rate conversion does take processor power, however, and can occasionally produce nasty audible artifacts; so, for best results, you should convert the sample rates of all your audio tracks to match the sequence settings. For more information, see "To export audio only from a clip or sequence" in Chapter 18.

Anatomy of the Audio Tab

The Audio tab in the Viewer window is where you perform review, marking, and editing tasks on single audio clips opened from the Browser or the Timeline. You can see the audio waveforms of audio clips, and in addition to the editing functions, you can use onscreen controls to adjust the level and stereo pan settings (**Figure 11.6**).

Before you start marking up audio clips, make sure you understand how and where FCE saves your changes. See the sidebar, "FCE Protocol: Clips and Sequences," in Chapter 3.

Figure 11.6 The Audio tab in the Viewer window.

Audio tab onscreen controls and displays

Editing digital audio requires different interface tools than editing digital video. When you open an audio clip in the Viewer, a graph of the audio waveform appears in the Audio tab, and the playhead travels across a stationary waveform image.

The Audio tab retains the transport controls from the Video tab interface in the lower part of the tab, but it has its own set of onscreen controls in the upper part.

Here's a brief rundown of the onscreen controls unique to the Audio tab (**Figures 11.7** and **11.8**):

◆ **Level slider:** Use to adjust the amplitude or volume of the audio clip.

◆ **Spread slider:** Use to adjust stereo panning or swapping of left and right channels. Single channel (mono) clips display a Pan slider here, for left/right positioning of audio.

◆ **Reset (X) button:** Use to delete all marked points in the audio timeline and reset the level and spread values to their original settings.

continues on next page

Figure 11.7 Controls displayed in the upper half of the Audio tab.

◆ **Drag hand:** This is your handle for drag-and-drop editing. Click and drag to move the audio clip with edits to another window, such as the Browser or the Timeline.

◆ **Audio tab ruler:** This displays the timecode for the audio displayed. Edit point overlays show along the ruler. You can adjust the time scale with the Zoom slider or the Magnifier.

◆ **In and Out points:** These appear in both the Scrubber bar and the ruler.

◆ **Level line graph:** Both a tool and an indicator, it graphs level changes by indicating the amplitude of the audio. You can also click and drag the Level line graph to adjust the overall level of your audio clip, or you can click and drag keyframes to create dynamic volume effects.

◆ **Spread (or Pan) line graph:** This has the same basic operation as the Level line graph. Click and drag to adjust the spread (for stereo clips) or pan (for mono clips).

◆ **Zoom selector:** Click to jump between different time scale views.

◆ **Zoom slider:** Use to scroll through an audio file and to adjust the time scale of your view.

✔ Tip

■ You can link two single audio clips to form a stereo pair. This is a quick way to apply identical level changes to a couple of clips. You can always unlink them after you have made your level adjustments. For more information, see "Modifying Audio Channel Formats," earlier in this chapter.

Figure 11.8 Controls displayed in the lower half of the Audio tab.

ANATOMY OF THE AUDIO TAB

Figure 11.9 When you review a long, unedited audio recording, the wide Viewer window is a great place to set markers in preparation for breaking the clip into subclips.

Figure 11.10 Click the Audio tab to access the audio portion of an audio+video clip.

Using the Viewer's Audio Tab

The capture settings for a clip determine how its audio appears in the Viewer. Stereo clips are panned full left and full right by default, and clips with one or two channels of discrete audio are panned center.

To open an audio clip:

Do one of the following:

- ◆ Double-click the clip icon in the Browser or the Timeline.

- ◆ Select a clip icon and press Enter.

- ◆ Select the clip in the Browser or the Timeline and choose View > Clip in New Window.

✔ Tip

- ■ Don't forget: You can stretch the Viewer window across your monitor to make a wide view—great when you're working with audio. You can see more of the clip, which makes marking and level adjustments easier (**Figure 11.9**). Resize it manually or click the green zoom button in the upper-left corner of the window.

To access the audio channel for an audio+video clip:

- ◆ Open the clip in the Viewer and click the Audio tab (**Figure 11.10**).

USING THE VIEWER'S AUDIO TAB

Scaling and scrolling an audio file

The Zoom slider is located along the bottom of the Audio tab. You use it to scroll through an audio file and to adjust the time scale of your view. You can view several minutes of audio in the window or focus on a fraction of a frame. The Zoom slider also appears on the Filters tab, Motion tab, and Timeline.

To scroll through your file:

◆ Drag the Zoom slider across the scroll bar (**Figure 11.11**).

To adjust the time scale:

Do one of the following:

◆ Press Command-+ (plus) to zoom in, expanding the time scale, and Command-- (minus) to zoom out, shrinking the time scale. These zoom keyboard shortcuts are useful in the Audio tab, because your view stays centered on the current playhead position.

◆ The thumb controls are the ribbed-looking ends of the Zoom slider (**Figure 11.12**). Click a thumb control and drag it to shrink the time scale and expose more of your audio file (**Figure 11.13**).

◆ Click the Zoom selector to the left of the Zoom slider to jump to a different time scale (**Figure 11.14**).

Figure 11.11 Drag the Zoom slider across the scroll bar to navigate through an audio file. This control doesn't move the playhead, just the view.

Figure 11.12 Drag the thumb control to vary time scaling. A smaller Zoom slider indicates an expanded time scale.

Figure 11.13 Drag the thumb control. A longer Zoom slider indicates a more compressed time scale.

Figure 11.14 Jump to a different time scale with one click using the Zoom selector.

Setting edit points in the Audio tab

You set In and Out points and markers in the Audio tab in the same way as on the Viewer's Video tab. The overlays for these markers show in the Audio tab ruler at the top of the waveform display.

Because video is captured and stored as frames, the smallest adjustment you can make to a video edit point is a single frame. Digital audio, however, is captured in subframes as samples forming a continuous waveform. In FCE, audio edit points can be set to an accuracy of $1/100$ frame. The Audio tab is the only place you can make subframe adjustments to an audio clip's In and Out points. Most likely, you'll need this kind of fine-tuning when you are finessing a music edit.

You can also place keyframes with the same precision—a lifesaver when you are working your way through a really good dialogue take with a couple of bad clicks or pops. The subframe precision allows you to use audio level keyframes to silence that audio just for the few milliseconds it takes to mute the click.

Lost in the Waveforms? Audio Tab Editing Tips

When you're trying to fine-tune an audio edit point in the Audio tab, it's easy to lose track of your location as you zoom and scroll through your audio clip's waveforms. Here's a navigation method to try while editing in the audio tab:

◆ Start by playing back the clip.

◆ When you hear the spot where you think your edit point should be, tap the spacebar to pause the playhead at that spot.

◆ Use the marquee selection feature of the Zoom tool to draw a narrow selection box around the playhead. You won't lose track of the playhead this way.

◆ While you're zoomed in, you can take advantage of the detailed waveform display to get a precision edit. Press I or O to mark your edit point at the current playhead position.

◆ When you finish tweaking, press Shift-Z to zoom out and fit the clip to the window with a single keystroke.

To make subframe adjustments to an audio clip's edit points:

1. Open the audio clip in the Audio tab; then jump the playhead to the edit point you want to adjust.

2. Use the marquee selection feature of the Zoom tool to zoom in until the playhead looks like a bar (**Figure 11.15**).

3. Hold down the Shift key; then click the Audio tab playhead and drag it to the (subframe) location of the new In or Out point (**Figure 11.16**).

4. Press I (or O) to stamp a new In (or Out) point (**Figure 11.17**).

✔ Tip

■ To add an audio keyframe in a location that's not on a frame line, you don't need to adjust the playhead; just zoom way in and use the Pen tool to add the keyframe.

Figure 11.15 Use the Zoom tool to drag a marquee right around the playhead. When the view zooms in, the playhead will still be in view.

Figure 11.16 Hold down the Shift key; then drag the Audio tab playhead to the exact location of the new In or Out point.

Figure 11.17 Press I (or O) to set a new In (or Out) point. This In point has been adjusted to trim out the little pop at the beginning of a word.

Figure 11.18 Click and hold to grab the drag hand.

To drag an audio clip into the Timeline or the Canvas window:

1. Start with an open clip and the Viewer window selected.

2. Position the pointer over the drag hand.

   When the pointer changes to a hand shape, you're in the right spot (**Figure 11.18**).

3. Drag from that spot to the Canvas or the Timeline. This inserts your audio clip into the open sequence (**Figure 11.19**).

Figure 11.19 Drag and drop to insert a clip into a sequence in the Canvas window.

Editing Audio in the Timeline

Editing in the Viewer is fine, but here are a few compelling reasons to do your audio editing right in the Timeline:

◆ The Timeline is the only place where you can view all your audio tracks at once.

◆ You can set audio keyframes and sculpt audio levels right in the Timeline.

◆ Canvas and Timeline playback are locked together, so the Timeline is the only place you can trim audio on the fly as you watch your sequence play back.

Most of the tools and techniques collected here are discussed in Chapter 9, "Editing in the Timeline and the Canvas." These techniques can give you more control when you need to fine-tune a particular bit of dialogue or a sound effect in a busy soundtrack (**Figure 11.20**).

Turn off track visibility to mute selected tracks

Use snapping to line up clips

Display audio waveforms

Use clip overlays to set and adjust audio keyframes

Select the right track size for the job

Place markers during playback to mark sync points

Figure 11.20 Use these tools to gain more control over audio editing in the Timeline.

EDITING AUDIO IN THE TIMELINE

◆ **Track Size:** Use the largest track size for fine-tuning and close work; use the smallest size to get a multi-track overview. Press Shift-T to cycle through the track sizes.

◆ **Turn on Audio Waveforms:** Displaying audio waveforms in the Timeline is a big help when you edit audio, but displaying waveforms slows the Timeline's performance. Toggle audio waveforms off and on by pressing Command-Option-W.

◆ **Markers:** When you're trying to hit the perfect spot for a sound effect or music cue, tap the M key as you watch your sequence play back to set a Timeline marker right at the sweet spot. You can also hold the M key down as you watch and then set a marker by releasing the key at the perfect moment.

◆ **Track solo:** As you build up your audio tracks, *track soloing*—silencing all but one audio track so you can concentrate on one sound—is a big help. Option-click the Track Visibility icon on the track you want to hear. For more information, see "Making a Timeline track invisible" in Chapter 9.

◆ **Snapping:** Snapping makes certain points in the Timeline "sticky." With snapping turned on, the edges of clips snap together, or a clip will snap to an edit point on an adjacent track when dragged close to it. When you're making fine adjustments to your audio, snapping can be a help (such as trying to line up a stack of audio clips to a marker or the playhead position) or a hindrance (trying to drag a sound effect to the perfect location and snapping jerks your clip to the nearest edit point). Remember, you can toggle snapping on or off *at any time*— even mid-move—by pressing the N key.

◆ **Audio Scrubbing:** Audio scrubbing plays your sound at high or low speeds— even when you step through your clip one frame at a time. This is useful for locating the precise point for an edit. Scrubbing is great while you use it, but the constant low- and high-speed audio as you shuttle around a sequence can get annoying. Toggle audio scrubbing off or on at any time by pressing Shift-S.

EDITING AUDIO IN THE TIMELINE

Recording Audio with the Voice Over Tool

The Voice Over tool is a nifty gadget designed to record synchronous audio as FCE plays back a selected portion of your sequence. Here's a brief rundown of its features:

◆ You can monitor your existing tracks through headphones as you record.

◆ Each completed audio take is automatically placed on a new Timeline track in the portion of the sequence you specified.

◆ When you record multiple takes, FCE automatically creates a new Timeline track for each take's clip.

◆ The Voice Over tool automatically records before and after your Mark In and Mark Out points, so your recorded track won't be cut off if your voiceover runs over.

◆ Once you complete your recording, you are free to reposition, trim, and polish your new voiceover tracks just as you would any other FCE clip.

Anatomy of the Voice Over tool

The Voice Over tool is a self-contained audio recording interface within FCE. When you set up for your recording session, use the Input controls to configure your audio input hardware settings and set audio recording levels, and the Headphones controls to set monitoring levels. When you're ready to record, use the transport controls for preview and capture. The status display helps you keep in step with FCE's playback without having to watch the picture.

To open the Voice Over tool:

◆ Choose File > Voice Over.

◆ The Tool Bench appears with the Voice Over tool displayed (**Figure 11.21**).

Transport controls

Record/Stop button: Click to start audio recording and Timeline playback. Once recording starts, this button changes to the Stop button. Click again (or press the Escape key) to stop recording.

If you stop recording before your specified Out point, the audio you recorded is saved to disk, and the partial clip is placed in the Timeline.

◆ **Review button:** Click to play back the Timeline section you've specified, without recording. Use Review while you rehearse your voiceover.

◆ **Discard button:** Click to delete the clip and media file from the previous take. The Discard button is dimmed until you've recorded your first voice-over clip. *Using the Discard button to delete a take is not undoable.*

Status display

◆ **Status area:** A progress bar indicates what proportion of your specified Timeline section has been recorded, along with a message indicating the Voice Over tool's current state.

Status messages include:

◆ **Ready to Record:** Indicates that the Voice Over tool is standing by to record.

◆ **Starting:** Displays during the 5 second countdown before Timeline playback reaches your specified In point. FCE records audio during this pre-roll period, to ensure that your performance is preserved even if you jump the gun and start speaking too soon.

continues on next page

RECORDING AUDIO WITH THE VOICE OVER TOOL

Review button
Record/Stop
Discard button

Status area
Status message
Progress bar

Target sequence name and track number for your next take

Enter your audio track name here or use the auto-naming feature

Choose recording device from Source pop-up menu

Level meter displays audio input level

Select from multiple inputs in Input pop-up menu

Choose Offset to compensate for audio processing delay

Choose sample rate for recording from Rate pop-up menu

Use Gain slider to set input audio level

Use Volume slider to set playback levels for headphone mix

Check to enable sound cue beeps

Figure 11.21 An overview of the Voice Over tool controls.

◆ **Recording:** Appears when Timeline playback reaches your specified In point. The Recording status message displays a countdown (accompanied by audio cue beeps in your headphones) during the last 5 seconds before your specified Out point.

◆ **Finishing:** Appears when FCE reaches your specified Out point. FCE continues to record 2 seconds past your specified Out point to ensure that your last word won't be cut off, preserving your take if you run a little over.

◆ **Saving:** Displays while FCE saves your voiceover recording from RAM to a file on your specified scratch disk.

Audio File area

◆ **Target:** This field shows the sequence name and track number where your next voiceover take will be placed. The target track updates automatically, moving down to the next available track for each subsequent take.

◆ **Name:** Enter a name for your voiceover recording here. The file name will automatically increment as you record subsequent takes. This name is used for both the clip and for the source media file on disk. If the name is already in use by another clip in the same capture folder, FCE automatically appends a number to the duplicate name.

Input controls

Use the Input controls to select the source, configure the format, and adjust the incoming audio signal that you're recording. These settings are for the Voice Over tool only; they won't affect your capture preset settings.

◆ **Level:** This audio meter displays the input recording levels you set with the Gain slider, located at the bottom right of the Input controls section.

◆ **Source:** Choose your audio input device from this pop-up menu. The specific external recording equipment you have connected will determine your menu choices.

◆ **Input:** If your audio input device has multiple inputs, select which input you want FCE to record from this pop-up menu.

◆ **Rate:** Choose an audio sample rate for your recording from this pop-up menu. Only sample rates that your selected audio device supports should appear. If you can, select the rate that matches the audio sample rate of your sequence settings. If your audio device doesn't support your sequence's sample rate, choose the highest available sample rate.

◆ **Offset:** Choose an offset to compensate for any processing delay in your incoming audio signal.

◆ **Gain:** Use this slider to adjust the input levels from your microphone or other recording device.

Headphones controls

◆ **Volume:** Use this slider, or enter a value in decibels, to adjust the playback volume in your headphones.

◆ **Sound Cues:** Check this box to hear audible cue beeps in your headphones during recording. The beeps won't be recorded in your voiceover recording.

✔ Tips

■ DV camcorders typically introduce a delay of 3 frames; an average USB capture device introduces a delay of 1 frame. If you use the Voice Over tool to record replacement dialogue, even a couple frames of delay can be a bother when you are trying to judge quickly whether the lip sync in a take is good enough.

■ If you don't plan to monitor your program's existing soundtrack during your voiceover recording, be sure to mute any speakers that are within range of your microphone or mute the playback here in the Headphones control panel. Set the Volume slider to –60dB and disable the Sound Cues check box.

Voice Over tool set-up checklist

The Voice Over tool may streamline your recording process, but remember: you're still setting up for a recording session. If you intend to use these tracks in a final product, you should plan on running a full test to check your audio quality before starting your recording session. Here's a list of set-up tasks:

◆ **Set up your external recording device.** You can hook up any audio recording device that's compatible with the Apple Sound Manager; options include the built-in DV microphone on your DV camera, a PCI audio card, or a USB audio capture device. If your Mac has one (and you're not too picky), you can use the built-in microphone port on the back of the computer.

◆ **Set up headphones.** Plug headphones into your computer's built-in headphone jack. You may want to configure your setup to allow headphone monitoring for both the recordist and the voiceover talent.

◆ **Calculate the offset of your audio recording device.** Digital recording devices typically introduce a short delay while the device processes the analog audio signal from your microphone. This delay can offset your voiceover clips from your performer's original timing. You could go back and adjust all your clips by hand, but the Voice Over tool allows you to set a compensating offset that will put your tracks right back in sync. See Chapter 17, "Using the Voice Over Tool," in Apple's *Final Cut Express User's Manual* for details on the offset calibration process.

◆ **Test your setup.** Listen to playback of your audio away from the whir and whine of your editing workstation. Better yet, set up an external video monitor away from your computer and drives and isolate your voiceover talent from the sound of your CPU and drives when recording your voiceover.

✔ Tip

■ If you select your DV camera's microphone as your audio recording device, you won't be able to record until you turn off your external video feed by choosing View > Video > Real-Time.

To record synchronous audio with the Voice Over tool:

1. Follow the Voice Over tool setup procedure outlined earlier.

2. In the Timeline, mark In and Out points to specify the duration of your recording by defining the section of your sequence you want to record over (**Figure 11.22**). If you do not set In and Out points, recording will start at the playhead position and stop at the end of the last clip in the Timeline.

3. Specify the target location of your new voiceover audio clip by choosing the Timeline audio track immediately *above* your desired voiceover track position, and set that track as the Channel 2 target track (**Figure 11.23**).

4. Choose Tools > Voice Over.

   The Tool Bench appears with the Voice Over tab displayed.

5. On the Voice Over tool tab, click the Record button (**Figure 11.24**).

   The Timeline playhead jumps back 5 seconds before your specified In point,

   FCE starts playback and recording and displays the "Starting" status message during this 5-second pre-roll countdown.

   When FCE reaches your specified In point, the status message area displays "Recording" (**Figure 11.25**).

Figure 11.22 Define the section of your sequence you want to record by marking In and Out points in the Timeline.

Figure 11.23 FCE will place your new audio on a new track immediately below the track you set as the Channel 2 target track.

Figure 11.24 Click the Record button or press Shift-C to start recording and playback.

Figure 11.25 When playback reaches your specified In point, the Voice Over tool status display turns red, and the message switches to "Recording."

Figure 11.26 Your new audio clip appears in the Timeline.

Figure 11.27 Click the track light to turn off the Timeline track of the previous take before you record a second take. This will mute the audio from the previous take.

Figure 11.28 Additional takes appear as audio clips on new Timeline tracks inserted below your first take.

6. Start speaking, or cue your voiceover talent.

   FCE continues recording for 2 seconds after the playback reaches your specified Out point, and the Status message area displays "Finishing."

   FCE saves your new audio clip in the capture folder specified in your scratch disk preferences.

   Your new audio clip appears in the Timeline (**Figure 11.26**), and the Voice Over tool is reset so that it displays the "Ready to Record" status message.

7. If you want to record additional takes, mute the previous take by turning off its Timeline track before you record (**Figure 11.27**).

8. Repeat steps 5 and 6 to record additional takes in the same Timeline location.

   Your additional takes appear as audio clips on new Timeline tracks that appear below your first take (**Figure 11.28**). The Channel 2 track target automatically moves down one track, and you're ready to record another take on the newly created track.

✔ Tips

■ Did your voiceover take get cut off at the head or tail of the clip? Never fear. FCE was recording during the entire pre- and post-roll. You can adjust the In and Out points of your truncated take's audio clip (**Figure 11.29**) and retrieve your first consonant or your last gasp.

■ Does this sound familiar? You got tongue-tied when you recorded "VO Take 1," so you deleted that take from your Timeline and you're ready to record a new take 1. Maybe you're wondering why the Voice Over tool stubbornly refuses to let you re-use the name "VO Take 1". Here's why—you deleted the clip reference to "VO Take 1" from the Timeline, but the audio file created when you recorded the first "VO Take 1" remains in your capture folder. FCE wisely forbids two files having the same name to exist in the same folder. If you want to reuse the name "VO Take 1," delete the audio file with that name from your capture folder.

Figure 11.29 Adjusting the Out point of an audio clip to restore the end of the take that extended past the specified Out point during recording.

Cue Beep Choreography

The Voice Over tool offers the option of hearing cue beeps along with the audio track playback in your headphones. These beeps are invaluable if you can't watch the screen because your eyes are glued to the script you're about to read. Unfortunately, you can't easily adjust the beep level separately from the rest of the headphone playback mix, and a little beep goes a long way.

Here's the sequence and timing of the cue beeps:

1. Three beeps mark off the first 3 seconds at the start of the 5 second pre-roll. The last 2 seconds before playback reaches your In point are beepless.

2. Exactly 15 seconds before playback reaches your Out point, you'll be cued with a single warning beep.

3. During the last 5 seconds of recording, you'll hear five beeps—the last beep is longer and has a lower pitch. Try not to panic. Remember—you still have those 2 seconds of post-roll recording as protection.

Figure 11.30 Dragging the Level slider to the right increases the clip volume.

Figure 11.31 Dragging the Level line graph higher increases the volume.

Figure 11.32 Choose Modify > Audio and make a Gain selection from the submenu. Note the keyboard shortcuts listed to the right of the submenu choices.

Finishing Audio

This section covers all the ways you can adjust your audio clip's levels, stereo pan position, and sound quality.

Setting audio levels

You can set the volume (level) for individual audio clips in the Viewer's Audio tab by visually editing the line graph that appears as an overlay on your audio waveform.

In the Timeline, you can use the Modify > Levels command to set levels for multiple audio clips in a single operation. See Chapter 9, "Editing in the Timeline and the Canvas."

To set audio clip levels:

1. Start with an open clip and the Viewer window selected.

2. *Do one of the following:*

   ◆ Drag the Level slider to the right to increase clip volume, or to the left to lower clip volume (**Figure 11.30**).

   ◆ Drag the pink Level line graph displayed over the audio waveform: higher increases volume, lower decreases volume (**Figure 11.31**).

   ◆ Press Control-+ (plus) or Control-- (minus) to adjust audio levels by single decibel increments.

   ◆ Choose Modify > Audio, and make a Gain selection from the submenu (**Figure 11.32**).

To set computer audio levels:

There's no way to adjust computer audio levels within Final Cut Express. Instead, adjust your levels from your Mac's Sound preference pane (**Figure 11.33**).

FINISHING AUDIO

Figure 11.33 The Macintosh Sound preference pane.

Monitor Levels and Mixing

It's important to keep your speaker levels constant when you adjust audio levels for a sequence. There's more than one place to adjust your monitoring level. Take a moment before you start working to set up everything, and note your settings so that you can recalibrate if necessary.

If you'll be recording out to an external video deck or camera, check the audio output levels on the recording device's meters. Play the loudest section of your program. If your recording device has no meters, record a test of the loudest section and review the audio quality.

Check the Sound preference pane to make sure your computer's sound output level is set high enough. Next, set a comfortable listening level on the amplifier that drives your external speakers. Now you are in a position to make consistent volume adjustments to the audio in your sequence.

Figure 11.34 Move the playhead to the location where you want the level change to start.

Figure 11.35 Adjust the level with the Level slider and click the level line with the Pen tool to set a keyframe.

Figure 11.36 At the next location where you want a level change, use the Pen to drag the level line to the new level setting.

To create dynamic level changes within a clip:

1. Start with an open clip and the Viewer window selected.

2. Park the playhead where you want to start the level change (**Figure 11.34**).

3. Adjust the level using the Level slider.

4. Select the Pen tool from the Tool palette, then set a keyframe by clicking on the level line with the Pen tool (**Figure 11.35**).

5. Move the playhead to the next location where you want a change in the level.

6. With the Pen tool, drag the level line to the new audio level (**Figure 11.36**).

   Another keyframe is set automatically as you drag the level line with the Pen tool.

✔ Tip

- Click the Set Keyframe button in the lower part of the window to set a keyframe on both the Level and Spread line graphs at the current playhead position.

FINISHING AUDIO

Adjusting the pan position

The pan position is the left/right placement of sound for single audio channels. Clips with one or two channels of discrete audio will initially open with pan set to the center.

To set a pan position:

1. Start with an open clip and the Viewer window selected.

2. *Do one of the following:*

   ◆ Drag the Pan slider to the right to pan toward the right; drag the slider to the left to pan toward the left (**Figure 11.37**).

   ◆ Drag the purple Pan line graph displayed over the audio waveform. Drag higher to pan right; drag lower to pan left (**Figure 11.38**).

   ◆ Choose Modify > Audio and make a Pan selection from the submenu.

Figure 11.37 Dragging the Pan slider to the left pans your track toward the left channel.

Figure 11.38 Dragging the Pan line graph lower pans your track toward the left channel.

FINISHING AUDIO

Figure 11.39 Spread slider settings.

Figure 11.40 The Spread slider at its base setting of –1. This setting replicates the original mix of a stereo source track.

Figure 11.41 Dragging the Spread line toward the center for a –1 setting.

Adjusting the spread

The Spread control adjusts the degree of stereo separation, and it adjusts left and right channels simultaneously and equally.

You can use the Spread slider or the Level line graph to adjust the spread. The setting options on the Spread slider are as follows (**Figure 11.39**):

◆ The base setting of –1 outputs the left audio channel to the left and the right audio channel to the right. This setting accurately reproduces the stereo mix of a track from a music CD.

◆ A setting of 0 outputs the left and right audio channels equally to both sides.

◆ A setting of +1 swaps the channels and outputs the left audio channel to the right and the right audio channel to the left.

To adjust the spread on a stereo audio clip:

1. Start with an open clip and the Viewer window selected.

2. *Do one of the following:*

   ◆ Drag the Spread slider to adjust the stereo pan positioning (see **Figure 11.40**).

   ◆ Drag the purple Spread level line graph displayed over the audio wave-form at the center line between the two stereo channels. Drag away from the center line for a +1 setting; drag toward the center for a –1 setting (**Figure 11.41**).

Modifying audio transitions

Final Cut Express has only two audio transitions to choose from, but they're very useful. One is a 0 decibel cross-fade. The other is a +3 decibel cross-fade. How do you decide which one works best to finesse your audio edit? Try them out and trust your ears.

To modify the duration of an audio transition:

◆ With the Selection tool, drag one edge of the transition to adjust its length (**Figure 11.42**).

Or do this:

1. Control-click the transition; then choose Duration from the shortcut menu.

2. In the Duration dialog box, enter a new duration.

3. Click OK.

✔ Tip

■ Duration is the only adjustable parameter for the audio cross-fade transitions in Final Cut Express, but you can build your own cross-fades. Set up the audio clips you want to transition between on adjacent tracks. You can adjust the clips' overlap and then set Level keyframes and sculpt your special-purpose cross-fade.

Figure 11.42 Adjusting the start point of an audio transition in the Timeline. Dragging a transition's edge affects the length of the transition effect but does not alter any underlying edit points.

FINISHING AUDIO

Figure 11.43 Make a short test clip from a representative section of your audio track.

Adjusting Audio Filters

Final Cut Express's suite of audio filters is geared toward repairing problems in production audio. That's good, because production audio frequently has problems—problems that don't come to light until you review your footage in the editing room. FCE's equalization, compression, and noise reduction filters are tools you can use to reduce rumble in an exterior street recording or improve the crispness in a dialogue track. (Before you ask, there is no filter that will strip background music out of dialogue.)

You apply FCE's audio filters in the same way that you apply video filters.

Like video filters, most audio filters in FCE have to be rendered before you can hear the results of your settings adjustment. Unfortunately, the lack of real-time feedback makes adjusting audio filters in FCE more challenging. Try the method described here to reduce the lag time between adjusting an audio filter's setting and hearing the results.

To adjust an audio filter's settings:

1. Make a short test clip from a representative section of your audio track (**Figure 11.43**). If you're trying to fix a problem, pick out a worst-case section and then maybe an average-case section to try your worst-case settings on. Make the section long enough so you can evaluate your work, say 5 to 10 seconds.

2. Open your test clip in the Viewer, apply the filter, and start tweaking the filter settings.

3. You'll hear a series of beeps (FCE's rendering indicator for audio) when your test clip requires rendering. You need to render the audio before you can hear the effect of the audio filter you've applied. Your short test clip should render quickly.

continues on next page

4. Enable looped playback and then try to get into a rhythm of adjusting, rendering, and listening. When you think you've zeroed in on your filter settings, copy and paste the filter (and its settings) from the test clip to your full-length audio track in the sequence (**Figure 11.44**). Use the Paste Attributes command to paste just the filters (**Figure 11.45**).

✔ Tips

■ Audio filters applied to audio that is formatted as a stereo pair are applied to both channels equally, and only one set of controls appears on the Viewer's Filters tab.

■ You can copy an audio filter with all its current settings and paste it onto other clips or onto an entire nested sequence. If you perfect the EQ setting that cancels out the sound of your camera, you can easily apply the same filter setting wherever it's needed. See "Copying and pasting clip attributes" in Chapter 9.

■ Chapter 16 of Apple's *Final Cut Express User's Manual* contains a complete list of FCE's audio filters and over 50 pages on working with audio in FCE.

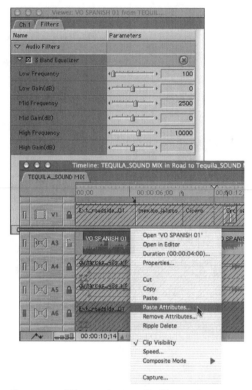

Figure 11.44 When you've tuned in filter settings, copy and then use the Paste Attributes command to paste the filter and its settings from the test clip to your full-length audio track in the sequence.

Figure 11.45 In the Paste Attributes dialog box, paste just the filters from your test audio clip onto the longer audio clip you're filtering.

CREATING TRANSITIONS

Transitions are a small, but essential, part of film grammar. Over the years, transitions have developed an important role in film story language. Filmmakers rely on the audience's knowledge of the transition "code." This grammar of transitions and what they signify in movie language has grown up with the movies. These days, viewers are hardly aware of the translations that they make while watching film: fade-out/fade-in means the passage of time, a ripple dissolve means "it was all a dream," and a heart-shaped iris wipe means you're watching reruns of "Love: American Style."

Final Cut Express offers a library of more than 50 transition effects, which range from simple dissolves to complex 3D transitions. This chapter introduces the procedures for working with transitions in an editing context. For information on modifying effects settings to sculpt transitions, see Chapter 13, "Compositing and Effects Overview."

Adding Transition Effects

You can add transitions along with clips as you assemble your sequence by performing one of the two transition edit types available in the Canvas edit overlay, or you can apply transitions to edit points after you have assembled your sequence. Once transitions are applied, you can go back and modify them as you refine your cut.

Final Cut Express displays transitions as overlays within a single Timeline track—an efficient use of screen real estate (**Figure 12.1**). You can adjust a transition directly in the Timeline window, or you can make more complex adjustments in the Transition Editor. The following procedures for adding a transition to a sequence are performed in the Timeline.

Figure 12.1 Transitions appear as overlays within a single Timeline track. The darker gray diagonal shading on the transition's Timeline icon indicates the direction, alignment, and speed of the transition.

FCE Protocol: Transitions

◆ Because transitions are created by overlapping material from two adjacent clips, each source clip requires additional frames equal to half of the transition's duration for Final Cut Express to create the effect. If a source clip is too short to create the transition at your specified duration, Final Cut Express will calculate and apply the transition with a shorter duration, or not apply it at all if you have no additional frames.

◆ You can add transition effects as you edit a clip into a sequence, or you can add transitions to a previously edited sequence.

◆ You can place a transition so that it is centered on the cut, starts at the cut, or ends at the cut.

◆ A transition edit always centers the transition on the cut between the two clips. If you want to add a transition that either starts or ends at the cut, add the transition after the clips are placed in the sequence.

Figure 12.2 Selecting an edit point in the Timeline.

Figure 12.3 Choosing Cross Dissolve from the Effects menu.

Figure 12.4 The Cross Dissolve applied to the selected edit point in the Timeline.

To add a transition effect that's centered on a cut:

1. In the Timeline, select the edit point between two clips on the same Timeline track (**Figure 12.2**).

2. To add the transition effect, *do one of the following:*

   ◆ Choose Effects > Video Transitions; then select from the submenu's list of effects (**Figure 12.3**).

   ◆ Drag a transition effect from the Effects tab in the Browser onto the cut, centering it over the cut.

   ◆ To add the default transition, Control-click the edit point; then choose Add Transition from the shortcut menu.

   The transition is applied to the selected edit point (**Figure 12.4**).

✔ Tip

■ You can change the alignment of an existing transition by Control-clicking the selected transition in the Timeline and then choosing a different alignment from the shortcut menu.

ADDING TRANSITION EFFECTS

359

To add a transition effect that starts or ends at a cut:

◆ Drag a transition effect from the Effects tab in the Browser onto the edit point in the Timeline, aligning it so that it starts or ends at the cut (**Figure 12.5**).

✔ Tips

■ Create a fade-to-black transition by dragging the Cross Dissolve transition from the Effects tab of the Browser to the final clip in your sequence, aligning it so that it ends at the cut.

■ To fade up from black, drag the Cross Dissolve transition onto the beginning of the first clip in your sequence, aligning it to start at the first frame of the sequence.

Figure 12.5 Dragging the transition from the Effects tab of the Browser to the edit point in the Timeline. This Dip to Color transition is aligned to end at the cut, creating a fade up from black.

FCE Protocol: Saving Changes to Modified Transitions

When saving changes to a transition, remember that transitions follow the same protocols as clips and sequences. (For more information, review "FCE Protocol: Clips and Sequences" in Chapter 3.) Here's a summary of the main points:

◆ When you add a transition to a sequence by dragging it from the Browser to the Timeline, a copy of the transition is inserted into the sequence.

◆ You can open a transition from the Browser (outside a sequence) or from the Timeline (within a sequence).

◆ If you modify a transition from the Browser before you insert the transition into a sequence, the transition that is placed in the sequence includes the changes made in the Browser.

◆ Any changes you make to a transition from within a sequence are not made to the transition in the Browser. If you want to reuse a transition you've designed within a sequence, drag a copy of your revised transition from the Timeline back to the Browser.

ADDING TRANSITION EFFECTS

Figure 12.6 Select the transition you want to replace.

Figure 12.7 Choose a replacement transition from the Effects menu.

Figure 12.8 Control-click the edit point; then choose Paste from the shortcut menu.

To delete a transition from a sequence:

◆ In the Timeline, select the transition; then press the Delete key.

To replace one transition with another:

1. In the Timeline, select the transition you are replacing (**Figure 12.6**).

2. Choose Effects > Video (or Audio) Transitions; then select a replacement transition from a submenu (**Figure 12.7**).

To copy a transition and paste it in another location:

1. In the Timeline, select the transition you want to copy; then press Command-C.

2. Control-click the edit point where you want to paste the transition; then choose Paste from the shortcut menu (**Figure 12.8**).

✔ Tip

■ You can copy and apply a transition to another edit point in one stylish move. Select your desired transition and then hold down Option while dragging the transition to another edit point in the Timeline. This technique works with clips, too.

Working with Default and Favorite Transitions

Final Cut Express offers one default video transition—a 1 second cross dissolve (**Figure 12.9**), and one default audio transition—a 1 second cross fade (**Figure 12.10**). The default transitions are available from the Effects menu, the edit point's shortcut menu, and as keyboard commands. A transition edit, available in the Canvas edit overlay, automatically includes the default transition at the time you perform the edit. You can also designate a transition (or any other type of effect) as a Favorite by dragging the effect from the Browser, Viewer, or Timeline and placing it in the Favorites bin on the Effects tab in the Browser. Using Favorites is an easy way to save a transition's settings so you can reproduce the effect later. You can build up a small group of favorite transitions for a particular project.

To apply the default video transition:

Do one of the following:

◆ Select the edit point where you want to place the transition; then choose Effects > Default - Cross Dissolve.

◆ Control-click the edit point; then choose Add Transition 'Cross Dissolve' from the shortcut menu (**Figure 12.11**).

◆ Select the edit point; then press Command-T.

Figure 12.9 FCE's default video transition is a 1 second cross dissolve.

Figure 12.10 The default audio transition is a 1 second, +3dB cross fade.

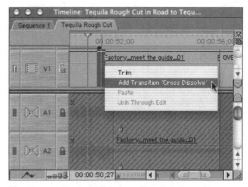

Figure 12.11 Control-click the edit point; then choose Add Transition 'Cross Dissolve' from the shortcut menu.

WORKING WITH DEFAULT AND FAVORITE TRANSITIONS

Figure 12.12 Control-click the edit point; then choose Add Transition 'Cross Fade (+3dB)' from the shortcut menu.

Figure 12.13 Dragging a modified transition from the Timeline to the Favorites bin, located on the Effects tab of the Browser.

To apply the default audio transition:

Do one of the following:

◆ Select the audio edit point where you want to place the transition; then choose Effects > Default - Cross Fade (+3dB).

◆ Control-click the edit point; then choose Add Transition 'Cross Fade (+3dB)' from the shortcut menu (**Figure 12.12**).

To create a favorite transition by saving its settings:

◆ In the Transition Editor or the Timeline, click and drag the transition icon to the Favorites bin on the Effects tab in the Browser (**Figure 12.13**).

To create a favorite transition before changing its settings:

1. On the Effects tab in the Browser, double-click the transition (**Figure 12.14**).

   The transition opens in the Transition Editor.

2. Adjust the transition's settings in the Transition Editor; then use the drag handle to drag the modified transition into the Favorites bin (**Figure 12.15**).

3. In the Favorites bin, rename the new transition (**Figure 12.16**).

To delete a favorite transition from the Favorites bin:

◆ In the Favorites bin, select the transition you want to delete, then press Delete.

Figure 12.14 Double-click the transition you want to customize to open it in the Transition Editor.

Figure 12.15 Adjust the transition settings in the Transition Editor, and then drag the customized transition into the Favorites bin.

Figure 12.16 Rename your modified transition in the Favorites bin.

Figure 12.17 The Timeline playhead positioned at the selected edit point; the playhead position will be used as the sequence In point.

About transition edits

There are two types of transition edits: Insert with Transition and Overwrite with Transition. A transition edit automatically places your default transition at the head of the edit. When using either of the transition edit types, you'll need enough footage in your source clip to create the transition. Each source clip will need additional frames equal to half of the transition's duration.

To perform a transition edit:

1. Set the sequence In point by positioning the Timeline playhead where you want the edit to occur (**Figure 12.17**).

2. In the Viewer, set source In and Out points to define the part of the source clip you want to add to the sequence (**Figure 12.18**).

3. Drag the clip from the Viewer to either the Insert with Transition or the Overwrite with Transition edit overlay in the Canvas (**Figure 12.19**).

Figure 12.18 Set Source In and Out points in the Viewer. Be sure to leave at least 15 extra frames at the beginning of your clip to accommodate the transition.

Figure 12.19 Drag the source clip from the Viewer to the Canvas edit overlay; then drop the clip on the Overwrite with Transition edit area.

WORKING WITH DEFAULT AND FAVORITE TRANSITIONS

Editing Video Transitions

You can make dramatic changes to a video transition even after you have added it to your sequence. You can adjust duration and placement and customize its appearance. Opening your transition in the Transition Editor will give you maximum access to the transition's settings, but you can perform many adjustments directly in the Timeline.

Figure 12.20 shows an overview of the Transition Editor interface.

Transition placement buttons: Click the corresponding button to align the transition to end on, center on, or begin on the cut

Recent clips: Select a recently opened clip from this pop-up menu

Begin on cut

Transition duration display: Enter a new duration in the field to modify the transition duration

Center on cut

End on cut

Drag handle: Click and drag to an edit point in the Timeline to apply a transition

Transition name

Incoming clip: Drag this clip edge with an edit tool to ripple the edit point underlying the transition

Outgoing clip: Drag this clip edge with an edit tool to ripple the edit point underlying the transition

Transition: Drag a transition edge to adjust one side of the transition duration; Shift-drag to adjust both sides

Transition settings controls: Use the controls to adjust transition parameters; the controls displayed vary with the transition

Reverse Transition button: Click to reverse the direction of the transition effect

Reset button: Click to reset all transition controls to their default values

Figure 12.20 The Transition Editor opens in the Viewer window.

Figure 12.21 The Transition Editor with Thumbnail Display set to Filmstrip.

Using the Transition Editor

The Transition Editor (sometimes called the Transition Viewer) is a special version of the Viewer window that you use to make detailed adjustments to transition settings. Use the Transition Editor to do the following:

◆ Adjust the duration of the transition.

◆ Reverse the direction of the transition.

◆ Trim the edit point underlying the transition.

◆ Adjust the placement of the transition relative to the edit point. You can set a transition to end on the cut, center on the cut, begin on the cut, or occur anywhere in between.

◆ Adjust the starting and ending effect percentages. A simple cross-dissolve's default settings would start at 0 and end at 100 percent. However, in a transition effect that incorporates a motion path, effect percentages specify the portion of the full path that will be included in the transition.

The Timeline's Thumbnail Display option controls the way clips appear in the Transition Editor (**Figure 12.21**). You can adjust the thumbnail display on the Timeline Options tab of the Sequence Settings window.

To open a transition in the Transition Editor:

Do one of the following:

◆ Control-click the transition; then choose Open (name of transition) from the shortcut menu (**Figure 12.22**).

◆ In the Timeline, double-click the transition to open it in the Transition Editor.

◆ Select the transition's icon in the Timeline; then choose View > Transition Editor.

To change the duration of a transition in the Transition Editor:

Do one of the following:

◆ Type a new duration in the Duration field; then press Enter (**Figure 12.23**).

◆ Drag either end of the transition.

The change in duration applies equally to both sides of the transition (**Figure 12.24**).

✔ Tip

■ FCE transitions apply equally to both sides of an edit point, so if you need an asymmetrical effect—where the transition effect is not applied to an equal number of frames on either side of the edit point—you must build it yourself. Here's how to build an asymmetrical dissolve. Place the incoming and outgoing clips on separate Timeline tracks, and allow the areas you want to include in the dissolve to overlap. Then ramp the opacity levels to cross-dissolve from one clip to the other.

Figure 12.22 Control-click the transition; then choose Open from the shortcut menu.

Figure 12.23 Type a new duration in the Duration field of the Transition Editor.

Figure 12.24 Dragging the edge of a transition to adjust just its duration.

EDITING VIDEO TRANSITIONS

Figure 12.25 Positioning the cursor on the incoming clip's In point in the Transition Editor.

Figure 12.26 Performing a Ripple edit on the incoming clip's In point. Drag the edge of the clip to perform a Ripple edit on the edit point underlying the transition.

Figure 12.27 Drag the Roll Edit tool on the transition to perform a Roll edit on the edit point underlying the transition.

To perform a Ripple edit on a transition in the Transition Editor:

1. Position the cursor on the edit point you want to trim (**Figure 12.25**).

   In the Transition Editor, the edit points appear on the clip icons displayed in the tracks above and below the transition icon.

   The cursor changes to the Ripple Edit tool.

2. Drag the edit point (**Figure 12.26**).

   A Ripple edit is performed on the edit point underlying the transition as the Canvas display changes to show your new In point.

To perform a Roll edit on a transition in the Transition Editor:

◆ Place the pointer anywhere on the transition. When the pointer changes to the Roll Edit tool, drag it on the transition to perform a Roll edit on the edit point underlying the transition (**Figure 12.27**).

   A Roll edit is performed on the edit point underlying the transition. The Canvas display changes to show your new In point.

To change the settings for a transition:

Do one or more of the following:

◆ To change the starting and ending effect percentages, drag the Start and End sliders (**Figure 12.28**) or type percentage values in the text boxes.

◆ To change the direction of the effect, click the Reverse button.

◆ To have the transition center on, begin on, or end on the edit, click the corresponding placement button at the top center of the Transition Editor. Once you've changed the center point of a transition, these controls won't remember the original edit point.

◆ Make other settings as desired for the transition. For more information on modifying effects settings, see Chapter 13, "Compositing and Effects Overview."

To preview a transition in the Canvas:

1. Open the transition in the Transition Editor.

2. Position the Transition Editor's playhead at any point in the transition (**Figure 12.29**).

3. Adjust the transition settings.

   The Canvas display updates to reflect any adjustments made to the transition settings (**Figure 12.30**).

4. To preview a frame at another point in the transition, reposition the Transition Editor playhead.

✔ Tip

■ Hold down the Option key as you scrub the Canvas's Scrubber bar to preview your transition. You can also step through a transition one frame at a time by pressing the right arrow key to advance the transition by single frames. Press the left arrow key to step backward. A slow-motion view of the transition appears in the Canvas.

Figure 12.28 Using the slider to adjust end position settings for a wipe transition.

Figure 12.29 Position the Transition Editor's playhead at any point in the transition. The Canvas displays a preview of the transition at the selected playhead location.

Figure 12.30 The Canvas display updates to reflect an adjustment to the transition's border width settings.

EDITING VIDEO TRANSITIONS

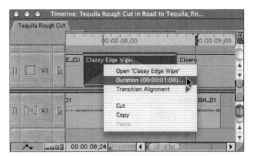

Figure 12.31 Control-click the transition; then choose Duration from the shortcut menu.

Figure 12.32 Enter a new duration for your transition.

Editing transitions in the Timeline

You can streamline transition editing in the Timeline by using the shortcut menus. One shortcut menu is accessed by Control-clicking the transition itself. A different shortcut menu is available for the edit point underlying the transition. Edit points that have transitions applied to them can still be trimmed in the same way as other edits; you can use the Trim Edit or Viewer windows or drag directly in the Timeline. For more information on trimming operations, see Chapter 10, "Fine Cut: Trimming Edits."

To adjust the duration of a transition in the Timeline:

◆ With the Selection tool, drag one edge of the transition to adjust its length.

Or, do this:

1. Control-click the transition; then choose Duration from the shortcut menu (**Figure 12.31**).

2. In the Duration dialog box, enter a new duration (**Figure 12.32**).

3. Click OK.

✔ Tip

■ Control-D is the keyboard shortcut to open the Duration dialog box for a selected clip or transition.

EDITING VIDEO TRANSITIONS

To trim an edit point underlying a transition:

Do one of the following:

- From the Tool palette, select the appropriate edit tool; then drag the edit point underlying the transition (**Figure 12.33**).

- With the Selection tool, double-click an edit point to open the Trim Edit window.

Modifying audio transitions

Final Cut Express has only two audio transitions to choose from; both are cross-fades. Only the duration of audio transitions can be adjusted. For more information on audio transitions, see Chapter 11, "Audio Tools and Techniques."

Rendering transitions

Unless you are using a real-time system, you must render transitions before you can play them back.

To render a transition:

1. Select the transition (**Figure 12.34**).

2. Choose Sequence > Render Selection (**Figure 12.35**).

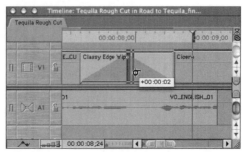

Figure 12.33 Trim an edit point underlying a transition by dragging the edit point with an edit tool. This Ripple edit will trim two frames off the incoming clip's In point.

Figure 12.34 In the Timeline, select the transition you want to render.

Figure 12.35 Choose Sequence > Render Selection.

Real-Time Transitions

If your Final Cut Express system is capable of supporting real-time effects, you can play certain transitions without rendering them first. The real-time transitions that are available on your particular system appear in bold type in the Effects menu and on the Browser's Effects tab (**Figure 12.36**). For more information on real-time systems and rendering, see Chapter 17, "Rendering."

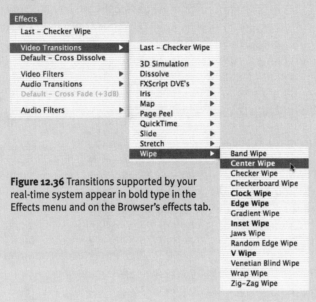

Figure 12.36 Transitions supported by your real-time system appear in bold type in the Effects menu and on the Browser's effects tab.

Part V:
Adding Titles
and Effects

Part V: Adding Titles and Effects

The effects tools in Final Cut Express are like a whole program within a program. This part provides basic information and a few step-by-step procedures to give you a feel for how techniques combine to create simple effects. It also includes some single-purpose tasks that show how the interface and tools operate. However, these chapters are not a comprehensive survey of Final Cut Express's effects capabilities. There are many more options, adjustments, keyboard commands, and possibilities than are described in here, but you will be in a better position to explore them yourself after going through the basic procedures.

COMPOSITING AND EFFECTS OVERVIEW

Creating digital motion effects could be the most fun you'll ever have without getting arrested. Modern mass media relies heavily on the same techniques you'll be introduced to in this chapter. Once you understand the role of each basic building block of effects creation, you'll never look at movies and TV in the same way again, because you'll be able to see how complex visuals are constructed.

The effects creation tools found in Final Cut Express are designed to be easy to use, but effects tools are the most challenging part of the FCE interface to master.

This chapter offers an overview of the basic elements you combine and sculpt to create effects, offers details on how to apply effects to your sequence, and shows where you can modify those effects.

As you start to apply effects, it's important to keep this in mind: Adding a clip from the Browser to a sequence in the Timeline places a *copy* of the clip in the sequence. By placing a clip in a sequence, you create a new instance of the clip. Before you modify a clip with effects, be sure you have selected the correct copy of the clip you want to change. This rule is central to understanding editing in Final Cut Express. For more information, see "FCE Protocol: Clips and Sequences" in Chapter 3.

Basic Building Blocks of Effects Creation

The basic building blocks you use to create video effects are fairly simple. You can generate complex effects by combining and then animating images using the basic processes described here.

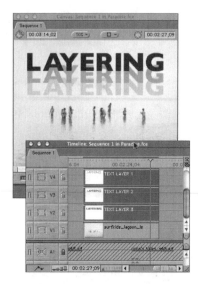

- **Layering** is an arrangement of multiple clips at one point in time, each in its own track. Superimposing a title over a video clip is a simple example of layering, with the video clip forming the background layer and the title forming the foreground layer. Other layering arrangements require making the upper layers semitransparent, so you can see the image in the background layer.

- **Compositing** can be any process that combines two or more image layers to create an effect. Compositing techniques can include adjustment of the transparency of one or more of the image layers and selection of a Composite mode, which is the algorithm that controls the way the image layers are combined.

- **Motion properties** are image modification tools that control a clip's size and shape, its position in the frame, and its designated center point, among other characteristics. The tools that are grouped together on the Motion tab don't always have an obvious connection to image movement; for example, the Opacity controls are located on the Motion tab. However, making incremental adjustments to a clip's size, position, and angle of rotation are basic steps in animating a static element—that's when things start to move.

◆ **Filters** are image modifiers that process the image data in a clip. Over time, filters have developed into a diverse effects category that includes everything from basic tools, such as brightness, contrast, and color controls, to complex 3D simulators.

◆ **Opacity** refers to a clip's level of transparency. A clip with an opacity level of 100 percent is completely opaque; one with an opacity level of 0 percent is completely transparent. Adjusting opacity is a basic procedure in compositing layers of images. Alpha channels and mattes are a means of adjusting opacity in selected portions of an image. You can adjust a clip's opacity on the Viewer's Motion tab or by using the opacity clip overlay in the Timeline.

◆ **Generators** are effects that create (or generate) new video information, rather than modify existing video. Generators are useful for producing utility items such as black frames (known as slugs), a plain-colored background, or text titles.

Locating and Applying Effects

You can access Final Cut Express's effects features in a variety of places:

◆ The Browser's Effects tab (**Figure 13.1**) displays bins containing all the types of effects available in Final Cut Express except motion properties.

◆ The same effects found on the Browser's Effects tab are also available from the Effects menu (**Figure 13.2**).

◆ Motion properties are automatically applied to every clip. Open a clip in the Viewer and click the Motion tab to access a clip's motion controls.

You can apply effects to clips and sequences in the following ways:

◆ Select a clip in the Timeline, and then choose an effect from the Effects menu.

◆ Select an effect from a bin on the Effects tab of the Browser and drag it onto the clip.

◆ Select a customized effect or motion from the Favorites bin on the Effects tab of the Browser and drag it to the clip to apply it.

◆ Choose a generator from the Generator pop-up menu in the lower-right corner of the Viewer.

◆ Open a Timeline or a Browser clip in the Viewer; then use the controls on the clip's Motion tab to apply motion effects.

◆ Open a Timeline clip in the Canvas; then use the Canvas's Wireframe mode overlay to animate a motion path.

Figure 13.1 The Browser's Effects tab organizes available effects in bins.

Figure 13.2 The same library of effects is available from the Effects menu.

Onscreen effects controls

You can make adjustments to effects you've already applied in the following ways:

◆ Double-click the clip in the Timeline; then select the Audio, Filters, or Motion tab in the Viewer and use the controls to make your adjustments. **Figure 13.3** illustrates the operation of the controls found on the Filters, Motion, and Controls tabs.

Color controls:
- *Click the triangle to open HSB controls*
- *Use the eyedropper to pick colors from Video windows.*
- *Click the arrow to perform color cycling for sweep direction*
- *Click the square to bring up the Apple Color Picker*

Adjustable column width: Drag separator lines

Effects tabs: Click to access a tab containing effects controls

Triangle: Click to show or hide controls

Toggle switch: Check box to turn effect on or off

Reset button: Click to reset all controls to default values

Slider controls: Drag the slider to set a value

Incremental controls: Click tiny arrows to change value by one

Clip control: Drop other clips here to affect the filtering of this clip

Text field: Enter exact parameter values

Dial controls: Drag the needle to set a value

Current Timecode field: Shows playhead's timecode location; enter time to move playhead

Point control: Set point values, such as X,Y positions, by clicking the image area

Figure 13.3 Overview of the effects controls found on the Filters, Motion, and Controls tabs in the Viewer window.

◆ In the Timeline, adjust opacity or audio level keyframe locations in the clip's overlay level line. **Figure 13.4** shows an overview of the effects tools and procedures available in the Timeline window.

◆ In the Canvas, turn on Wireframe mode and adjust a clip's motion properties or use motion keyframes to animate a motion path.

Clip & Sequence markers: Linked to markers in Viewer; used to align keyframes over multiple tracks

Opacity keyframe

Video clip: Double-click to access the Effects tab in the Viewer

Clip level line overlays: Displays opacity level for video and audio level for audio clips

Clip overlays: Toggle to view level line overlays for opacity and audio level

Clip overlay keyframe shortcut menu: Control-click a keyframe to switch between corner and curve keyframe types

Figure 13.4 Overview of effects tools in the Timeline.

LOCATING AND APPLYING EFFECTS

Effects Production Shortcuts

Creating effects can be time consuming and repetitive. Here are a few production shortcuts.

Copying and pasting clip attributes: Clip attributes are settings applied to a particular media file in Final Cut Express. You can copy and paste selected settings from one clip to another clip in the Timeline or in the Canvas, or use the Remove Attributes command to restore a clip's default settings. For more information, see Chapter 9, "Editing in the Timeline and the Canvas."

Nesting sequences: When you place, or create, a Final Cut Express sequence within another sequence, it's called *nesting* a sequence. Nested sequences can streamline and enhance your effects work in a variety of ways. You can use nested sequences to protect render files, to force effects to render in a different order, or to group clips so you can apply a single filter or motion path to all of them in one operation. Nested sequences are discussed in Chapter 3, "How to Manage an FCE Project."

"Effecting" multiple clips: FCE allows you to adjust opacity levels for a group of clips. You can also adjust audio levels for multiple clips in a single operation. See "Setting a clip's opacity in the Timeline" in Chapter 14.

Favorites: Favorites are customized effects presets. For example, if you need to apply the same color correction to a large group of clips, you can tweak the settings once, save that filter configuration as a Favorite, and apply it to the whole group without having to make individual adjustments. Favorites are discussed in the next section.

Saving Effects Settings as Favorites

You can designate an effect, transition, or generator as a Favorite. Favorite effects are placed in the Favorites bin on the Browser's Effects tab. Favorites provide an easy way to save an effect that you want to reproduce later. For more information on creating and using Favorites, see "Working with Default and Favorite Transitions" in Chapter 12.

To create a Favorite effect by saving its settings:

1. In the Timeline, double-click the clip with the effect you want to make a Favorite. The clip opens in the Viewer.

2. Select the Filters or the Controls tab to access the selected effect's controls.

3. Select the effect in the Name column (**Figure 13.5**); then drag the effect's name from its control bar to the Favorites bin on the Browser's Effects tab.

✔ Tip

■ If you've created a set of Favorite effects for use in a particular project, you can archive those effects by dragging the Favorites folder (or selected Favorite effects) from the Browser's Effects tab onto your project tab. Your project's Favorite effects are saved with the project file.

Figure 13.5 Save customized effects settings by selecting an effect in the Name column and dragging it to the Favorites bin.

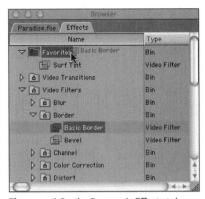

Figure 13.6 On the Browser's Effects tab, select an effect and drag it to the Favorites bin.

Figure 13.7 Configure the effect's settings.

Figure 13.8 In the Favorites bin, rename the customized effect.

To create a Favorite effect before changing its settings:

1. On the Effects tab in the Browser, select an effect and drag it to the Favorites bin (**Figure 13.6**).

2. Open the Favorites bin; then double-click the effect.

   The effect opens in the Viewer.

3. Adjust the effect's settings (**Figure 13.7**); then close the Viewer.

4. In the Favorites bin, rename the new effect (**Figure 13.8**).

✔ Tip

■ You can also select an effect in the Browser and then choose Edit > Duplicate. A copy of the effect appears in the Favorites submenu of the Effects menu.

Tuning in Effects: Using Dial, Slider, and Point Controls

Here are some keyboard/mouse combos you can use to enhance your control over any effect parameter with a dial interface:

◆ Hold down the Shift key to constrain the dial to 45-degree increments.

◆ Hold down the Command key to "gear-down" the dial's movement and make precise adjustments.

◆ Drag way, way out of the dial to reset the effect to the previous value.

Here are a few tips for effect parameters with slider interfaces:

◆ Expand the horizontal throw of any slider by widening the Parameters column in the column title bar. A longer slider makes it easier to adjust values.

◆ Hold the Command key to "gear-down" the slider's movement and make precise adjustments.

◆ Hold down the Shift key to add two decimal places of accuracy to a slider's value. This command could be more useful if it incorporated "gear-down" as well. You need to expand the horizontal throw of the slider by widening the Parameters column in the Filters or the Controls tab before the "double-digit accuracy" becomes useful.

◆ The Point control is that little crosshairs button you use to select location coordinates for a clip's center point. You can select the Point control and then click in the Canvas to specify a center point. That's very handy, but here's a way to use the point control that's even better. Once you've clicked, keep the mouse button pressed, and you can drag your center point location around the canvas until you find a position you like. The Canvas will update even while you have the mouse button down.

Keyframe Navigation Shortcuts

Table 13.1 shows keyboard shortcuts for jumping forwards and backwards through a series of keyframes, and for adding a motion keyframe. These keyboard shortcuts work for the Timeline's level line overlays and the Canvas's wireframe overlay. These shortcuts will boost your speed and accuracy, and are highly recommended.Creating effects can be time consuming and repetitive. Here are a few production shortcuts.

Table 13.1

Keyboard Shortcuts for Keyframes

FUNCTION	KEY COMMAND
Go to Next Keyframe	Shift-K
Go to Previous Keyframe	Option-K
Add Motion Keyframe	Control-K

Using Keyframes

Whenever you create motion paths, sculpt audio levels, or just fade to black, you need to use keyframes. Think of a keyframe as a kind of edit point—you set a keyframe at the point at which you want to change the value of an effect's parameter. Keyframes work the same way wherever they are applied.

You don't need keyframes to set a single level or value that applies to an entire clip; keyframes are required only if you want to change the value at some point within the clip. After you have added the first keyframe to a clip, Final Cut Express adds a new keyframe automatically whenever you change an effect setting for that clip at a different point in time.

When you use a keyframe to change a parameter, you have the option of making that keyframe a "curve-type." Curve-type keyframes have two added controls: *Bézier handles*, which you can use to fine-tune the shape of the motion path's curve, and *ease handles*, which you can use to fine-tune a clip's speed immediately before and after the keyframe location. You can also use curve-type keyframes to fine-tune the rate of change in an effect parameter's level. Converting a keyframe from a "corner-type" to a "curve-type" is sometimes called smoothing a keyframe. For more information on keyframe types, see "Adjusting motion path curves and corners" in Chapter 14.

continues on next page

USING KEYFRAMES

Final Cut Express has two types of keyframe graphs: level line overlays and motion paths.

Level line overlays (or *clip overlays*) are displayed as line graphs right on top of the track display in the Timeline (**Figure 13.9**) and over the waveform display on the Viewer's Audio tab. Keyframe overlays indicate clip opacity (for video clips) and volume level and stereo pan position (for audio clips).

For more information, see "Working with Keyframes in the Timeline" in Chapter 9.

Motion keyframes are set and sculpted in the Image+Wireframe display in the Canvas (**Figure 13.10**) or in the Viewer.

For information about working with motion keyframes, see Chapter 14, "Motion."

Figure 13.9 Level line overlays are displayed as line graphs right on top of the track display in the Timeline. The overlay in this figure controls opacity. Corner-style keyframes appear at the beginning of the clip; a curve-type keyframe with Bézier handles appears at the clip's end. Hide and show level line overlays by clicking the Clip Overlays button in the lower-left corner of the Timeline.

Figure 13.10 Motion keyframes appear on the wireframe overlay in the Canvas (or the Viewer), when Image+Wireframe mode is enabled.

USING KEYFRAMES

Figure 13.11 Shift drag the keyframe to change both the value and the keyframe's point in time simultaneously.

Figure 13.12 Enter timecode values to set keyframes at frame-accurate intervals.

Precision control of a keyframe's positioning

Even in a compact screen layout, FCE offers a variety of techniques to help you get a grip on your keyframe's positioning:

◆ In the effect's Viewer tab, use the incremental controls (the tiny arrows at either end of the effect parameter control sliders) to nudge values by +1 or by –1, or enter an exact numeric value in the parameter's text field.

◆ In the Timeline or the Viewer, hold down the Command key while you drag a keyframe. This enables "gear-down" dragging, which allows you to move the keyframe in precise increments.

◆ Shift-drag to change both the value and the keyframe's point in time simultaneously (**Figure 13.11**).

◆ To set keyframes at precise intervals, use timecode entry to jump the Timeline or Canvas playhead by a precise number of frames (**Figure 13.12**); then add your keyframe.

MOTION

Unlike filters or generators, motion properties are already present on every clip. You can access them by loading a clip or sequence into the Viewer and then selecting the Motion tab.

A few of the controls you find on the Motion tab don't have any obvious connection to movement; the Opacity, Crop, Distort, and Drop Shadow controls are all found on the Motion tab.

The first part of this chapter introduces motion properties as static image modification tools, which can be used in either static or animated compositions. The second part of the chapter, "Animating Clip Motion with Keyframes," discusses motion paths: the time-based uses of motion properties.

Setting motion properties

The motion properties listed below are present automatically on every clip, and their controls can be adjusted on the clip's Motion tab in the Viewer (**Figure 14.1**), or on the clip's Image+Wireframe mode overlay in the Canvas (**Figure 14.2**) or in the Viewer.

◆ **Scale:** Adjusts the size of the clip to make it smaller or larger than the sequence frame size.

◆ **Rotation:** Rotates the clip around its anchor point without changing its shape. Clips can be rotated up to plus or minus 24 complete rotations.

◆ **Center:** X,Y coordinates specify the center point of the clip.

◆ **Anchor Point:** X,Y coordinates specify another point relative to the clip's center point to use as a pivot point for rotating, scaling, or animating the motion path of the clip.

◆ **Crop:** Crops (removes) a portion of the clip from the side you specify. Use the Edge Feather option to create a soft border at the crop line.

◆ **Distort:** Changes the shape of the clip by adjusting its corners. The Aspect Ratio parameter sets the clip's height:width proportions.

◆ **Opacity:** Makes a clip opaque or translucent; 100 percent is completely opaque, and 0 percent is completely transparent.

◆ **Drop Shadow:** Places a drop shadow behind the selected clip, with a color, softness, and opacity you specify. You also specify the drop shadow's offset.

◆ **Motion Blur:** Blurs moving images by a specified percentage, by combining the images of adjacent frames to create the effect.

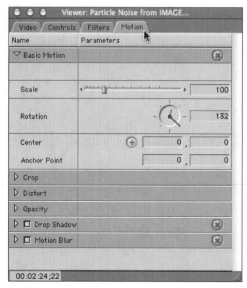

Figure 14.1 Use the controls on the Viewer's Motion tab to adjust motion properties.

Figure 14.2 You can also adjust motion properties graphically, using the Canvas wireframe overlay.

Locating X,Y coordinates

Final Cut Express uses X,Y coordinates to specify a clip's position in the frame. For example, in the DV-NTSC (720 by 480 pixel) frame size, you can specify locations outside the visible frame by using coordinate values greater than plus or minus 360 on the X axis, or plus or minus 240 on the Y axis. You'll often see X,Y coordinates specified like this: (50,25). The first number (50) is the X coordinate, and the second number (25) is the Y coordinate. **Figure 14.3** is a diagram of X,Y coordinate locations in a DV-NTSC (720 by 480 pixel) frame.

Figure 14.5 X,Y coordinates for a DV-NTSC (720 by 480 pixel) frame size.

Motion Properties Modify an Image or Make It Move

Motion properties perform basic image modifications when used as static composition tools, but they can also create motion effects when you adjust their values over time. For example, you might use the Rotation control as a static composition tool to display a title at a 90-degree angle (**Figure 14.4**) or animate rotation by setting incrementally increasing values over time (**Figure 14.5**).

Figure 14.4 Use the Rotation control as a static composition tool to set a title clip at a 90-degree angle.

Figure 14.5 Use the Rotation control to animate the title clip's rotation by setting incrementally increasing values over time.

Using Wireframes

Enabling Image+Wireframe mode in the Canvas or the Viewer activates a wireframe overlay that appears on your clip image. You must be in Image+Wireframe mode in order to graphically manipulate a clip's motion properties in the Canvas or the Viewer.

The elements of the wireframe aren't just indicators; they're also onscreen controls you can use to manipulate the size, shape, and position of your clip's image. Select the appropriate tool from the Tool palette; then click and drag a handle on the clip's wireframe in the Canvas or the Viewer. **Figure 14.6** offers a key to wireframe handles and tools.

✔ Tip

■ While you work in Wireframe mode, note that the selected track's number appears just above the clip's center point. The track number helps you remember which layer you have selected. If you're working on an effects sequence with many layered elements, that's a big help.

Green dot *indicates the upper-left corner of the clip*

Crop handle: *Drag to crop the clip*

Track number: *Identifies the clip by its Timeline track number*

Center point handle: *Drag to reposition the clip*

Anchor point handle: *Drag to reposition the pivot point of the clip*

Rotation handle: *Drag the borders to rotate the clip*

Scale/Distort handle: *Drag to scale or distort the clip*

Selection cursor: *Select Arrow tool and use within frame to reposition clip*

Distortion cursor: *Select Distort tool and use it on corners to distort clip*

Crosshair cursor: *Select Arrow tool and use on corner points to resize clip*

Rotation cursor: *Select Arrow tool and use it on borders to rotate clip*

Crop cursor: *Select Crop tool and use it on borders or corners to crop clip*

Figure 14.6 To manipulate motion properties in Image+Wireframe mode, select a tool; then click and drag the appropriate handle on the clip's wireframe.

Wireframe keyframe indicators

Wireframe mode uses green highlighting to indicate whether a keyframe is present on a frame and what type of keyframe it is (**Figure 14.7**).

To enable Wireframe mode:

Do one of the following:

◆ Press W once to place the Viewer or the Canvas in Image+Wireframe mode. (Press W again to return to Image mode.)

◆ Choose Image+Wireframe from the View pop-up menu at the top of the Viewer or the Canvas (**Figure 14.8**).

◆ Choose View > Image+Wireframe.

Figure 14.8 Choose Image+Wireframe from the View pop-up menu at the top of the Viewer or Canvas.

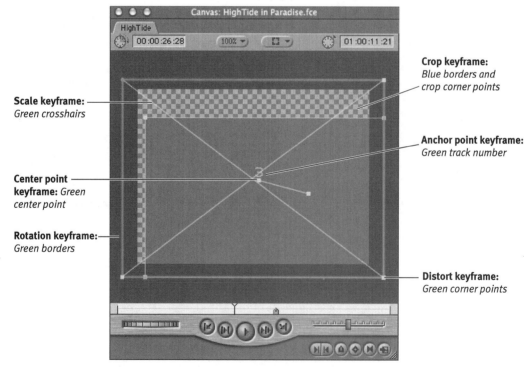

Scale keyframe: *Green crosshairs*

Center point keyframe: *Green center point*

Rotation keyframe: *Green borders*

Crop keyframe: *Blue borders and crop corner points*

Anchor point keyframe: *Green track number*

Distort keyframe: *Green corner points*

Figure 14.7 Wireframe mode uses highlighting to indicate the presence of keyframes.

USING WIREFRAMES

Using Motion Properties to Change a Clip's Appearance

In Final Cut Express, when you want to make a clip's image larger or smaller, tilted or skewed, opaque or transparent, you adjust the clip's motion properties—even if the clip's not moving. Not very intuitive, is it?

As long as you're not animating the clip (changing the size and shape of the clip's image over time), you don't need to add any motion keyframes. Simply open the clip and adjust the clip's default motion properties settings. Final Cut Express offers two ways to modify a clip's motion properties—by adjusting the controls and entering numerical values on the clip's Motion tab in the Viewer, or by using the Tool palette's image modification tools to manipulate the clip's image directly in the Canvas wireframe overlay. When you're going for precision and consistency, you'll probably end up working both numerically and graphically.

All of the operations described in this section can be performed in both places. Start each operation by following the general setup procedure for each respective mode; the setup tasks are described in the sections that follow.

Pressin', Clickin', and Draggin': Using Keyboard Shortcuts with Wireframes

Many of the scaling and positioning tools have keyboard modifiers—keys you press as you drag the tool on the wireframe handles in the Canvas or in the Viewer—that you can use to create complex alterations to a clip.

◆ **Option key:** Use this modifier to force automatic rendering while you drag the clip.

◆ **Shift key:** Use this modifier to enable nonproportional scaling (modification of a clip's aspect ratio while scaling). You can use the Shift and Option modifiers together.

◆ **Command key:** Use this modifier to rotate and scale the clip simultaneously. You can use the Command and Option modifiers together.

MOTION PROPERTIES TO CHANGE APPEARANCE

To set up for motion properties adjustment in the Canvas Wireframe mode:

1. In the Timeline, select the clip you want to reposition (**Figure 14.9**). If you are working with a layered composition, be sure to choose the layer you want to affect.

2. From the Tool palette, choose the appropriate image modification tool for the motion property you want to adjust. Refer to the key to wireframe handles and tools in Figure 14.6.

3. If it's not already activated, press W to turn on the Canvas's Image+Wireframe mode.

   The outline of the wireframe overlay appears on the selected clip's image (**Figure 14.10**).

To set up for motion properties adjustment on the Viewer's Motion tab:

1. Double-click the clip in the Timeline or the Browser to open it in the Viewer.

2. In the Viewer, click the Motion tab.

Figure 14.9 In the Timeline, select the clip you want to reposition.

Figure 14.10 Press W to activate Image+Wireframe mode, and the wireframe overlay appears on the selected clip's image.

Figure 14.11 Click anywhere in the clip's wireframe and drag it to a new position.

Figure 14.12 Click the Point Select button located to the left of the Center value field.

Figure 14.13 Click a new center location in the Canvas to specify new center coordinates.

Positioning clips

Clips start out positioned at the center of the Canvas or the Viewer. You can reposition a clip's center point by dragging it to a new position in the Canvas or in the Viewer, or you can specify new center point coordinates on the clip's Motion tab. You can position a clip partially or completely outside the sequence frame.

To adjust a clip's center point using Wireframe mode:

◆ Follow the setup steps for Wireframe mode presented earlier; then click anywhere inside the clip's wireframe and drag it to a new position (**Figure 14.11**).

To adjust a clip's center point on the Viewer's Motion tab:

Follow the setup steps for the Motion tab mode described earlier; then *do one of the following:*

◆ Enter new X,Y coordinates for the clip's center location. Enter the X coordinate in the left value field and the Y coordinate in the right value field.

◆ Click the Point Select (+) button (**Figure 14.12**) (located to the left of the Center value field) and then specify new center coordinates by clicking the new center location in the Canvas (**Figure 14.13**) or on the Video tab of the Viewer.

Scaling clips

A clip placed in a Final Cut Express sequence plays at the same frame size at which it was captured, regardless of the sequence frame size. A clip whose native size is smaller than the sequence frame size appears in the center of the sequence frame; a clip whose native size is larger than the sequence frame size shows only the portion of the clip that fits inside the sequence frame dimensions.

You can adjust the scale of a clip to change its frame size (for the current sequence only). If you want to create a media file of your clip at a different size that does not need to be rendered before it can be played back, you should export a copy of the clip at the frame size you need.

To scale a clip in Wireframe mode:

1. Follow the setup steps for Wireframe mode presented earlier.

2. Drag a corner handle to scale a clip while maintaining its proportions (**Figure 14.14**).

✔ Tips

■ Smooth your keyframes with Bézier curves when you animate scale. Curve-type keyframes produce a change in the rate of scale at the beginning and the end of the scaling animation, making the movement less mechanical. To learn how to convert a keyframe to a Bézier curve type, see "To refine a keyframe," later in this chapter.

■ When you're scaling a clip, it's easy to drift away from the clip's original aspect ratio, but not easy to find the control that resets your clip to its native proportions. Go to the clip's Motion tab and scroll down to the Distort controls. That's where you'll find the Aspect Ratio parameter. Reset the value to 0, and you'll restore height:width sanity to your scaled clip.

Figure 14.14 Dragging a corner handle scales a clip while maintaining its proportions.

FCE Protocol: Center Point vs. Anchor Point vs. Origin Point

All three types of points—the center point, anchor point, and origin point—are used to define position, but each serves a different purpose:

◆ **Center point:** Establishes the clip's position inside the Canvas area. The center point's default position (0,0) is the same as the anchor point.

◆ **Anchor point:** Establishes the pivot point for a clip's movement inside the Canvas area. Rotation and Scale properties and motion paths are all based on the anchor point. The anchor point's default position (0,0) is the same as the Center point.

◆ **Origin point:** Origin appears on the Motion tab for text generators and establishes the positioning of the text elements placed inside the clip.

Figure 14.15 Adjust the Scale slider on the Motion tab to scale the clip.

Figure 14.16 To rotate a clip in Wireframe mode, drag in an arc around the clip's center point.

To scale a clip on the Viewer's Motion tab:

Follow the setup steps for Motion tab mode presented earlier; then *do one of the following*:

◆ Adjust the Scale slider (**Figure 14.15**).

◆ Enter a percentage in the text field located to the right of the slider; 100 percent is equal to the clip's native size.

Rotating clips

Rotation is an important part of modern video effects (as you know if you've watched a TV commercial break recently).

A clip rotates around its anchor point. The default anchor point location matches the clip's center point, but you can rotate a clip around a different pivot point by changing the location of the anchor point. You can position a clip at the edge of your sequence frame and rotate your clip partially or completely outside the Canvas, so it appears on the screen for only a portion of its rotation. You can also rotate a clip up to 24 revolutions in either direction or use the Rotation control to angle a clip as part of a static composition.

To adjust a clip's rotation angle in Wireframe mode:

Follow the setup steps for Wireframe mode presented earlier; then *do one of the following*:

◆ Click an edge of the border and drag in an arc around the clip's center point (**Figure 14.16**).

◆ Click a border edge, and then drag farther away from the clip's center point to get more precise control over the rotation.

◆ Hold down the Shift key while dragging to constrain the rotation positions to 45-degree increments.

◆ Drag around the clip multiple times without releasing the mouse to specify a number of rotations.

To adjust a clip's rotation angle on the Viewer's Motion tab:

Follow the setup steps for the Motion tab mode described earlier; then *do one of the following:*

◆ Drag the black rotation needle around the dial to set a rotation position (**Figure 14.17**); the red needle indicates the number of complete revolutions.

◆ Enter a new value in the text box.

The clip realigns at the new rotation angle for the selected frame. To create an animated rotation effect on the Motion tab, you must set individual keyframes for each rotation angle value (see "Animating Clip Motion with Keyframes," later in this chapter).

Cropping clips

You can crop a clip either by dragging with the Crop tool or by specifying the number of pixels to crop from the borders. You can also feather the edges of the frame to make them blend smoothly with the background.

When you use the Crop tool to remove part of a clip's image, the selected parts are hidden, not deleted. You can restore the cropped sections to view by clicking the Reset button next to the Crop controls on the Viewer's Motion tab.

Figure 14.17 Drag around the rotation control dial needle to set a rotation position. The black hand indicates the current angle of the clip, and the small red hand indicates how many total rotations forward or backward have been specified.

Figure 14.18 Click and drag from the edges of the clip to crop out elements in the image.

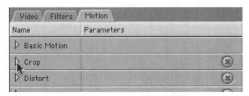

Figure 14.19 Open the Crop controls by clicking the Crop expansion triangle.

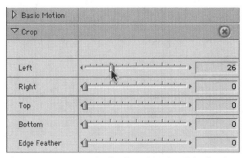

Figure 14.20 Crop a clip by dragging the slider for the side you want to crop and setting it to a new value.

To crop a clip in Wireframe mode:

1. Follow the setup steps for the Wireframe mode presented earlier; then select the Crop tool from the Tool palette.

2. *Do one of the following:*

   ◆ Click and drag from the edges of the clip to hide elements in the image (**Figure 14.18**).

   ◆ Shift-drag to constrain the clip's aspect ratio as you crop.

   ◆ Command-drag to trim both horizontal edges or both vertical edges simultaneously.

   ◆ Use Option in combination with Shift and Command to force rendering while performing a crop operation.

To crop a clip on the Motion tab:

1. Follow the setup steps for the Motion tab mode described earlier; then open the Crop control bar by clicking the expansion triangle on the left (**Figure 14.19**).

2. To crop the clip from a specific side, *do one of the following:*

   ◆ Drag the slider for that edge to a new value (**Figure 14.20**).

   ◆ Enter a new value in the corresponding text field.

3. To soften the cropped edges of the clip, *do one of the following:*

   ◆ Adjust the Edge Feather slider to specify the width of the feathered edge.

   ◆ Specify a value in the Edge Feather text field.

Distorting a clip's shape

Use the Distort tool when you want to make independent adjustments to each corner point of a clip's wireframe, or use the Viewer's Motion tab to numerically specify X,Y coordinates for the location of each corner point.

To distort the shape of a clip in Wireframe mode:

1. Follow the setup steps for the Wireframe mode presented earlier; then select the Distort tool from the Tool palette (**Figure 14.21**).

2. To distort the clip's image, *do one of the following:*

   ◆ Drag a corner handle of the clip's wireframe (**Figure 14.22**).

   ◆ Shift-drag to change the perspective of the image.

To distort a clip on the Viewer's Motion tab:

1. Follow the setup steps for the Motion tab mode presented earlier; then open the Distort control bar by clicking the expansion triangle.

2. To specify new locations for the corner points, *do one of the following:*

   ◆ Enter new values for the corner points you want to move.

   ◆ Adjust the Aspect Ratio parameter to change the clip's height:width ratio, relocating all four corner points. A clip's original aspect ratio has a value of zero.

Figure 14.21 Select the Distort tool from the Tool palette.

Figure 14.22 Drag a corner handle of the clip's wireframe to distort it.

MOTION PROPERTIES TO CHANGE APPEARANCE

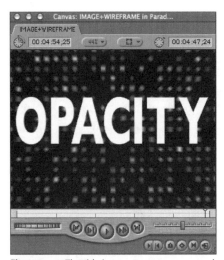

Figure 14.23 The title is 100 percent opaque and completely obscures the background.

Figure 14.24 The superimposed title with opacity set to less than 100 percent appears semitransparent.

Figure 14.25 Enter a value between 0 and 100 in the Opacity text field.

Adjusting opacity

Final Cut Express clips start out 100 percent opaque (**Figure 14.23**). If you superimpose a clip over another clip in the base track of your sequence, the background image will be completely hidden until you adjust the opacity of the superimposed clip to less than 100 percent, making it semitransparent (**Figure 14.24**).

Layering multiple, semitransparent images is a basic compositing technique, and one you may be familiar with if you have ever worked with Adobe Photoshop.

You can adjust a clip's opacity on the Viewer's Motion tab or with the opacity clip overlay in the Timeline.

To set a clip's opacity on the Viewer's Motion tab:

1. Follow the setup steps for the Motion tab mode described earlier; then open the Opacity control bar by clicking the triangle.

2. To set the opacity level, *do one of the following:*

    ◆ Use the slider control.

    ◆ Enter a value between 0 and 100 in the Opacity text field (**Figure 14.25**).

Setting a clip's opacity in the Timeline

A clip's opacity can be adjusted directly in the Timeline using the clip overlay for opacity, a level line graph that appears over the clip icon in the Timeline. To display clip overlays, click the Clip Overlays button in the lower-left corner of the Timeline.

For information on adjusting clip overlays in the Timeline, see "Working with Keyframes in the Timeline" in Chapter 9.

Use the Modify > Levels command to adjust opacity levels for a group of Timeline clips in a single operation.

To adjust opacity levels on a group of clips:

1. In the Timeline, select a group of clips whose levels you want to adjust (**Figure 14.26**).

2. Choose Modify > Levels.

3. In the Opacity Adjust dialog box, *do one of the following*:

    ◆ Choose Relative from the pop-up menu. Adjust each clip's opacity relative to its current level by specifying the percentage value (**Figure 14.27**).

    ◆ Choose Absolute from the pop-up menu; then set an absolute value for all clips' opacity by specifying a percentage value.

4. Click OK.

Figure 14.26 Select a group of Timeline clips whose opacity levels you want to adjust.

Figure 14.27 Choose Relative in the Opacity Adjust dialog box to adjust the opacity of all the selected clips by the percentage you specify.

Figure 14.28 Drop shadows add depth to a superimposed title.

Figure 14.29 Check the box to enable the Drop Shadow option.

Adding a drop shadow to a clip

Drop shadows add the illusion of dimensional depth to the 2D television screen (**Figure 14.28**). Titles pop out from the backgrounds, or clips softly float over other clips; complex silhouettes can add a special depth to your sequences. You can add a drop shadow to any clip whose display size is smaller than the sequence frame size.

You can apply drop shadows to clips that were captured at a smaller frame size and to clips that have been scaled, cropped, moved, or distorted. You can also display a drop shadow on a full-size clip with an alpha channel.

To add a drop shadow to a clip:

1. Double-click the clip in the Timeline or the Browser to open it in the Viewer.

2. In the Viewer, click the Motion tab; then check the Drop Shadow check box (**Figure 14.29**).

3. To adjust your drop shadow settings, *do any of the following:*
   ◆ Enter Offset settings to specify the shadow's distance from the clip.
   ◆ Enter Angle settings to specify the position of the shadow relative to the clip edge.
   ◆ Enter Softness settings to specify the degree of blending in the shadow's edge.
   ◆ Enter Opacity settings to specify the shadow's degree of transparency.

continues on next page

MOTION PROPERTIES TO CHANGE APPEARANCE

4. In the Color control bar, click the expansion triangle; then pick a color by *doing one of the following*:

- ◆ Drag the hue, saturation, and brightness sliders to new values.

- ◆ Enter color values numerically in the text fields.

- ◆ Click the eyedropper and click in the Canvas to sample a color.

- ◆ Click the color swatch and use one of the color pickers to choose the desired color (**Figure 14.30**).

Figure 14.30 Click the color swatch; then choose a color from one of the color pickers.

Figure 14.31 Motion blur produces soft-focus effects based on movement within your video image.

Figure 14.32 You can apply motion blur to a static graphic as well, but you must animate the graphic with a motion path first.

Adding a motion blur effect

The motion blur effect enhances the illusion of movement by compositing the images of adjacent frames (**Figure 14.31**). This is definitely one control to experiment with, particularly for creating interesting, animated, soft-focus background textures. If you're using graphics or stills, you must combine motion blur with other motion effects—scaling, rotation, or motion paths, for example—to see the motion blur effect, but you can use it to create a lot of action in your composition, even with static elements (**Figure 14.32**).

✔ Tip

- Nest a clip containing an element you want to blur. By increasing the frame size when you nest, you can create a roomier bounding box that will accommodate the larger size of your blurred element.

To add motion blur to a clip:

1. Double-click the clip in the Timeline or the Browser to open it in the Viewer.

2. In the Viewer, click the Motion tab; then check the Motion Blur check box (at the bottom of the tab) (**Figure 14.33**).

3. Click the Motion Blur expansion triangle to reveal the controls for blurring motion.

4. Use the % Blur slider or enter a value in the text field. Values range from 1000%, which blurs a frame's image across 10 frames, to 100%, which blurs the image on a single frame.

5. To change the quality of the motion blur, adjust the sample rate by choosing a value from the Samples pop-up menu (**Figure 14.34**).

✔ Tip

■ The sample rate is the number of in-between images FCE calculates when it compares two adjacent frames to calculate motion blur. A low sample rate produces more visible intermediate steps; a high sample rate produces a smoother look, but takes longer to render.

Figure 14.33 Check the Motion Blur check box to enable motion blurring.

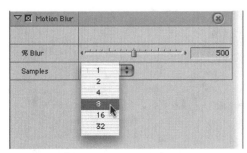

Figure 14.34 Specify a number of samples by selecting a value from the pop-up menu. The sample rate changes the quality of the motion blur. Fewer samples creates more visible intermediate steps.

Figure 14.35 Click the Add Keyframe button on the Canvas to set a keyframe.

Animating Clip Motion with Keyframes

The previous section explained how to use motion properties to alter a clip's shape, size, and transparency in a static composition. In this section you'll finally learn how to use motion properties to actually move your clips around.

Working with basic motion keyframe commands

There's only one location where you set and adjust motion keyframes—all of these operations must be performed with the clip open in the Canvas or the Viewer when it is in Image+Wireframe mode.

✔ Tip

■ You can work with motion keyframes in both the Canvas and the Viewer, but because keyframing more commonly happens in the Canvas, the directions in this section mention only the Canvas.

To set a motion keyframe:

1. In the Canvas, position the playhead at the frame where you want to set the keyframe.

2. Click the Add Keyframe button (**Figure 14.35**); or press Control-K.

The Best Way to Fine-Tune a Motion Sequence

The Canvas's wireframe overlay uses a system of green highlighting to indicate that a keyframe is present on a particular frame, but it's not always easy to tell when you are parked exactly on a motion keyframe. FCE's keyframe navigation keyboard commands are essential to animating motion because, even if you can't see green highlighting on the wireframe overlay—and, believe me, sometimes you can't—the keyboard command will move you to that next keyframe.

As you use Shift-K and Option-K to step through a series of keyframes, you can review your clip's motion settings at each keyframe. For best results, keep an eye on both the Canvas and the Motion tab—the Canvas wireframe overlay updates to show the way your composition looks, and the clip's Motion tab updates to show the precise value of each keyframe's settings.

3. To set an additional keyframe, move the playhead to the next location where you want to set a keyframe; then *do one of the following:*

- ◆ Add another keyframe, then adjust the Motion tab parameter control or make a graphical adjustment to the clip's wireframe.

- ◆ Make an adjustment to a Motion tab parameter control or make a graphical adjustment to the clip's wireframe.

Final Cut Express adjusts the values and then automatically adds the keyframe (**Figure 14.36**).

✔ Tip

- ■ Clicking the Add Keyframe button in the Canvas sets a motion keyframe across all motion parameters for the current frame.

Figure 14.36 Move the playhead to the next location; then adjust an effects parameter control, and FCE automatically adds the next keyframe.

ANIMATING CLIP MOTION WITH KEYFRAMES

Figure 14.37 To delete the keyframe, Control-click and choose Delete Point from the shortcut menu.

Figure 14.38 Another way to delete a motion keyframe is to Option-click it with the Pen tool.

To navigate between motion keyframes:

◆ Press Shift-K to move to the next motion keyframe.

◆ Press Option-K to move to the previous keyframe.

The playhead moves to the next keyframe in the appropriate direction, and the Canvas updates to show the new position of the clip

✔ Tip

■ In the Timeline, these keyframe navigation shortcuts step through opacity and audio level overlay keyframes.

To delete a motion keyframe:

In the Canvas wireframe overlay, *do one of the following*:

◆ Control-click the keyframe and choose Delete Point from the shortcut menu (**Figure 14.37**).

◆ Option-click the keyframe with the Pen tool (**Figure 14.38**).

To refine a motion keyframe:

1. Control-click the keyframe and choose Ease In/Ease Out from the shortcut menu (**Figure 14.39**).

   The keyframe changes into a curve type, and Bézier handles appear.

2. Drag the small blue circle at the end of the Bézier handle to adjust the motion path leading up to (or away from) the keyframe (**Figure 14.40**).

✔ Tip

- Refine opacity and audio level overlay keyframes in the Timeline by Control-clicking the overlay keyframe and selecting Smooth from the shortcut menu.

To move a motion keyframe:

- In the Canvas wireframe overlay, click the motion keyframe with the appropriate selection tool and drag it to a new location.

Figure 14.39 To smooth a corner-type keyframe to a Bézier curve type, Control-click the keyframe and choose Ease In/Ease Out from the shortcut menu.

Figure 14.40 Drag the small blue circle at the end of the Bézier handle to adjust the motion path leading away from the keyframe.

Figure 14.41 To add the first keyframe, click the Add Keyframe button on the Canvas.

Figure 14.42 Click the Current Timecode field at the bottom left of the Motion tab; then type +30 to add 30 frames to the playhead location.

Setting motion keyframes with timecode entry

Evenly spaced keyframes are essential for smooth, even changes in your effects and for precision synchronization to music or other effects. This is especially true for motion effects. When you animate a program element, using timecode ensures that your keyframes will be set at precise intervals. This task shows you how to rotate a clip using timecode entry to set keyframes.

To set keyframes using timecode entry:

1. In the Timeline, double-click the clip you want to rotate to open it in the Viewer.

2. In the Viewer, click the Motion tab; then press Home to jump the playhead to the first frame of your clip.

3. In the Canvas, click the Add Keyframe button (**Figure 14.41**); or press Control-K.

   The clip's first Rotation keyframe is set on the first frame.

4. Verify that the Rotation control is set to zero.

   This establishes the clip's orientation at the beginning of the rotation.

5. Click the Current Timecode field at the bottom left of the Motion tab; then type +30 to move the playhead 30 frames forward (**Figure 14.42**).

   The playhead advances 30 frames.

   continues on next page

6. Click the Add Keyframe button again; then *do one of the following*:

♦ In the Rotation control dial, drag the needle clockwise to set the keyframe value to 180 (**Figure 14.43**).

♦ Enter 180 in the Rotation text field.

7. Repeat steps 5 and 6, increasing the Rotation value to 360.

You have set three keyframes, exactly 30 frames apart, causing your clip to complete one full 360-degree rotation in 2 seconds (**Figure 14.44**).

8. Press Option-K to step backward through your three keyframes, noting that the clip flips and the Rotation value updates at each keyframe. Press Shift-K to step forward through the keyframes.

9. You must render your rotating clip before you can play it back. Select the clip; then choose Sequence > Render Selection.

10. Play back your rotation effect.

✔ Tip

■ Strictly speaking, it's not necessary to click the Add Keyframe button to set the second and third keyframes; you need only change the keyframe's value in the Motion tab. However, in FCE 1.0, rotation keyframes don't show up in the wireframe overlay even when they are present. Pressing the Add Keyframe button sets a keyframe across all motion parameters, so the green highlighting is visible.

Figure 14.43 Set the keyframe value to 180 by dragging the Rotation dial needle to the right.

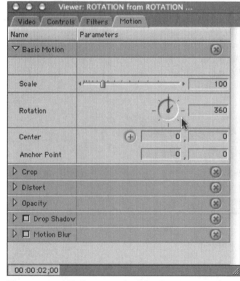

Figure 14.44 You have set three keyframes, exactly 30 frames apart, that program your clip to complete one full 360-degree rotation in 2 seconds.

Figure 14.45 Choose Image+Wireframe from the View pop-up menu.

Creating Motion Paths

If you are new to motion paths, try one—if your FCE system is powerful enough to support real-time previewing, you can play your moving clip back without rendering, and you will get a feel for how the Canvas function changes when you are working in Wireframe mode. You can work in Wireframe mode in the Viewer as well.

When you animate the center point, you move the whole clip. The following section explains the basic steps for animating a simple motion path.

✔ Tip

■ Motion paths are limited to single sequence clips; you must nest sequence clips if you want to create a motion path that includes two or more clips that have been edited together. For more information on nesting items, see Chapter 3.

To create a motion path in the Canvas:

1. In the Timeline, select a sequence clip; then position the playhead on the first frame in your clip.

2. Make the Canvas active; then choose 12% from the Zoom pop-up menu and Image+Wireframe from the View pop-up menu (**Figure 14.45**).

3. To add the first keyframe, click the Add Keyframe button in the Canvas.

   Final Cut Express sets the first keyframe across all motion parameters for that sequence frame.

continues on next page

4. In the Canvas, drag the wireframe's center handle to the left until the right side of the wireframe aligns with the left edge of the black background. Hold down the Shift key while you drag to constrain the motion path. This makes it easier to drag in a straight line.

Your clip is now positioned just off the screen, at the left (**Figure 14.46**).

5. In the Timeline, position the playhead on the last frame in your sequence clip.

6. In the Canvas, click inside the wireframe and Shift-drag it to the right. Drag the wireframe across the black background until its left side aligns with the right edge of the black background.

As you drag, the motion path appears across the center of the screen. The white line indicates the motion path of your clip's center point (**Figure 14.47**).

7. To preview your motion path, hold down the Option key while you scrub the Canvas Scrubber bar from side to side.

8. If your computer supports real-time previewing, you can play your moving clip immediately. If not, you must render before playback. Select the clip; then choose Sequence > Render Selection.

✔ Tip

■ When your clips and motion paths are so spread out that you need to make the Canvas or the Viewer view smaller than the smallest level listed on the Zoom control (12%), choose Fit All, which will zoom the view out enough to fit all elements of your multilayered composited sequence within the window.

Figure 14.46 Your clip is positioned just off the screen, at the left.

Figure 14.47 The white line indicates the motion path of your clip's center point.

CREATING MOTION PATHS

Figure 14.48 As you drag the motion path into a curve, the additional keyframes appear with little handles, called Bézier handles, that you drag to sculpt the motion path's curves.

Figure 14.49 Rotate the handle to change the direction of the curve relative to that keyframe.

Figure 14.50 Command-drag to restrict rotation to one side of the curve.

To add curves to a motion path:

1. If you don't already have a sequence clip with a motion path applied, follow steps 1 through 6 in the previous task, "To create a motion path in the Canvas."

2. To create a curve in your straight motion path, click the motion path and drag in the direction you want the path to curve.

   As you drag the motion path into a curve, additional keyframes automatically appear on the motion path; the keyframes have little handles, called Bézier handles, that are used to sculpt the motion path's curves (**Figure 14.48**).

3. Click the Canvas Play button to play back the first draft of your edited motion path. Watching real-time playback in Wireframe mode is the best way to evaluate your clip's speed and movement.

4. To adjust the curve, click a keyframe's Bézier handle; then *do any of the following*:

   ◆ Drag the handle away from the keyframe to deepen the curve.

   ◆ Drag the handle toward the keyframe to reduce the curve.

   ◆ Rotate the handle to change the direction of the curve relative to that keyframe (**Figure 14.49**).

   ◆ Command-drag to restrict rotation to one side of the curve (**Figure 14.50**). Release the Command key to set the new relationship between the two curves.

To reposition an entire motion path:

1. Choose the Selection tool from the Tool palette.

2. In the Canvas, hold down the Command and Shift keys; then place the cursor near the motion path that you want to reposition.

   The Selection tool turns into a Hand pointer when you position it correctly (**Figure 14.51**).

3. Drag the motion path to a new position.

   The entire motion path repositions but does not change its shape or timing (**Figure 14.52**).

Figure 14.51 Hold down the Command and Shift keys; then place the Selection pointer near the motion path that you want to reposition. The pointer turns into a Hand pointer when you're in the right spot.

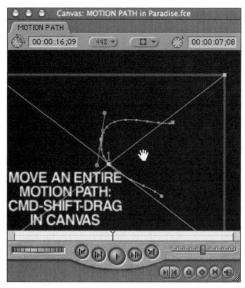

Figure 14.52 Drag the entire motion path to a new position without changing its shape or timing.

Editing a Motion Path

Once you have created it, you can adjust a motion path directly in the Canvas (or Viewer) by moving or deleting motion path keyframes. When you're working with a motion path in the Canvas, the playhead doesn't need to be over a keyframe for you to move or delete it, nor does the playhead location prohibit you from adding a motion path keyframe.

Remember that a keyframe is like an edit point: It signals a change in an effect. In a motion path, keyframes are placed automatically only when a motion path changes direction. A straight motion path requires only two keyframes: a start keyframe and an end keyframe.

The two motion path variables you are adjusting are your clip's speed of travel (determined by the ratio of duration to distance between keyframes) and the path's route (indicated by the shape of the white line that connects the start and end keyframes). The little round dots that appear in between the keyframes indicate the duration between path points.

Adjusting motion path curves and corners

Final Cut Express features two types of motion path keyframes: corners and curves. The default motion path keyframe is a corner, which creates an instant change in direction. If you want a smoother motion effect, the curve keyframes have Bézier handles, which you can use to fine-tune the shape of the motion path's curve, as well as ease handles, which you can use to fine-tune your clip's speed immediately before and after the keyframe location.

You switch a corner-type motion path keyframe to a curve type as the first step in smoothing your motion path and finessing its timing.

✔ Tip

■ You can use the Shift and Command keys while dragging a Bézier or ease handle to influence the connections between the angles of the curve.

To toggle a keyframe between corner and curve types in Wireframe mode:

With your clip displayed in Wireframe mode in the Canvas, Control-click a keyframe and *choose one of the following options:*

◆ Make Corner Point toggles the keyframe from a curve type to a corner type (**Figure 14.53**).

◆ Ease In/Ease Out accesses the ease handles, which are discussed later in this section.

◆ Linear applies a constant rate of speed to the path immediately before and after the keyframe location.

◆ Delete Point deletes the keyframe.

Figure 14.53 Control-click a keyframe on the Canvas; then choose Make Corner Point to toggle the keyframe from a curve type to a corner type.

Figure 14.54 Ease handles are located about midway between the Bézier handles and the keyframe's position point.

Adjusting speed along a motion path

You can increase the speed of a clip's movement by shortening the timecode duration between two keyframes without changing their spatial coordinates. The clip's speed increases, as it takes less time to travel between the two locations on your motion path. Or, keep the time interval the same and move the keyframes farther apart on the motion path, so the clip travels farther in the same amount of time. Other timing factors in your sequence composition will dictate your choice.

Ease handles, located in the Canvas between the Bézier handles and the keyframe's position point (**Figure 14.54**), fine-tune the rate of speed at which a clip approaches and leaves a curve keyframe. The default Ease In and Out setting slows the speed on the motion path by 33 percent before and after the keyframe, but you can customize that setting. Drag both handles to set the clip's ease in and ease out to the same rate, or drag the handles separately to set different ease-in and ease-out rates.

To make a clip ease in and out of a keyframe:

1. With the Canvas in Wireframe mode, start with a curve motion path keyframe.

2. Select the Selection tool.

3. Click the curve keyframe; then *do one of the following:*

   ◆ Drag the ease handle away from the keyframe to increase the clip's speed as it passes through the keyframe's location on the motion path (**Figure 14.55**).

   ◆ Drag the handle toward the keyframe to slow the clip's speed as it passes through the keyframe's location on the motion path (**Figure 14.56**).

   ◆ Drag either ease handle to adjust the path's timing on both sides of the keyframe equally.

   ◆ Shift-drag one ease handle to adjust the path's timing only on the selected side.

4. Play back in Wireframe mode to see your results.

✔ Tip

■ You can copy and paste Motion Paths between clips or sequences by using the Paste Attributes command on the Edit menu. Check the Scale Attributes box when you paste attributes onto your destination clip, and you can reuse a motion path on a different clip that's shorter or longer than the original.

Figure 14.55 Drag the ease handle away from the keyframe to increase a clip's speed as it passes through the keyframe's location on the motion path.

Figure 14.56 Drag the ease handle toward the keyframe to decrease a clip's speed as it passes through the keyframe's location on the motion path.

Setting a Single Motion Path for Multiple Clips

How can you easily apply a single motion path to multiple clips? There are a couple of different techniques available; your choice depends on whether you are dealing with a series of clips on a single track or with multiple clips stacked in layers on Timeline tracks.

One approach is to copy and paste just the series of clips into a separate sequence, which you edit back into your main sequence just as if it were a single clip. You can then apply a single motion path to the entire series, because it's contained in a single sub-sequence. You can use the same technique to convert multiple layers into a sub-sequence in order to apply a single motion path.

You also have the option of copying a clip and pasting only its motion path using the Paste Attributes function.

For more information on working with multiple sequences, see Chapter 3, "How to Manage an FCE Project."

For more information on the Paste Attributes feature, see Chapter 9, "Editing in the Timeline and the Canvas."

FILTERS AND COMPOSITING

15

Just as the term *motion properties* is used to describe a collection of tools that do a lot more than move things, so the term *filters* applies to a lot more than just tools for tinting or texturing an image. Final Cut Express comes with more than 50 video filters, with a wide variety of uses (**Figure 15.1** next page). In addition to a suite of image-control filters for color correction or tinting, Final Cut Express provides filters you can use to blur, twirl, emboss, ripple, flip, mask, and key. For a list of filters, refer to Chapter 21 in Apple's *Final Cut Express User's Manual*.

Final Cut Express can also make use of the QuickTime effects that are installed with QuickTime and some FXBuilder-based filters written for Final Cut Pro.

You'll find filters on the Browser's Effects tab or in the Effects menu. After installation, QuickTime effects and third-party filters are stored in separate bins within the main Video Filters bins.

For information on working with audio filters, see Chapter 11, "Audio Tools and Techniques."

To apply a filter to a clip:

1. *Do one of the following:*

   ◆ Drag the filter from the Browser's Effects tab and drop it on the clip in the Timeline (**Figure 15.2**).

   ◆ Select the clip in the Timeline, choose Effects > Video (or Audio) Filters, and make your filter selection from the submenu.

2. Position the playhead over a frame in the selected clip to see a preview of the effect in the Canvas (**Figure 15.3**).

✔ Tip

■ Many filters' default settings have no visible effect on a clip. You must make settings adjustments before you can detect a difference.

Figure 15.1 Final Cut Express comes with a library of more than 50 filters.

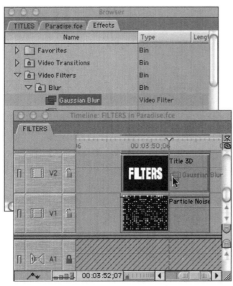

Figure 15.2 Drag the filter from the Effects tab and drop it on the clip in the Timeline.

Figure 15.3 Position the playhead over a frame in the filtered clip to see a preview of the effect in the Canvas.

Figure 15.4 Choose the Range Selection tool from the Tool palette.

Figure 15.5 Choose Effects > Video Filters; then select a filter from the submenu.

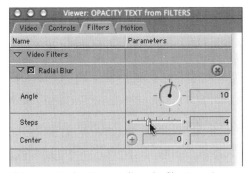

Figure 15.6 In the Viewer, adjust the filter's settings on the clip's Filters tab.

To apply a filter to a range of clips or part of a clip:

1. From the Tool palette, choose the Range Selection tool (**Figure 15.4**).

2. In the Timeline, drag to select whole or partial clips.

3. Choose Effects > Video (or Audio) Filters and select a filter from the submenu (**Figure 15.5**).

   If you selected multiple clips, Final Cut Express adds a separate copy of the filter to each clip.

4. Position the playhead over a frame in the selected clip range to see a preview of the effect in the Canvas.

To adjust a filter:

1. In the Timeline, double-click a clip to which you've added a filter; it opens in the Viewer.

2. In the Viewer, click the Filters tab to access the filter's controls.

3. Configure the filter's settings (**Figure 15.6**). The items you can change vary according to the type of filter.

4. To see the changes you've made, use the arrow keys to move through the clip frame by frame. You must render the clip before you can play it with a video filter applied.

To disable a filter:

1. In the Timeline, double-click a clip to which you've added a filter; then select the clip's Filters tab.

2. Uncheck the box next to the filter's name on the Viewer's Filters tab.

   The filter is disabled but is still applied to the clip. To toggle it back on, recheck the box.

✔ Tips

- Final Cut Express renders a clip's filters in the order they appear on the Filters tab. You can drag a filter up or down in the list to rearrange the filter order. Rendering order affects your final results.

- If you need more space to adjust sliders (or just to read the full name of a filter control), expand the width of the columns containing the effect controls on the Filter, Control, and Motion tabs. Drag the column header separators to adjust column width (**Figure 15.7**).

To remove a filter:

To remove a filter from a clip, *do one of the following*:

◆ Select the filter in the Filters tab and press Delete.

◆ Control-click the filter and choose Cut from the shortcut menu.

◆ Select the filter and choose Edit > Clear.

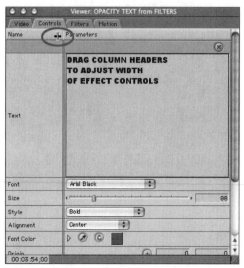

Figure 15.7 Drag the column headers on the Filter, Control, and Motion tabs to adjust the width of the effect controls.

Useful Filters

There's a boatload of filters in Final Cut Express. Some of them do really useful and cool things that you might not normally associate with the idea of a filter.

Here's the rundown of a few interesting ones that you might have missed:

Flop: This Perspective filter flip-flops the image horizontally, vertically, or both directions at the same time. John Huston used this effect in his World War II documentary "The Battle of San Pietro" to keep the Allied forces heading right to left, and the Axis forces heading left to right, regardless of which direction they were actually moving during filming.

De-interlace: This Video filter can improve the stability of still images by duplicating either of the two fields that make up a video frame. De-interlace is also useful for correcting jittery high-speed movement, if you can accept a slightly softened image quality. Try the Flicker options for the best control over the effect.

View Finder: This Video filter simulates footage from security cameras, home cameras, or pre-production screen tests. Other filters in the Video group—**Blink, Strobe,** and **Image Stabilizer**—are also interesting and can be applied creatively. Check 'em out.

Sepia: This Image Control filter tints the clip to an old-time, faded film color. Why use this filter when the Tint filter does that as well? Well, with Sepia, you can change the color in the same way as you can using the Tint filter, but you have the advantage of being able to tweak the contrast as well, which you can't do using the Tint filter. If you need to adjust color *and* contrast, why not have just one filter doing the math instead of two?

Echo and Reverb: These two Audio filters help make that pickup dialogue you recorded in your bedroom sound believable when you cut it into the scene you shot in the gymnasium.

Film Noise: This QuickTime filter adds hair, scratches, dust, and the look of old film to your video. Lots of people skip the dust and scratches completely and use Film Noise just for a faded-color-film look that renders quickly. This is not, however, a filter that can be found on the Effects tab in the Browser. To use Film Noise, you have to export your clip as a QuickTime movie and access the Filters as described in "To export a clip or sequence in another QuickTime format" in Chapter 18. Be sure to set your movie settings to match your audio and video sequence settings. Re-import your processed clip into your project and enjoy your film noise.

Joe's Filters: Joe Maller's custom filters, originally written for Final Cut Pro, work just fine in Final Cut Express (with the sole exception of the legendary "Joe's Time Bender," which requires FCP's filter keyframing capabilities). Demo versions of these filters are available online. Be sure to check out Joe's documentation for each filter, including the beautiful color illustrations of each filter at work; you can learn a lot about how filters work just by reading his descriptions. Highly recommended. www.joesfilters.com.

Using Color Correction Filters

Like editing, color correction is an invisible art. It's an essential part of post-production that can have a significant impact on a show, but it's not a high-profile part of the process. Final Cut Express introduces an improved set of image-quality measurement and color correction tools that make it feasible to complete a broadcast-quality finished product without leaving the desktop.

At the most basic level, you can use these tools to ensure that the video levels in your finished program don't exceed broadcast-legal limits. If the video in your program already looks good, careful color correction can make it look even better—if you have exposure problems or intercut shots that don't match, color correction can salvage your show. You can also use color correction tools to completely transform the look of your footage or to create an illusion—one example is "day for night," an old movie trick where scenes shot during the day are printed very dark to simulate night lighting.

This section serves as a brief overview of the tools and the basics of working with the Color Correction filter interface, but does not delve into the complexities of color correction (there are entire books written on the subject).

Always Be Color Safe!

It's a fact of life: It's easy to produce video with colors and luminance levels that look great on your Macintosh, but look scary, overblown, and distorted on a home television set. With DV footage you shouldn't need to worry about color levels, but images created in the computer need to be created correctly. Many colors, including black, white, and quite a few reds, are considered outside the color-safe guidelines. While this may not matter so much if you are creating content for the Web, it will matter if you are intending your masterpiece to be premiered on broadcast or cable TV.

It's easy to exceed NTSC broadcast limits for luminance and color intensity; Photoshop and other programs allow you to create images with colors and levels well outside the legal broadcast limits. Use FCE's color correction tools to tone down your graphics after you import. See "Using the Broadcast Safe filter," later in this chapter.

Be sure to check your work on an external TV monitor as you proceed. The best way to get out of trouble is not to get in.

If your project is headed for national broadcast, you might want to re-create your edit at a professional post-production house for a proper online session, where all the technical demands of broadcast TV can be honored in style.

For more information on FCE's role in handling the conversion of digital video levels to analog video levels, see Apple Knowledge Base article 60864, "Final Cut Pro: About Luminance," available online at the Apple web site.

Figure 15.8 These five filters make up FCE's color correction suite. Some, like the Color Corrector, are general-purpose color correction tools; others, like the Desaturate Highlights filter, have specialized uses.

The color correction filter suite

You'll find five filters in FCE's Color Correction filter bin (**Figure 15.8**). Some of the filters are general-purpose color correction tools; others have specialized applications. It's common to use more than one filter type on a single color-corrected clip.

- ◆ **Broadcast Safe:** This filter is designed to *clamp* (filter out) any illegal luma and chroma levels in your clip. See "Using the Broadcast Safe filter," later in this chapter.

- ◆ **Color Corrector:** This filter is for general-purpose color correction, and offers both numerical controls and graphical onscreen controls. For more information, see "Anatomy of the Color Corrector tab," later in this chapter.

- ◆ **Desaturate Highlights/Desaturate Lows:** These two filters (actually the same filter with two different default settings) are designed to solve a common color-correction problem: altering or increasing the intensity of a color in your image without tinting the highlights or black areas of the image. These filters desaturate (reduce the chroma levels) in those areas of the image, keeping your whites and blacks pure.

- ◆ **RGB Balance:** This simple RGB color balance filter has separate highlight, midtone, and blacks controls for reds, greens, and blues.

USING COLOR CORRECTION FILTERS

Using the Broadcast Safe filter

The Broadcast Safe filter is a quick fix you can apply to any NTSC or PAL video in your program. The filter offers a menu of preset settings (**Figure 15.9**) designed to clamp any illegal luma or chroma levels in your clip to within legal limits. The default setting should work well for most clips, but if you want to tweak the settings yourself, you can choose the Custom setting, which enables the individual luma and chroma level controls. The filter displays NTSC or PAL broadcast-safe presets based on your sequence settings.

✔ Tip

- You can apply a single Broadcast Safe filter to your entire sequence by nesting the sequence inside a parent sequence before you apply the filter. To learn more about the care and feeding of nested sequences, see "Working with Multiple Sequences" in Chapter 3.

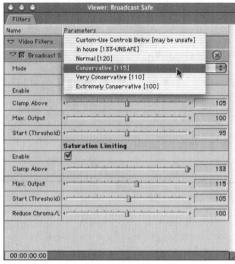

Figure 15.9 The Broadcast Safe filter offers a menu of presets designed to clamp illegal luma or chroma levels in your clip to broadcast-legal limits. The filter's default settings work fine in most cases.

Monitors and Color Correction

A properly calibrated, broadcast video monitor is an essential tool for accurate color correction (and most other post-production tasks). Use the best broadcast video monitor you can afford. Follow the procedures outlined in Apple Knowledge Base article 36550, "Final Cut Pro 3: How to Calibrate Your Broadcast Monitor," (available online at the Apple web site) before you color correct your first clip. You should not color correct based on the color you see in the image areas of the Viewer or the Canvas.

Anatomy of the Color Corrector tab

The Color Corrector filter —one of the five filters available in FCE's Color Correction filter bin— features graphical onscreen controls in addition to the standard numeric controls found on the Filters tab of the Viewer. The visual controls appear on their own Viewer tab after you apply the Color Corrector filter (**Figure 15.10**).

✔ Tip

■ Position the cursor over a filter control in the interface to display a tooltip with the name of the control and its keyboard shortcut equivalent.

The top section of the tab contains clip controls for keyframing the color correction filter and for copying the filter's settings to other clips in your sequence.

◆ **Color Corrector Viewer tabs:** The filter's visual controls appear on their own Viewer tab. If you have multiple copies of the Color Corrector filter applied to the clip, a separate numbered tab appears for each copy.

◆ **Numeric button:** Click this button to switch to the filter's numeric controls on the Filters tab.

◆ **Enable Filter check box:** Check to enable this filter. Uncheck to disable the filter.

continues on next page

Figure 15.10 The Color Corrector filter's visual controls appear on their own tab in the Viewer.

USING COLOR CORRECTION FILTERS

- **Copy Filter controls:** The Copy Filter feature (**Figure 15.11**) is one of the secret weapons of the Color Corrector filter. Once you have color-corrected a representative shot in your sequence to your satisfaction, you can use the Copy Filter controls to copy your filter's settings to other clips in your sequence with a single mouse click.

  - **Copy from 2nd Clip Back:** Copies settings from the Color Corrector filter that is applied two clips upstream from the currently selected clip, and pastes the settings into this copy of the Color Corrector filter, replacing any previously applied settings. If the source clip has no color correction filter, this control is dimmed.

  - **Copy from 1st Clip Back:** Copies settings from the Color Corrector filter that is applied to the first clip upstream from the currently selected clip, and pastes the settings into this copy of the Color Corrector filter, replacing any previously applied settings. If the source clip has no color correction filter, this control is dimmed.

  - **Copy to 1st Clip Forward:** Copies the settings of this Color Corrector filter into the next downstream clip in your sequence. If no Color Corrector filter is present on the destination clip, FCE applies one automatically.

  - **Copy to 2nd Clip Forward:** Copies the settings of this Color Corrector filter into the clip located two clips downstream in your sequence. If no Color Corrector filter is present on the destination clip, FCE applies one automatically.

- **Drag Filter control:** Drag this button to another Timeline clip to copy the current Color Corrector filter and its settings into that clip.

Figure 15.11 Use the Copy Filter controls to copy your filter settings to other clips in your sequence with a single mouse click.

USING COLOR CORRECTION FILTERS

The tab's center section contains the filter's Color Balance controls and Level and Saturation controls, your everyday color balance tools.

◆ **Color Balance control:** Use the Balance control like a virtual trackball control. Click the dot at the center of the control and drag it across the circular face of the control to adjust the color balance of your clip. The center of the circle represents pure white; drag farther from the center to increase the saturation of your color shift.

Hold down the Shift key while dragging to constrain the angle of the adjustment—a useful technique for adjusting the intensity of a color without shifting its hue.

Hold down the Command key while dragging to "gear up" the control, increasing the magnitude of the color balance adjustments in response to your mouse movements. (This is the opposite of the Command-drag "gear down" modifier implemented elsewhere in FCE, which enables precision adjustments.)

◆ **Whites Select (Auto-balance) eyedropper:** Click the Whites Select eyedropper icon; then click on a highlight in your image. The Color Balance control analyzes the color value of the selected pixel, and then automatically adjusts the overall color balance of the image to turn that pixel white; for example, selecting a light-green highlight will result in an overall color shift toward magenta to correct the green highlight to neutral white.

◆ **Balance Reset button:** Click to reset the Balance control to its default settings. Shift-click the button to reset the Levels and Sat(uration) sliders to their default values as well.

◆ **Hue control:** Click the outer edge of the Hue control's circular face and rotate the dial to make an overall adjustment to the clip's hue.

◆ **Hue Reset button:** Click to reset the Hue control to its default settings. Shift-click the button to reset the Levels and Sat(uration) sliders to their default values as well.

◆ **Levels sliders:** Use these sliders to make overall adjustments to the luminance levels in your clip. Click the tiny arrow at either end of a slider to nudge the value by a single increment.

  ◆ **Whites slider:** Use the slider to adjust the clip's maximum white level.

  ◆ **Mids slider:** Use the slider to adjust just the midtones in the clip, leaving any black or white areas untouched.

  ◆ **Blacks slider:** Use the slider to adjust the clip's minimum black level.

◆ **Sat(uration) slider:** Move this slider to make overall adjustments to the color saturation levels in your clip. Click the tiny arrow at either end of the slider to nudge the value by single increments. Moving the slider all the way to the left removes all color from the clip, leaving a grayscale image. Moving the slider all the way to the right will almost certainly push your color values into distortion, so use caution and check your work on your broadcast video monitor.

◆ **Auto White Level button:** Click to find the maximum white level in the current frame and automatically adjust the Whites slider to set the maximum white level.

◆ **Auto Contrast button:** Click to set Auto black and Auto white levels in a single operation.

◆ **Auto Black Level button:** Click to find the maximum black level in the current frame and automatically adjust the Blacks slider to set the maximum black level.

Compositing

Compositing can be any process that combines two or more image layers to create an effect. A compositing process can also include filters and motion that have been applied to modify individual layers or to modify the composited image.

Setting Composite mode

A Composite mode is an algorithm, a mathematical formula that controls the way the colors in a clip combine with the clip colors in underlying video layers.

All compositing happens from the top down; the highest-numbered track's image sits on the front plane and obscures the image on a track beneath it, unless the foreground image is made transparent. Each clip's opacity setting influences the final effect of the Composite mode.

For a complete list of the Composite modes in Final Cut Express, refer to Chapter 20 of Apple's *Final Cut Express User's Manual*.

To set the Composite mode for a clip:

1. Select the clip in the Timeline.

2. Choose Modify > Composite Mode, and then select a Composite mode from the submenu (**Figure 15.12**).

Figure 15.12 Choose Modify > Composite Mode, and then select a composite mode from the submenu. You can also access composite modes from a Timeline clip's shortcut menu.

Figure 15.13 A still graphic image.

Using Alpha Channels

An RGB image is composed of three 8-bit grayscale images—the red, green, and blue color channels—that express color information as a gray scale: 256 brightness values (ranging from 0 for black to 255 for white), plus an alpha channel. An alpha channel is a fourth 8-bit channel that can be assigned to an RGB image to track which areas of the image are transparent.

Figures 15.13, 15.14, and **15.15** illustrate how an alpha channel can be manipulated to mask selected areas in an image.

Figure 15.14 The graphic's alpha channel. With the alpha channel set to Straight, the white area will be interpreted as transparent.

Figure 15.15 The graphic frame superimposed over video. With the frame's alpha channel set to Straight, the white areas in the alpha channel shown in Figure 15.14 are made transparent in this figure, allowing the video background to show through.

Alpha channels are useful critters with a variety of applications in digital imaging. Final Cut Express video clips automatically have alpha channels assigned to them; it's the alpha channel that's being manipulated when you adjust the opacity of a clip or apply a key or matte filter.

◆ When you import an image that has an alpha channel, Final Cut Express interprets the clip's alpha channel and sets the alpha channel to Straight, Black, or White (corresponding to the background setting for the clip at the time the clip was created).

◆ When you place a clip in a sequence, Final Cut Express automatically makes the alpha channel area transparent. You can override the automatic setting by modifying the alpha channel type.

◆ You can reverse an alpha channel if you want to invert the transparency of an image, or you can choose to ignore the clip's alpha channel altogether.

To view or modify a clip's alpha channel type:

1. Select the clip.

2. Choose Modify > Alpha Type and select a different alpha channel type from the submenu (**Figure 15.16**).

✔ Tip

■ DV clips do not retain their alpha channel information if you export them in a DV format. If you want to save a clip's alpha channel when you export, use the Animation codec, set to Millions of Colors+. If you're exporting FCE elements for processing in a digital effects creation program such as Adobe After Effects, this is the way to go. Use the Animation codec again when you export from After Effects.

Figure 15.16 Choose Modify > Alpha Type and select a different alpha channel type from the submenu.

USING ALPHA CHANNELS

Figure 15.17 Final Cut Express offers a toolbox full of special-purpose matte and key filters. When you create multi-layer compositions, use these filters to mask out portions of the frame.

Working with Mattes

Mattes are filters that you shape to define which areas of opaque video clips are to be made transparent during compositing. For example, you could use a circular matte to isolate a clock face from its background, or you could create a matte in the shape of a keyhole to simulate peeking through a keyhole in a door.

Final Cut Express offers many types of matte filters (**Figure 15.17**). "Garbage mattes" are used to quickly rough out large areas of the frame. A Key is a type of matte that uses a clip's color or luminance information to determine which opaque areas will be made transparent (bluescreen effects are created with color key mattes set to make blue areas transparent). You can combine layers of different types of mattes to create very complex composite shapes.

To apply a matte:

1. *Do one of the following:*
   ◆ Drag the Key or Matte filter from the Browser's Effects tab and drop it on the clip in the Timeline.
   ◆ Select the clip in the Timeline, choose Effects > Video Filters, and then select a filter from the Key or Matte submenu.

2. Position the playhead over a frame in the selected clip to see a preview of the effect in the Canvas.

Travel mattes

A travel matte allows one video clip to play through another. The alpha information in a third clip is used as a matte that defines the transparent and opaque areas of the composited image.

When you create a travel matte effect, there are usually three video tracks involved; this is sometimes called a "matte sandwich." The background clip is placed on V1, or the lowest video track available. The Matte clip, preferably a high-contrast, grayscale motion clip or still image, goes on the video track just above the background clip, on V2, and the foreground clip sits on V3, or the video track above the Matte clip. A Composite mode specifically for creating travel mattes, called Travel Matte - Luma, is applied to the foreground clip. If the matte clip is placed on video track V1 without a background clip, then the background is automatically black.

To create a travel matte:

1. In the Timeline, drag your background clip (**Figure 15.18**) to V1.

2. Drag the clip selected to be the matte clip (**Figure 15.19**) to V2.

3. Drag your foreground clip (**Figure 15.20**) to V3.

Figure 15.18 Drag your background clip to track V1.

Figure 15.19 Drag your matte clip to track V2. The white areas in this clip will define the opaque areas of the foreground clip.

WORKING WITH MATTES

Figure 15.20 Place your foreground clip on track V3.

4. To establish the travel matte, select the foreground clip on V3 (**Figure 15.21**) and choose Modify > Composite Mode > Travel Matte – Luma.

The completed travel matte effect (**Figure 15.22**) uses the matte clip's luminance (or grayscale) levels as the mask. The matte clip's black area creates the shape of the foreground clip's transparent areas, and the matte clip's white area creates the shape of the foreground clip's opaque areas—that's where you see the foreground clip's video.

continues on next page

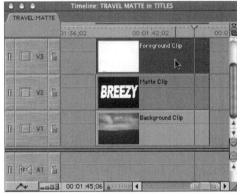

Figure 15.21 To composite the travel matte, select the foreground clip on V3 and choose Modify > Composite Mode > Travel Matte – Luma. The foreground clip on V3 is now composited with the matte clip on V2.

Figure 15.22 The completed travel matte effect.

WORKING WITH MATTES

✔ Tips

- After you composite your travel matte, you can refine the effect by adjusting the matte clip's brightness and contrast.

- You can apply animated filters and effects, as well as any other standard clip motion, to the travel matte in V2 for some very interesting looks.

- Play with Edge Feather and Edge Thin to soften the halo effect you might find around your matted objects when working with color keys.

- DV video is not the best video format for creating effects that require critical color key mattes, for example, blue or green-screen effects. DV compression throws out too much color information to give you the best control over edges.

TITLES AND GENERATORS

Generators are a class of effects that create (or generate) new video information rather than modify existing video. After you have generated it by rendering, a generated clip can be used just like any other clip. Text is a high-profile member of the generator class of effects; using the text generator to produce titles is covered later in this chapter.

Final Cut Express's generators include the following:

◆ Bars and Tone, which generates NTSC or PAL color bars and includes a 1-kHz audio tone with an adjustable level.

◆ Matte, which generates solid single-color clips.

◆ Render, which generates color gradients and different types of "noise."

◆ Shape, which generates an opaque geometric shape on a black background. You can scale or color the shape.

◆ Slug, which generates solid black frames and silent audio. (There are no controls for this effect.)

◆ Text, which generates simple titles using TrueType fonts loaded in your system.

◆ Title 3D and Title Crawl, two text generators from third-party developer Boris, offer much more precise control over title text, such as individual letter control over kerning. See "Creating titles with Boris Calligraphy," later in this chapter.

To add a generator to a sequence:

1. In the Viewer, choose an item from the Generator pop-up menu in the lower-right corner (**Figure 16.1**).

   The generator effect is loaded into the Viewer as an unrendered clip.

2. Click the Controls tab to access the generator controls.

3. Adjust the generator's controls (**Figure 16.2**); then click the Video tab to view the generator clip in the Viewer.

4. Edit the generator into your sequence just as you would a clip.

5. You must render your generated clip before you can play it back. Select the clip; then choose Sequence > Render Selection.

✔ Tips

■ When you are configuring settings for a generator clip, it's much easier to see what you're doing if you drag the generator clip's Controls tab out of the Viewer window first. Now you can view the generator image on the Viewer's Video tab as you configure the settings on the Controls tab.

■ Some generators, such as the Shape options, require that you change their Composite Mode to make sure they don't obscure the clips below them. For example, a Circle shape generator with a Composite Mode of Multiply displays the video beneath it in the middle of the circle. See "Setting Composite mode" in Chapter 15.

To edit a generator in a sequence:

1. Double-click the generator clip in the Timeline to open it in the Viewer.

2. Click the Controls tab; then make your adjustments.

Figure 16.1 Choose a generator from the Generator pop-up menu in the lower-right corner of the Viewer window.

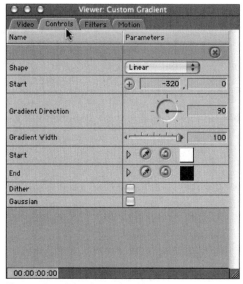

Figure 16.2 Adjust the settings for your generated clip on the clip's Controls tab.

Particle Noise = Generator Fun

When you're stuck for a way to add a little flash and color to a title sequence, load up Particle Noise. This generator is a ready source of animated textured backgrounds that range from serene (**Figure 16.3**) to trippy (**Figure 16.4**). Remember, you can stack multiple copies in layers, apply filters, and animate generators with motion keyframes. Now your only problem is how to stop fooling with Particle Noise and finish your title sequence.

Figure 16.3 The Particle Noise generator in a misty mood.

Figure 16.4 Make trippy animated backgrounds in seconds with the Particle Noise generator and the Whirlpool distortion filter.

Generating Text

Use text generators to create text elements and title screens in Final Cut Express. A text generator can create titles using any TrueType font currently loaded in your System Folder. You can specify text size, style, color, tracking, and kerning.

Final Cut Express offers six built-in text generators, which appear in the Text submenu of the Viewer's Generator pop-up menu (**Figure 16.5**) (for fancier text options, flip ahead in this chapter to read about the Boris Calligraphy text generators):

◆ **Text:** Generates static text in a single size and style. This option allows carriage returns.

◆ **Lower 3rd:** Generates two lines of static text. Each line has separate font, style, and size controls. The Lower 3rd generator is designed to create the standard titles used to identify interview subjects in news and documentary programs.

◆ **Crawl:** Generates a single line of animated text that scrolls horizontally across the screen. Crawl speed is determined by the duration of the clip—a longer clip duration results in a slower crawl speed.

◆ **Outline Text:** Generates static text with an adjustable outline stroke and background matte. You can also matte graphics into the text, outline, or background elements.

◆ **Scrolling Text:** Generates animated text that scrolls vertically up or down the screen. A longer clip duration results in a slower scrolling speed. Scrolling text allows carriage returns.

◆ **Typewriter:** Generates animated text that appears on the screen one letter at a time, as if typed.

Figure 16.5 Six text generator options are available from the Text submenu of the Generator pop-up menu in the Viewer window.

Assembly-Line Text Generation

If you have a big stack of title or text screens to produce, this assembly-line production technique may help:

1. To produce a title template, create a standard text generator that specifies all basic formatting: font, size, color, position, and so on. Save it as a Favorite Effect.

2. Select all the clips that get titled and apply your template Favorite to all of them in one operation.

3. Choose File > Open and open a text document in a new window that contains all your title copy.

4. Open your text generator clips one at a time; then copy and paste from the title copy in the text window to the Text field in the text generator clip.

These built-in generators are the simplest means of adding text to your sequences, but there are some limitations: Although text generators offer extensive control over the font, size, style, and positioning of text, with the exception of the Lower 3rd generator, you're limited to a single font per text generator.

Final Cut Express also comes with two optional, third-party plugin text generators: Boris Title 3D and Title Crawl. These generators allow you to use as many fonts as you want (and probably more than you should); read the section later in this chapter, "Creating titles with Boris Calligraphy," for more details.

You can edit a text generator clip into a sequence in the Timeline and apply effects, just as with other clips. You can also animate static text by using keyframes to make dynamic adjustments to a text generator clip's motion properties.

Your animation applies to all text in the generator—you cannot individually control each letter, word, or sentence.

✔ Tip

- The simplest way to fade titles in and out is to keyframe opacity at the head and tail of the text generator clip. If you're building a title sequence, you can copy and paste just the opacity attribute to ensure a consistent look.

Complex Text: Other Options

If you need to build more complex text elements, your best bet is to use Title 3D and Title Crawl, the (free) Boris Calligraphy text generator plugins that are included on your Final Cut Express CD. These third-party text generators offer a number of additional titling features you can use within FCE. For more information, see "Creating titles with Boris Calligraphy," later in this chapter.

Here's another option—create your text outside of FCE in a professional graphics program, such as Adobe Photoshop, Illustrator, or After Effects, or Macromedia FreeHand, and then import the text elements as motion clips.

Text generator options checklist

On the Controls tab, you can specify the following text control settings (**Figure 16.6**):

- ◆ **Text:** Enter your text in this field or cut and paste from a word processing program.

- ◆ **Font:** Choose a font from this pop-up menu.

- ◆ **Size:** Use the slider or enter a point size for your type.

- ◆ **Style:** Choose a font style (Plain, Bold, Italic, and so on) from this pop-up menu.

- ◆ **Alignment:** Choose Center, Left, or Right alignment from this pop-up menu.

- ◆ **Font Color:** Click the expansion triangle to reveal the full set of color controls; then *do one of the following:*
  - ◆ Drag the hue, saturation, and brightness sliders to new values.
  - ◆ Enter color values numerically in the text fields.
  - ◆ Select the eyedropper and click the Canvas to sample a color.
  - ◆ Click the color swatch and use one of the color pickers to select a color.

- ◆ **Origin:** Click the Point Select (+) button (located to the left of the Origin value field), and then specify new coordinates for your text's origin point relative to the frame by clicking the new Origin location in the Canvas or on the Video tab of the Viewer. Animating the Origin point (rather than the Center point) of your text allows you to position your text at a starting point outside your frame.

- ◆ **Tracking:** Use the slider or enter a value to specify the space between letters.

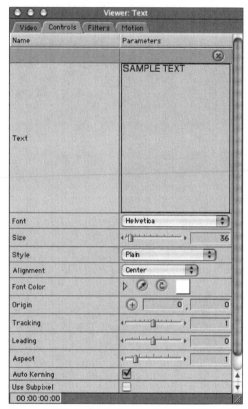

Figure 16.6 Style your text generator on the Viewer's Controls tab.

GENERATING TEXT

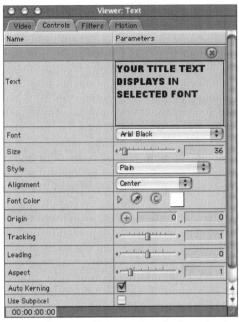

Figure 16.7 Enter and format text on the Controls tab.

Figure 16.8 Drop the text clip on the Superimpose area of the edit overlay. A Superimpose edit automatically places your text clip on a new Timeline track above the target track, starting at the sequence In point.

◆ **Leading:** Use the slider or enter a value to specify the space between lines of text.

◆ **Aspect:** Use the slider or enter a value to specify the height:width proportion of your selected font.

◆ **Auto Kerning:** Check the box to enable automatic adjustment of the spacing between individual letters.

◆ **Use Subpixel:** Check the box to enable subpixel accuracy in your rendered text generator. Subpixel rendering takes longer.

To generate a basic title screen:

1. To generate a title screen, *do one of the following:*

   ◆ From the Generator pop-up menu in the lower right of the Viewer window, choose Text.

   ◆ On the Browser's Effects tab, choose Text from the Video Generator bin.

   The text generator appears in the Viewer.

2. In the Viewer, click the Controls tab to access the generator's controls; then specify your text control settings (**Figure 16.7**). You can specify only one font per text generator.

3. Click back to the Viewer's Video tab and edit the text clip into your sequence in the Timeline. If you want to superimpose your text over video, choose the Superimpose edit type when you perform your edit (**Figure 16.8**).

   You can edit, filter, and animate text clips as you would any other video element.

GENERATING TEXT

Tips for Better-Looking Titles

◆ Always check your type on an actual television monitor. (If you are outputting for home viewing on videotape, preferably test it on the absolute worst-case television set and VCR you can find in the nearest back-alley junkyard.)

◆ Text size should be larger than 24 points if you want your text to be legible on TV.

◆ Black-and-white titles will never look their best if you use pure white and pure black; these extreme values exceed DV video's capacity to handle contrast. Try using a 10% gray over 90% black. (Compare the results on your video monitor to a title composed with pure white over pure black.) The same principle can be applied to color titles; using pure red, green or blue will produce that "bad, late-night infomercial" look you are probably trying to avoid.

◆ When you superimpose a solid color title over production video, try setting the title's opacity to 90%.

◆ Don't forget the simple drop-shadow effect found on the Motion tab of any clip. With some tweaks, you can create a professional-quality drop shadow that really pops your title out from any background.

Always Be Title Safe!

Every TV set is different: different colors, different screen geometries, different projection skews—never the same color, never the same combinations. Since even the middle area of the screen is not reliably centered (especially on home sets!), it's important to keep your text and graphic elements within a screen area that television engineers call *title safe*.

With the Title Safe overlay on, two boxes are superimposed on your clip—the inside border outlines the Title Safe boundary. Keep your graphic elements inside this box, and the edges won't get cropped off, even on consumer TVs. The slightly larger box surrounding the Title Safe boundary is known as the Action Safe boundary. Any visual elements critical to your project should occur within the Action Safe region. For more information, see "Viewing Title Safe and Action Safe boundaries" in Chapter 7.

When creating graphic elements in an external program (such as Photoshop), remember to respect the Title Safe area. Import a quick test screen into Final Cut Express before you invest too much time on your layout.

One final note: Title Safe and Action Safe areas apply only to program material displayed on a TV (both NTSC and PAL). If you plan to show your FCE project on the Web or via some other computer-based format, remember that web-based video displays the entire frame, so check the edges for unexpected surprises—microphones, shadows, dolly grips, and so on. The same caveats apply if you're compositing a Picture in Picture (PiP) effect—every pixel in your frame is included. (In fact, a PiP effect is likely to show some of the edges of the technical part of the video stream, so try experimenting with cropping a pixel or two into your clip or adding a border.)

GENERATING TEXT

Figure 16.9 The Outline Text generator is composed of three customizable elements: text, an outline stroke, and a rectangular background matte.

Figure 16.10 You can matte graphics into any of the generator's three elements. This composition has a clip matted into the text element.

The Wonders of Outline Text

The Outline Text generator offers three customizable elements in one text generator: text, an outline stroke, and a rectangular background matte (**Figure 16.9**)—perfect for punching titles over hard-to-read backgrounds or creating subtitles that maintain their legibility. You can insert a clip into any of the three elements by dropping the clip on the element's clip well on the Controls tab; the clip's image will be matted into the outline text element you specify (**Figure 16.10**).

To create outline text:

1. To generate an outline text title, *do one of the following:*
   - From the Generator pop-up menu in the lower right of the Viewer window, choose Outline Text (**Figure 16.11**).
   - On the Browser's Effects tab, choose Outline Text from the Video Generator bin.

   The new Outline Text generator appears in the Viewer.

2. In the Viewer, click the Controls tab to access the generator's controls; then specify your text control settings as outlined earlier in this chapter, in the section "Text generator options checklist" (**Figure 16.12**).

3. You can also specify any of the following outline text parameters:
   - **Line Width:** Specify the width of the text's outline.
   - **Line Softness:** Specify the amount of edge feathering applied to the text's outline.

continues on next page

- **Text Opacity:** Specify the text's transparency level.

- **Center:** Specify X,Y coordinates for the text's center point.

- **Text Color:** Select a color for the text.

- **Text Graphic:** Drag and drop a graphic clip to be matted into the text element.

- **Line Color:** Select a color for the text's outline.

- **Line Graphic:** Drag and drop a graphic clip to be matted into the outline element.

4. Use the sliders in the Background settings section to specify the size, edge feathering, opacity, color, and graphic for an optional rectangular matte that sits behind the text and outline. The default Size values are set to zero, so you must increase the size settings to see the background matte.

5. Click back to the Viewer's Video tab and edit the text clip into your sequence in the Timeline. If you want to superimpose your text over video, choose the Superimpose edit type when you perform your edit.

Figure 16.11 Choose Outline Text from the Viewer's Generator pop-up menu.

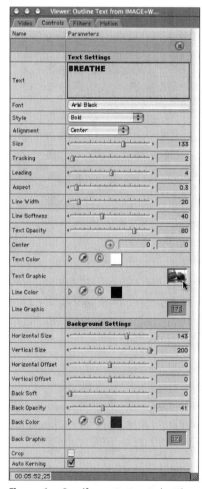

Figure 16.12 Specify your text control settings as outlined in the section "Text generator options checklist."

Using Animated Text Generators

Final Cut Express offers three animated text generators: Scrolling Text, Crawl, and Typewriter. These generators offer the font styling and positioning controls of the static text generators, plus simple animation routines built into the generator. You set up the animation on the text generator's Control tab.

Because these animated titles typically start offscreen, you will not see any text onscreen if your playhead is parked at the beginning or end of the clip. You have to scrub the playhead through the clip to see how your animated title is shaping up.

Creating scrolls

Scrolls are most often found as credit sequences at the end of a show (or at the beginning of *Star Wars* parodies). Scrolling text displays a lot of information in a little time, but take care not to roll your text too quickly. If you set your scroll speed too high, the titles will stutter (won't appear to scroll smoothly), and no one will be able to read them.

There are several ways to create the scrolling graphic elements. The easiest is to use the Scrolling Text generator found in the Video Generator list, but if you plan to use multiple fonts or specialized tracking, sizing, and kerning, then your best bet is to use the free Boris Calligraphy Title Crawl text generator plugin found on your Final Cut Express CD. See "Creating titles with Boris Calligraphy" later in this chapter.

To generate a scrolling text title:

1. *Do one of the following:*

    ◆ From the Generator pop-up menu in the lower right of the Viewer window, choose Scrolling Text (**Figure 16.13**).

    ◆ On the Browser's Effects tab, choose Scrolling Text from the Video Generator bin.

    The Scrolling Text generator appears in the Viewer.

2. In the Viewer, click the Controls tab to access the generator's controls; then specify your text control settings as outlined earlier in this chapter, in the section "Text generator options check-list" (**Figure 16.14**).

3. You can also specify any of the following scrolling text parameters:

    ◆ **Spacing:** Use the slider or enter a value to specify the space between letters (as with Tracking).

    ◆ **Leading:** Use the slider or enter a value to specify the space between lines of text.

    ◆ **Indent:** Use the slider or enter a value to set the X axis (left-right) positioning of the scroll's aligned edge, expressed as a percentage of the screen. Indent is enabled only for left- or right-aligned scrolls. The title-safe area begins inside 10% of the screen.

    ◆ **Gap Width:** Use the slider or enter a value to specify the width of the gap between any two text entries separated by an asterisk (*).

Figure 16.13 Choose Scrolling Text from the Viewer's Generator pop-up menu.

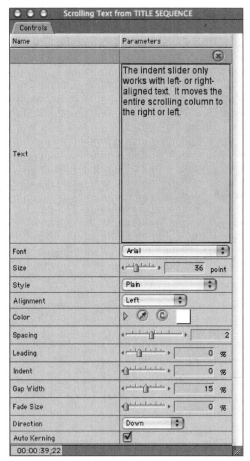

Figure 16.14 Specify your text control settings as outlined in the section "Text generator options checklist."

USING ANIMATED TEXT GENERATORS

◆ **Fade Size:** Use the slider or enter a value to set the vertical display area of your scrolling text, expressed as a percentage of the screen. The scrolling text will fade in as it enters (and fade out as it exits) the vertical display area you specify.

◆ **Direction:** Choose Up or Down from this pop-up menu to specify the direction in which the generated text will scroll.

4. Click back to the Viewer's Video tab and edit the text clip into your sequence in the Timeline. If you want to superimpose your text over video, choose the Superimpose edit type when you perform your edit.

✔ Tip

■ Use the Gap Width setting to create a double-column credit scroll with a center gutter. Here's how: Set the Gap width parameter to specify the width of the gap between any two text entries separated by an asterisk (*). When you assemble the text for your credit scroll, type Production Credit*Name, for example Visual Effects*Xochi Studios, and the gutter in your credit scroll will be set to the Gap Width value. How*about*that?

Creating crawl titles

Like the stock market tickertape creeping along the bottom of your TV screen, a text crawl is an animated title that scrolls horizontally. Text crawls can be useful for displaying short phrases—but keep them short, unless you are trying to annoy your audience. (Are you listening, CNN?)

Stuttering is more pronounced during a text crawl than during any other type of text effect. Take care to test your crawl on an NTSC monitor and watch for optical jumpiness. Possible remedies include using a wider-stroked font, a larger font size, a slower crawl speed, or a motion blur.

To generate a crawl text title:

1. *Do one of the following:*
   - From the Generator pop-up menu in the lower right of the Viewer window, choose Crawl (**Figure 16.15**).
   - On the Browser's Effects tab, choose Crawl from the Video Generator bin.

   The Crawl text generator appears in the Viewer.

2. In the Viewer, click the Controls tab to access the generator's controls; then specify your text control settings as outlined earlier in this chapter, in the section "Text generator options checklist" (**Figure 16.16**).

Figure 16.15 Choose Crawl from the Viewer's Generator pop-up menu.

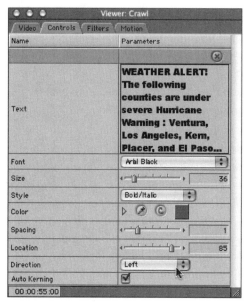

Figure 16.16 On the generator's Controls tab, specify your text control settings as outlined in the section "Text generator options checklist."

Figure 16.17 Choose Typewriter from the Viewer's Generator pop-up menu.

3. You can also specify any of the following crawl text parameters:

♦ **Spacing:** Use the slider or enter a value to specify the space between letters (as with Tracking).

♦ **Location:** Use the slider or enter a value to specify the Y axis (top-bottom) positioning of your crawl.

♦ **Direction:** Choose Left or Right from this pop-up menu to specify the direction in which the generated text will scroll.

4. Click back to the Viewer's Video tab and edit the text clip into your sequence in the Timeline. If you want to superimpose your text over video, choose the Super-impose edit type when you perform your edit.

Creating animated typewriter text

The cute, little Typewriter text generator automates the animation of single letters popping onto the screen; that's why it's called Typewriter. It's a real time-saver, as anybody who has manually animated simulated typing will tell you.

To generate a typewriter text title:

1. *Do one of the following:*

♦ From the Generator pop-up menu in the lower right of the Viewer window, choose Typewriter (**Figure 16.17**).

♦ On the Browser's Effects tab, choose Typewriter from the Video Generator bin.

The Typewriter text generator appears in the Viewer.

continues on next page

2. In the Viewer, click the Controls tab to access the generator's controls; then specify your text control settings as outlined earlier in this chapter, in the section "Text generator options checklist" (**Figure 16.18**).

3. You can also specify any of the following typewriter text parameters:

   ◆ **Spacing:** Use the slider or enter a value to specify the space between letters (as with Tracking).

   ◆ **Location:** Use the slider or enter a value to specify the Y axis (top-bottom) positioning of your text element.

   ◆ **Indent:** Use the slider or enter a value to specify the X axis (left-right) positioning of your text element, expressed as a percentage of the screen.

   ◆ **Pause:** Use the slider or enter a value to specify the timing of your typewriter animation. A larger Pause value results in a longer hold at the end of the clip. The speed of the type-on effect is calculated based on the overall duration of the generator clip minus the pause value you set here.

4. Click back to the Viewer's Video tab and edit the text clip into your sequence in the Timeline. If you want to superimpose your text over video, choose the Superimpose edit type when you perform your edit.

✔ Tips

■ If you're looking for an old-fashioned typewriter font, try Courier.

■ Use a techno-style font like Andale Mono or VT 100 for simulating computer input (and don't forget to add the Blink filter!).

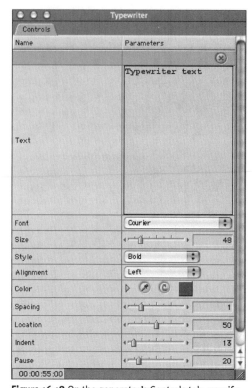

Figure 16.18 On the generator's Controls tab, specify your text control settings as outlined in the section "Text generator options checklist."

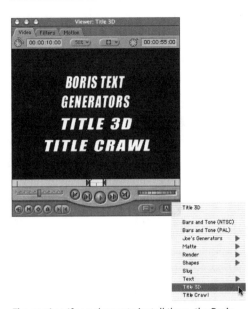

Figure 16.19 If you choose to install them, the Boris Text generators appear in the Generator pop-up menu along with the standard FCE generators.

Figure 16.20 Boris text generators feature a large text input window and a myriad of text styling options.

Creating titles with Boris Calligraphy

Two Boris Calligraphy text generators, Title 3D and Title Crawl, are available as an installation option in the Final Cut Express installer. Once you install them, these third-party generators show up in the Viewer's Generator pop-up menu along with the standard FCE generators (**Figure 16.19**).

Title 3D features vector-based text you can manipulate in 3D space with pivot control, animated tracking, and a host of text transformations.

Title Crawl is an automated roll and crawl title generator.

Both generators share the following features. You can:

◆ Enter text in a larger text-entry field (**Figure 16.20**).

◆ Create static titles.

◆ Set font, size, style, and color properties for individual characters.

◆ Apply drop shadows and borders.

◆ Choose from other 2D title animation options.

◆ Copy and paste text from a word processor.

Note that you can set individual parameters such as font, size, color, and tracking for every character, but you cannot animate individual character properties over time.

For more information about Boris Calligraphy, see the "Boris Calligraphy User Manual," a 43-page, illustrated, Acrobat PDF file, located in the Extras folder on the Final Cut Express CD.

USING ANIMATED TEXT GENERATORS

461

Part VI: Finishing

Part VI: Finishing

You've invested blood, sweat, and tears (okay, maybe it was just a couple of hours of blood, sweat, and tears) in your project. Now it's time to take the final steps: rendering any processed audio and video in your project and choosing your final output format.

Digital media offers a wide variety of output options, and many media makers output in a variety of formats, each to suit a special purpose; for example, you might archive your finished project on DV tape, make a DVD for showing to audiences, and output a trailer version in a web-friendly, compressed, streaming QuickTime format.

RENDERING

Rendering is the process of combining your raw clip media with filters, transitions, and other adjustments to produce a new file. This new file, called the render file, can be played back in real time.

Final Cut Express offers many, many ways to manipulate your raw media—a wild world of complex effects. Someday soon (we all hope), computer processing will speed up enough to dispense with the need to render in Final Cut Express. Until then, you'll need to render clips with effects before you can play back your final result. Most Final Cut Express sequences (containing transitions, motion, and filters) must be rendered before they can be played in real time.

Real-time systems use the power of your Mac's CPU to process added effects on the fly, allowing you to play them back without rendering them first. G4 Real-Time Effects, FCE's effects previewing feature, doesn't require additional hardware. For editors (and their clients) who work extensively with effects, these systems can dramatically improve efficiency and creativity.

This is a chapter with more protocol than most. Understanding rendering protocols can be a big factor in making your post-production work efficient while producing high-quality results. This chapter lays out the rules governing video and audio render files and lays out some strategies for minimizing render time.

Rendering Protocols

Here are some general guidelines to help you understand Final Cut Express's rendering protocols.

What needs to be rendered

In general, you must render any transitions, effects, and composited layers to play a sequence smoothly.

Also, before your sequence can be exported or printed to video, you have to render any source media with frame rate, frame size, or video or audio compression settings that differ from those settings in your sequence.

Audio tracks with transitions or filters, as well as multiple audio tracks over your real-time playback limit, have to be rendered before playback.

Clips whose speed has been changed must also be rendered before playback.

What doesn't need to be rendered

Final Cut Express sequences consisting of cuts only can be played back in real time without rendering, as long as the sequence size and frame rate match those of the original source material.

Multiple tracks of audio can be played back in real time without rendering. (See Table 17.1, "Final Cut Express Audio Track Costs," later in this chapter, for more information.)

Rendering order

Video frames in sequences are rendered in the following order:

- Effects applied within individual tracks are processed first. Speed changes, filters, motion, motion blur, opacity, and transitions, are processed next, in that order.

- After all the individual tracks have completed processing, the processed tracks are composited, starting with the top layer of video (the highest-numbered track), which is composited onto the track below it.

It is possible to change the order of rendering by using nested sequences. For more information, see "Working with Multiple Sequences" in Chapter 3.

Figure 17.1 The "Unrendered" screen appears in the Viewer or the Canvas when you try to play back video that cannot be played back in real time without rendering.

Rendering indicator

Figure 17.2 The rendering indicator is located above the Timeline ruler. The upper bar indicates the render status of video tracks. The lower bar shows the audio track status.

Rendering indicators

As you build your sequence, you'll encounter the following indicators:

◆ When you try to play video material that requires rendering in the Viewer or the Canvas, a blue background with the word "Unrendered" appears (**Figure 17.1**), indicating that the video can't play in real time.

◆ When you try to play audio material that requires rendering in the Viewer or the Canvas, you'll hear a steady beeping sound, indicating that the audio can't play in real time.

◆ In the Timeline, the rendering indicator above the ruler (**Figure 17.2**) consists of two thin bars. These bars indicate which sections of the sequence currently require rendering to play back smoothly. The upper bar indicates the render status of video tracks; the lower bar shows the audio track status.

Non-real-time FCE systems use the following status codes in the rendering indicators:

◆ **Red:** The material needs to be rendered.

◆ **Gray:** No rendering is required.

◆ **Blue-gray:** The material has already been rendered.

Real-time effects previewing adds two more color codes to the render status indicator:

◆ **Green:** The material does not need rendering and can be played in real time.

◆ **Yellow:** The results are a real-time approximation of the final effect. To get the true final effect, you still need to render the material. You'll see the final effect when playback is stopped or during scrubbing.

Rendering

The Render All command (in the Sequence menu) creates render files for all audio and video tracks in the current sequence.

The Render Selection command processes only the material you select in the Timeline.

You can also choose to render audio only or real-time effects only. See "Rendering audio" and "About Real-Time Effects," later in this chapter.

To render an entire sequence:

1. Open the sequence you want to render in the Timeline.

2. Choose Sequence > Render All (**Figure 17.3**).

    A progress bar displays the percentage of completed processing while the sequence is being rendered (**Figure 17.4**). Click Cancel if you want to stop rendering. Final Cut Express saves all the rendered frames it has processed, even if you cancel rendering.

✔ Tips

■ To render just the audio in your sequence, choose Sequence > Mixdown Audio.

■ If your project involves multiple sequences and lots of rendering, you can consolidate your rendering chores into a single operation. Check out the batch render feature discussed later in this section.

Figure 17.3 Choose Sequence > Render All.

Figure 17.4 A progress bar tracks the speed of the rendering process. More complex effects will take more time to render than simple effects or audio processing.

Quick Preview Tips

The "instant-preview" techniques listed here can show you a quick, temporary preview of an effect or transition before you commit to rendering it. Place the Timeline playhead at the section you want to preview and then use one of these methods:

◆ Press Option-P (the Play Every Frame command) to force a frame-by-frame preview of your unrendered material. FCE displays the frames as fast as they can be processed.

◆ Use the left and right arrow keys to step through your footage a frame at a time.

◆ Scrub the playhead across the Scrubber bar in the Canvas or the Timeline's ruler.

Figure 17.5 Set the Sequence In and Out points to select the area you want to render. (This figure shows split edit points, marking Video In and Video Out.)

Figure 17.6 Choose Sequence > Render Selection.

To render a section of a sequence:

1. *Do one of the following:*
   - ◆ In the Timeline, select a portion of a clip or one or more clips or transitions.
   - ◆ In the Timeline or the Canvas, set the sequence In and Out points to mark the area that you want to render (**Figure 17.5**).

2. *Do one of the following:*
   - ◆ Choose Sequence > Render Selection (**Figure 17.6**); or press Command-R to render both video and audio in the selected area.
   - ◆ Press Control-Option-R to render just the audio in the selected area.

   A progress bar displays the percentage of completed processing while the selected area is being rendered.

3. Click Cancel if you want to stop rendering. Final Cut Express saves all the rendered frames it has processed, even if you cancel rendering.

To disable rendering:

- ◆ Press the Caps Lock key to temporarily disable rendering. Press Caps Lock again to cancel.

RENDERING

Batch Rendering

Batch rendering is a lifesaver for projects with multiple sequences that require rendering.

You can select multiple sequences from multiple projects and kick off a batch render that processes overnight (or while you're at your day job). Final Cut Express queues the sequences you select and renders them sequentially.

To batch render multiple sequences:

1. Select the sequences in the Browser (**Figure 17.7**).

2. Choose Sequence > Render All (**Figure 17.8**).

   You'll see a progress bar displaying the percentage of completed processing for the sequence that's currently processing.

3. Click Cancel if you want to stop rendering.

   You'll have to cancel each render operation in the batch separately. Final Cut Express saves all the rendered frames it has processed, even if you cancel rendering.

Figure 17.7 Select the sequences that you want to batch render in the Browser.

Figure 17.8 Choose Sequence > Render All to batch render the selected sequences sequentially.

Table 17.1

FINAL CUT EXPRESS AUDIO TRACK COSTS		
ITEM	TYPE	TRACK COST
Each mono track	Track	1
Each mono track with transitions applied	Transition	2
Pair of stereo tracks	Track	2
Sub-sequence containing one stereo track	Track	4
Each track referencing a sub-sequence	Track	Number of audio tracks in sub-sequence
Compressor/limiter	Filter	6
Expander/gate	Filter	6
Vocal de-esser	Filter	6
Vocal de-popper	Filter	6
Reverb/echo	Filter	Must be rendered
All other filters	Filter	3

Rendering audio

Although real-time video playback in Final Cut Express is usually limited to a single, cuts-only track, FCE can mix and play back up to eight tracks of audio in real time, so audio rendering is not always necessary.

The number of tracks you specify in the Real-Time Audio Mixing preference (located in the General tab of the Preferences window) determines how many tracks Final Cut Express attempts to play back before it asks for audio rendering.

There's an additional factor that determines whether you have maxed out your real-time audio playback capabilities: All audio tracks are not created equal. When you apply filters or transitions to an audio track, Final Cut Express must allocate processing power to calculate those effects on the fly in order to play back the result in real time—which brings us to track costs. (See the sidebar "FCE Protocol: Track Costs" and **Table 17.1**.)

BATCH RENDERING

FCE Protocol: Track Costs

Final Cut Express uses the concept of track equivalent costs, or track costs, to calculate the total processing power needed to play back multiple channels of audio. Under certain conditions, you may be able to play back audio tracks with filters or transitions applied.

You can calculate the real-time audio capabilities available in your sequence by adding up the audio track costs. Track costs can accumulate quickly when even a couple of unmixed tracks are combined, if you have used filters and transitions. If you exceed your real-time playback capability, you'll hear beeps instead of your audio when you attempt playback. Before you can play back, you'll need to render by selecting the Mixdown Audio command from the Sequence menu.

To render a single audio sequence clip:

1. In the Timeline, select the audio clip you want to render (**Figure 17.9**).

2. Choose Sequence > Render Selection (**Figure 17.10**); or press Command-R.

   All the audio tracks at your audio clip's location, along with any filters, levels, and transitions you have applied, are processed into a render file.

Figure 17.9 Select the audio clip you want to render.

✔ Tip

■ If you want to exclude tracks from the processed audio file, turn off track or clip visibility before you render. For more information on toggling track and clip visibility, see "Making a Timeline track invisible" in Chapter 9.

Figure 17.10 Choose Sequence > Render Selection.

BATCH RENDERING

FCE Protocol: Estimating Render Processing Time

Render processing times can range from a couple of seconds to many hours. How do you know whether you've got just enough time for a quick break or enough time for a two-hour lunch? Read on.

◆ Final Cut Express expresses the progress of your rendering operation as estimated time remaining. Even so, the time displayed on the progress bar is based on how long the current frame takes, multiplied by the number of remaining frames; so, if your effects differ drastically in complexity, predicting the time required to render is difficult—even for Final Cut Express. Watch the progress bar for a few minutes and make a guess, based on the speed of the progress bar and your knowledge of the sequence.

◆ After rendering, or whenever you move a large number of clips, Final Cut Express rebuilds the QuickTime movie used for computer playback of your sequence, so it will be ready to play—wherever you put your playhead. While it's rebuilding, you may see a dialog box that says "Preparing video for display."

Figure 17.11 The Mixdown Audio menu item is dimmed, and a checkmark indicates that the sequence audio has been mixed.

To render just the audio in a sequence:

◆ Choose Sequence > Mixdown Audio.

Your audio tracks, along with all applied filters, levels, and transitions, are processed into a render file. The Mixdown Audio menu item is dimmed, and a checkmark indicates that the sequence audio has been mixed (**Figure 17.11**). The Mixdown Audio command remains dimmed until you modify the audio tracks.

✔ Tips

■ The Mixdown Audio command produces a render file with a computed mix. Even though the command is called "Mixdown," you still have individual control over all your audio tracks. Think of Mixdown Audio as a "temp mix" you can use while you're working.

■ Rendered audio behaves differently than rendered video in one crucial way: If you reposition an audio clip that's been rendered, you lose the render file. Workarounds are available to deal with this small wrinkle. For more information, see "Preserving Render Files," later in this chapter.

BATCH RENDERING

About Real-Time Effects

G4 Real-Time (G4 RT) Effects take advantage of the PowerPC G4 chip's graphics handling power to compute and display previews of many effects in real time.

You need a fast G4-based Mac to take advantage of this feature (that's why they're called G4 effects), but if your computer qualifies, you'll be able to preview many effects on the desktop and render only when it's time to prepare your final output.

If your G4 supports G4 RT Effects, FCE will identify your G4 model and display the G4 RT Effects it supports in boldface type. The boldface indicators appear both on the Browser's Effects tab (**Figure 17.12**) and in the Effects menu (**Figure 17.13**).

The Timeline's render indicator bars are color coded to let you know which sections of your sequence will play back in real time, and which sections still require rendering before you can play them. (See "Rendering indicators," earlier in this chapter.)

Like most cutting-edge technologies, G4 RT Effects come with a list of caveats and trade-offs attached, so let's get those out of the way up front.

◆ G4 RT requires a Power Mac G4 running at 500 MHz or faster for a single-processor model or at 450 MHz or faster for a dual-processor model; or, you can use a PowerBook G4 at 450 MHz or faster. The level of real-time performance you get depends on the speed of your Mac. You also need a minimum 384 MB of RAM.

Figure 17.12 Real-time effects appear in boldface type on the Browser's Effects tab.

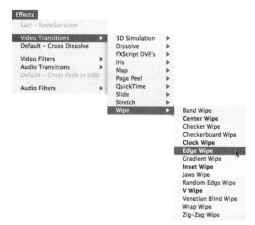

Figure 17.13 Real-time effects also appear in boldface in the Effects menu.

Check the Tech Specs page of the Final Cut Express web site (www.apple.com/finalcutpro/specs.html) for a list detailing which real-time effects are supported on which G4 system. If you're already working on an FCE system that supports G4 RT Effects, check the list of effects on the Browser's Effects tab. The effects listed in boldface type are G4 RT-enabled on that system.

◆ G4 RT's real-time magic works only on DV format footage.

◆ G4 RT Effects are computed on the fly and play back only in the Canvas and the Viewer. You have to disable your DV FireWire to enable G4 RT's real-time previewing, so you won't be able to see anything on your external TV monitor while you're enjoying your real-time previews. However, you can purchase and install an extra ATI Radeon video display card in your G4 tower and then route the G4 RT previews to an external TV monitor via S-video. If you're using a qualifying PowerBook G4, you can use the PowerBook's S-video output to feed your external monitor.

◆ Remember that G4 RT previews are optimized for real-time processing, not resolution. They work great for judging timing and composition, but for critical judgment of color and detail, be sure to render at least a few test frames and view them on your external NTSC or PAL monitor at final output resolution.

Warnings and limitations aside, the G4 Real-Time Effects feature offers an amazing productivity boost to FCE users.

Rendering Real-Time Effects

Most real-time systems, including G4 RT Effects, don't write permanent, usable render files as they process and play back the real-time effects they do support. You must render everything in your sequence before you output the final version of your program.

To render real-time effects only:

1. *Do one of the following:*
   - ◆ In the Timeline, select the clips or transitions that you want to render (**Figure 17.14**).
   - ◆ In the Timeline or the Canvas, set sequence In and Out points to mark the area that you want to render.
   - ◆ Leave the entire sequence unselected to render all real-time effects in the entire sequence.

2. Choose Sequence > Render RT Effects (**Figure 17.15**) to render only the real-time effects in the selected area.

   You'll see a progress bar displaying the percentage of completed processing while the sequence is being rendered. Click Cancel if you want to stop rendering. Final Cut Express saves all the rendered frames it has processed, even if you cancel rendering.

✔ Tips

- ■ Real-time proxy effects (indicated by a yellow render indicator bar) are effects that your real-time system is equipped to preview only at a reduced resolution or in a simplified form. Choose Sequence > Render Proxy Effects to render a final output quality version of these effects.

Figure 17.14 Select the real-time effect clip or transition in the Timeline. This Center Wipe transition can play back in real time only as a reduced-resolution proxy effect; you must render it in order to play back the final version of the effect.

Figure 17.15 Choose Sequence > Render RT Effects to render the real-time effects in the area you selected.

- ■ Looking for the green and yellow indicator bars or the Render RT Effects menu? If you've turned off your external video feed and these still don't appear, it means your machine doesn't support G4 RT Effects. Time to upgrade!

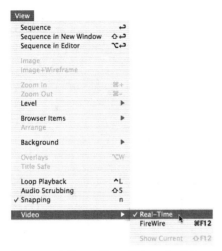

Figure 17.16 Choose View > Video > Real-Time to disable your external video output—this enables G4 Real-Time Effects.

To enable G4 Real-Time Effects:

◆ Choose View > Video > Real-Time (**Figure 17.16**).

Your external video output is disabled, and real-time previewing is enabled.

✔ Tip

■ Endlessly switching back and forth between Real-Time preview mode and external video (FireWire) mode? Wish there was a keyboard shortcut to toggle External Video output on and off? Wish no more: Command-F12 does exactly that.

G4 Real-Time Effects Menu

Here's the complete list of G4 RT supported effects. Depending on your G4's performance level, your mileage may vary.

◆ **G4 RT transitions:** Cross Dissolve.

◆ **Wipe transitions:** Center Wipe, Clock Wipe, Edge Wipe, Inset Wipe, V Wipe.

◆ **Iris transitions:** Cross Iris, Diamond Iris, Oval Iris, Point Iris, Rectangle Iris, Star Iris.

◆ **G4 RT motion effects:** Opacity, Scale, Center, Offset, Crop, Aspect.

◆ **Real-time still frames:** Still frames and imported graphics play back in real time at preview resolution. The total number of still images you can preview is determined by the size of the RT Still Cache setting on the General tab of the Preferences window.

FCE Protocol: Real-Time Rendering Options

◆ The Sequence > Render All command renders all real-time and non-real-time effects.

◆ The Sequence > Render Selection command renders real-time and non-real-time effects for clips you select in the Timeline.

◆ If you've set sequence In and Out points to mark a section of your sequence, but haven't selected any Timeline clips:

   ◆ Choose Sequence > Render RT Effects to render just the real-time effects.

   ◆ Choose Sequence > Render Proxy Effects to render proxy and non-real-time effects only.

   ◆ Choose Sequence > Render All to render all real-time and non-real-time effects.

RENDERING REAL-TIME EFFECTS

Managing Render Files

Render files are valuable media elements, stored as actual media files on your hard disk, like your original captured media files. Final Cut Express names the render files according to its own internal naming protocols. You will not be able to identify individual render files by their file names, so planning your render file management strategy is a critical part of your post-production work. This will become clear the next time you invest considerable time in a single complex rendering process.

Specifying storage locations for render files

You can specify up to 12 disks for storing captured video, captured audio, or render files. As you create render files, Final Cut Express stores them on the disk with the most available space. If you don't specify disk locations, Final Cut Express saves video and audio render files in separate folders (called Render Files and Audio Render Files), which are located, along with your Capture Scratch folder, in the Final Cut Express Documents folder (**Figure 17.17**). Render files are media files and should be stored on the same media drives as your captured media.

Specify storage locations for your render files on the Scratch Disks tab in the Preferences window. For more information on setting scratch disk preferences, see Chapter 2, "Installing and Setting Up."

Figure 17.17 Render files are stored in the Final Cut Express Documents folder, along with your Capture Scratch folder.

MANAGING RENDER FILES

Figure 17.18 Select obsolete render files in a project's Render folder, and move them to the Trash. The Date sort function in the Finder can help you find older render files.

Deleting rendered files

When you are working on multiple projects, each with multiple sequences, render files can build up quickly.

Freeing up disk space by dumping old render files is an attractive proposition, but use caution if you are deleting render files for your current projects. Final Cut Express uses render file names that are useful to the program but unintelligible to you.

Final Cut Express will automatically delete any render file in your project that has been directly superceded by a replacement render file, but it doesn't throw out leftover render files or render files in old versions of projects. To delete render files, you'll have to sort through your project's render folder, manually weeding out obsolete files and moving them to the Trash (**Figure 17.18**).

For more information, see "Deleting Media" in Chapter 3.

Rendering Strategies

To take full advantage of the media manipulation techniques that are possible with Final Cut Express, you will need to render to produce your finished results; you'll also need to render to review your sequence and evaluate any effects you've created. The rendering strategies in this section fall into three basic categories:

◆ Tips for avoiding unnecessary rendering

◆ Techniques for speeding up rendering times

◆ Schemes for preserving render files

Avoiding unnecessary rendering

Final Cut Express allows you to add source material whose frame rate and compression settings do not match your sequence settings. However, if the frame rate, frame size, or video or audio compression settings in your source media are different from the settings in your sequence, those frames need to be rendered before the sequence can be exported or printed to video.

If a particular group of source clips looks normal when you open it from the Browser window (**Figure 17.19**), but it requires rendering or it changes size or shape when you add it to a sequence and view it in the Canvas window (**Figure 17.20**), you probably have a settings mismatch between your source clips and your sequence settings.

Figure 17.19 This clip looks normal when opened from the Browser.

Figure 17.20 The same clip as it appears in the Canvas. The mismatched sequence settings override the clip settings, causing the clip to appear distorted and to play back poorly.

Figure 17.21 Choose Properties from the clip's shortcut menu.

Figure 17.22 In the Item Properties window, check the clip's video rate, frame rate, frame size, and compression settings. Highlighted settings must match sequence settings for the sequence to play in real time.

Important: To avoid rendering when creating a sequence with cuts only, make sure that the sequence's editing timebase, frame rate, and compression settings are the same as the frame rate, frame size, and compression settings of your source media.

How do you compare source clip and sequence settings? Follow the instructions here for viewing both source clip settings and sequence settings. To learn more about specifying source clip settings, see Chapter 4, "Capturing Video." For information on specifying sequence settings, see Chapter 2, "Installing and Setting Up."

To view settings for a clip:

1. Control-click the clip in the Browser or the Timeline, and then choose Properties from the shortcut menu (**Figure 17.21**). The Item Properties window appears.

2. In the Item Properties window, note the clip's video rate, frame rate, frame size, and compression settings (**Figure 17.22**).

To view settings for a sequence:

1. *Do one of the following:*

   - Control-click the sequence in the Browser or the Timeline (for a nested sub-sequence), and then choose Item Properties from the shortcut menu (**Figure 17.23**).

   - Choose Edit > Item Properties.

   The Item Properties window appears.

2. Note the sequence's frame size, compression settings, and video rate; these should match the clip's frame size, compression settings, and video rate (**Figure 17.24**).

Figure 17.23 Control-click the sequence in the Browser; then Choose Item Properties from the shortcut menu.

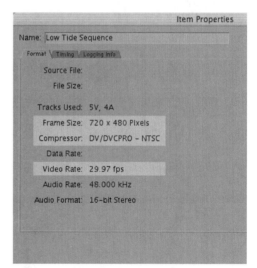

Figure 17.24 In the sequence's Item Properties window, check the clip's video rate, frame rate, frame size, and compression settings. Highlighted settings must match clip settings.

Reducing Rendering Time

Following are two strategies that can help you minimize your rendering time.

Render in stages

If you are building a highly complex effects sequence, you may want to render your elements in stages. For example, you might perfect just the motion paths and interactions of your composited layers and then render just that portion of your sequence in high quality by exporting and re-importing your rendered elements. The export process creates a new piece of source media, and you can continue to sculpt your sequence using the new composited clip as a fully rendered base track. Exporting to preserve a render file is described later in this chapter.

Batch render

Use the batch render feature to render all your projects while you're busy elsewhere.

Preserving Render Files

You can spend days creating a polished effects or title sequence in Final Cut Express, and then wait hours for your final product to be rendered. How can you protect your time investment?

Following are a few strategies to help you hold onto your render files.

✔ Tip

- Final Cut Express allows multiple undos (**Figure 17.25**). If you just want to try a new idea on material you've already rendered, when you're done, you can undo (Command-Z) your experiment until you have reverted to your previously rendered file. Careful use of the Undo function can give you freedom to experiment without risking rendered sequence material. See Chapter 2 for information on setting the number of Undo levels.

Using nested sequences to preserve render files

You can select a group of sequence clips or a portion of a Final Cut Express sequence and, by cutting and pasting it into a separate sequence (which you then edit back into your master sequence), convert that selection into a self-contained sub-sequence. As a sub-sequence inside a parent sequence, nested sequences are treated the same as other clips in a sequence. But unlike clips, nested sequences are actually pointers, or references, to the original sequence, not copies.

Figure 17.25 You can specify up to 32 levels of undo in Final Cut Express.

FCE Protocol: Salvaging Renders with Undo

FCE protocol dictates that when you invalidate a render file by making changes to a sequence, the invalid render file becomes unrecoverable either when you next save the project, or when you are past the point where you can use Undo to make the render file valid again, whichever is later.

A nested sequence can help preserve your render files, because even though it can be edited into another sequence in pieces just like a clip, the render files associated with the nested sequence are preserved within the nested sequence. Even if you make a change in the parent sequence that requires the nested sequence to re-render, when you open the nested sequence, your original render files created within the nested sequence will still be available.

However, like everything else associated with rendering, you need to be aware of particular protocols governing the preservation of render files when a sequence is nested as a sub-sequence in another, parent sequence.

To learn how to create nested sequences, see Chapter 3, "How to Manage an FCE Project."

✔ Tip

■ Final Cut Express cannot reliably track down all nested sub-sequence material that requires rendering when performing a Render All process. If you have built multiple levels of nested, unrendered sub-sequences into your project, this tip's for you: Try rendering at least one element in each nested sequence to help FCE track down the nested rendering required. Double-check your rendered sequences before you invite your client in for a screening.

FCE Protocol: Nested Sequences and Rendering

When you nest, or place a sequence inside another sequence, render files for the nested sequence are saved separately, with the nested sequence.

Nested sequences may require separate rendering in a parent sequence under the following circumstances:

◆ If a parent sequence modifies a nested sequence, the nested sequence must be re-rendered. Modifications include any compositing, filters, transitions, speed changes, and so on.

◆ If movement, such as rotation, has been applied to a sequence and then rendered, the sequence needs to be re-rendered if it is nested inside another sequence.

◆ If a nested sequence is placed inside a parent sequence, its alpha channel type is set to Straight. If you set the alpha channel for that nested sequence to None, the clips it contains won't need to be re-rendered. Its rendered files will be retained as long as they do not need to be combined with other tracks in the sequence, but because you've turned off the alpha channel, the clip will be opaque.

Using nested sequences to preserve audio render files

Unlike video clips, which can be moved and retain the linkage to their render files, audio clips will lose the linkage to their existing render files and require re-rendering if you move them to a different location in your sequence. This section contains some workarounds for this problem.

When you nest an audio clip, you redefine it as a new sub-sequence within your main sequence. Audio contained within its own sub-sequence can be moved and retain its render files.

To preserve a rendered audio track:

1. In the Browser, create a new, empty sequence to receive the audio clips you wish to render (**Figure 17.26**), and then open it as a tab in the Timeline

2. In the Timeline, select the audio clips in your main sequence that require rendering (**Figure 17.27**); then press Shift-A to mark In and Out points at the boundaries of your selection.

3. Press Command-X to cut the selected audio clips from the main sequence.

4. Switch to your new empty sequence by clicking its tab, and then paste the audio clips (**Figure 17.28**).

Figure 17.26 Create a new, empty sequence to hold the audio clips you wish to render.

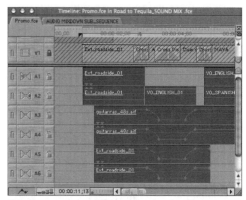

Figure 17.27 In the main sequence, select the audio clips to be rendered, press Shift-A to mark the boundaries of selection with In and Out points, and then press Command-X to cut the clips.

Figure 17.28 Paste the audio clips into your empty sequence.

Figure 17.29 Choose Sequence > Mixdown Audio.

Figure 17.30 Edit the sub-sequence (containing your processed audio track) into the main sequence, just as you would a clip. Use the In point you marked in step 2 to help you line up the audio sub-sequence.

5. Choose Sequence > Mixdown Audio (**Figure 17.29**).

The audio in the new sub-sequence is rendered.

6. Edit the new sub-sequence containing the rendered audio at the clip's former location in the main sequence (**Figure 17.30**). Use the In and Out points you marked in step 2 to help you accurately position the nested audio sub-sequence.

7. If you want to make further adjustments to your rendered audio, double-click the new sub-sequence in the Timeline to open the nested sub-sequence that contains just the audio. Then, make your adjustments.

8. Re-render the nested sequence.

✔ Tip

■ Pre-process a raw, unedited audio track that requires filtering in its own sequence, render once, and then edit that rendered processed audio into your main sequence just as if it were a clip. You'll preserve your treated audio track's render file.

Export to preserve render files

Exporting creates a physical copy of your rendered file on your hard disk. Exporting is the safest way to preserve rendered material. Once you have exported render files, you can re-import and use them just as you would raw captured media. For your render file to be exported without re-rendering, the export settings must match the render file's settings. If you wish, you can archive an effects sequence by re-rendering it as you export; your selection of export settings will determine the quality of your exported copy.

To export an existing render file without re-rendering:

1. In the Timeline, select the sequence or portion of a sequence for which you want to export the render file (**Figure 17.31**).

2. Choose File > Export > Final Cut Movie.

3. In the Save dialog box, select a destination for your exported render file from the pop-up menu near the top.

4. Type a name for the file in the Save As field.

5. From the Include pop-up menu, choose Video Only (**Figure 17.32**). Leave the Markers pop-up menu set to None.

6. Check the Make Movie Self-Contained check box (**Figure 17.33**).

7. Click Save.

   Your render file is copied into the selected location.

Figure 17.31 A portion of a sequence, selected for exporting. The sequence In and Out points form the boundaries of the selection.

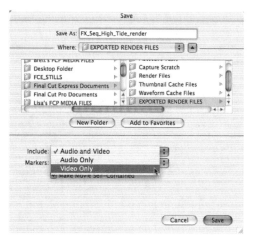

Figure 17.32 In the Save dialog box, select Video Only from the Include pop-up menu.

Figure 17.33 Check the Make Movie Self-Contained check box to export a copy of your render file.

PRESERVING RENDER FILES

CREATING FINAL OUTPUT

You've come this far. Now it's time to send your masterpiece out into the world.

Final Cut Express has a variety of output options. How do you choose the right one? The best output format for your Final Cut Express project depends on where you plan to take it next.

◆ Are you going to distribute it on VHS?

◆ Do you need a broadcast-quality master?

◆ Will you distribute your project as a DVD?

◆ Are you preparing a webcast?

◆ How about "all of the above"?

This chapter walks you through the output options in Final Cut Express and helps you decide which one will deliver what you need.

In the first part of this chapter, you'll learn about two different methods for outputting your project to tape: recording Timeline playback and printing to video.

The second part of the chapter is devoted to file export options. You can also use a file export option to convert your FCE sequence or clip to another digital format for use in computer-based media.

One of the beautiful things about digital video is the wide variety of output options available to you—right at your desktop.

Using Tape Output Modes

Final Cut Express is designed to support external video monitoring at any time using your camcorder or deck, so you can always record FCE's output. You don't need to process your FCE material unless you are exporting your sequence in a computer-compatible format.

Final Cut Express offers two tape output modes:

- **Recording Timeline Playback:** One of the easiest ways to record Final Cut Express's output to videotape is simply to start recording on your video camcorder or deck; then play your sequence in the Timeline. For more information, see "Recording Timeline Playback," later in this chapter.

- **Print to Video:** Use Print to Video to output a Final Cut Express sequence or clip to videotape. The Print to Video function lets you configure pre- and post-program elements such as color bars and a 1-kHz tone, leader, slate, and countdown. Print to Video's loop feature allows you to print your sequence multiple times automatically.

  You don't need device control to use Print to Video. Use Print to Video if you want to make a videotape copy of your FCE sequence that includes customized pre-program elements, or if you want to loop your sequence.

Figure 18.1 Set your camcorder or deck to VTR (or VCR) mode.

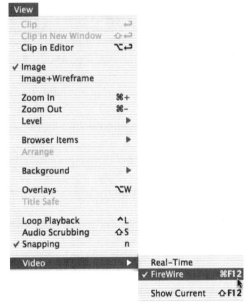

Figure 18.2 Enable the external video feed by choosing View > Video > FireWire.

Setting up for recording to tape

Before you record FCE's output on video-tape, make sure that your recording device is connected and receiving output from Final Cut Express, and that the sequence or clip you're outputting is set up correctly.

Use this setup checklist for both tape output modes:

◆ Make sure your camcorder or deck is set to VTR (or VCR) mode. Final Cut Express can't record to devices set to Camera mode (**Figure 18.1**).

◆ Make sure your video camcorder or deck is receiving output from Final Cut Express. Your external video setting should send FCE's video signal out to the external video device you want to record to. Enable the video output feed to your camcorder or deck by choosing View > Video > FireWire. (**Figure 18.2**).

For more information, see "How To Choose an Easy Setup" in Chapter 2.

continues on next page

USING TAPE OUTPUT MODES

◆ If you want to print only a selected portion of a sequence or clip, open the clip or sequence and then set In and Out points to specify the portion you want to record (**Figure 18.3**).

◆ You should enable the Report Dropped Frames During Playback preference on the General tab of the Preferences window. Feedback on dropped frames is especially critical during final output.

See "Optimizing Performance" in Chapter 2 and "Is Your System Capture-Ready?" in Chapter 4 for more tips on eliminating dropped frames by improving FCE's performance.

◆ Test your setup by recording a section of your show to tape. Play back the test recording and scrutinize the results in your external monitoring setup. Do the rendered sections of the program match quality with the rest of the footage? Are your titles crisp? Are your video levels within the recommended brightness range for your output format, or has your video image developed hot spots? Is the audio playback level healthy, but not overmodulated? Are both stereo tracks properly balanced and panned correctly? A little extra care and patience now, when you're producing your final product, will protect all the care and patience you've lavished on your project up until now.

Figure 18.3 Set In and Out points to specify the portion you want to record.

Figure 18.4 Cue your sequence in the Timeline. You don't need to set In and Out points unless you want to record less than the entire sequence.

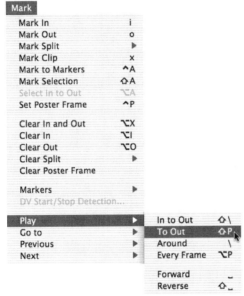

Figure 18.5 Choose Mark > Play, and then select a play option from the submenu. In to Out plays only the portion of your sequence between the In and Out points.

Recording Timeline Playback

If you are receiving Final Cut Express's output in your video camcorder or deck, you don't need to use Print to Video to record your FCE sequence to tape. Print to Video provides mastering options (color bars, slate, and so on). Otherwise, recording Timeline playback directly provides exactly the same output quality, and you may find it more convenient.

To record Timeline playback onto tape:

1. Cue your videotape to the point where you want to start recording.

2. Cue your sequence in the Timeline (**Figure 18.4**).

3. Render any unrendered sections of your sequence. Unrendered material appears as blue unrendered graphics when you record Timeline playback to tape.

4. Start recording on your video deck.

5. Choose Mark > Play, and then select a play option from the submenu (**Figure 18.5**).

   Final Cut Express plays the contents of the Timeline as you specified and then holds on the final Timeline frame marked for playback. A freeze frame is recorded on your tape until you stop recording.

6. Stop recording on your camcorder or deck when Timeline playback is done.

Touching Up Your Timeline Playback

Recording your Timeline playback can be a real time-saver, but because you are making a live recording of Final Cut Express's output, you need to do a few things differently to get smooth-looking results. Here are a few pointers:

◆ You don't have to use Print to Video just because you want to add pre-program elements to your tape output. Black leader, color bars, and audio reference tone are available in the Viewer's Generator pop-up menu. You can edit your pre-program elements into the Timeline. For more information, read the introductory material in Chapter 16.

◆ When you record Timeline playback, your camcorder or deck records whatever is sent to Final Cut Express's external video output from the instant you press your device's Record/Play button. If the Viewer or the Canvas is active, you'll record whatever is currently displayed until you start playback of your Final Cut Express sequence. Even if you have positioned the Timeline playhead at the start of your sequence, you'll record a freeze frame of the first frame of the sequence until you start Timeline playback. Make sure your external video output is displaying black by inserting a frame of black before the first frame in your sequence. Now the freeze frame will appear as a solid black leader at the start of your recording.

◆ Place another frame of black at the end of your sequence, so that when FCE reaches the end of the Timeline and freezes the final frame, that frame is black as well.

◆ Wait a few seconds after you start recording before you start the Timeline playback. You'll give your videotape time to get up to speed, and your picture will be rock solid from the first frame of your sequence.

Printing to Video

The Print to Video command is the correct choice when you want to make a videotape copy of a Final Cut Express sequence or clip that includes pre-program elements, such as color bars, slate, and countdown. Print to Video is also your best choice if you want to loop playback and print multiple passes of your sequence on the same tape. If you have a controllable camcorder or deck, you can set up your device control preset so that FCE controls your deck during a Print to Video operation, but you don't need a deck that supports device control to use Print to Video. For information on hardware setup, see Chapter 2, "Installing and Setting Up."

If you don't need customized pre-program elements at the beginning of your dub, playing your sequence in the Timeline and recording the output directly may give you satisfactory results and save you some time as well. See "Recording Timeline Playback" earlier in this chapter.

Print to Video: Rendering Tips

◆ If you have multiple layers of sub-sequences in your sequence, (sub-sequences within sub-sequences inside the master sequence), it's a good idea to render things in the nested items at the lowest root, or sub-sequence, level first—at least for the first render. Subsequent adjustments and re-renders can be processed at the parent level, and Final Cut Express will more reliably find all the nested sub-sequence material that requires re-rendering.

◆ The pre-program elements discussed in the section "Print to Video settings checklist" must be rendered before you can print to video.

◆ If you use the same pre-program sequence frequently, you might want to use the Print to Video function to assemble your color bars, leader, slate, and countdown in advance. After your pre-program sequence has been rendered, print it to video and then capture it as a clip. You can drop your prepared pre-program clip into sequences before you print, speeding up the final output process.

Print to Video settings checklist

The Print to Video dialog box (**Figure 18.6**) displays a list of formatting options. Select the elements you want to include in your videotape copy. You can specify durations for all options.

◆ **Leader:** Select the pre-program elements you want to include in your videotape copy. Your pre-program sequence will be assembled in the same order that the elements are listed in the dialog box, which is why there are two separate Black options. Check the elements you want to include, and then specify a duration (in whole seconds) for each option in the field next to the option. These elements must be rendered before printing to video can begin.

Figure 18.6 Select the pre-program elements you want to include in your videotape copy from the Print to Video dialog box.

◆ **Color Bars:** Check this box to include color bars and a 1-kHz tone, preset to –12 dB, before the beginning of the sequence or clip.

◆ **Tone Level:** If necessary, adjust this slider to change the level of the preset, –12 dB, 1-kHz audio reference tone. Note that this slider does not adjust the output level of your audio track, just the level of the reference tone.

◆ **Black:** Check this box to add black frames between the color bars and the slate.

Figure 18.7 Final Cut Express uses Final Cut Pro's countdown screen as its default.

◆ **Slate:** Check this box to include the slate information specified in the Slate Source pop-up menu in the adjoining field.

- **Slate Source pop-up menu:** Select a source for the information that appears on your slate from this pop-up menu. You can specify the sequence or clip name, a file on disk, or multiple lines of custom text.

- **Black:** Check this box to include black frames between a slate and a countdown (or before the beginning of the sequence or clip, if you aren't adding a slate and a countdown).

- **Countdown:** Check this box to add a 10-second countdown before the sequence or clip (**Figure 18.7**). Choose FCE's built-in 10-second SMPTE standard countdown or use the File pop-up menu and Browse button to specify your own custom countdown file.

◆ **Media:** Specify the material you want to include in the program section of your tape copy. You can print an entire sequence or clip, or only a marked portion. You can also loop the sequence or clip selection and insert black at the end of each loop.

- **Print pop-up menu:** Choose Entire Media if you want to print the entire sequence or clip. Choose In to Out if you want to print a portion of the selected item. Specify the portion to be printed by setting In and Out points in the sequence or clip.

- **Loop:** Check this box to print your selection multiple times.

- **Times:** Specify the number of repetitions for Loop.

- **Black:** Check this box to insert black frames between repetitions for the duration specified in the Black field.

- **Trailer:** Check the Black box to add a black trailer at the end of the printed sequence or clip; then specify the duration in the Seconds field. If you are looping the sequence or clip, the trailer appears after the last repetition.

- **Duration Calculator:** These fields display the total duration of all the media you selected to print, as you have specified it.

✔ Tip

■ Be sure your tape is long enough to record the entire program running time as calculated by the Duration Calculator. Most tape stock has a little extra capacity over the program length printed on the packaging, but it's a good idea to respect the official program length capacity.

PRINTING TO VIDEO

To print a sequence or clip to video:

1. Read and follow the setup process described earlier in "Setting up for recording to tape."

2. In the Browser, select the sequence or clip you want to print (**Figure 18.8**). Open the sequence and make the Timeline active.

3. Choose File > Print to Video.
   The Print to Video dialog box will appear.

4. Select the program elements you want to include in your program. Refer to the "Print to Video settings checklist" earlier in the chapter for explanations of your options. If you need to change any of the settings, do so now.

5. Click OK (**Figure 18.9**).
   If the sequence you select needs to be rendered before it can be printed, Final Cut Express automatically renders any unrendered sequence material, plus any additional program elements you've specified. When the rendering is complete, FCE displays a dialog box telling you to go ahead and start recording on your camcorder or deck.

Figure 18.8 In the Browser, select the sequence you want to print to video.

Figure 18.9 Select the pre-program elements you want to include in your videotape copy and then click OK.

Start video recorder now and click OK to begin playback.

Cancel   OK

Figure 18.10 Click OK to start playback of your Final Cut Express sequence.

6. Start recording on your camcorder or deck and, when the device is up to speed, click OK to start playback of your Final Cut Express sequence (**Figure 18.10**).

7. When your program material has finished printing, stop recording on your camcorder or deck. Final Cut Express doesn't provide any end-of-process beep (the large black box disappears from the screen, and the interface returns), so check in at the scheduled end-of-program if you plan on recording unattended.

8. Play back your recorded sequence and check the quality.

✔ Tips

■ If you don't specify a post-program black trailer, Final Cut Express will hold on the last frame of your sequence, creating a freeze-frame that will be recorded onto your tape until you stop recording.

■ Once the Print to Video process is complete, you'll have access to the render files created for Print to Video in your regular Timeline version of the sequence.

PRINTING TO VIDEO

Exporting Sequences and Clips

If you want to convert your Final Cut Express sequence to another digital format for use in computer-based media, exporting is the right choice for you. You can also export sound files, snippets of clips, or single-frame images. Final Cut Express offers a variety of export formats.

When you export, Final Cut Express uses QuickTime's compression codec and file format conversion features to generate a media file on your hard drive in the format you choose.

Here's how FCE's export options are organized:

When you choose File > Export, you'll see two media export options: Final Cut Movie and QuickTime (**Figure 18.11**).

◆ The Export > Final Cut Movie command is designed to streamline your export configuration chores by offering you very limited settings options (**Figure 18.12**). Use Export > Final Cut Movie to export your sequence as a single movie using the same format settings as your sequence.

The Final Cut Movie format is the only option that allows you to export your sequence as a reference movie. (See "What's a Reference Movie?" later in this chapter.). Final Cut Movie is also the correct export choice if your export destination is iDVD 3.

Figure 18.11 When you choose File > Export, you'll see FCE's two media export options.

Figure 18.12 Use Export > Final Cut Movie to export your sequence as a single movie using one of your sequence presets or to export a reference movie for use with a third-party compression program, or iDVD 3.

Figure 18.13 One of your QuickTime export format options, the QuickTime Movie format, is a good choice for producing highly compressed QuickTime movies for multimedia or the Web.

- The Export > QuickTime command gives you access to the full range of QuickTime-supported file formats. Export > QuickTime is your starting point when you want to export anything, from still images to compressed audio files.

One of the QuickTime format options, the QuickTime Movie format (**Figure 18.13**), is a good choice for producing highly compressed QuickTime movies or media files in full-resolution, uncompressed formats. The QuickTime Movie format option also offers video filters that you can apply as you export a sequence.

FCE Protocol: Exporting Audio Tracks for Finishing

If you need more control over your audio tracks than you can get inside FCE, you can export your edited sequence audio tracks out of Final Cut Express as individual AIFF files, and then continue your audio finishing in a dedicated, digital audio editing program such as Pro Tools. FCE's audio export capability features are limited; there's a 2-channel limit for each export operation, and the exported audio files are continuous—you lose your edit points. Yuck.

If you have access to a Final Cut Pro workstation, you can open your project created in FCE and export your audio tracks in the Open Media Framework (OMF) file exchange format. The exported OMF file contains the audio files, plus the audio edit information from your project file. That means you can export audio tracks with the original track separations, edit points, cross-fades, and video sync intact, and then import them into an OMF-compatible, digital audio workstation, the kind used at most professional, audio post-production facilities. For more information, see "To export audio only from a clip or sequence," later in this chapter.

✔ Tips

- When you export a clip or sequence, Final Cut Express includes only the material between the In and Out points. You can set In and Out points to select a portion of your clip or sequence, but be sure to clear In and Out points before you export if you want to export the entire clip.

- Apple Knowledge Base Article #36655, "Final Cut Pro 3: QuickTime Export of Video, Images, and Sound" introduces a series of linked articles that provide detailed instructions on exporting to the various QuickTime file formats—recommended reading for FCE users faced with an export format decision.

- The two tables that follow provide a sketch of the codecs and the file formats you are most likely to use with Final Cut Express and the way they're most commonly used. Note that these tables do not contain a complete list of QuickTime formats and codecs, and the summary of uses and characteristics is not comprehensive. **Table 18.1** lists the codecs most commonly used with Final Cut Express. **Table 18.2** lists the most commonly used file formats.

What's a Reference Movie?

The Export > Final Cut Movie feature offers the option of exporting your FCE clip or sequence as a reference movie. A reference movie is a bit of QuickTime media-handling wizardry. A small file that contains no media (except for a render file of your mixed sequence audio, plus video render files for parts of your exported sequence that haven't been rendered yet), a reference movie simply points to the original media files used in the exported sequence. Third-party media compression programs, such as Cleaner, can use the reference movie pointer information from that small file to process the compressed version of your sequence using the larger original media files. iDVD 3 can also use FCE reference movies to create a DVD disk image of your sequence.

Reference movies work with any QuickTime-compatible compression application that's installed on the same computer as your Final Cut Express system. The compression program must have access to the original QuickTime source media files for your reference movie to work.

You won't see a "Make Reference Movie" option in the Save dialog box for the Export Final Cut Movie function. The only way to export your Final Cut Express clip or sequence as a reference movie is to leave Make Movie Self-Contained unchecked. Pretty esoteric, huh?

Table 18.1

Some Useful QuickTime Codecs

FILE FORMATS	TYPE	USED FOR	ALPHA CHANNEL?
Sorenson	A/V	CD-ROM	No
Cinepak	A/V	Older CD-ROM	No
QuickTime Fast Start	A/V	Web movies	No
QuickTime Streaming	A/V	Web movies	No
Animation	V	High-res digital export	Yes
Uncompressed	V	Uncompressed digital export	Yes
M-JPEG A/M-JPEG B	V	Compressed files for editing	No
DV-NTSC/DV-PAL	A/V	Importing DV into FCP	No

Table 18.2

Some Useful QuickTime File Formats

FILE FORMATS	TYPE	USED FOR	ALPHA CHANNEL?	COMPRESSION?
QuickTime Movie	A/V/Graphic/+	Cross-platform multimedia	Yes	Available
DV stream	A/V	iMovie DV media files	No	Yes
JPEG	Graphic	Graphics, video still frames	No	Available
Photoshop	Graphic	Multilayered graphics	Yes	No
PICT	Graphic	Mac format	Yes	Available
PNG	Graphic	Graphics	Yes	No
TIFF	Graphic	Graphics	Yes	Available
AIFF	A	Common audio format	N/A	Available
WAVE	A	Windows audio format	N/A	No

Codec vs. File Format

A codec is an algorithm, or mathematical formula, for compressing and decompressing digital media. The word codec is techie shorthand for COmpression/DECompression. Whenever you see compression options in the QuickTime interface, you're looking at a list of codecs.

A file format is one standardized way of organizing data so it can be recognized and used by an application or operating system. You could use the same compression codec in a variety of file formats, and vice versa. QuickTime Movie is an example of a file format that supports many, many codecs.

Exporting a Final Cut Movie

The Export > Final Cut Movie command is the right choice when you want to export a sequence using the same sequence settings you used in the project.

The Save dialog box for the Export Final Cut Movie function opens with your current sequence preset settings already loaded. Specify whether to include audio or video, or both, specify your marker export preference, and you're done.

Final Cut Movie is the only export format that offers the option of exporting your sequence as a QuickTime reference movie.

Because the Final Cut Movie format supports export of both chapter markers and reference movies, it's the also the right export choice when you want to use iDVD 3 to create a DVD of your FCE project.

To export a clip or sequence as a Final Cut Movie:

1. *Do one of the following:*
   - Select a clip or sequence in the Browser.
   - In the Timeline, open the sequence you want to export.

2. Set In and Out points in your clip or sequence to mark the section you want to include in the exported file. If you want to export the entire item, clear any In and Out points from the item before export (**Figure 18.14**).

3. Choose File > Export > Final Cut Movie. The Save dialog box appears. This is your opportunity to review and confirm the export format settings.

4. From the Include pop-up menu, choose Video and Audio, Audio Only, or Video Only (**Figure 18.15**).

Figure 18.14 If you want to include the entire length of your sequence, be sure to clear any In and Out points before you export.

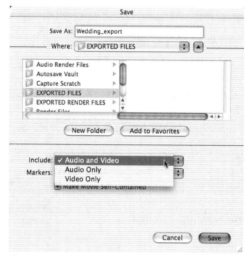

Figure 18.15 Make a selection from the Include pop-up menu. You can export audio plus video, or video or audio only.

EXPORTING SEQUENCES AND CLIPS

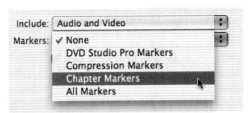

Figure 18.16 Choose Chapter Markers from the Markers pop-up menu to export chapter markers for use in iDVD 3.

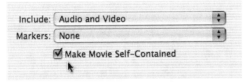

Figure 18.17 Check the Make Movie Self-Contained box to create a stand-alone movie.

5. If you want to export markers along with your file, select which kind of markers you want to export from the Markers pop-up menu (**Figure 18.16**).

6. *Do one of the following:*

◆ Check Make Movie Self-Contained to export a QuickTime movie that duplicates all audio, video, and render files in one self-contained media file (**Figure 18.17**).

◆ Leave Make Movie Self-Contained unchecked to export a reference movie—a small movie file that contains only pointers to the original audio, video, and render files.

7. Type a name for your file in the Save As field and select a destination folder; then click Save.

✔ Tip

■ If your clip or sequence doesn't have an audio track, select Video Only from the Include pop-up menu. Even empty audio tracks will increase the file size of your exported clip.

To export a Final Cut movie for use in iDVD 3:

1. Follow steps 1 through 4 in the previous task, "To export a clip or sequence as a Final Cut Movie."

2. If you want to export chapter markers along with your file, choose Chapter Markers from the Markers pop-up menu.

3. *Do one of the following:*

   ◆ Check Make Movie Self-Contained to make a stand-alone file that can be used with iDVD 3 on this or on another computer.

   ◆ Leave Make Movie Self-Contained unchecked to export a reference movie—a small movie file that contains only pointers to the original audio, video, and render files—that can be used only with a copy of iDVD 3 that is located on the same computer as your Final Cut Express project (**Figure 18.18**).

4. In the Save dialog box, type a name for your file in the Save As field and select a destination folder; then click Save.

   The exported movie contains any sequence markers you have designated as chapter markers (**Figure 18.19**).

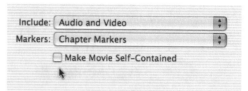

Figure 18.18 Uncheck the Make Movie Self-Contained box to create a compact reference movie you can use in another processing program like iDVD 3.

Figure 18.19 Open your exported reference movie in QuickTime Player, and you'll see a pop-up menu containing your exported chapter markers.

iDVD 4 choose export all markers not just chpt. markers

FCE Protocol: DVD Chapter Markers

It's very simple to export a Final Cut Movie with chapter markers that you can import into iDVD3, but you should be aware of a few rules governing the number and placement of chapter markers:

◆ Final Cut Express chapter markers must be sequence markers, not clip markers.

◆ You can set a maximum of 36 chapter markers per iDVD project.

◆ Chapter markers must be set more than one second apart, and more than one second from the start or the end of a sequence.

Figure 18.20 Select the sequence in the Browser.

Figure 18.21 Choose File > Export > QuickTime. Choosing QuickTime gives you access to the full range of QuickTime's output formats.

Exporting Other QuickTime Formats

The Export > QuickTime option gives you access to the full range of QuickTime-supported file formats. Use this option to convert your FCE media to any of the following:

◆ Compressed QuickTime movies (use the QuickTime Movie format)

◆ Uncompressed, full-resolution file formats that include an alpha channel

◆ Still images in a variety of graphics file formats

◆ Audio tracks in a variety of compressed and uncompressed formats

To export a clip or sequence in another QuickTime format:

1. *Do one of the following:*

   ◆ Select a clip or sequence in the Browser (**Figure 18.20**).

   ◆ In the Timeline, open the sequence you want to export.

2. Set In and Out points in your clip or sequence to mark the section you want to include in the exported file. If you want to export the entire item, clear any In and Out points from the item before export.

3. Choose File > Export > QuickTime (**Figure 18.21**).

   The Save dialog box opens.

   continues on next page

4. In the Save dialog box, choose an export file format from the Format pop-up menu (**Figure 18.22**); *then do one of the following:*

◆ Choose one of the export settings presets from the Use pop-up menu (**Figure 18.23**).

◆ Click the Options button to access the full QuickTime settings for the format you have selected. In the settings dialog box (or boxes) that follow, confirm or modify the export format settings and click OK. Export options will vary according to the format you have selected (**Figure 18.24**).

Figure 18.22 Choose an export file format from the Format pop-up menu.

Figure 18.23 Choose one of the export settings presets from the Use pop-up menu. These are the export presets available for the QuickTime Movie export format.

Figure 18.24 In the settings dialog boxes, confirm or modify the export format settings and click OK. Export options will vary according the format you have selected. These are the settings dialog boxes for the Sorenson video codec.

Figure 18.25 Type a name for your file in the Save dialog box's Save As field.

Figure 18.26 Click the Filter button in the Movie Settings window to access a palette of QuickTime filters you can apply as part of your export operation. QuickTime filters are available only in the QuickTime Movie format.

5. In the Save dialog box, type a name for your file in the Save As field (**Figure 18.25**), and then select a destination folder from the Where pop-up menu.

6. Click Save.

✔ Tip

- The QuickTime Movie format gives you the option of applying QuickTime's suite of video filters, and you can choose from a range of effects and image control filters (check out the Film Noise filter!). Select the filters as you are configuring your export options, and they will be processed as part of the export operation. You can access the filters by clicking the Filter button in the Movie Settings dialog box (**Figure 18.26**).

FCE Alert: Web Video Uses the Whole Video Frame

If you are converting your FCE sequence to a compressed format for web or CD-ROM distribution, be aware that your exported file will show the entire video frame when viewed on a computer screen.

External video monitors typically don't display the edges of the video frame; that's why you're advised to keep your titles inside the "title safe" area. If you have unwanted elements, such as microphones, hovering about the edges of your video frame, you may never have seen them if you've been monitoring your framing only on an external video monitor.

So check your whole video frame by viewing it on your computer monitor. If you do find that your frame has unsightly edges, you can always crop your frame before you export.

To export a still image from a Canvas or a Viewer frame:

1. In the Canvas or the Viewer, position the playhead on the frame you want to export (**Figure 18.27**).

2. Choose File > Export > QuickTime.

3. In the Save dialog box, choose Still Image from the Format pop-up menu (**Figure 18.28**); then *do one of the following:*

   ◆ Choose one of the Still Image settings presets from the Use pop-up menu.

   ◆ Click the Options button to access a complete list of QuickTime still image formats and their settings. In the Export Image Sequence Settings dialog box, select an export format from the pop-up menu at the top of the dialog box (**Figure 18.29**), and then click OK.

EXPORTING OTHER QUICKTIME FORMATS

Figure 18.27 Position the Canvas or the Viewer playhead on the frame you want to export as a still frame.

Figure 18.28 Select an Export format from the Format pull-down menu.

Figure 18.29 Selecting Photoshop as the export format from the pop-up menu in the Export Image Sequence Settings dialog box.

Figure 18.30 In the Save dialog box, type a name for your still frame in the Save As field; then select a destination folder from the Where pop-up menu and click Save.

4. In the Save dialog box, type a name for your still frame in the Save As field and select a destination folder from the Where pop-up menu near the top of the dialog box.

5. Click Save (**Figure 18.30**).

   Final Cut Express automatically adds the correct image file extension to the name you typed.

✔ Tip

■ Whenever you're exporting a still frame, you can ignore the frames-per-second settings—they don't apply to still-frame export.

To export an image sequence:

1. *Do one of the following:*
   - Select a clip or sequence in the Browser.
   - In the Timeline, open the sequence you want to export.

2. Set In and Out points in your clip or sequence to mark the section you want to export as a numbered image sequence (**Figure 18.31**). If you want to export the entire item, clear any In and Out points from the item before export.

3. Choose File > Export > QuickTime.

4. In the Save dialog box, choose Image Sequence from the Format pop-up menu (**Figure 18.32**); then *do one of the following:*
   - Choose one of the Image Sequence settings presets from the Use pop-up menu.
   - Click the Options button to access a complete list of QuickTime still image formats and their settings. In the Export Image Sequence Settings dialog box, select an export format from the Format pop-up menu, select a frame rate for your image sequence (**Figure 18.33**), and then click OK.

5. In the Save dialog box, type a name for your still frame in the Save As field, and then select a destination folder.

6. Click Save.

   Your image sequence is saved as a series of still graphics in the file format you selected.

Figure 18.31 Set In and Out points in your clip or sequence to mark the section you want to include in the exported image sequence file.

Figure 18.32 Select Image Sequence from the Format pop-up menu.

Figure 18.33 Select an export format from the pop-up menu at the top of the dialog box, select a frame rate for your image sequence, and then click OK.

Figure 18.34 Choose File > Export > QuickTime, and then select an audio format from the Format pop-up menu. AIFF, Wave, μLaw, and System 7 Sound are all audio formats.

Figure 18.35 Select sample rate and compression settings from the Sound Settings dialog box, and then click OK.

To export audio only from a clip or sequence:

1. Select a clip or sequence in the Browser or open the sequence in the Timeline.

2. Set In and Out points in your clip or sequence to mark the section you want to export as an audio file.

3. Choose File > Export > QuickTime.

4. In the Save dialog box, choose an audio export file format from the Format pop-up menu (**Figure 18.34**); *then do one of the following:*

   ◆ Choose one of the audio export settings presets from the Use pop-up menu.

   ◆ Click the Options button to access the full QuickTime settings for the format you have selected. In the Sound Settings dialog box, select sample rate (**Figure 18.35**) and compression settings, and then click OK.

5. In the Save dialog box, type a name for your audio file in the Save As field; then select a destination folder and click Save.

✔ Tips

- Use this export method to convert the 44.1 kHz sample rate of a CD audio track. In the Sound Settings dialog box, choose 48 (or 32) kHz—the sample rate that matches your sequence audio's rate. Once you have completed the export/sample rate conversion, import the exported copy back into your project.

- FCE allows you to mix audio tracks with different sample rates in the same sequence, converting the sample rate of nonconforming audio on the fly as you play back a sequence. Real-time sample rate conversion can occasionally produce nasty audible artifacts, so for best results, convert the sample rates of all your audio tracks to match the sequence settings.

513

ONLINE RESOURCES

Apple Computer Links

www.apple.com/finalcutexpress/

Apple's Official Final Cut Express Home Page is the place to go for program updates; the latest FCE news; updates on Final Cut Express and QuickTime; and the list of Apple-approved video hardware and software. Check in at the FCE home page on a regular basis.

www.apple.com/finalcutpro/directory.html

The **Final Cut Pro Directory page** contains a variety of resource links that Final Cut Express users will also find helpful: links to discussion groups, a complete list of Final Cut Pro user groups, general DV reference resources, and a list of software and plugins you can use in conjunction with Final Cut Pro.

www.apple.com/finalcutexpress/qualification.html

The **Final Cut Express Qualified Devices page** contains a complete list of DV decks and camcorders qualified to work with FCE, and the correct device control setting to use with each and every one. You'll also find links to web sites of qualified hardware manufacturers.

www.apple.com/quicktime/

Apple's QuickTime Home Page

www.apple.com/firewire/

Apple's FireWire Home Page

www.info.apple.com/usen/finalcutexpress/

Apple's Final Cut Express Support site
You cannot access Apple's support services—its Knowledge Base or discussion forums—without registering for an official Apple User ID. Apple Support should be your first stop if you've never registered with Apple before. You can access the registration page and get an overview of the offerings in the Support area. A couple of specifics are listed below. Apple changes the names and URLs of their data sites regularly. Try these:

kbase.info.apple.com

Apple's Knowledge Base (formerly known as the Tech Info Library, or TIL) is Apple's library of product information, technical specifications, and troubleshooting information. Search the Knowledge Base with keywords "Final Cut Express" for a complete list of Apple technical documents relating to FCE.

To access a specific Knowledge Base article: This book makes occasional reference to specific Knowledge Base reference articles. You can go directly to a specific article by using the following URL, where *XXXXX* is the document number:

`http://www.info.apple.com/kbnum/nXXXXX`

✔ Tip

■ Check the Knowledge Base regularly. Apple posts updates on "known issues" (a.k.a. bugs) affecting Final Cut Express in the Kbase—and nowhere else.

Online Users Forums

http://discussions.info.apple.com/ WebX/finalcutexpress/

This is **Apple's Final Cut Express Discussion**, Apple's official online support forum. Currently, this is the most active discussion forum exclusively devoted to FCE. If you think a Final Cut Pro user might be able to assist you, try the 2-pop forums as well.

www.2-pop.com

When Final Cut Pro was released in April 1999, the 2-pop.com site quickly became the central exchange forum for Final Cut Pro users to share information. 2-pop is primarily a Final Cut Pro hangout, but its popularity makes it a good place to go for answers, FCP/FCE news and gossip, new ideas, and product critique. A gold mine.

The action at 2-pop is centered around the discussion forums. Click the Discussion link on 2-pop's front page to navigate to a complete listing of 2-pop's discussion forums.

Be sure to take advantage of the Search feature located at the top of most discussion boards; you'll find a wealth of detailed information by searching the archives of the 2-pop message boards.

ONLINE RESOURCES

Reference

www.dv.com

DV Magazine would be my first stop if I were looking for product reviews, industry analysis, and "long view" technical evaluations of the current state of the digital video world.

www.adobe.com

In addition to product specific information on Photoshop and After Effects, **Adobe's web site** is a great source of general information on digital imaging.

www.techweb.com/encyclopedia/

Simple to use, the **TechEncyclopedia** offers more than 20,000 definitions of computer terms and concepts.

Mavens

If you are seeking alternatives to marketing department hype, these sites offer a bracing dose of opinionated candor and experienced insight, along with valuable reference material and more great links.

www.adamwilt.com/DV.html

Adam Wilt's Amazing DV FAQ. I'm an Adam Wilt fan. See for yourself.

www.nonlinear4.com

Michael Rubin (and co-editor Ron Diamond) are keepers of **nonlinear4.com**, a great reference and resource site for all things digital and video. You should also visit this site to purchase *Nonlinear4* (the fourth edition of Michael Rubin's really good "field guide to digital video and film editing").

www.joesfilters.com

Joe's Filters is a great resource for anyone interested in using learning to use filters and transitions in Final Cut Express. Joe offers demo versions of his custom filters, and the illustrated documentation that accompanies each filter description is a great way to learn more about using filters to create digital effects.

www.dvcentral.org

Get subscription information at **DV & FireWire Central** for the excellent DV_L mailing list.

www.kenstone.net

Ken Stone has been quietly building an impressive online library of illustrated Final Cut Pro tutorial reviews, as well as articles by Ken and other FCP scholars. Well worth the visit for FCE users.

FCP User Groups

At this time, there are no Final-Cut-Express-only user groups out there, so you'll have to crowd in with the FCP folk.

www.apple.com/finalcutpro/directory.html

Apple's Resource Directory page contains links to all members of the **Final Cut Pro User Group Network** (19 groups and counting). Check here to see if there's a user group meeting near you.

www.2-pop.com

2-pop's User Groups Announcement Forum is a good place to check for user group action in your town. If you don't see any users posting from your area, this is a good place to try to round up your neighborhood Final Cut users and start a user group of your own.

www.lafcpug.org

The **Los Angeles Final Cut Pro User Group** is a triumph of ad-hocracy (and a tribute to the energy of its prime mover, Michael Horton). Founded in June 2000, LAFCPUG now has over 1500 members on its mailing list. LAFCPUG holds well-attended monthly meetings. The LAFCPUG web site is updated regularly, and is worth a visit for the archive of fine "how-to" articles contributed by community-minded FCP mavens.

www.sfcutters.org

The **San Francisco Final Cut Pro User Group web site**. These guys started the first FCP user group, and gleefully nagged Southern California FCP users until they started the LAFCPUG. The rest is history.

KEYBOARD SHORTCUTS

Keyboard Shortcuts

General controls

FUNCTION	KEY COMMAND
Open file	Cmd O
Open selected item	Return
Open in separate window	Shift Return
Open item editor	Option Return
Close window	Cmd W
Help	F1
Quit	Cmd Q
Save	Cmd S

General controls *(continued)*

FUNCTION	KEY COMMAND
Save all	Cmd Option S
Undo	Cmd Z
Redo	Cmd Y
Audio scrub on or off	Shift S
Snapping on or off	N
Looping on or off	Ctrl L
Close Tab	Ctrl W
Open text generator	Ctrl X

To open application windows

FUNCTION	KEY COMMAND
Viewer	Cmd 1
Canvas	Cmd 2
Timeline	Cmd 3
Browser	Cmd 4
Audio Meters	Option 4
Effects	Cmd 5
Favorites bin	Cmd 6
Trim Edit	Cmd 7
Log and Capture	Cmd 8
Item Properties	Cmd 9
Sequence Settings	Cmd 0 (zero)
Preferences	Option Q

Select, cut, copy, and paste

FUNCTION	KEY COMMAND
Copy	Cmd C
Cut	Cmd X
Duplicate	Option D
Make In/Out a selection	Option A
Paste	Cmd V
Paste attributes	Option V
Paste Insert	Shift V
Select all	Cmd A
Deselect all	Cmd D

Navigation

FUNCTION	KEY COMMAND
Forward one frame	→
Back one frame	←
Forward one second	Shift →
Back one second	Shift ←
Match frame	F
Next edit	Shift E
Previous edit	Option E
Next gap	Shift G
Previous gap	Option G
To beginning of media	HOME
To end of media	END or Shift HOME
To next edit or In/Out	↓

Navigation *(continued)*

FUNCTION	KEY COMMAND
To previous edit or In/Out	⬆
To next marker	Shift ⬇
To previous marker	Shift ⬆
To master clip	Shift F
Shuttle backward fast	J (tap repeatedly to increase speed)
Shuttle backward slow	J + K
Pause	K
Shuttle forward fast	L (tap repeatedly to increase speed)
Shuttle forward slow	L + K
Next edit	' (single quote) or Shift E
Previous edit	; (semicolon) or Option E

Finding items

FUNCTION	KEY COMMAND
Find	Cmd F
Find Next (in Find results)	Cmd G *or* F3
Find previous (in Find results)	Shift F3

Scrolling

FUNCTION	KEY COMMAND
Horizontal scroll left	Shift Page Up
Horizontal scroll right	Shift Page Down
Vertical scroll up	Page Up
Vertical scroll down	Page Down

Screen layout and display

FUNCTION	KEY COMMAND
Custom layout 1	Shift U
Custom layout 2	Option U
Standard Layout	Ctrl U

Projects and sequences

FUNCTION	KEY COMMAND
New project	Cmd E
New sequence	Cmd N
New Sequence with Presets prompt	Cmd Option N
Import file	Cmd I

Browser

FUNCTION	KEY COMMAND
Insert bin	Cmd B
Open bins (list view)	→
Close bins (list view)	←
Make Favorite	Option F
Show logging columns	Option B
Show standard columns	Shift B
Toggle list/icon view	Shift H
Make Favorite motion	Ctrl F

KEYBOARD SHORTCUTS

Timeline

FUNCTION	KEY COMMAND
Create or break link	[Cmd] L
Create or break stereo pair	[Option] L
Toggle track sizes	[Shift] T
Clip Keyframes on or off	[Option] T
Clip overlays on or off	[Option] W
Delete and leave gap	[Delete]
Ripple delete (no gap)	[Shift] [Delete]
Ripple Cut to Keyboard	[Shift] X
Fit sequence in window	[Shift] Z
Lock video track + track number	[F4] + track number
Lock all video tracks	[Shift] [F4]
Lock audio track + track number	[F5] + track number
Lock all audio tracks	[Shift] [F5]
Toggle Audio Waveforms	[Cmd] [Option] W
Linked selection on or off	[Shift] L
Modify Duration	[Ctrl] D
Zoom Timeline In	[Option] - (minus sign)
Zoom Timeline Out	[Option] + (plus sign)

Logging and capturing

FUNCTION	KEY COMMAND
Capture Project	[Ctrl] C
Capture Now	[Shift] C

KEYBOARD SHORTCUTS

Playing video

FUNCTION	KEY COMMAND
Play	L *or* Spacebar
Pause/Stop	K *or* Spacebar
Play around current	\ (backslash)
Play every frame	Option P
Play here to Out	Shift P
Play in reverse	Shift Spacebar *or* J
Play In to Out	Shift \ (backslash)

In and Out points

FUNCTION	KEY COMMAND
Set In point	I *or* / (slash) on keypad
Set Out point	O *or* * (asterisk) on keypad
Clear In	Option I
Clear Out	Option O
Clear In and Out	Option X
Mark In and Out at selection boundaries	Shift A
Mark clip	X
Mark to Markers	Ctrl A
Go to In point	Shift I
Go to Out point	Shift O
Set video In only	Ctrl I
Set video Out only	Ctrl O
Set audio In only	Cmd Option I
Set audio Out only	Cmd Option O

Tool selection

FUNCTION	KEY COMMAND
Tool Selection	A
Tool Edit Select	G
Tool Group Select	G+G
Tool Range Select	G+G+G
Tool Track Forward Select	T
Tool Track Backward Select	T+T
Tool Track Select	T+T+T
Tool All Tracks Forward Select	T+T+T+T
Tool All Tracks Backward Select	T+T+T+T+T
Tool Roll Edit	R
Tool Ripple Edit	R+R
Tool Slip	S
Tool Slide	S+S
Tool Razor Blade	B
Tool Razor Blade All	B+B
Tool Hand	H
Tool Zoom In	Z
Tool Zoom Out	Z+Z
Tool Crop	C
Tool Distort	D
Tool Pen	P
Tool Pen Delete	P+P
Tool Pen Smooth	P+P+P

KEYBOARD SHORTCUTS

Markers

FUNCTION	KEY COMMAND
Add marker	M
Add and name marker	M + M
Delete marker	[Cmd] ` (accent grave)
Extend marker	[Option] ~ (tilde)
Reposition marker	[Shift] ` (accent grave)
Next marker	[Shift] M
Previous marker	[Option] M
Clear All Markers	[Ctrl] ` (accent grave)
Mark to Markers	[Ctrl] A

Editing

FUNCTION	KEY COMMAND
Select Closest Edit	V
Add Edit	[Ctrl] V
Toggle Ripple / Roll Tool Type	U *or* [Shift] R
Apply Default Video Transition	[Ctrl] T
Apply Default Audio Transition	[Cmd] [Option] T
Extend edit	E
Insert edit	[F9]
Insert with transition	[Shift] [F9]
Overwrite	[F10]
Overwrite with transition	[Shift] [F10]
Replace	[F11]
Fit to fill	[Shift] [F11]

Editing *(continued)*

FUNCTION	KEY COMMAND
Superimpose	[F12]
Make subclip	[Cmd] U
Slip edit	[Shift] Click In *or* Out point
Split edit	[Option] Click In *or* Out point
Set target video + track number	[F6] + track number
Set target video to None	[Shift] [F6]
Set target Audio 1 + track number	[F7] + track number
Set target Audio 1 to None	[Shift] [F7]
Set target Audio 2 + track number	[F8] + track number
Set target Audio 2 to None	[Shift] [F8]
Trim backward one frame	[(left bracket) *or* , (comma)
Trim backward x frames	[Shift] [(left bracket) *or* [Shift] , (comma)
Trim forward one frame	] (right bracket) *or* . (period)
Trim forward x frames	[Shift]] (right bracket) *or* [Shift] . (period)

Output

FUNCTION	KEY COMMAND
Display frame	[F15] *or* [Shift] [F12]
Print to video	[Ctrl] M
Toggle External Video	[Cmd] [F12]

KEYBOARD SHORTCUTS

Compositing and special effects

FUNCTION	KEY COMMAND
Add Motion Keyframe	Ctrl K
Add Audio Keyframe	Cmd Option K
Go to Next Keyframe	Shift K
Go to Previous Keyframe	Option K
Make still frame	Shift N
Render selection	Cmd R
Render sequence	Option R
Render single frame on or off	Caps Lock
Speed	Cmd J
Toggle Image/Wireframe view	W
Toggle RGB/RGB+A/Alpha	Shift W
Fit in window	Shift Z
Nudge position down	Option ↓
Nudge position left	Option ←
Nudge position right	Option →
Nudge position up	Option ↑
Sub pixel down	Cmd ↓
Sub pixel left	Cmd ←
Sub pixel right	Cmd →
Sub pixel up	Cmd ↑
Zoom in	Cmd = (equal sign)
Zoom out	Cmd - (minus sign)
Mixdown Audio	Cmd Option R

Quick navigation keys and modifiers

This group of Keyboard shortcuts for marking and navigation are arranged in what is known as a "Set-Clear-Go" scheme.

◆ The simple key command sets the edit, marker, or point.

◆ [Shift] plus the key command advances to the next edit, marker, or point.

◆ [Option] plus the key command advances to the previous edit, marker, or point.

KEY	NO MODIFIER	[Shift] + KEY	[Option] + KEY
I	Set In	Go To In	Clear In
O	Set Out	Go To Out	Clear Out
M	Set Marker	Next Marker	Previous Marker
E	Extend Edit	Next Edit	Previous Edit
G		Next Gap	Previous Gap
K		Next Keyframe	Previous Keyframe
[Ctrl] K	Add Motion Keyframe		

INDEX

INDEX

INDEX

motion keyframes, 294, 388, 411–416
navigation, keyboard shortcuts, 387, 413
overlays (*See* keyframe overlays)
overview, 294, 387
precision positioning, 389
scaling when copying attributes, 289
Knowledge Base articles
Apple's Knowledge Base (web page), 515–516
"Final Cut Pro: About Luminance," 432
"Final Cut Pro: Dropped Frames and Loss of Audio Sync," 109
"Final Cut Pro: How to Calibrate Your Broadcast Monitor," 434
"Final Cut Pro 3: QuickTime Export of Video, Images, and Sound," 502

L

L key, 184
Last Modified column, Browser, 83, 155, 157
layered images
compositing, 378, 438
opacity, 405–406
layered Photoshop files
importing, 142–143
increasing length of, 143
updating in FCE, 140–141
layering, 378
layouts. *See* screen layouts
Leader options, 496–497
Leading slider, 450, 456
Length column, Browser, 155
length of clips, adjusting. *See* trimming edits
level controls, Timeline, 250
Level line graph, 332, 334, 350, 354
level line overlays, 388
Level meter, 343, 345
Level sliders
Audio tab, 332, 333, 350, 352
Color Corrector tab, 435, 437
Levels of Undo setting, 41, 64
Lift edits, 226
Limit Capture/Export File Segment Size To: setting, 48
Limit Capture Now To: setting, 48, 120
linear editing systems, 6
Link indicators, 253

linked clips. *See also* linked selection; stereo pairs
audio clips, 328, 329
linking unrelated clips, 279
overview, 280
Timeline display, 253
unlinking, 279
linked selection. *See also* linked clips
enabling or disabling, 254
locked tracks and, 280
overriding, 302
overview, 303
trim edits and, 302
turning on or off, 280
Linked Selection control, 250, 254
List of Recent Clips setting, 41
List view, 160, 161
live footage, capturing, 122
Location setting, 460
Lock Track control, Timeline, 251, 270
locking tracks
in Timeline, 251, 270, 271
linked selection and, 280
locked target tracks, 213, 214
target tracks compared to, 271
trim edits and locked tracks, 302
Log Note column, Browser, 155
Log Note field, 89, 107
logging clips
adding markers to clips, 114, 119, 120
auto-incrementing naming fields, 115
automatic naming function, 113
Capture Clip *vs.* Capture Now, 117
clip names, 112–113
file names, 116
media In and Out points, 113
overview, 110
reel names, 112
tips, 110
Logging Info tab, Item Properties window, 89
Logging tab, Capture window, 106–107, 110–116
logging video footage, Final Cut Pro capabilities, 22
Loop option, 497
looping playback, 184
Los Angeles Final Cut Pro User Group (web page), 518
Lower 3rd generator, 448
luminance, 432, 434, 441

M

INDEX

N

P

INDEX

INDEX

INDEX

Look to **Peachpit Press** for your digital video needs!

Adobe After Effects 5.0 Classroom in a Book
Adobe Creative Team
ISBN: 0-201-74131-8 • 384 pages • $45.00

After Effects 5 for Macintosh and Windows: Visual QuickPro Guide
Antony Bolante
ISBN: 0-201-75043-0 • 608 pages • $34.99

Adobe Premiere 6.0 Classroom in a Book
Adobe Creative Team
ISBN: 0-201-71018-8 • 480 pages • $45.00

DVD Studio Pro 1.5 for Macintosh: Visual QuickPro Guide
Martin Sitter
ISBN: 0-321-11547-3 • 400 pages • $24.99

Editing Techniques with Final Cut Pro
Michael Wohl
ISBN: 0-201-73483-4 • 400 pages • $44.99

Final Cut Pro for Beginners
Michael Rubin
ISBN: 0-321-11802-2 • 176 pages • $34.99

Final Cut Pro 3 for Macintosh: Visual QuickPro Guide
Lisa Brenneis
ISBN: 0-321-11583-X • 672 pages • $29.99

FireWire Filmmaking
Scott Smith
ISBN: 0-201-74163-6 • 176 pages • $39.99

iMovie 2 for Macintosh: Visual QuickStart Guide
Jeff Carlson
ISBN: 0-201-78788-1 • 216 pages • $19.99

The Little Digital Video Book
Michael Rubin
ISBN: 0-201-75848-2 • 192 pages • $19.99

LiveStage Professional 3 for Macintosh and Windows: Visual QuickStart Guide
Martin Sitter
ISBN: 0-201-77142-X • 416 pages • $21.99

Making iMovies
Scott Smith
ISBN: 0-201-70489-7 • 156 pages • $39.99

QuickTime 5 for Macintosh and Windows: Visual QuickStart Guide
Judith Stern and Robert Lettieri
ISBN: 0-201-74145-8 • 440 pages • $19.99

Premiere 6 for Macintosh and Windows: Visual QuickStart Guide
Antony Bolante
ISBN: 0-201-72207-0 • 592 pages • $19.99

Pro Tools 5 for Macintosh and Windows: Visual QuickStart Guide
Steven Roback
ISBN: 0-201-79534-5 • 448 pages • $21.99

Video on the Web with Adobe Premiere
Thomas Luehrsen
ISBN: 0-201-77184-5 • 352 pages • $39.99

www.peachpit.com